Liberalism and Modern Society

Liberalism and Modern Society

An Historical Argument

Richard Bellamy

Polity Press

First published in 1992 by Polity Press
in association with Blackwell Publishers

Editorial office:
Polity Press
65 Bridge Street
Cambridge CB2 1UR, UK

Marketing and production:
Blackwell Publishers
108 Cowley Road
Oxford OX4 1JF, UK

ISBN 0 7456 0533–8
ISBN 0 7456 1070–6 (pbk)

A CIP catalogue record for this book is available
from the British Library.

Typeset in Palatino on 10/11½ pt
by Graphicraft Typesetters Ltd, Hong Kong
Printed in Great Britain
by TJ Press (Padstow) Ltd, Padstow, Cornwall

This book is printed on acid-free paper.

For Louise

Contents

Preface and Acknowledgements

Writing a book over some five years has led me to incur a number of debts. My most general and in many respects deepest debt arises from the opportunity of teaching and researching in different departments and faculties of various universities. This experience has helped me drop conventional disciplinary distinctions between philosophy, politics, law, economics, sociology and history. The thinkers examined here regarded these subjects as complementary to each other, and employed them all in framing their theories. Only later commentators have sought to hive off bits of their work as contributions to particular fields of study. A subtheme of this book, therefore, concerns the importance for social and political theorists today to emulate these earlier writers' combination of historical sensitivity, sociological awareness and philosophical sophistication. In attempting to employ a similar mixture in my analysis of their writings, I hope to have contributed in some small measure to this goal.

I began this project as an Economic and Social Research Council (ESRC) post-doctoral research fellow at Nuffield College, Oxford. I am very grateful to David Miller and Raymond Plant, then a visiting fellow at the college, for the interest they have shown in my work from its first tentative beginnings. Raymond also made some extremely helpful and encouraging comments on a full draft of the manuscript. A period as a teaching fellow at Jesus College, Cambridge provided me with the incentive for researching the historical context of chapters 1–4. Conversations there with Richard Tuck, Jeremy Butterfield, John Mullan and John Thompson also proved extremely instructive as well as enjoyable, even if they were unaware of giving such help at the time. Colleagues in Edinburgh have been similarly kind in debating my ideas and reading sections of the manuscript. I am particularly indebted to Malcolm Anderson, Zenon Bankowski, Martin Clark, Richard Gunn, Vinit

Haskar, John Holmwood, Neil MacCormick, Michael Menlowe, John Orr and Paul Smart for rendering this service. Peter Baehr was especially kind in allowing me to trespass on his time as a visiting fellow in the Sociology Department at Edinburgh and for sharing his knowledge of Weber so generously with me. I also wish to thank the following friends and colleagues in other universities for having supplied all kinds of information and comments vital in the preparation of this book: Walter Adamson, David Beetham, Jon Brooks, David Held, Jeremy Jennings, Peter Jones, Susan Mendus, John Morrow, Peter Nicholson, Bob Stern, Richard Vernon, Jo Wolff and Danilo Zolo. To Quentin Skinner I owe a special debt of gratitude for his support of my research over many years. Last but far from least, Louise Dominian has gone well beyond the call of duty in the emotional and intellectual help she has lent me in the writing of this work. Even if the royalties prove insufficient to fund the long-distance telephone calls often required to deliver this necessary assistance, I hope she thinks the book was worth the effort. It is dedicated to her.

Introduction: from Ethical to Economic Liberalism

Twentieth-century liberalism has suffered the curious fate of steadily declining in most countries as an electoral force exclusive to a particular party, whilst prevailing and even growing as a background theory or set of presuppositions and sentiments of a supposedly neutral and universal kind which dominates political thinking across the ideological spectrum. Today all major groupings employ the liberal language of rights, freedom and equality to express and legitimize their views and demonstrate a corresponding general acceptance of liberal conceptions of democracy and the market. From New Right conservatives to democratic socialists, it seems we are all liberals now.

To some extent, this situation is unsurprising given that liberal ideals and politics fashioned the states and social and economic systems of the nineteenth century, creating the institutional framework and the values within which most of us in the West continue to live and to think. This circumstance, however, does not justify the widely accepted assertion that the apparent triumph of liberalism forms part of 'a universal human evolution in the direction of free societies' grounded in 'the empirically undeniable correlation between advancing industrialization and liberal democracy'.[1] On the contrary, the empirical evidence suggests just the opposite – a fact of some concern for liberal thinkers in the past. If many earlier liberals shared the belief of their contemporary epigone in a guaranteed progress towards a bourgeois utopia, they also came to feel badly let down by the historical process as a number of their core assumptions were called into question by the further development of the very social order they had helped to create. The consequent undermining and eventual transformation of liberalism under the impact of the structural forces generated by advanced industrial societies *c*.1870–1930 forms the subject of this book. I shall argue that an analysis of this crucial period of liberal political thought throws doubt on the adequacy of much of our liberal heritage as a basis for a viable political order today. Far from being a sign of its intellectual and practical ascendency, liberalism's recent mutation from ideology to meta-ideology is indicative of its current theoretical and political bankruptcy. No longer part of the dynamic of history, liberalism has simply been reduced to presenting itself as the culmination of the historical process in a desperate attempt to circumscribe and contain those social forces which threaten to undermine it.

This study examines the fortunes of a particularly influential strand of the liberal tradition, which I call ethical liberalism. Its principal originators were British liberals such as Adam Smith, Herbert Spencer and J. S. Mill, although Kantian and Hegelian inspired thinkers developed parallel ideas on the Continent which were easily assimilable to it. Ethical liberalism combined a philosophical and a social thesis, the latter providing the former with a coherence it otherwise lacked. The philosophical core of this school of liberalism stemmed from the priority it assigned to increasing individual liberty.[2] In spite of differences amongst liberal theorists over the exact interpretation of liberty, all assumed that a coherent theory of freedom existed and that it was possible to maximize an equal set of harmoniously coexisting liberties for all members of society. The problem with this doctrine is the normative and practical one of how we decide between different sets of conflicting liberties so as to arrive at the greatest possible liberty on balance. What metric do we use to sort out the potential clashes between, say, freedom of association and the freedom not to be discriminated against, or between freedom of speech and the freedom of privacy, so as to increase freedom over all? Can any one of these liberties be judged greater or lesser than the others? Practically, such choices are unavoidable. They arise, for example, in legislation aimed to secure equal opportunities and freedom of information respectively. In these sorts of cases, prioritizing liberty in itself proves indeterminate, for many different sets of equal liberties could be assigned consistently to all people, with each set emphasizing some liberties at the expense of others. Thus, judgements about the greatest liberty are necessarily qualitative rather than quantitative. They can only proceed on the basis of some view of the value of different human activities, which regards certain liberties as being more intrinsic to human flourishing and well-being than others. In general, liberals have steered clear of such controversial evaluations, for they threaten the entire liberal project. If no objective ideal of liberty exists, then claims to expand freedom will depend at least in part on differing subjective understandings of the relative importance of various liberties which are themselves likely to collide. In such a situation, it may not be possible even rationally to agree when conflicts between liberties occur, let alone to resolve such disputes.

Traditionally, liberals avoided this problem by tacitly relying on the social thesis. They assumed society would develop in a direction which would lead to the harmonization of individual life plans. A view originally based on theological foundations, as in Locke and possibly Smith, it gradually became a secularized theory of progress about the evolution of society and the nature of human development.[3] The gradual transformation of British society by the industrial revolution was held up as exemplifying this progressive process of social, economic and political change. Ethical liberals idealized the market relations between small-scale entrepreneurs characteristic of early capitalism. They saw them as the basis of a meritocratic society of self-reliant and responsible citizens, who freely contracted with each other for their mutual advantage and were moved via an invisible hand towards individual, social, material and moral improvement. Freedom, reason, morality and progress came in this way to be identified, with the social thesis supporting an implicitly ethical naturalist philosophical thesis concerning the compatibility of different forms of self-realization.

From about 1870 the social thesis appeared increasingly implausible. Perfectly competitive market relations had never existed, but the concentration of capital and the rise of organized labour distorted them even further. The liberal model assumed free competition between individual producers of approximately equal standing. Independent prices were supposed to secure the optimal equilibrium between production and consumption for the economy as a whole, so that *laissez-faire* achieved the most efficient employment of the available natural and human resources possible. In the event, this result proved to be contingent on a pre-existing equilibrium between economic actors, rather than an automatic function of the market system regulating itself. Once this equilibrium became disturbed, market forces alone were incapable of re-establishing it. Temporary market advantages, for example, provided firms or workers with privileges which enabled them to maintain their advantageous position in ways which undermined the market's future competitiveness. By such means, large corporations came to control the supply of goods and services in a particular area, thereby distorting the operation of the price mechanism. Differences amongst consumers had similarly corrosive effects on market operations. Perfect competition assumed that consumers were fully informed both about their needs and about the available services on offer to meet them, and that they were equally able to make their demands felt. In reality, however, they rarely possessed such knowledge, and could only imperfectly influence the economy even if they did, since the inequitable distribution of wealth resulted in the whims of the rich often being met before the more urgent needs of the poor. Such factors meant that in practice the market economy gave rise not to a co-operative society of mutually improving individuals, but to a world of conflicting group interests.

The ethical liberal's theory of the market had been opposed to the sort

of possessive individualism that came to characterize it in practice.
The optimal allocation of resources aimed at by the perfect competition
model ultimately precluded profit, since profit resulted from a dis-
equilibrium between supply and demand, cost and price. The pursuit of
profit in itself motivated just those tendencies, such as the creation
of monopolies, which destroy the competitiveness and freedom of the
market. Accordingly, ethical liberals condemned it.[4] They believed that
the profit motive could be superseded by the desire to do something
well for its own sake. Liberals acknowledged that some state regulation
was necessary both to preserve the market from attempts to undermine
it and to remedy its deficiencies in providing certain public goods.[5]
However, they hoped the evolution of human sentiments would ultimately overcome these anti-social tendencies. When this moral improvement failed to materialize, the state took on a commensurately greater
role as the ethical educator of a recalcitrant populace.

The ethical liberals had regarded the state as the preserve of a
public-spirited elite. These men (women being almost always excluded)
were deemed worthy by virtue of their education and moderate landed
wealth to represent the nation in a responsible fashion, and to deliberate
rationally and disinterestedly on the common good within the framework of a shared moral code. The social and political changes wrought
by the industrial revolution and the creation of a mass electorate
rendered this idealized conception of notable politics an anachronism.
The radical belief that it could simply be extended through increased
popular participation to include the entire citizen body has proved
an illusion. Unfortunately, the same self-interested motivations which
drove people to seek their advantage in the market encouraged them to
pursue their ends by political means as well. The introduction of universal suffrage made the state the arena of the social conflicts it was supposed to regulate. Far from controlling society, the state itself became an
instrument of the very economic interests it sought to curb.[6]

The comparison of liberal theories and regimes in Britain, France, Italy
and Germany at the turn of the century (chapters 1–4) serves to develop
this account of the overcoming of ethical by economic liberalism. The
examination of the fate of liberal ideas within a variety of intellectual
and social contexts reveals the historically contingent nature of many
of liberalism's key propositions. When the favourable constellation of
social forces linking the bourgeois class with liberal institutions and
values was absent, the philosophical assumptions of ethical liberalism
proved untenable and had to be drastically rethought. Each chapter
contains two elements: a brief examination of the liberal tradition and
the social and political situation in the country concerned, and an analysis of one or more of the prominent thinkers of the period. Although
individual chapters or sections may be taken in isolation from the rest,
they form part of a single narrative which is best read in sequence. My
principal aim has been to provide an historical argument concerning the

impact of the evolution of modern society upon liberal thought, rather than a straightforward history of the doctrine during this period.[7]

Chapter 1, on Britain, examines the social and philosophical assumptions behind ethical liberalism. Nineteenth-century British liberals appreciated the threat posed by modern societies to their doctrine and sought to rework its categories to cope with the political, social and economic demands of a mass industrial world. Left- and right-wing commentators respectively have regarded the resulting new liberalism as either a progressive extension or a regressive reformulation of classical liberalism. Both these apparently contradictory views contain an element of truth. Changes within British society, not least the rise of organized labour, made it increasingly difficult for liberals to portray their own values as transcending class and defining the common good. The new liberals sought to adapt the old ethical language to meet the imperatives of a collectivist and democratic age. For the most part, this programme involved the progressive adaptation of traditional liberal concepts to new groups of people. However, the contentious and regressive nature of many of these categories frequently rendered this project more coercive and reactionary than its past or present champions have allowed. Chapter 2 continues this theme via an examination of the views of Durkheim and the Solidarists. Their apologetics for the French Third Republic provide one of the most detailed blueprints for an ethical liberal regime available. They were forced to articulate the social principles upon which they sought to construct a liberal morality and politics far more explicitly than their British counterparts. The gradual nature of Britain's social development allowed British liberals to take the existence of a liberal society for granted for much of the nineteenth century. As a consequence, British liberalism tended to emphasize the self-creating power of the individual. Elsewhere, liberal social structures had to be created, so that they became the central object of attention. Durkheim's theory brings out particularly well both the dependence of liberal individualism upon a particular type of society, and the normative bias of the putatively natural laws of social and economic development which underpinned liberal philosophy.

In Britain and France the shortcomings of this liberal project were partially hidden by the comparative hegemony of bourgeois interests. The social structures of Italy and Germany, in contrast, proved considerably less amenable to the liberal ethos. Much later to industrialize, their economies took on a more pronounced corporate and statist character and at an earlier stage than either the British or French. The challenge of working-class parties excluded from the social and political system was also commensurately greater in these countries. As a result, the transition from ethical to economic liberalism occurred here in a starker form. Chapters 3 and 4, on Italy and Germany respectively, explore this development.

Pareto's political sociology and Croce's liberal historicism, the principal theories studied in chapter 3, reveal how the Italian situation forced a drastic rethinking of liberal politics and morality. The Italian liberal elite consisted of progressive landlords rather than an entrepreneurial bourgeoisie. They sought to modernize the rural economy without disturbing traditional hierarchical social relations. Thus, in Italy liberal ideas and institutions were compromised in decisive ways by the constraints of a predominantly agrarian society. In spite of the rapid industrial growth at the turn of the century, the new class of industrialists remained secondary both economically and politically to the landowners until the First World War. Rather than contesting the morality and privileges of the pre-industrial elites, the Italian bourgeoisie adapted them to their own interests and continued to uphold the old order. Moreover, the very backwardness of Italian society made it harder than in Britain to portray the creation of a liberal economic order as the unharnessing of natural social forces. Instead, the new relations of production had to be created by an increasingly intrusive state. Far from representing a hegemonic project for the progressive transformation of society, Italian liberalism became associated with the narrow economic interests of privileged classes who cynically exploited the political system to manipulate and coerce the population into acceptance of their dominance. The harmony of individual ends, posited by classical ethical liberalism, gave way to an economic liberalism characterized by the clash of warring material interests. Pareto's cynical politics reflected his frustration at Italy's failure to live up to the model of the British liberals he had so admired in his youth. Although perfect competition in the market remained his ideal, he divested this conception of its ethical packaging and so rendered it practically unrealizable without the intervention of a strong state supposedly separated from social and political conflict. This conclusion led him into support for fascism. Croce initially followed a similar path to Pareto. However, he was unwilling to grant the state the moralizing role accorded it by fascist ideologues. Instead, his historicist liberalism offered a non-foundationalist defence of liberal morality. Liberalism, on this view, consisted of no more than the practices of a particular kind of society and culture. It had no intrinsic value beyond its historical importance for us as the product of West European civilization.

Max Weber continued the rethinking of liberal politics and ethics along similar lines to those taken by Pareto and Croce. Germany's intellectual traditions and social and political development have been regarded by liberals as even more of an aberration from the putative Anglo-French norm than Italy's. They argue that the German bourgeoisie failed to demand the social and political reforms warranted by their economic dominance. As a result, industrialization was effected within a social structure in which power was still held by the pre-industrial elites. This backward and authoritarian political system failed to contain the social tensions generated by a dynamic economy. The First World War and the rise of Hitler are seen as the indirect consequences of an illiberal social and political order which attempted to diffuse domestic conflicts through foreign aggression. However, as chapter 4 shows, Weber appreciated that the problems confronting liberalism in Germany were far from peculiar to that country alone. Rather, they revealed in a particularly acute manner general difficulties for the survival of liberal democratic values and forms of organization within advanced capitalist societies. The enhanced bureaucratization of state and society alike, the replacement of small-scale entrepreneurs by corporations, the increasing complexity of economic life, the advent of a mass electorate and vocal working class – everywhere these factors had served to undermine the traditional social and philosophical bases of liberalism. Instead of domestic and international harmony, markets and the division of labour had occasioned class struggle and imperialist rivalry. A rationally objective conception of human liberty grounded in an agreed set of natural human rights proved unsustainable once the social environment which had supported this thesis and rendered it plausible ceased to exist. Weber's solution, a pluralistic restatement of the political practices and ethical framework of traditional liberalism, attempted to provide the most satisfactory defence of individual liberty possible in a disenchanted and conflict-riven world.

Chapter 5 rounds off the book with a discussion of contemporary liberal theories. Much recent work in political philosophy has centred on a debate between liberal theorists and their communitarian critics. The first group claims that today a workable liberal theory must be neutral between conceptions of the good. The presence of competing cultures and interests within modern societies renders an ethical conception of liberalism unacceptably offensive to too many people. Agreement on a single general moral framework of this kind could only be maintained by the oppressive use of state power. The second group retorts that no theory can be so abstract. All moral and political theories draw on an implicit view of social relations. To remove this social foundation is to deny those formative experiences which make us moral and political agents in the first place. The argument of this book suggests that the communitarian critics are to a certain extent right. The allegedly neutral liberal theories of both New Right and social democratic thinkers are shown to rely on the traditional social assumptions of ethical liberalism. However, if my analysis is correct and these social conditions have been eroded, then contemporary liberal philosophy is untenable. Liberal political principles can have no foundation in reason or history within today's post-modern, post-industrial societies. Instead, they become mere matters of subjective opinion. To cope with this situation, liberalism must transform itself from an ethical to a political theory, in which the central place is occupied, not by liberal values, but by institutions or procedures capable of giving expression to a plurality of points of view and arranging agreements between them. In the conclusion, I tentatively outline such a democratic conception of liberalism, that drops the moralism of the ethical tradition for the realist approach of Weber.

1

Britain: Liberalism Defined

European intellectuals generally regarded Britain as the embodiment of the liberal ideal. They attributed the nation's relative stability and industrial predominance to the virtues of its intellectual tradition and institutions. For contemporary observers, Victorian liberalism constituted a broad political culture, part response and part cause of the social transformation occasioned by the impact of the industrial revolution and the ascendency of the middle and labouring classes over an aristocratic and predominantly agrarian social order. The first section of this chapter will explore this dual relationship between liberal values and the social structure of mid-nineteenth-century Britain. I shall argue that this context provides the key to understanding the ideas of three major liberal thinkers – J. S. Mill, T. H. Green and L. T. Hobhouse. In particular, I relate the metamorphosis of liberal discourse over this period to the contemporary evolution of British society, which these thinkers sought both to explain and to influence. Only thus can the peculiarities of this liberal tradition, comprising both its strengths and weaknesses, be understood and evaluated.

VICTORIAN VALUES: CHARACTER AND SOCIAL PROGRESS
c.1840–80

During the late eighteenth and early nineteenth centuries Britain underwent a profound social revolution associated with the process of industrialization. The transition from an agrarian to an industrial society involved the displacement of the old aristocratic social order based on vertical connections of dependency and patronage by the horizontal solidarities of class. Liberal ideology reflected the pivotal position played by the middle classes in the creation and maintenance of this new order. They looked upon the new industrial techniques, enhanced prosperity, the growing urban population and the political reforms of 1832 and 1867 as parts of a single complex process of progress or 'improvement', whereby Britain had come to occupy its prominent position as the workshop of the civilized world. They attributed this achievement to the moral revolution resulting from the freeing of individuals from the constraints of the old aristocratic order. Behind the various causes of liberal pressure groups, such as the Corn Law repeal, disestablishment, land reform, the extension of the franchise, etc., lay a central unifying theme – the breaking down of the barriers created by privilege and the interests of the landowning aristocracy, and the opening up of opportunities to talented and hardworking individuals from amongst the 'middle and industrious classes' of the new manufacturing centres.[1]

This ethos should not be interpreted as the championing of 'bourgeois' individualism, the pursuit of a narrowly conceived self-interest summed up in the right to maximize the consumption and acquisition of material goods.[2] As Stefan Collini has shown, the Victorian self-made man possessed the rather different attributes attached to the notion of 'character'.[3] Far from being a licence for the unrestricted satisfaction of one's wants and desires, 'character' consisted in the ability to rise above sensual, animal instincts and passions through the force of will. A variety of conventional Victorian middle-class virtues clustered around this key concept. These included, to cite some of those gathered together by the high priest of Victorian 'character' building – Samuel Smiles (1812–1905) – self-culture, self-control, energy, industry, frugality, thrift, prudence, patience, perseverence, honesty, integrity, temperance, sobriety, independence, manliness and duty.[4] In a series of books, the most important of which were *Self-Help* (1859), *Character* (1871), *Thrift* (1875) and *Duty* (1880), Smiles sought to illustrate through the lives of numerous inventors, explorers, entrepreneurs and other moral paragons, ranging from George Stephenson to Nelson, how these virtues were responsible for Britain's greatness. Taken together, they constituted the legitimizing creed of the new classes and the new age.

Economic, moral and political elements were fused within character discourse, so that its component parts can only be separated with difficulty. At the most fundamental level it reflected the logic of Ricardian political economy. According to Ricardo, capital served as the mainspring of the economy, it formed 'that fund by whose extent the extent of the productive industry of the country must always be regulated'. The result of the capitalist's self-denying abstention from consumption was that capital savings were reinvested in production, thus raising wages and, through the consequent increased demand for food, enabling the landlords to charge higher rents. In this way, capital secured the prosperity of the whole of society. It could never be too large: 'There is no amount of capital which may not be employed in a country, because demand is only limited by production.' The chief threat to economic progress came from the diminution of the capital fund either by the selfishness or fecklessness of workers calling for excessive wages and overbreeding beyond the capacity of the system to maintain them, or by landowners taxing profits and falsely raising the wage bill through Corn Laws.[5] Economic activity, within this schema, reflected moral discipline, with the manners of the 'unproductive class' of landowners on the one hand and of 'improvident' workers on the other unfavourably compared to those of the hardworking entrepreneurial factory owner-managers. Wealth or poverty was firmly linked to the collective character of the country: 'National progress', Smiles declared, 'is the sum of individual industry, energy and uprightness as national decay is of individual idleness, selfishness and vice.'[6] In this way, the 'partisan', 'class interests' of the aristocracy and unskilled labourers were set against the self-declared 'national interests' of the artisans, businessmen and professionals, for, in James Mill's words, 'in this country at least, it is this class which gives the nation its character.'[7]

Character doctrine gained much of its moral tone from nonconformity, 'the backbone of English Liberalism', possessing as it did the classic Weberian 'elective affinity' to the Protestant dissenter's concern with the individual's responsibility for his or her own redemption through the overcoming of sin.[8] Classical political economy and the nonconformist conscience both concurred in approving 'the power of resisting present gratification for the purpose of securing a future good' as 'the ascendency of reason over the animal instincts'.[9] A convenient symmetry existed between commercial and moral success or ruin. Smiles's books contained numerous homilies and cautionary tales concerning the corruption of those who had wasted their natural endowments with 'low-living', or who had confused self-help with 'selfishness', 'mere money-making', or simply 'getting-on'. Mere 'riches', he observed, 'are no proof whatever of moral worth'. If 'some of the finest qualities of human nature' were related to 'the right use of money', wealth could equally testify to the 'avarice' and 'selfishness' of the 'inordinate lovers of gain', or tempt its possessor to the 'vices of thriftlessness, extravagance, and improvidence'.[10]

Collini has emphasized how this 'Manichaean view of the self' exercised a strong hold over Victorian political thought generally. The danger of falling into bad ways formed a perennial temptation for the liberal; a fear reinforced not only by religion but also by the associationist psychology of the time, with its emphasis on the formative role of habit and custom on human behaviour.[11] There was a growing worry that the nation's commercial achievements might undermine the very qualities which had produced them. In a typical piece of culture critique, Smiles observed how 'in their pursuit of riches, the English are gradually losing sight of their higher characteristics.'[12] The growth of cities, increased factory size, greater mobility of labour with the new railway system, even improved prosperity, all seemed to be destroying the environment necessary for the Victorian virtues to flourish. As early as 1857, the free trade campaigner Richard Cobden remarked: 'The social and political state of [Birmingham] is far more healthy than that of Manchester; and it arises from the fact that the industry of the hardware district is carried on by small manufacturers...whilst the great capitalists in Manchester form an aristocracy.'[13] Only competition could provide the necessary antidote, for it placed 'the lazy man...under the necessity of exerting himself.'[14] It disciplined businessman and worker alike, rewarding merit and effort and punishing the indolent. Smiles feared that as the division of labour increased, the beneficial aspects of competition lessened. Selfishness replaced the desire to shine as the motive to work, and the sympathy uniting master and servant degenerated into 'simply a money bargain' between antagonistic classes.[15]

Politically, the character ethos contained a goodly dose of bourgeois priggishness mixed with resentment directed at the wasteful debauchery of a 'decadent' aristocracy. Smiles looked on the emulation of 'genteel' ways as the surest road to moral and financial downfall. Only the landowners escaped the rigours of the competitive system, their rents reflecting the 'unearned income' accruing from the efforts of others. Their hereditary wealth and privileges gave them great resources for patronage and corruption, making them, in J. S. Mill's phrase, 'the great demoralising agency in the country'.[16] Smiles warned that the new men should not forget their common origins: 'in recognising the great parvenu spirit of this age, we merely recognise what, in other words, is designated as the dignity of labour, the rights of industry and the power of intellect.'[17] In such ways, the Smilsean ethic served to reinforce the respectable classes' sense of their own worth. Growing out of the radicalism of the 1840s, it represented the aspirations of the 'men of active and aspiring talent': the craftsmen, retailers, small producers, merchants, manufacturers and members of the professions who were anxious for the power and prestige they felt was their due.[18] They presented this political challenge in the guise of a struggle of ideals rather than as naked class conflict. As Harold Perkin notes, 'active capital, open competition and the productive entrepreneur were a standing indictment of passive property, closed patronage and the leisured gentleman.'[19] The battle with the landowners, epitomized in the anti-Corn Law agitation, became 'part of the eternal duel between good and evil'.[20] This attitude drew additional sustenance from a view of English history, centred on the Civil War, as the triumph of the righteous over the damned, of 'almost Judaic narrowness'.[21]

If the assault on the position of the aristocracy was one aspect of the liberal moral revolution, the elevation of the working classes into sober and diligent habits was another of equal importance. In liberal eyes the political ascendency of the masses had to be linked to their moral improvement if a destructive anarchy was not to result. This was achieved in two ways: first, by apparently extending the rewards and values of the Victorian ethos to ever larger sections of the community, and second by reinforcing the practice of its distinctive virtues through a vast network of institutions – from elementary schools and Mechanics Institutes to friendly societies, co-operatives and savings banks.[22] The extensions of the franchise in 1832 and 1867, for example, were championed for their usefulness as a moralizing agency capable of encouraging the virtues of self-reliance and mutual respect between the social classes.[23] It was not the rights of citizens but the workers' 'self-command and power of endurance' as exemplified in 'that magnificent moral spectacle' of the self-sacrificing Lancashire cotton operatives who supported the North in the American Civil War, which warranted Gladstone including them within the pale of the constitution.[24] In a similar vein, Smiles told the Leeds workers, to whom his lectures were originally addressed, that self-help was not 'to be regarded merely as a means of gaining a higher position in society than that which you now hold...The grand object aimed at should be to make the great mass of people virtuous, well-informed, and well-conducted; and to open to them new sources of pleasure and happiness.' With prudence and foresight workers could become capitalists themselves. 'Little things' added up: 'a glass of beer a day is equal to forty-five shillings a year...Placed in a savings bank, it would amount to a hundred pounds in twenty years.' By such measures, the average citizen could gain independence, attain an equal standing in contractual relations, and have no need to call on charity – thereby escaping the paternalistic and 'demoralising' clutches of the aristocratic ideal. The concerns of the working class were thereby harnessed to those of middle-class radicals, Smiles remarking that 'those who do society's work – who produce, under the direction of the most intelligent of their number, the wealth of the nation – are entitled to a much higher place than they have yet assumed.'[25]

Through the language of character, therefore, Victorian liberalism fashioned a new way of life, which because of its religious and historical roots was capable of cementing together a totally different class structure from the predominately agrarian and hierarchical order of the old society. The view of a natural hierarchy was abandoned and replaced by the notion that individuals were born free and equal and possessed of rights deriving from their innate capacities as human beings. Contract replaced status as the organizing principle of society. Rather than constraining individuals, the social order reflected the compacts and associations they had freely entered into for their own advantage. Individuals were no longer confined to their respective stations and their duties, but had an obligation to work hard and reap the rewards their talents entitled them to. Beatrice Webb's recollection of her mother's beliefs sums up this ethos in exemplary fashion:

...it was the bounden duty of every citizen to better his social status; to ignore those beneath him, and to aim steadily at the top rung of the social ladder. Only by this persistent pursuit by each individual of his own and his family's interest would the highest general level of civilisation be attained...No one of the present generation realises with what sincerity and fervour these doctrines were held by the representative men and women of the mid-Victorian middle class.[26]

This liberal morality drew on the social experience of the entrepreneurs, traders, shopkeepers and artisans of early capitalism. It invoked the image of an idealized market society, in which an individual's social position and success rested on his or her ability and effort. The labour theory of value codified this linkage of desert and the market. As David Miller has observed, 'if the value of an object is equal to the quantity of labour embodied in it, if the system of exchange ensures that (in the long run) objects exchange in proportion to their values, and if, finally, quantity of labour is an adequate measure of desert, then a market system must reward producers according to their deserts.'[27] That deserving individuals might fail through no fault of their own, either through sickness or because their services were not needed at a particular time, was rarely considered. It was assumed that human talents would ultimately prove mutually compatible, with each person's proving complementary to those of everyone else. A liberal society would therefore prove self-regulating.

The writings of Herbert Spencer (1820–1903) offer a particularly clear picture of this liberal ethos, for his ideas largely corresponded to the goals of the provincial nonconformist radicals of the 1840s to whose ranks he had belonged.[28] Responding to the need of the age for scientific proof of essentially religious doctrines, Spencer sought to justify liberal ideals as immanent laws of organic life. He argued that societies evolved from a feudal 'militant' order to an egalitarian and meritocratic 'industrial' form of organization. Although his coining of the phrase 'the survival of the fittest' gained him the reputation of being a Social Darwinist, his evolutionary theory drew its support from the Lamarckian model of adaptation to the environment and the inheritance of acquired characteristics, rather than Darwin's thesis of the competitive struggle for existence. Lamarck's view fitted the Victorian notion of the development of character through the judicious reward of effort far better than Darwin's. In general, Spencer defended *laissez-faire* not because he thought the weakest should go to the wall, but so that people would be forced to adapt themselves through their own efforts and their improvements would become 'organic' (that is, biologically incorporated) in the race.

Spencer's fully evolved society consisted of a purified form of mid-nineteenth-century market society. The dominant business unit of the time, the small private partnership, was plainly the inspiration for Spencer's model of a future 'industrial' social order composed of individual producers who grouped themselves into associations for mutual advantage through 'voluntary co-operation'. This social ideal assumed a natural harmony would issue from individuals striving towards self-betterment. The notion of character predisposed Spencer to regard any failure to succeed or fit in as the product of a perverted life. In any case, those whose talents were not required did not suffer any impairment of their liberty, only misfortune, and so were fit subjects for benevolent charity. Such cases were exceptional, however. The belief that individual development took a particular form, that there was a moral order to the universe, was so deeply entrenched that few Victorian thinkers recognized the difficulties which would arise should it be called into question. Spencer's Law of Equal Freedom,[29] for example, failed to address the problem of choosing between divergent sets of incompatible and incommensurable liberties, because he never considered the possibility of the existence of different qualities of freedom.[30] In both domestic and international affairs, irresolvable conflict was attributed to vestigal remnants of the aristocratic and hierarchical 'militant' society, in which particular individuals possessed the illegitimate power to place their private interests in opposition to the common good. Once unearned privilege was removed, such damaging opportunities ceased to arise.[31] Spencer even hinted at an eventual third stage, 'aesthetic' society, where work was subordinated to 'higher activities' of a spiritual and intellectual kind.[32]

Spencer personally remained wedded to the ideals of the 1840s throughout his long life. However, the growth of corporate capitalism towards the end of the century cast doubt on the plausibility of this model of industrial production and the view of human agency it embodied, as we shall see. The early liberal ethos increasingly came under pressure from the further evolution of those very social forces which had created it. The traditional view is that this development gave rise to a reorientation of British liberalism in the latter half of the nineteenth century. This account will dispute the traditional historiography and show no real shift occurred.

The assumed transition from the 'classical' liberalism of the 1840s to the 'new' liberalism of the 1880s is usually associated with the supposedly contrasting ideas of J. S. Mill and T. H. Green.[33] However, both thinkers shared the basic assumptions of Victorian liberalism outlined above. These ideals provided a common denominator between their respective theories, which undercut those differences of approach which have usually been employed to distinguish them. The dissimilarities between the two thinkers reflected a change of emphasis, the beginnings of which were already present in Mill's later writings. This alteration occurred within the conventions of Victorian liberal thought and reflected the ambiguity of its understanding of the relationship between society and the individual. Character discourse tended to fudge the degree to which changes in social structure were the cause or effect of

alterations in individual morality. As the new industrial social environment came to seem increasingly inimical to the character ideal, this
ambivalence was brought to the fore. Rather than seeing society as the
spontaneous product of individual effort, liberals became preoccupied
with ensuring the requisite social preconditions for character development. The rest of this section will explore the ambiguities of the
common core uniting Mill and Green before turning to an examination
of their respective variations on these shared themes in the next two
sections. The final section will cast doubt on the allegedly progressive
nature of the 'new liberalism', which further extended their redefinition
of liberal ideas and practices. It will be argued that the social dimension
of this movement often stemmed from a more regressive desire to
preserve the liberal ideal from many of the incoherences which the
modern industrial order had revealed it to contain.

The putative transformation of British liberalism in the late nineteenth
century has been attributed to a variety of epistemological, conceptual
and political shifts: from utilitarianism to idealism, from 'negative' to
'positive' liberty and from individualism to collectivism respectively.
However, once Victorian liberal thought is located within the framework of 'character' discourse, these conventional historiographical dicho-
tomies lose much of their interpretative force. I shall briefly consider
each of them in turn in relation to Mill and Green.[34]

Green's moralism has often been put down to his reliance on German
metaphysics and contrasted with the sound common sense of the native
empiricist tradition. Yet this attitude clearly belonged to the prevailing
spirit of the age and was prominent in thinkers holding very different
epistemological positions. Mill ascribed his famous break with his
Benthamite past to the failure of his father and mentor to recognize that
'man…is a being capable of pursuing spiritual perfection as an end;
of desiring for its own sake the conformity of his own character to his
own standard of excellence.'[35] Bentham's version of utilitarianism could
enforce an individual's external conformity to morality, either through
fear of pain or via an anticipated increase in pleasure, but could not
provide an internal motivation to act morally from a disinterested desire
to do good. Mill's revised utilitarianism sought to remedy these defects
by amending Bentham's notion of happiness to include a distinction
between those enjoyments which employed the 'higher faculties' and
those which appealed to the 'beast's pleasures'. As a result, he was able
to connect an increase in human happiness with the development of
character. Mill claimed that, given sufficient experience, the rational
satisfaction of wants would lead the individual from a 'lower' to a
'higher' self. Regression seemed inconceivable, for:

A being of higher faculties requires more to make him happy, is capable
probably of more acute suffering, and certainly accessible to it at more
points, than one of an inferior type; but in spite of these liabilities, he can

never really wish to sink into what he feels to be a lower grade of existence.

Elaborating this thesis in an infamous passage, Mill remarked how:

> It is better to be a human being dissatisfied than a pig satisfied; better to be Socrates dissatisfied than a fool satisfied. And if the fool, or the pig, are of a different opinion, it is because they only know their own side of the question. The other party to the comparison knows both sides.[36]

The only people who would willingly chose the lower pleasures over the higher were those who had either never experienced the latter or who had somehow lost the capacity to enjoy them. 'Human dignity' rendered it inconceivable that anyone could be truly happy with less.

Green agreed with the sentiment expressed by Mill, but disputed the coherence of his revision of utilitarianism.[37] By appealing to human dignity, Mill indicated 'his virtual surrender of the doctrine that all desire is for pleasure',[38] for 'he regards it as a counter motive to desires for animal pleasure.'[39] Mill had acknowledged tacitly a distinction between what humankind naturally was and what it could be, which the language of morals sought to bridge, without revising his theory of human psychology accordingly. He maintained that we developed our character through judging the desirability of different pleasures as defined by our existing wants. Green contested this model. He noted that different pleasures are often incommensurable. Comparing them only made sense when we discriminated between motivations, and did not take our desires as fixed and all-determining in relation to the goals we wanted to pursue. Thus the possession of character could not simply be a matter of doing what you wanted, but involved choosing to be a certain type of person and guiding your actions in conformity to this ideal.

The character ethos similarly bridges the divide usually held to separate Green's conception of liberty from Mill's.[40] In a famous article, Isaiah Berlin accused Green of having placed a putative transcendent self over and above the empirical self and of asserting that only the latter represented our 'true' personality.[41] On this basis, he supposedly distorted the notion of liberty from its usual 'negative' sense, of non-interference with the pursuit of our present wants, into a 'positive' power to realize our 'real' selves. Berlin maintained that whereas negative liberty consisted in freedom from external hindrances placed in the way of individuals satisfying their desires, positive liberty included the removal of restrictions on them conceiving those desires in the first place. He feared that the latter theory could justify the imposition of a code of conduct upon an individual because it fulfilled his or her putative better self, erroneously defending this action in the name of liberty.

This criticism has a number of problems deriving from the notoriously elusive nature of the negative/positive liberty distinction itself. As Berlin conceded, they 'seem concepts at no great logical distance from each other'. Indeed, earlier in his essay he clearly combined the two himself when arguing that negative liberty is asserted in 'every protest against exploitation and humiliation, against the encroachment of public authority, or the mass hypnosis of custom or organized propaganda'.[42] The first three cases are examples of external constraints on individual liberty, but the last two are surely internal. Thus it is not clear that mixing the two notions of constraints does involve any logical confusion of two different concepts of liberty. Rather, the concentration on purely external constraints renders the concept of negative liberty unacceptably narrow. If liberty is simply not to be prevented by others from doing what you want, then you could increase your freedom by trimming your desires. The paradigm case is the contented slave, who is conditioned to accept his or her slavery as natural, and whose expectations therefore match the opportunites available to him or her. Berlin granted this point when replying to his critics, but as he remarked this strengthens rather than weakens a fuller understanding of negative liberty. If, for example, my agoraphobia (internal constraint) is removed by psychoanalysis I am not thereby obliged to walk about in open spaces, I merely have the choice, previously denied me, to do so or not. This interpretation appears fully consistent with Berlin's revised definition of negative liberty as 'the removal of obstacles not merely to my actual, but to my potential choices...due to the closing of such doors or failure to open them, as a result intended or unintended, of alterable human practices'.[43] It can be distinguished from positive liberty on the grounds that there is 'no requirement that an agent actually realise an end for him to be free from all constraints to realise an end'.[44]

Recent accounts of freedom now usually agree on its conceptual structure as the liberty to make an autonomous choice, that is, without the hindrance of removable internal or external constraints resulting from human actions.[45] Both Mill and Green understood freedom in this sense. Green explicitly countered the sort of accusation Berlin levels at him by denying that 'it is the business of the state...directly to promote moral goodness, for that, from the very nature of moral goodness, it cannot do, but to maintain the conditions without which a free exercise of the human faculties is impossible.'[46] The freedom required for moral action was thus of a negative kind, in 'the primary or juristic sense, [of] power to act according to preference', that is, without internal or external constraints. Green did not state that only the good person was free, merely that only such individuals valued their liberty since 'freedom is precious...because it is an achievement of the self-seeking principle.'[47]

Mill employed a similar line of reasoning. It has been argued that his *On Liberty* contained two logically distinct doctrines of liberty. The first, encapsulated in Mill's 'very simple principle', limited the reasons which could be adduced to interfere with the individual to the prevention of harm to others. The second, his theory of individuality as the development of the 'higher' pleasures, outlined in chapter three of the essay, was a metaphysical doctrine defining what liberty consisted in.[48] However, by including 'the moral coercion of public opinion' on his list of impediments to 'liberty of action',[49] Mill invoked this fuller notion even when he formulated the simple principle. He believed the main threat to freedom in modern societies came from the pressure to conform, a danger arising from the power of majority opinion in democracies and the enervating effects of industrial labour. A society of contented slaves presented too real a prospect for Mill to limit political liberty to the narrow negative version often attributed to him.

Agreement on the general structure of the concept means that debate usually hinges on the degree to which particular human practices can be held to inhibit an individual's liberty, an issue which often shades into a discussion of our moral obligations towards others.[50] For example, advocates of the market as an unplanned catallaxy dispute the socialist opinion that those disadvantaged by market fluctuations have been denied any liberty by those seeking a profit. Similarly, whilst most commentators agree that the idea of freedom implies a weakly normative condition about an agent's ability to make a reasonable choice, disagreements arise about the degree to which social conditioning can induce 'false consciousness' and inhibit an individual's selection of his or her own way of life. Self-consciousness in these respects can no doubt only be pushed so far if it is not to be disabling and generate undue paranoia, but the limits will be largely those of conventional wisdom rather than of logic.

Victorian discussions of freedom were heavily conditioned by the ideal of character in this respect.[51] It set limits to the kinds of obstacle individuals could reasonably surmount themselves and to the duties they owed not to inhibit others. In different ways this enabled them to gloss over an important problem with autonomy-based liberalism central to Berlin's fears about 'positive' liberty. Berlin's original formulation sought to prevent any confusion between freedom and rationality. He believed that concentration on a person's inner motives for choosing a course of action ran the risk of replacing the natural, unplanned web of actions by a crude, rationalist set of rules, which the individual was obliged to obey.[52] Those who adopt the autonomy view of negative liberty counter the objection by arguing that reason could not determine action in this way because the range of possible rational choices is so large that one is always faced with numerous alternatives of equal reasonableness. In common with Berlin, they believe acceptance of this conflict of values marks the true liberal. Indeed, the commitment to autonomy implies such a pluralistic attitude, since one can only exercise it when there is a range of reasonable choices available. Nevertheless, as Tom Baldwin notes, this argument leaves negative libertarians 'with a profound antinomy', and he appositely quotes Sidgwick's conclusion that 'unless we assume or prove a moral order of the world there is a conflict between rational convictions.'[53]

The language of character, however, allowed Mill and Green (in common with other liberals) to ignore this quandry. Persons of character were supposed to practise self-restraint. Self-improvement entailed an abandonment not only of sensual gratification, but also of narrow selfishness. Although liberals praised competition as a means of maintaining individual vigour, they did not see it in terms of a clash between competing interests. Rather, it stimulated the exercise of the various virtues discussed above. Whilst individuals might have different aptitudes and abilities, when they employed them in the right manner they were revealed as being complementary.

Laissez-faire might be expected to form the natural counterpart to this view of human nature. The belief that social progress depended upon the elevation of individual morality through self-help provided for most Victorian liberals a prima facie case for adopting an individualist rather than a collectivist approach. For if, in Smiles's words,

> the nation is only an aggregate of individual conditions...then it follows that the highest patriotism and philanthropy consist, not so much in altering laws and modifying institutions, as in helping and stimulating men to elevate and improve themselves by their own free and individual action.[54]

According to the Smilsean school of thought, no better stimulus to self-help existed than the experiences of life's hardships and the necessity of making one's own way. Whilst he admitted 'human character is moulded by a thousand subtle influences,...by the world we live in as by the spirit of our forefathers', he considered 'it is nevertheless equally clear that men must be the active agents of their own well-being and doing.'[55] Removing the obstacles to human happiness or goodness by state action, or even indiscriminate charity, would produce an effeminate people, lacking in moral backbone and engender national decline – a thesis which Spencer gave a spurious 'scientific' backing in evolutionary theory.[56] The improvement of the nation depended upon self-improvement.

However, even Smiles distinguished this general preference for individualism and *laissez-faire* from a blanket advocacy of doing nothing. 'Character' and 'Duty' were largely interchangeable in his eyes, and an obligation to help those who could not, as opposed to would not, help themselves, runs through his writings. In common with most radical liberals, he accepted the need to provide certain 'public goods' such as bridges or a sewage system which were necessary for the functioning of society at large, but insufficiently remunerative for any single individual to provide. In a famous passage, he railed against the view that when typhus and cholera broke out, 'nobody is to blame.'[57] As administrative historians have pointed out, if *laissez-faire* is taken to mean a complete absence of government intervention then the nineteenth century, which saw a veritable explosion of state activity, failed to practise what it preached.[58] However, despite the dramatic increase in the quantity of such interference, Dicey was quite right not to regard this as a move from 'individualism' to 'collectivism'. Its justification and the principles regulating its funding and administration remained impeccably individualist.

The later blurring of individualism and collectivism was less obvious because far more deeply rooted in liberal assumptions. The tension between the two notions arose from the paradoxical manner in which character formed both the mechanism of social advance and its end product. An entirely individualist interpretation of this conception of progress seems to suggest the existentialist fantasy of the 'brave and naked will', whereby individuals with no fixed biological and social nature created themselves as they go along. Most nineteenth-century liberals were prevented by either the predominately sensationist psychological theories, or biological views stressing the importance of inherited characteristics, from swallowing this thesis in its entirety. They conceded that the right kind of environment formed a pre-condition for the possession of character. However, to modern eyes at least, this risks falling into the trap of justifying a character-promoting paternalism and an intolerance to uncharacterful ways of life. By and large contemporaries fudged the issue. If poverty, to take the commonest contemporary example, was treated as entirely within the individual's power to control his or her fate regardless of social conditions, welfare was opposed on the grounds that it would present temptations to indolence most individuals could not withstand and 'sap forever the self-reliance of a class'. Once self-reliance and self-management became synonomous with self-realization and self-development, the shift from individualist policies to collectivist ones in the 1880s became much easier to justify.[59] Even so, the advocacy of collective arrangements involved no fundamental disagreement with the moral goals of individualism, and social reformers consistently argued that they aimed at 'the freest and fullest development of human quality and power'.[60]

These last two aspects of Victorian liberal thought, the assumption of the progressive supersession of conflict by co-operation and the paradoxical relationship of character to conditions, provided both the linchpin and the Achilles' heel of the doctrine. A fuller consideration of the writings of Mill and Green will reveal how both ideas were stretched to the limit as liberal discourse interacted with the emerging industrial society of nineteenth-century Britain, finally being undermined by the world it had helped to shape.

J. S. MILL: A COLLECTIVIST INDIVIDUALISM

More than any other thinker, John Stuart Mill (1806–73) came to epitomize Victorian liberalism. *On Liberty*, in particular, has been treated as a paradigmatic statement of the liberal tradition. Yet too frequently this essay is read outside the context of Mill's other works and the political language and preoccupations of the day. This more historical interpretative angle reveals a far more ambivalent message.

Concentration on Mill's defence of the 'one very simple principle' in *On Liberty*,[61] that the only justifiable interference with another's liberty is to prevent harm to others, has led to a relative neglect of the 'single truth' this principle was intended to serve; namely, 'the importance, to man and society, of a large variety in types of character, and of giving full freedom to human nature to expand itself in innumerable and conflicting directions'.[62] This championship of character formed the core of Mill's advocacy of liberty. For Mill the possession of character distinguished human beings from the brutes. It entailed an overcoming of sin – usually defined as animal pleasure, notably sexual lust – and was the mark of one 'whose desires and impulses are his own – are the expression of his own nature, as it has been developed and modified by his own culture'.[63] Indeed, Mill asserted that 'civilization in every one of its aspects is a struggle against the animal instincts',[64] so that 'the laws of national character' became for him 'by far the most important of sociological laws', character being 'the power by which all those of the circumstances of society which are artificial, laws and customs for instance, are altogether moulded'.[65] In Mill's argument, liberty was only vital to self-realization and social progress when linked to character, therefore. Without character, he thought personal liberty degenerated into mere animal licence.

Mill's conception of character involved three interrelated elements: liberty or autonomy, individuality or diversity and progress or improvement.[66] The error of many modern commentators rests in separating his case for the first from its links with the other two within the discourse of character. As we saw in the previous section, Mill adopted the standard view of autonomy as the capacity for self-directed choice, free from internal or external constraints of a psychological or physical nature. Mill thought it was important that people be given the opportunity to make their own way in the world rather than being dictated to by others – no matter how well-meaning or better informed those interferences might be. In Mill's opinion, a person's 'own mode of laying out his existence is best, not because it is best in itself, but because it is his own mode'.[67] Even if individuals fell into error as a result of going their own way, it was better for them to learn from their own mistakes than to have the right course of action forced upon them.

Part of the reason for Mill valuing autonomy so much arose from his belief in the diversity or individuality of human beings.[68] His own education at the hands of his father had been behaviourist and mechanical. At the end of the process he had felt like a 'manufactured man' who had 'had a certain impress of opinion stamped upon me which I could only reproduce'.[69] In reacting against his upbringing, Mill was moved to adopt an organic view of human nature. Individuals, like trees, must be allowed to develop 'according to the tendency of the inward forces which make it a living thing'. We were not like 'a machine to be built after a model'. In keeping with this horticultural metaphor, he insisted that just as different sorts of plants flourish in different kinds of soil and climate, so 'different persons also require different conditions for their spiritual development.'[70] The diversity of human beings therefore entailed that they be provided with a variety of situations in which to develop autonomously their particular talents and aptitudes.

The issue of development brings us finally to the nub of Mill's argument – the importance of autonomy for individual progress and improvement. Mill famously decided 'to forego any advantage which could be derived to my argument from the idea of abstract right as a thing independent of utility'. Much Mill scholarship has been taken up with trying to prove the inadvisability of this decision. However, it was vital to Mill's argument. For Mill had in mind his own revised version of Benthamite utilitarianism, based upon a notion of 'utility in the largest sense, grounded on the permanent interests of man as a progressive being'.[71] We noted in the previous section that Mill had attacked Bentham's doctrine for ignoring human perfectibility – the ability to pursue excellence and virtue for their own sakes. He accused Bentham of having treated human desires as fixed and essentially base. They could be manipulated but never improved – a theory with potentially totalitarian implications. Mill, in contrast, contended that the mechanical manipulation of human sentiments must be replaced by their natural improvement within a society which encouraged their free development. Bentham's theory fell foul of what Hayek has called the constructivist fallacy. Although Mill thought one could employ the concept of utility to explain the spontaneous emergence of a social order, he denied that you could apply it directly in order to evaluate specific policies. As John Gray has pointed out, Mill's utilitarianism was of an indirect nature.[72] Mill's utility principle was an axiological principle defining the goal of human conduct, namely 'that pleasure and freedom from pain are desirable as ends', not a moral axiom that we maximize happiness. The individuality of self-development, which he defended in *On Liberty*, did not conflict with his utilitarianism, because Mill did not believe we could maximize happiness in a direct manner. Since human beings were so diverse and their improvement potentially infinite, they had to be given full reign to develop according to their inner natures through trial and error. Bentham's managerial attempt to obtain the greatest happiness of the greatest number at any given moment would arbitrarily halt human progress at the lowest level. Mill maintained that maximal happiness of the superior sort could only be obtained by allowing individuals to form their characters for themselves.

Although Mill's linking of autonomy with a utilitarian view of human progress was coherent, it rested on dubious foundations. Mill's theory traded on an implicitly teleological and optimistic view of human nature, in which free agents naturally opted for 'higher' pleasures over the 'lower', 'Socratic dissatisfaction' over 'swinish contentment'. Moreover, Mill assumed that this refinement of human pleasures brought with it 'the better development of [the individual's] nature' and especially 'the feelings and capacities which have the good of others for their object'.[73] Thus, Mill could endorse autonomy and diversity on two counts: they were necessary not only for the natural development of the individual but also for the moral and intellectual improvement of society at large. Since the character of society depended on the character of its individual members, only a society committed to autonomy could progress. If Mill never elaborated a teleological theory of historical progress along the lines of most other nineteenth-century social thinkers, he certainly assumed some such thesis.[74] As Stefan Collini has pointed out, 'he frequently resorted to the claim that there had been a discernible line of moral improvement, not dissimilar to what T. H. Green was to call "the extension of the area of the common good".'[75] Thus, the coherence of Mill's position rested on the dual claim that autonomous individuals would not choose a 'lower' over a 'higher' pleasure, and that the higher pleasures were essentially social in nature.

The second aspect of this dubious claim was in many respects more important than the first. For example, Mill identified the 'harm' principle as the sole allowable justification for the restriction of individual liberty. Harm is notoriously difficult to define in a neutral manner, however. Mill avoided employing it to adjudicate between conflicting types of liberty on the grounds that certain freedoms might be deemed more or less harmful than others. Indeed, his indirect utilitarianism went against such direct applications of the utility principle. But he seems to have thought that only the lower pleasures could clash in a harmful way. He did not consider that clashes between conflicting higher freedoms might take place – that freedom of speech might conflict in certain instances with the freedom of privacy, for instance. Hence, his tendentious exclusion of offence as a form of harm. He simply assumed that individual liberty amongst autonomous agents of character could be expanded in a non-conflictual fashion. However, this belief rested on the highly unlikely presumption that all autonomous individuals were Millian utilitarians.

So long as individuals and society progressed in the manner Mill supposed, his liberalism was relatively straightforward, fitting with the traditional picture of him as an anti-paternalist keen to remove the restraints on individual freedom. Unfortunately for his peace of mind,

Mill was all too aware that our desire for self-improvement was easily inhibited and that the:

> capacity for the nobler feelings is in most natures a very tender plant, easily killed, not only by hostile influences, but by the mere want of sustenance; and in the majority of young persons it speedily dies away if the occupations to which their position in life has devoted them, and the society into which it has thrown them, are not favourable to keeping that higher capacity in existence.[76]

In tackling this problem, Mill's theory built upon a crucial distinction, inherent to the assumptions behind character discourse, between the capacity for autonomy and the exercise of autonomy.[77] On the one hand, Mill argued that the exercise of autonomy must be self-willed. To impose it would be to infringe that capacity, since 'he who does anything because it is the custom makes no choice' and 'has no need of any other faculty than the ape-like one of imitation'. Mill stressed that it was 'of importance, not only what men do, but also what manner of men do it'.[78] To act autonomously simply because one had no option in the matter would be insufficient to generate a truly autonomous character. Hence Mill's insistence that people should have the opportunity to drink themselves to death if they so chose, always providing, of course, that they harmed no one else in the process. On the other hand, Mill recognised the impossibility of someone autonomously becoming autonomous. Mill's empiricist psychology committed him to the thesis that we were largely formed by our environment and history. The capacity for autonomy, therefore, was a product of antecedent circumstances. Mill attempted to resolve the dilemma this fact posed to the notion of autonomy in the section of his *System of Logic* devoted to a discussion of 'Liberty and Necessity'. He acknowledged that 'the will to alter our own character is given us, not by any effort of ours, but by circumstances we cannot help: it comes to us from external causes or not at all.' However, once obtained, 'the desire to mould [our character] in a particular way' became 'one of those circumstances, and by no means the least influential'.[79] As a result of this compatibilist thesis, Mill could justify considerable intervention and provision on the part of the state or well-placed individuals in order to give people the capacity for autonomy, whilst at the same time claiming that the exercise of autonomy only required the freedoms guaranteed by the harm principle and a 'variety of situations' so that people could make experiments in living.

Mill made it clear that the argument of *On Liberty* applied 'only to human beings in the maturity of their faculties'. Such persons possessed character and so had acquired the capacity for autonomy. He explicitly excluded from his doctrine the non-autonomous, such as children and 'those backward states of society in which the race itself may be considered in its nonage'. Indeed, he asserted 'despotism is a legitimate mode of government with barbarians, provided the end be their improvement, and the means justified by actually effecting that end.'[80] Paternalistic interference with those who had yet to become autonomous was both acceptable and imperative for Mill, so long as the attainment of autonomy was the purpose and effect of the measures. The difficulty with this position concerns how we identify whether someone acts out of choice or not. Mill's belief in human perfectibility made this question a particularly tricky one for him, since on this view it became almost inconceivable that anyone with the capacity for autonomy who was placed in conditions of freedom should fail to use it to mould his or her character in a desirable way. If Mill accepted 'that many who are capable of the higher pleasures, occasionally, under the influence of temptation, postpone them to the lower', he could not believe that they did so 'voluntarily': 'before they devote themselves to the one, they have already become incapable of the other.'[81] The pitfalls of Mill's linking of autonomy to moral progress now become clear. Mill had identified autonomy with acting in accordance with his ideals. As a result, all actions which did not aim at social improvement of the approved kind became *ipso facto* non-autonomous and hence legitimate cases for paternalistic interference. In fact, Mill positively denied us the right to give up the capacity for free action. 'The principle of freedom', he declared, 'cannot require that [a person] should be free not to be free. It is not freedom to be allowed to alienate his freedom.' To enter an irrevocable contract, such as marriage or slavery for example, involved an abdication of liberty and 'defeats...the very purpose which is the justification of allowing him to dispose of himself'. Nothing stood in the way of restraining such actions, therefore, since 'he is no longer free; but is thenceforth in a position which has no longer the presumption in its favour, that would be afforded by his voluntarily remaining in it.'[82] As we shall see, in spite of Mill's personal stand on the drink question, Green employed an analogous argument to justify temperance legislation.

The ambiguity within Mill's liberalism arising from his linking of freedom and improvement can be found throughout his writings. Although he claimed to be in the vanguard of progress, he increasingly found himself at odds with the dominant opinions or social trends of his age. His proposals for rectifying the blockages on the road to improvement highlight the dangers of Mill's doctrine. They reveal the possibility that the despotic methods suited to barbarians might become permanent measures to keep people on the straight and narrow.

Mill's mentalist theory of human progress made the potential inhibition of people's capacity for autonomy as a result of internal constraints a particular worry for him. He regarded this fear to be especially well founded in modern societies. For an unfortunate by-product of civilization was its tendency to produce social conformity to a base and materialistic ethos, suitable only for Benthamite pigs.

In a famous early essay on the theme of 'Civilization', he noted how commercial prosperity had produced 'moral effeminacy', 'torpidity and cowardice', rendered people 'less heroic', unable to support pain or difficulty, or even 'disagreeable ideas'. The lower orders were placed in a new form of 'dependency' by the division of labour, whilst their superiors neglected public service and confined their energies to 'money-getting'. The 'salutary influence' of public opinion was 'lost in the hubbub' of modern cities. Tradesmen in small country towns, for example, acquired the reputation that their conduct entitled them to. If their goods were of poor quality or over-priced in a relatively circum-scribed market, they lost their customers. In a 'crowded city', in contrast, 'success…depends not upon what a person is, but upon what he seems: mere marketable qualities become the object instead of substantial ones.' 'This growing insignificance of the individual in the mass' corrupted the 'private virtues'. Mass communication and education rendered culture more homogeneous and increased the 'despotic' power of custom. Even intellectuals had succumbed to the temptations of the new popular press, and only told the public what they wanted to hear. In these ways, the mass nature of the democratic age moved it inexorably towards 'collective mediocrity'.[83] The pressures of modern social production were like the binding on a Chinese lady's foot, stultifying the natural development and diversity of individuals and forcing them to conform to a uniform 'pinched and hidebound' type of character. Mill was horrified that contemporary Britain was moving towards the nemesis of 'Chinese stationariness'.[84]

Mill's remedy for these evils was to devise forms of economic co-operation which would revive the value of competition and to design 'national institutions of education and forms of polity, calculated to invigorate the individual character'.[85] Although he never wrote his planned science of ethology (or character formation), a number of less precise principles guided his suggestions for social and political reform. He provided the clearest exposition of these ideas in the opening chapters of his *Considerations of Representative Government*. Government, he declared, served two purposes: it operated 'as an agency of national education' and it supplied 'arrangements for conducting the collective affairs of the community in the state of education in which they already are'.[86] Unfortunately, in outlining his thesis the first purpose became subordinated to the second. He contended that the machinery of govern-ment was much the same under any constitution. The laws of economics and the principles of good administration were of universal application. However, not all governments had the same desire or interest in apply-ing them with equal diligence. The central problem of politics, therefore, consisted in placing the people in a position to ensure these duties were effectively carried out. A country's political institutions played a decisive part in this respect, by educating the people in promoting and securing the general interest. Education and a correct evaluation of one's own interests went hand in hand. It had been his father's and Bentham's error in uncoupling the utilitarian argument from the educative case for democracy that gave rise to fears of the 'tyranny of the majority'. Thus, the form of government had to be adapted to the prevailing stage of development of the populace and foster their passage 'to the next step which it is necessary for them to take'.[87]

Mill distinguished between 'rude' and 'civilised' peoples, or between those who did not possess the capacity for autonomy associated with character and those who did. A 'rude' people could not practise the necessary forbearance, and their passions were too violent, to forgo private conflict. 'In such a case', Mill observed in his best East India Office manner, 'a civilised government, to be really advantageous to them, will require to be in a considerable degree despotic.' 'Uncivilized races', moreover, avoided 'continuous labour of an unexciting kind'. Since Mill regarded such work as vital to civilization, preparing the material world for its reception and disciplining the mind, 'even personal slavery' might be justified. For:

> by giving a commencement to industrial life, and enforcing it as the exclusive occupation of the most numerous portion of the community, [slavery] may accelerate the transition to a better freedom than that of fighting and rapine.

A 'civilized' people, in contrast, deserved much better. Possessing an 'active and energetic character', as opposed to the 'passive' type encountered in less advanced nations, they could both maintain and benefit from the more participatory forms of government. Even at this stage, 'its principal element' was 'the improvement of the people themselves'. A 'completely popular government' not only favoured good administration, but by making citizens responsible for their own affairs 'promotes a better and higher form of national character than any other polity whatsoever'.[88]

Communities had to traverse numerous 'intermediate stages' between these two extremes. Indeed, Mill devoted the rest of the book to outlining the various institutional arrangements suitable for the degree of mental development he considered to exist amongst his fellow citizens. Disavowing the radical orthodoxy of his father, he argued that one could not assume that the interests of the numerical majority would naturally coincide with the general welfare. 'Unskilled workers' were unlikely to follow the enlightened counsel of middle-class intellectuals or sacrifice an immediate benefit for a longer term advantage.[89] Instead, such habits had to be inculcated in them, and Mill proposed a number of measures – from Hare's scheme of proportional representation to open ballots and fancy franchises weighted in favour of the more intelligent – to secure a balanced representation of interests, increase the educative benefits of political participation, and habituate the populace to choosing their representatives from amongst the best minds and deferring to their opinions.

Mill's policy towards the regulation of the economy reflected an analogous desire slowly to inculcate character and with it the capacity for autonomy. His general advocacy of *laissez-faire* did not stem from his commitment to individual rights against state interference in moral matters.[90] 'Trade', as he said, 'is a social act' and hence 'other-regarding'. As such it was a fit subject for government regulation.[91] What mattered was whether a particular economic system enhanced or constrained the opportunities for the development of character. Mill favoured free trade for three main reasons: efficiency, fear of the rigidity and potentially authoritarian nature of state bureaucracy and, most importantly, to stimulate individual morality. All three reflected the requirements of character, and could be overridden when they conflicted with them.

Free trade favoured efficiency because, all things being equal, 'leaving people to themselves...is always better than controlling them.' In most cases, people knew their own interests better than others' and gained from being made more self-reliant. Competition usually encouraged innovation, secured better-quality goods at cheaper prices, and hence increased the prosperity of the people and indirectly their freedom. 'Restrictions on trade', therefore, 'are wrong solely because they do not really produce the results which it is desired to produce by them.'[92] In consequence, Mill happily entertained 'large exceptions to laissez-faire' where he felt they were beneficial. Many of these reflected the standard judgements of nineteenth-century political economists. Gas and water, for example, being natural monopolies were less likely to be exploited for private gain when managed by a government agency.[93] Other public services, such as lighthouses, were too unprofitable for individuals to want to provide them.[94]

Mill's second reason for supporting *laissez-faire* arose from his fear of any growth in the power of the state. Mill was particularly perturbed about the likely effects of a burgeoning state bureaucracy. His objections anticipate in many ways the much better-known views of Weber, examined here in chapter 4. In a planned economy, the bureaucracy would endlessly expand as societies became more technologically complex and new functions had to be taken over by the state. As the main source of power, it would naturally attract all the talented and ambitious individuals within the society. This concentration of talent would ultimately prove self-defeating. The mass of the population would become like slaves as a result of being permanently dictated to. Lack of competition and the complacency which comes with absolute power would likewise cause the elite themselves to stultify. Creative thought would be replaced by the drudgery of bureaucratic routine, resulting in social stagnation. Such, he believed, had been the fate of the Chinese Mandarinate and the Tsarist administration.[95]

The third and chief set of reasons behind Mill's prejudice against the extension of the state were neither economic nor political, however, but moral. In contrast to some of his contemporaries, he rejected:

> the complacent optimism, which represents the evils of life as desirable things, because they call forth qualities adapted to combat with evils...As practical beings it is our business to free human life from as many as poss-ible of its difficulties, and not to keep up a stock of them as hunters pursue game, for the exercise of pursuing it.[96]

Up to a point, human progress went together with the improvement of our material circumstances. A certain standard of material well-being was necessary to provide us with the leisure and means for the higher pursuits. Mill saw no reason for preventing the general population from benefiting from the enhanced levels of wealth available in civilized societies. All the same, he believed self-reliance and the spirit of volun-tary co-operation had to be encouraged because, even if the need for them might 'diminish', it was unlikely, to 'wither away'. Moreover, a people:

> who expect to have everything done for them, except what can be made an affair of mere habit and routine – have their faculties only half devel-oped; their education is defective in one of its most important branches.[97]

Such persons would lack the ability to be free, and would ultimately fall into a condition of slavery.[98] The aim of 'good government', therefore, was to 'give all its aid in such a shape as to encourage and nurture any rudiments it may find of a spirit of individual innovation'.[99] Wherever possible the role of the state was to encourage self-help and voluntary enterprise. Indeed, he maintained that 'a government cannot have too much of the kind of activity which does not impede, but aids and stimulates individual exertion and development.'[100] Mill's defence of the Poor Law was in this respect entirely conventional. This legislation provided the bulwark of the Victorian social order, and Mill, like most of his class, had few qualms about forcing the supposedly feckless and indolent to be free.

Thus, state interference was wrong for Mill whenever it inhibited the moral resources stemming from character. However, the reverse side of this principle was that it was justified to implement programmes when-ever these resources were either absent or required fostering. Indeed, he believed that:

> in the particular circumstances of a given age and nation, there is scarcely anything really important to the general interest, which it might not be desirable, or even necessary, that the government should take upon itself, not because private individuals cannot effectively perform it, but because they will not.[101]

In Mill's opinion, such a situation was likely to arise whenever collective action might be needed to implement policies. In these instances, everyone might desire the benefits of a particular measure, such as Green Belt legislation, but lack the solidarity to act in concert so as to achieve it without the sanction of the law.[102] In cases like these, Mill's faith in individualism frequently faltered and gave way to a paternalist collectivism. Mill's example in his *Principles of Political Economy*, the achievement of a reduction of working hours from ten to nine, represented an early instance of those two bugbears of modern public choice theory, the free rider problem and the prisoners' dilemma.[103] Mill observed that 'unless all the operatives bind themselves together to abide by it', individual workers would gradually erode the agreement by seeking to increase their wages by working the extra hour. The only way to prevent employers from taking advantage of such free riders was to force them to limit the working day to nine hours. Mill claimed that such intervention increased freedom, since all workers really desired to work less. He elaborated his case by comparing compulsory factory regulations with Sabatarian Legislation. The second directed that we employ the free day in a particular way. The first, in contrast, was only necessary to prevent a selfish or ill-informed operative sacrificing the long-term general interest for immediate personal gain by undermining the bargaining power of the others by working overtime for additional pay.[104] Factory labour apart, workers could use their extra time as they pleased. This example suggests that Mill aimed solely to enhance the scope for human beings to pursue activities of their own choosing by increasing their 'free time' from the imposed tasks of the workplace. However, presumably some workers might wish to work longer hours, either because they had nothing better to do or in order to save up for a house or expensive holiday, etc.

The paternalistic potential of Mill's argument becomes evident when we turn to another of his examples of a breakdown of collective behaviour, birth control. A rigorous Malthusian, Mill followed Ricardo's teaching that the only possibility for the working classes to maintain reasonable wages and a comfortable standard of living was by refraining from procreation. When voluntary restraint was lacking, Mill had no doubts about the justice of legally controlling sexual activity:

> In a country either over-peopled, or threatened with being so, to produce children, beyond a very small number, with the effect of reducing the reward of labour by their competition, is a serious offence against all who live by the remuneration of their labour...Such laws are interferences of the State to prevent a mischievous act.[105]

When it came to denouncing 'the animal instinct of sex', Mill was a true Victorian. A 'degrading slavery to the brute instinct', such 'swinish' pleasures formed no part of human dignity or freedom for him. Such

examples show the narrowness of Mill's moralized account of autonomy. They also reveal that even Mill sometimes doubted his fellow
human beings' capacity for moral improvement. Once his optimism
about human nature deserted him, there was nothing the benevolent
state might not do to realize the 'real' interests of its citizens.[106] In spite
of his disavowal of Benthamism, Mill's doctrine provided every bit as
much of a charter for the rational planner of human souls.

So far we have concentrated on the paternalist consequences of Mill's
association of autonomy with moral progress. Much of the discussion
reveals that this coupling severely qualified his avowed commitment to
diversity as well. Onora O'Neill has remarked that when the institutions
of society themselves shape the capacity for freedom of its members,
one can no longer invoke a premise concerning their capacity for free
action to work out what the optimal set of liberties is.[107] Mill's praise of
freedom in *On Liberty* suffered from just this difficulty, for the civilized
individuals presupposed by his theory had no choice but to act as
Millian rational self-developers. Practising self-cultivation constituted
the only way to thrive in a Millian society. In many respects it formed
the only permissible life style. Even the coercive effects of public dis-
approval had Mill's heartiest endorsement when directed at 'a person
who shows rashness, obstinacy, self-conceit – who cannot live within
moderate means –who cannot restrain himself from hurtful indulgences
– who pursues animal pleasures at the expense of those of feeling'.[108]
As we observed above, he rejected the possibility that a choice of a
non-autonomous life style could ever be a free decision. However, this
belief will only issue in a genuinely tolerant society, if one thinks (as
Mill generally did) that human beings naturally want to be Millian
individuals.

Even his championing of 'individuality', 'manysidedness', and 'the
essential importance of human development in its richest diversity',
implied a modified version of his preferred model of human agency.
Unlike many liberals today, such as Berlin, Mill's espousal of this
doctrine did not stem from a belief in value pluralism. Not only did he
assume human beings naturally acted as Millian utilitarians, ranking
poetry over push-pin, abstinence over sex, Socratic discontent over
piggish pleasure, so that the loss of the latter entailed no real diminution
of freedom; he also maintained that genuine expressions of human
individuality were mutually enhancing and complementary. Conflicts
only arose from the 'lower' pleasures, which were essentially self-
interested and materialistic in nature. The 'higher', in contrast, involved
'a better development of the social part of [human] nature, rendered
possible by the restraint put upon the selfish part'.[109] The sort of
contrasts and combinations he had in mind were of 'Coleridge' and
'Bentham', 'the most passionate virtue and the sternest self-control'. His
conception of the ideal marriage as a combination of feminine intuition
and masculine abstract reason between two largely assexual partners

offers a particularly striking example of the narrowness of forms of individual self-expression that Mill's moralized view of human nature allowed for.[110] He did not envisage the hard choices between incommensurable sets of compossible liberties that make up most of the hard practical decisions facing politicians and individuals. No doubt the fact that Victorian culture was more homogeneous than our own made this question easier to ignore in Mill's time than it is now. Yet, given that he regarded himself as confronting the forces of narrow conformity, this denial of genuine conflict between different conceptions of the good life considerably weakens the force of his case for liberty and tolerance.

These points need to be borne in mind when considering Mill's later 'socialism'. Mill's tentative espousal of this creed referred only to the moral ideal of a co-operative, altruistic society where the common good was pursued by collective effort. This 'ethical socialism', which rejected 'the materialist or Epicurean way of life' and advocated a 'genuine regard to the interests of others', was perfectly acceptable to contemporary liberals.[111] Mill's position on property illustrates particularly clearly the individualist basis of his apparent concessions to collectivism.[112] Mill did not regard property rights as flowing from some putative natural liberty to dispose of our goods as we pleased, they were social privileges. Their justification arose from utilitarian considerations of incentive and security. Whilst the production of wealth had to follow the 'laws' of economics, distribution was 'a matter of human institution solely'.[113] The only valid claim to property he acknowledged was 'as a guarantee to individuals of the fruits of their own labour and abstinence'.[114] This view fitted in with standard liberal prejudices against the inherited wealth of the aristocracy and income from land. Mill advocated limitations on the amounts an individual could inherit, seeing 'nothing objectionable in fixing a limit to what any one may acquire...without any exercise of his faculties'.[115] Similarly, landowners only deserved the income which derived from their own improvements.[116] Rent, in contrast, 'constantly tends to increase without any exertion or sacrifice on the part of the owners', so that landlords 'grow richer, as it were, in their sleep, without working, risking or economising'. A land tax on increased revenue from rising site values:

> would not properly be taking anything from anybody; it would merely be applying an accession of wealth, created by circumstances, to the benefit of society, instead of allowing it to become an unearned appendage to the riches of a particular class.[117]

Although these notions proved to be a Trojan horse, allowing later new liberals to justify progressive taxation, Mill never countenanced redistribution on the basis of need, or because individual liberty was increased by enhancing people's welfare. The few instances when he advocated redistributive measures derived their rationale from linking property more firmly to desert as a result of effort and merit. They supposedly increased freedom by stimulating self-reliance.

His proposals for Irish Land Reform provide a classic example of his thinking in this respect.[118] On his analysis, the famine had resulted from the inefficient management of the landowners and the excessive breeding of the peasants. The former had forfeited their property rights by their neglect of the land.[119] Mill proposed buying up estates by compulsory purchase and the reclamation of wastelands, and selling or leasing them to the peasantry. The possession of property would, he maintained, stimulate a 'new spirit of industry' and 'prudence and self-control', resolving the twin causes of the disaster, overpopulation and underproduction. Characteristically, he regarded the government's policy of extending the Poor Law and outdoor relief as 'insane', sapping the peasant's willingness to work and practise birth control. The 'main superiority' of his remedial measures, in contrast, was:

> that they would surround the peasant with a new moral atmosphere; they would bring a set of motives to operate upon him which he has never before experienced, tending in the strongest manner to correct everything in his national character which needs correction.[120]

Fourierist socialism held similar attractions for him. Unlike 'Communism', at least as Mill understood it, Fourierism did not 'withdraw any of the motives to exertion which exist in present society'.[121] Its merit consisted in the strengthening of these motivations by making it more certain that the individuals would reap the rewards of their mental or bodily skill or effort. Co-operative societies, moreover, would help direct these energies away from the attainment of purely personal advantages. 'The deeprooted selfishness which forms the general character of the existing state of society', he maintained, 'is *so* deeply rooted, only because the whole course of existing institutions tends to foster it.'[122] The 'general meanness of English life', typical of the 'uncultivated herd' of labourers and the majority of employers, could nevertheless be superseded. Mill believed 'the hindrance is not in the essential constitution of human nature.' 'By slow degrees, and a system of culture prolonged through successive generations', he thought 'education, habit and the cultivation of the sentiments will make a common man dig or weave for his country, as readily as fight for his country.'[123] No contradiction existed between Mill's defence of individuality and his account of 'the probable futurity of the labouring classes'. In both cases, the attainment of freedom rested on self-control, with self-management of industry, like self-government in politics, resulting from the piecemeal construction of an institutional framework which offered no other real alternative to a life of self-improvement. It would be 'a time when society will no longer be divided into the idle and the industrious', because 'the rule that they who do not work shall not eat, will be applied not to paupers only, but impartially to all.'[124] Even so, he continued to rely on the supposition that different life styles were naturally harmonious for his vision of a moralized capitalism in which the competition of beggar-my-neighbour had given way to one in which each tries to outdo the other in civic virtue. Once again the transition was achieved by stages, at first piece-work, then profit-sharing, and ultimately co-operative ownership and management 'schooled' individuals in 'generous sentiments' and brought about the:

> healing of the standing feud between capital and labour; [and] the transformation of human life, from a conflict of classes struggling for opposite interests, to a friendly rivalry in the pursuit of a good common to all.[125]

Since Mill shared the Malthusian belief that natural resources did not admit of an infinite extension through new forms of technology, the future could not be one of continuous economic growth. The need for material rewards for effort and merit would have to be transcended, as would the sex drive and the irresponsible desire for large families. Human progress in the economically 'stationary state' would be of an intellectual or moral nature or not at all. None of Mill's writings gives a better picture of the limited nature of his praise of individuality than this utopian vision of a thoroughly moralized society engaged in the collaborative pursuit of the higher pleasures to the virtual neglect of the lower.

Mill's conclusion dovetails with Green's premise. Caught between the Scylla of according individuals an implausibly high degree of autonomy in the creation of their moral worlds, and the Charybdis of an autonomy-maximizing paternalism, Mill avoided the dilemma by presuming that we naturally realize ourselves in a moral way. He achieved this largely because the liberal notion of character conflated freedom and self-development, so that only 'a person of confirmed virtue is completely free'.[126] Only his optimism that a civilized people would reject their selfish and animal desires, together with his faith in progress, allowed him to anticipate the loosening of the reins of government regulation. It was left to Green, who attempted to elucidate in a more direct manner the type of society needed to sustain this ideal, to reveal some of the contradictions within Mill's virtuous community.

T. H. GREEN: AN INDIVIDUALIST COLLECTIVISM

T. H. Green (1836–82) took over the Millian mantle as the schoolmaster of British liberalism. Although he endorsed Mill's radicalism, the epistemological underpinning of his theory was very different. His idealism had definite religious overtones that would have offended the utilitarian's aggressive secularism. Yet, we have already noted how the political discourse of the day was permeated with theological concepts deriving from the evangelical background of so many liberals, an experience Green shared. As we saw, this common conceptual framework resulted in greater similarities between the ideas of Mill and Green than their divergent philosophical commitments might suggest.

Green's philosophy derived much of its appeal from the way it offered a rational foundation for a variety of Christian beliefs – a project in many ways more congenial to the troubled minds of his contemporaries, assailed by religious doubts stemming from scientific and historical scholarship, than Mill's search for a secular social science.[127] Unlike Mill, Green was a professional academic, and although active as a town councillor in Oxford, he was not a prominent national political figure. Nevertheless, in spite of the impenetrability of his style, his university lectures attained an influence of almost Parisian proportions.[128] His achievement, if such it may be called, consisted in translating the political and emotional beliefs associated with the liberal conscience into the non-doctrinal terms of philosophical idealism.

Green's politics cannot be separated from his ethics and his metaphysics. He originally delivered his *Lectures on the Principles of Political Obligation* sandwiched between those later published as the *Prolegomena to Ethics*, and the two formed part of an integral course. Green argued, in Kantian manner, that the view of the world, essential to science, as a related series of objects and events was not a product but a presupposition of knowledge.[129] But he went beyond Kant to regard these relations not simply 'as fictions of our combining intelligence', but as explicable only on the assumption of the existence of a divine consciousness present in both mind and nature and guaranteeing their ultimate unity.[130] Adopting a parallel argument, he maintained that morality consisted of similar synthetic a priori judgements by which the eternal consciousness 'reproduced itself' in people's lives.[131] Humankind's striving after self-realization formed the operative force behind the transformation and development of human societies, the product of the progressive unfolding of the divine principle within the consciousness of individuals.[132] However, Green wished to avoid the suggestion that history was the work of a spiritual demiurge rationally ordering human affairs in a benign manner. Only individual effort could bring about this gradual moralization of social relations. Moreover the divine unity upon which it was premised remained beyond both time and space, and hence only imperfectly realized within existing institutions which could regress from it no less than advancing towards its fulfilment.[133] Thus, he used the development of character both as a hermeneutic principle for studying past societies and as a critical standard whereby they could be judged.

According to Green, we can only realize ourselves within the context of society.[134] Personal identity derived not from a number of pre-social biological or psychological determinants, but through the medium of social roles and relationships 'just as language of some sort is necessary to the real existence of thought'.[135] A community consisted of a number of shared ways of experiencing and interpreting the world, via which the individual formed his or her tastes and goals. Even when isolated from society we necessarily retain part of this cultural baggage when performing actions from other than pure biological necessity or arbitrary impulse. Robinson Crusoe remained an eighteenth-century gentleman even on his island.[136] Green denied that this thesis reduced the individual to a cypher of society, or of some other supra-individual entity such as the nation or spirit. If the content of our conception of self was constrained by the available social opportunities, 'the ultimate standard' remained 'an ideal of personal worth'. The social framework made personal development possible, but did not direct how we acted any more than grammar and vocabulary dictate what we say, so that 'to speak of any progress or improvement or development of a nation or society or mankind, except as relative to some greater worth of persons, is to use words without meaning.'[137]

The above reasoning provided Green with his definition of the common good. This did not refer to a number of particular goods individuals commonly desired, but rather to the common pursuit of self-realization by the members of a given society. Like Mill, Green did not believe individual freedom could be secured simply by protecting an individual's right to non-interference from others. Self-development could occur only when certain broader preconditions obtained. Some of these related to the person concerned, such as the ability for rational thought, others to the prevailing social circumstances. These consisted of the available range of options from which the individual could choose, for the character of one's life depended on the choices one made. Character could not be achieved by simply accepting whatever came your way, or by acting constantly from fear of coercive threats or the struggle to survive the perils of starvation or disease, but only through selecting from amongst a variety of significant and desirable possibilities.[138] Yet, neither could the state impose a course of action upon someone by making them take advantage of these opportunities:

No one can convey a good character to another. Everyone must make his character for himself. All that one can do to make another better is to remove obstacles and supply conditions favourable to the formation of a good character.[139]

Although often we had a personal interest in the common good, individual and collective interests conflicted frequently – notably when the temptation to 'free ride' occurred. As Mill and, with more force, Sidgwick acknowledged, the abnegation exercised by individuals pursuing their own happiness, and the injunction to cultivate the greatest happiness of the greatest number, were logically independent and the move from the first to the second difficult to derive from the psychological premises of utilitarianism.[140] Thus, support for the common good had to be separated from any interest a given individual might have in any one of the options secured by it. Against individualist rights theorists, Green denied that you could distinguish the rules governing self-regarding actions from those dealing with our transactions with others. A general injunction to respect other people's interests was too vague, since it potentially imposed implausible standards of forbearance. One could not identify the limits upon one's own actions without a consciousness of one's obligations towards one's fellow citizens, nor understand either in ignorance of what gives value to life both personally and in general.[141] The conduct of a civilized community depended upon finding space for a wide range of openings making possible a wide variety of worthwhile lives. The 'general fabric of rights', therefore, followed from a shared respect for the intrinsic value of the common good as a source both of personal self-development and of our duties towards others.[142]

In common with many nineteenth-century liberals, including Mill,[143] Green thought this attachment to the common good derived from national feeling. Mazzinian democratic nationalism, in particular, had convinced a number of Victorian intellectuals that the nation provided the focus of our moral unity with others.[144] The Italian had conceived nationality in ethical rather than straightforwardly racial, geographical or linguistic terms. The citizen owed to the nation a duty greater than self-interest, because it provided the environment within which each person fashioned his or her identity. Green, following his usual custom, simply took up this contemporary platitude – so essential, for example, to Gladstone's foreign policy and his commitment to Irish Home Rule – and gave it a Germanic gloss largely borrowed from Kant.[145] Unlike the 'loyal subject', who recognized the rights of others merely because the state compelled him to, the 'intelligent patriot's'

> judgement of what he owes to the state is quickened by a feeling of which the *patria*...is the natural object only in so far as it is an organisation of a people to whom the individual feels bound by ties derived from a common dwelling place with its associations, from common memories, traditions and customs, and from the common ways of feeling and thinking which a common language and still more a common literature embodies.[146]

As we saw, Green rejected the Fichtean or Hegelian view, which treated this national spirit as somehow superior to the personal character of the individuals who contributed to its formation.[147] Self-determination formed a vital part of the Mazzinian version of the doctrine, because he claimed a common sense of mutual obligation only came about through each citizen participating in the creation of national laws. Similarly, Green argued that only if the individual had a share 'in making and maintaining the laws which he obeys...will he learn to regard the work of the state as a whole'.[148] This type of patriotism did not display itself in war, but in so organizing society 'that everyone's capacities have free scope for their development'.[149]

Green hoped that the new society would be created by the unfolding will of its members as a result of human moral progress, rather than through the bureaucratic state. He regarded the growing complexity of modern societies as going hand in hand with a gradual diffusion of reason amongst their members; a process reflected in the development of a regular system of laws protecting the complex of rights upheld by conventional morality. This testified to the increasingly self-conscious awareness of a shared morality amongst humankind, itself the product of an eternal divine principle of self-realization immanent in all our actions.[150] Thus, a democratic nation could reasonably legislate to provide certain public services such as education and housing, or restrict particular practices, such as unhealthy factory conditions or drinking, without violating the voluntary principle or being paternalistic.[151] In this respect, he had even greater faith in human nature than Mill – a reflection of the improved mood occasioned by the phenomenal boom of the late 1860s and early 1870s, when liberal causes were in the ascendent. However, as the optimism which greeted Gladstone's first administration waned with electoral defeat, economic decline and a heightened awareness of the extent of the 'social problem', a similar tension between the power of character and the influence of conditions to that which we noted in Mill began to make itself apparent. Once more, the model of the rational, self-improving, altruistic individual turned out to be doing most of the work in his theory. When this paragon of virtue failed to materialize spontaneously, Green fell to employing state intervention to bring such citizens into existence. In attempting to justify the more 'constructive' policies of Gladstone's second term, Green revealed the ambiguities not just of his own theory, but of an entire ethos.

According to Green, the role of the state was to secure sufficient personal freedom for its members to act as rational moral agents. Yet his condemnation of attempts 'to enforce acts as virtuous which lose their virtue when done under fear of legal penalties'[152] entrenched the liberal presumption against excessive state interference within his philosophy at a fundamental level. However, his definition of the purpose of government as 'the removal of obstacles' to the moral life was not exhausted merely by securing the individual from external interference. As we saw, it also included the attack on restrictive practices which reduced the availability of aspects of social life important for autonomy. Green's practical proposals, therefore, turned upon identifying what counted as a hindrance to moral action. Three factors guided, and ultimately weakened, his thinking here. The first consisted of conventional Victorian assumptions about how far the individual was responsible for his or her acts. Although Green's theory could presumably accommodate new information concerning the operation of social processes, etc., it could never challenge the Victorian ideal itself. His whole philosophy was premised upon seeing human history as the outcome of this Smilsean ethic of self-help – even God had the attributes of the Victorian Moral Man! This weakness was exacerbated by the second feature, which blurred conflict between self-realization and personal satisfaction, moral freedom and autonomy, by assuming a universal rational will harmonising individual endeavours. Because living within any society involves a certain accommodation of personal goals to the benefits and requirements of coexistence, Green tended to gloss over the difference between being socialized into adopting the prevailing customs and a genuinely independent search to achieve goodness. Finally, this last tendency frequently led to an uncritical approval of the tenets of Victorian liberalism, already deeply imbued with a vulgar Kantian moralism. If the major internal hindrance came from a weakness of will, the principal external barrier remained the landowners and the uneducated and dependent masses. As he told his audience in his famous defence of Liberal legislation, behind all the new reforms one 'can discern the same old cause of social good against class interests, for which, under altered names, liberals are fighting now as they were fifty years ago'.[153] Thus, Green criticized liberal practices for falling short of their declared moral purpose, not in themselves.

Green's anti-paternalist strictures seem to epitomize Victorian moralism. He listed three instances when 'laws have been made which check the development of the moral disposition.' The first cited the attempts of the Established Church to set legal requirements on religious observance – a reference to the Thiry-Nine Articles, which Green had been obliged to endorse on taking up his Balliol fellowship. The second, more vaguely, referred to 'prohibitions and restraints, unnecessary, or which have ceased to be necessary, for maintaining the social conditions of the moral life, and which interfere with the growth of self-reliance, with the formation of a manly conscience and sense of moral dignity – in short with moral autonomy which is the condition of the highest goodness'. Finally, he offered the example of 'legal institutions which take away the occasion for the exercise of certain moral virtues (e.g. the Poor-Law, which takes away the occasion for the exercise of parental forethought, filial reverence, and neighbourly kindness)'.[154]

All of these criteria were conventional enough, but Green also backed causes supported by only a minority of liberals which might seem to contravene them. His promotion of temperance reform appears to conflict with the second argument, for example.[155] The Oxford Liberal MP, Harcourt, made just this observation, remarking that 'what really makes sobriety valuable is the voluntary self-control – the deliberate self-denial which resists temptation and leads a man, for the sake of himself and others, to abstain from vicious indulgence.'[156] Indeed, Green seemed condemned out of his own mouth, for he too criticized '"paternal government"' for 'narrowing the room for the self-imposition of duties and for the play of disinterested motives'.[157] Initially he got around the problem by supporting the so-called 'local option', which proposed giving ratepayers the possibility of voluntarily decreasing and even abolishing local licences, a measure Harcourt himself came to promote.[158] Green then dropped this solution for compulsory prohibition because he believed that significant numbers of poor people had got trapped into a cycle of deprivation which reduced their will-power to overcome their dependence. Green did not doubt the contention of his fellow liberals that given sufficient character people could leave the poverty trap and fashion their own lives. However, a 'drunken population naturally perpetuates and increases itself' because such people lacked the incentive to self-improvement offered by a favourable environment.[159] Their condition was already so low, that escape through alcohol provided as valid an option as any other. Green countered the charge of paternalism, because he denied that a person enthralled to drink had a moral capacity to lose. Finally, he justified the compulsion of moderate drinkers and the sellers of liquor on grounds stemming from the common good. The existence of ginshops and beer houses created an obstacle to the moral autonomy of drunkards which government had an obligation to remove, especially as it caused 'such a very slight inconvenience as it must be for those who take such a little drop'.[160] Contrary to Mill, although adopting a parallel reasoning to his, Green treated the very existence of liquor stores as a species of public harm. He claimed that 'however decently carried on, the excessive drinking of one man means an injury to others in health, purse and capability, to which no limits can be placed' – presumably because we were so interdependent that everyone suffered from this 'social evil'.[161] Green looked upon the drink trade as a vested interest of the Conservatives to hinder the progress of the labouring classes, a view reinforced by the Liberal electoral defeat of 1874 despite the reformed franchise of 1867, and given extra weight by the successful tactics of the Tory Oxford brewer Hall, who exploited the unpopularity of the temperance issue in a later by-election.[162]

Green's arguments were thus fully consistent with his general belief that the state should merely 'hinder hindrances' to moral autonomy. The intolerant aspects arise not from the formal nature of the theory, so much as the underlying Victorian assumption that full autonomy meant overcoming such bestial pleasures as drink so that no civilized community lost out by its suppression, an opinion which would certainly have astonished the poets and philosophers of antiquity! Moreover, by emphasising the iniquities of drink to such a degree, Green reinforced rather than challenged the Victorian liberal belief that we

have sole responsibility for our lives. His concern was not the improvement of the material conditions of the poor *per se*, merely their stature as
moral agents: securing the second would bring the first in its wake.
Blaming their destitution on drink obviated the need to search for social
causes beyond the individual's control.

Green adopted similar arguments to justify the Factory, Public Health
and Employers' Liability Acts. The regulation of hours and conditions of
work might appear, according to his third criterion, as a paternalist
interference with spontaneous benevolence and freedom of contract. As
with temperance, Green's position was strongest with regard to the
oppressed themselves. Their self-reliance was not endangered by laws
assuring them good housing, fair terms of employment and a healthy
environment, because they had none to lose. All the 'authorised
accounts' of royal and parliamentary commissions showed:

> Left to itself, or to the operation of casual benevolence, a degraded popu-
> lation perpetuates itself…Given a certain standard of moral and material
> well-being, people may be trusted not to sell their labour, or the labour of
> their children, on terms which would not allow that standard to be
> maintained. But with large masses of our population, until the laws we
> have been considering took effect, there was no such standard.[163]

Amongst the poor, enlightened self-interest, if not a directly moral will,
would provide an adequate incentive for self-improvement when they
had something worth striving for.

Green had greater difficulty explaining why the successful capitalist
should sacrifice a personal advantage for the sake of others. C. B.
Macpherson regards it as an insuperable problem for him due to
Green's adherence to a 'possessive' theory of property.[164] Green certainly regarded some private possessions as basic to an individual's
capacity for self-realisation,[165] and justified inequalities of property as
indications of people's different talents and tastes and of the divergent
forms personal development could take.[166] However, he denied that the
accumulation of goods within capitalist relations necessarily produced a
destitute mass of wage labourers possessing nothing beyond the means
of subsistence.[167] Once more his thinking followed a largely traditional
route. Green distinguished conspicuous consumption from the employment of goods as part of a rational plan of life. He assumed the former
inherently involved enslavement to impulse, 'the wild beast in man',[168]
which the progress of society gradually brought into check through
the growing consciousness of a rational will common to all people's
projects. Since only social recognition secured an individual's rights,
'there result[ed] a common interest in the free play of the powers of all.'
An individual's 'positive condition' of possession rested, therefore, on
the correlative 'negative condition' of respecting the power of appropriation of others.[169] Green contended that in an ideal free market property

would be treated as an aspect of the common good and the possibilities for possession as part of one's self-realisation would become open to all.

Green knew of 'the many characteristics of the institution of property, as it actually exists, which cannot be derived from the spiritual principle which we have assigned as its foundation'.[170] Following Mill, and radical opinion generally, he associated these aberrations almost entirely with the inherited landed wealth of the aristocracy. They were products of the lawless feudal era, evidence of a period when impulse had ruled over will. The most conspicuous remnant of this earlier degenerate period existed amongst the urban proletariat 'whose ancestors...were trained in habits of serfdom'.[171] Green attributed the present low condition of the masses to 'this debased population' which 'gluts the labour market and constantly threatens to infect the class of superior workmen'.[172] Their servile habits made them easy prey for unscrupulous employers seeking a cheap source of labour, for they lacked the moral backbone to combine for better terms thus undermining the bargaining power of those who did. The situation was further exacerbated by the continued existence of the aristocratic landlords themselves, whose inherited wealth derived from no effort of their own and, unlike industrial capital, remained largely unproductive. Like Mill, Green adopted a quasi-Lockean proviso based on his view of property as an aspect of the common good. Rights to non-renewable natural resources such as land depended upon rendering them 'more serviceable to society as a whole...than if they were held in common', for 'the capital gained by one is not taken from another...if it is compensated by the acquisition of other wealth on the part of those extruded from the soil.'[173] With Irish landlords particularly in mind, Green considered the descendants of feudal barons, whose acquisition came from conquest rather than labour, as hereditarily corrupted as their former dependents. They used the land for game and sport rather than cultivating it, and in innumerable ways had 'taken away the interest, and tied the hands, of the nominal owner – the tenant for life – in making the most of his property'. The Ground Game Act, which featured so prominently in his famous lecture on 'Liberal Legislation and Freedom of Contract', was a measure of considerable symbolic force. Green surmised that a genuine free market in land, rather than the system of entailed estates, combined with an adequate protection of the interests of tenants, would remove the problem and encourage 'the formation of that mainstay of social order and contentment, a class of small proprietors tilling their own land'.[174]

Thus blame for the chief abuses of the contemporary economic system lay not with the 'capitalism or the free development of individual wealth' but with 'the violent manner in which rights over land have been acquired and exercised'.[175] Only the historical accident whereby Britain had missed the clean sweep of the French Revolution accounted for the continued influence of 'unrestrained landlordism',[176] and its attendant evils of 'exaggerated luxury at the top, flunkeyism in the middle and recklessness at the bottom'.[177] The wealth generated by the successful capitalist, in contrast, was 'constantly distributed throughout the process in the shape of wages to labourers and of profits to those who mediate in the business of exchange'.[178] The 'large masses of hired labourers' required by the mines and manufacturing industries did not risk sharing the fate of their forefathers, the 'landless countrymen', because they could become 'small scale capitalists themselves'. The better-paid workers owned houses and furniture, and even clubbed together in benefit societies so as to match the investment power of the 'great' capitalists.[179] Green, in true liberal spirit, imbued the market with the ethical purpose of moulding character and eroding unearned privilege, the main source of moral laxity. He assumed that the accumulation of the 'great' capitalist went beyond mere material gain, reflecting instead the moral impulse for self-development. In consequence, he foresaw no clash between individual attempts at self-realisation, for all were aspects of the same spiritual principle. Green's view of the likely contours of a fully evolved industrial system was very similar to those of Mill and Spencer. Like them, he envisaged it tending towards the voluntary co-operation of individual producers, grouped together in associations for mutual advantage. The resulting domestic harmony would be mirrored at an international level. One of the chief proofs of the benevolence of capitalism within the liberal catechism was the supposed unifying and pacifying effects of free trade between nations.[180] Green, with his accustomed consistency, saw 'special class interests' lurking behind all wars, evidence of the continued predominance of 'old *dynasteiai*'.[181]

Green's acceptance of the liberal characterisation of the market blinded him to its potential failings. The capitalist worked for the challenge involved, ploughing profits back into the system for the benefit of everyone rather than retaining them for personal use. Yet even assuming a society of altruists, problems of scarcity and divergent views of the good life, or simple misinformation about other people's requirements, can give rise to incompatible priorities for the use of available resources. Green skirted around these and other difficulties because he assumed a harmonious moral order existed between rational individual goals. Since self-realization tended to shade into an overcoming of material pleasures, he did not envisage the distributional disputes between caviar addicts and those with more modest demands beloved of modern welfare economists. He regarded market distributions as a correct reflection of individual merit and need, overlooking the way the market disproportionately rewards those talented in money-making rather than in other directions.[182] Green made no provision for a planned redistribution of goods to remedy these defects. In any case, he thought welfare measures undermined individual independence and charitable feelings.[183] Similarly, he thought the common ownership of property 'incompatible with that highest object of human attainment, a free morality',[184] although an unpublished manuscript suggests that, like Mill and Spencer,[185] he did not rule out the possibility that human 'sympathy' might voluntarily bring this about in a distant future.[186]

Despite the conventionality of many of Green's opinions they were not without their subversive influence once liberalism failed to live up to its lights. According to Green's theory, societies improved in their internal organization as the possibilities for self-development were extended to larger numbers of people.[187] Once this right became widely recognized, then any attempt by an entrenched 'powerful class' to resist it would ultimately justify revolution.[188] A view strongly influenced by Mazzini's struggle for Italian unification and reinforced by his support for the North in the American Civil War, Green even countenanced force in 1867 should suffrage reform be stopped.[189] If this issue demonstrates the impeccable democratic and liberal nature of his intentions, it also illustrates the shaky foundations on which they rested. For the ensuing electoral defeat of 1874 bitterly disappointed him. Characteristically, he sought the explanation in the servility of the working classes, their 'lack of moral progress', which had rendered them incapable of coping with an 'unexampled commercial prosperity' so that 'political enthusiasm' was lost 'in what I may call a general riot of luxury' in which 'the beer and the money flowed freely.'[190] Once again, Green was forced into finding mitigating circumstances to bolster his belief that freedom brought enlightenment and a common morality.

Alan Milne pointed out that the British Idealists 'assumed that self-realization and rational moral conduct were one and the same thing, that to the extent that a man was a rational moral agent he achieved genuine selfhood'.[191] In fact, the two frequently conflict, for moral action may well involve some sacrifice of personal well-being. Green maintained that the possibilities for autonomous action generally available to individuals within society depended upon everyone acting morally and putting a regard for the common good above their own immediate gain. But he underestimated the degree of self-sacrifice this called for, because the doctrine of character tended to conflate self-discipline with self-realization. He shared the Victorian hostility towards licence and appetite. 'Moral freedom', he observed, 'is not the same thing as control over the outward circumstances and appliances of life. It is the end to which such control is a generally necessary means, and which gives it value.'[192] Genuine freedom, on this view, resulted from acting rationally and well.

Green's argument assumed that in aiming at higher goods, we divested ourselves of the animal passions of self-interest. Competition between individuals arose from the pursuit of material goods alone. When individuals aimed solely at moral goodness, then their efforts at self-development benefited the rest of society as well as themselves. To use Green's example, when we treated education as an end in itself, we both added to our own self-culture and augmented the knowledge and skills available to the wider community. When we pursued learning merely to enhance our own standing and power, it became what Hirsch termed a 'positional good'.[193] An orchestra perhaps offers the best illustration of the sort of collaborative and self-realizing endeavour Green had in mind. However, it remains highly dubious how far many of the collaborative activities of modern industrial societies could be assimilated to this model. More important, Green appreciated that the commercial spirit worked directly against this ethos: 'In the stream of unrelenting competition...the weaker has not a chance.' Whilst the labouring masses had been admitted to the 'negative rights' of citizenship, 'the good things to which the pursuits of society are in fact directed turn out to be no good things to them.' In Green's opinion, the difficulty arose 'because the good is being sought in objects which admit of being competed for', so that 'the success of some in attaining them is incompatible with the success of others.'

> Until the object generally sought as good comes to be a state of mind or character of which the attainment, or the approach to attainment, by each is itself a contribution to its attainment by everyone else, social life must continue to be one of war.[194]

Once everyone valued the 'higher' goods for themselves, then the market would be transformed into a mechanism for mutual service in the pursuit of the common good. Reviewing the *Prolegomena*, Sidgwick rightly questioned whether a personal appreciation of the 'higher' pleasures entailed conceding everyone an equal right to their enjoyment:

> The thoughtful trader knows that wealth will enable him to provide himself and those he loves with books, pictures, prolonged education, varied travel, opportunities of intellectual life: and knowing this, he allows himself to adopt methods of dealing which sometimes, perhaps, are hardly compatible with Green's ideal of justice...In short, Green seems to me to have unconsciously tried to get the advantages of two distinct and incompatible conceptions of human good: the one liberally comprehensive, but palpably admitting competition, the other non-competitive but stoically or puritanically narrow.[195]

He disparagingly dismissed Green's work as offering little more than 'a vague emotional thrill'.

Sidgwick's severe judgement could apply with equal justice to Mill. Both believed not only that people naturally opted for autonomy but also that it took the same narrow pattern. By confusing self-determination with self-abnegation, they could endorse the liberal prejudices of their day and ascribe imperfections to the incomplete realization of the ideal. Neither thinker crossed the divide from individualism to collectivism as we understand it today. Those social reforms they proposed were directed invariably at moral purposes: sobriety, sexual modesty and increasing individual exertion and co-operation. Their intervention was intended to increase voluntary effort, not to substitute for it.[196] The economist Arnold Toynbee revealed the limits of their position when, in an essay generally defending state help, he remarked: 'Even if the chance should arise of removing a great social evil, nothing must be done to weaken those habits of individual self-reliance and voluntary association which have built up the greatness of the English people.'[197] But such action risked becoming coercive, as the enforcement of the Poor Law amply demonstrated,[198] once individuals had to be forced into character development. For their successors, the contrast between the ideal and the reality of liberalism was even more conspicuous. Outside such a heavily moralized culture, the tension between the two began to reflect back on the liberal ethos itself.

THE STRANGE AFTER-LIFE OF LIBERAL BRITAIN: L. T. HOBHOUSE AND THE NEW LIBERALISM

From the 1880s onwards a number of changes within British society placed liberal ideals under a severe strain.[199] There was a noticeable downturn in the rate of economic growth due to the depression of the late 1870s and the impact of foreign competition. These events challenged Victorian confidence that Britain, no longer the world's workshop, offered the best possible social environment for technological innovation and industrial advance. The prospect of increased opportunities for social mobility and the fairer distribution of wealth through the reward of merit rather than of privilege, lay behind much liberal moralizing. Both these hopes proved unfounded, however. If real incomes had risen, the gap between rich and poor had widened considerably. Between 1850 and 1880 the average business profits went up by 60 per cent overall, compared to a rise of 45 per cent for wages over the same period. In 1803 the top 2 per cent shared a fifth of national income, in 1867 about two-fifths. The possibilities for social advancement had also declined. Even Smiles, who published his books in the 1840s and 1850s, had had to draw most of his industrial heroes from the eighteenth century. By 1880, businesses had outgrown the small-scale private partnerships run by owner-managers idealized by Spencer and Mill. Joint-stock companies managed by professional directors, a form of organization traditionally distrusted by liberal political economists,[200] became the norm – the number of registered companies (excluding railways and other chartered or parliamentary companies) growing from 1,000 in 1844 to nearly 3,000 in 1867 and over 10,000 in 1887. The giant family firms that survived were too large to be controlled at shop-floor level by their owners. The managerial corporation rendered the old-style entrepreneur, who rose from manual worker to captain of industry, an anachronism. These new businesses also undermined other aspects of the entrepreneurial ideal. For the new corporate capitalists, the distinction between earned income from capital and unearned income from land did not make much sense, whilst open competition seemed less in their interest than its limitation by price agreements, amalgamations and mergers. The greatest jolt to liberal assumptions, however, arose from the heightened awareness of the true extent of poverty and unemployment. The belief that the economic system normally could secure jobs and subsistence wages for all who were willing and able to work, that hardship and misery resulted from individual vice, improvidence and misery rather than from social mechanisms, had provided the rationale behind that quintessential piece of Victorian social legislation, the Poor Law. The Charity Organization Society, with its insistence on the rigorous application of the principle of making welfare relief 'less eligible' than a subsistence wage in order to prevent the demoralisation of the poor, had typified the liberal approach to the problem in the 1860s and 1870s. The surveys of Booth and Rowntree, conducted in London (1889) and York (1899), revealed a situation of devastating proportions. Nearly a third of the population in these urban areas had less than the 'minimum necessary expenditure for the maintenance of merely physical health'. By the early 1890s, debate on unemployment in particular acted as a catalyst in clarifying political discussion of the scale and nature of state intervention and the relationship between the individual and society.

A number of caveats and distinctions need to be made before discussing the new liberalism.[201] For a start, the intellectual movement, to be investigated here, cannot be fully identified with the New Liberal current within the party associated with Lloyd George and Churchill. Second, its arguments have to be distinguished from those of both Radicals and Liberal Imperialists, who on some issues adopted superficially similar views. Third, the development of liberal ideology cannot be adequately described either as a purely superstructural phenomenon, mechanically responding to the rise of organized labour, a revived conservatism and changed social conditions, or as an autonomous working out of traditional ideas. Rather, the interactions between the two require exploration. Failure to do this has often led historians to regard the new liberalism as somehow inevitable: the natural result of political pressures or the logical extension of liberal principles.

Spencer's reassertion of traditional Victorian values, against what he called the 'New Toryism' of the 1880s, show that the move towards a more social liberalism was not universally accepted. He continued to view unemployment and poverty as 'the normal result of misconduct'. He attacked the new welfarism for saving people 'from the natural penalties of dissolute living', and maintained it would eventually necessitate 'the infliction of artificial penalties in solitary cells, on tread-wheels, and by the lash' if the national character was to be preserved.[202] The dominant liberal trend, however, was less callous. Even so, the change must not be exaggerated. In fact, the terms of political discourse did not alter nearly as much as Spencer's lamentations might lead one to expect. Rather, they were deployed in different conceptual and practical contexts which modified their meaning. The escape from the strictures of Ricardian political economy played a particularly important role in shifting the intellectual consensus away from the sort of ideas espoused by Spencer. Orthodox economists had regarded wage increases as putting undue pressure on the fixed 'fund' available at any time for the payment of labour, putting a premium on reckless procreation and ultimately causing unemployment and poverty by overstretching the available resources. Although Mill had gone some way towards modifying the Malthusian logic of this picture, the decisive change came with the writings of Alfred Marshall from the 1870s onwards. Prosperity no longer seemed to carry with it the germs of future poverty, as Henry Fawcett, for example, had believed. For Marshall, the Malthusian trap only existed for 'the more ignorant and phlegmatic of races and individuals'. He remarked how 'education, and the raising of our moral and religious ideals, and the growth of the printing press and the telegraph have so changed English human nature that many things which economists rightly considered impossible thirty years ago are possible now.'[203] The notion that securing a reasonable standard of living for workers would act as an incentive for them to improve their character and productiveness removed an important hurdle to social reform, without unduly offending conventional liberal sentiments. This theoretical gain survived the economic downturn, enabling liberals to respond to the crisis in a constructive manner.

Historians have looked typically to L. T. Hobhouse's volume on *Liberalism* (1911) for 'the best formulation of the new English liberalism'.[204] Although recent scholarship has tended to modify this judgement, so long as due attention is paid to the various qualifications outlined above his status as a representative figure of the intellectual wing of the new liberalism remains intact. What the book most certainly was not, was a timeless statement of liberal ideals. Hobhouse's alignment with liberalism had been far from automatic. By the late 1880s and 1890s many political thinkers who would later call themselves new liberals had dropped the reservations of Green and his disciples and proudly admitted to being collectivists and socialists, a feeling reinforced by the disastrous administration of Gladstone and Rosebery from 1892 to 1895. Split by the issue of Home Rule, it had taken the opposition to the Boer War and Tariff Reform to provide a cause with the right historical resonances to revive traditional liberal enthusiasms and with them the party's fortunes, culminating in the landslide victory of 1906. The fight of organized Labour against the South African War and Chamberlain's protectionist policies, combined with the 'self-control' of the new model unionism exemplified by the behaviour of London dockers during the strike of 1889, rekindled the old Gladstonian faith in the masses' potential for virtue beyond class interests, and convinced Hobhouse that his conclusion that 'the work of the old Liberalism was done once and for ever' was 'too hasty'.[205] It was this altered atmosphere that influenced Hobhouse to strive for a progressive alliance of Liberalism and Labour by showing how 'the difference between a true, consistent, public spirited Liberalism and a rational Collectivism ought, with a genuine effort at mutual understanding, to disappear.'[206]

Hobhouse's case for the greater regulation of social life by the state rested upon the vision shared by Mill and Green of society as a co-operative association for the achievement of self-realization via the pursuit of the common good. Like them, he based this thesis upon the supposition that a moral community was naturally implied by individual self-development. He now gave the argument an additional twist, providing it with a putatively 'scientific' basis by dressing it up in the then fashionable terminology of evolutionary theory.[207] Via a dialectical *tour de force*, albeit of doubtful logical value, Hobhouse attempted to synthesize the epistemological positions of Mill and Green.[208] He hoped to offer a pseudo-empirical confirmation of Green's thesis of an 'eternal consciousness' by showing 'a coincidence between the views derived from an analysis of the pre-suppositions of knowledge, and those attained by a comprehensive review of experience'.[209] He claimed that contemporary evolutionary doctrine demonstrated that an unfolding spiritual principle within the consciousness of different individuals was an integral part of human development, in which the mind played an increasingly determinate role in controlling the instincts of the body.[210] He concluded that this process would culminate in an ethical order which 'will harmonize not merely individual with social interests, but a many-sided freedom, social and personal, with an orderly and disciplined co-operation'. Learning from experience, 'we develop character not by sheer coercion, but by self-conquest and the knowledge – or rather the full imaginative realization – of the meaning of good and evil. We approach assured social co-operation not by compelling obedience, but by winning assent.'[211] Social harmony ensued because the self-same process whereby one gradually brought one's own faculties under rational control took place in everyone else:

> Operating in every individual it moves to the fulfilment of personality, but operating alike in all individuals the development that it seeks must be self-consistent or harmonious, and it is as the condition of such development that liberty acquires its full, positive and social meaning.[212]

Given Hobhouse's faith that 'we get nearer to truth by letting error develop its fallacies than by stifling it at birth',[213] one might expect him to adopt a Spencerian libertarianism. However, he contended that as self-consciousness grew within a civilized society people naturally regulated their environment more rationally. Indeed, it was via this progressive organization of all the conditions of life by the mind:

> that modern civilisation had made its chief advance, that through science it is beginning to control the physical conditions of life, and that on the side of ethics and religion it is forming those ideas of the unity of the race, and of the subordination of law, morals and social constitutions generally to the needs of human development which are the conditions of the control that is required.[214]

Whereas Spencer had studiously avoided extending the organic analogy to society as a whole in order to escape the inference that the state acted as the controlling brain of the social body, new liberal theorists took just this step.[215] Like Green, Hobhouse escaped the charge of paternalism (at least formally) by regarding the state as expressing the democratic will of the people 'to secure a fuller measure of justice and a better organization of mutual aid', a response 'to the genuine desires not of a handful of superior beings, but of the great masses of men'.[216] Liberalism, so conceived, represented the empowerment of the people consciously to manage their collective destinies in such a way as to secure the maximal self-development possible for each and every citizen.

Echoing Mill, Hobhouse emphasised that 'social freedom...for any epoch short of the millenium rests on restraint', at the very least from the intentional physical injury of others.[217] In former times the state had represented class interests, and its coercive power had to be resisted in the name of individual liberty. In a democratic community, however, it provided the instrument for the planned 'reorganizing' of restraints by the people themselves.[218] Hobhouse begged the question of what rendered any particular arrangement of liberties freer than another, because, in an analogous manner to Mill and Green, he avoided the problem of how one decided what happened if one person's self-development involved restraining someone else's. Somewhat desperately, he pleaded that 'there *must* be a line of development open along which each can move in harmony with others.'[219] The premise supporting his liberalism was the by now familiar figure of the rational individual for whom 'liberty and compulsion have complementary functions', a claim buttressed in turn by some form of ethical naturalism which regarded human beings as naturally realizing themselves in the pursuit of certain moral ideals.[220]

Hobhouse issued the usual anti-authoritarian proviso:

> To try to form character by coercion is to destroy it in the making. Personality is not built up from without but grows from within, and the function of the outer order is not to create it, but to provide for it the most suitable conditions of growth. Thus, to the common question whether it is possible

to make men good by Act of Parliament, the reply is that it is not possible
to compel morality because morality is the character of a free agent, but
that it is possible to create the conditions under which morality can
develop.[221]

The identification of freedom with rational moral action, however,
undermined the potentially libertarian tenor of these remarks. Those
who were not free agents, because they were incapable of 'rational
self-determination', such as 'children,...the idiot, the imbecile, the
feeble-minded or the drunkard', could be legitimately restrained by the
state until such time as they attained the 'capacity of self-control'.[222]
Following Green and Mill respectively, Hobhouse regarded it as
permissible to prevent traders from tempting people into sinful ways by
selling drink, and to enforce collective action when necessary to give
effect to the general will. But the real novelty of his proposals arose
from his treatment of certain social and economic circumstances as
forms of coercion, and his call for a limited redistribution of wealth to
rectify this situation.

Hobhouse's rethinking of 'economic liberalism' reflected the New
Liberal desire simultaneously to woo working- and middle-class support without unduly compromising traditional liberal principles. He
based his case for social reform on a somewhat contentious distinction
between 'individual' and 'social' factors in the creation of wealth. Most
obviously, the 'social' element resulted from seeing the market, the
national infrastructure and the regular laws which made trade possible
as a species of public good. The progressive aspects of his thesis,
however, stemmed from the additional belief that both the production
of goods and their value had a social dimension deriving from
co-operation through the division of labour and the effects of demand
respectively.[223] Hobhouse claimed that if taxation only affected that
portion of wealth which was socially produced, then no damage was
done to the conventional liberal concern to protect the rights of
individuals to the products of their labour.[224] The opposition of the
House of Lords to the tax proposals within the 1909 'People's Budget'
helped Hobhouse to present his case as an extension of the liberal cause
against aristocratic class interests and privileges. Earlier liberals had had
no objections to taxing the 'unearned income' deriving from rent on
land, and Hobhouse followed other radical political economists in
treating his proposals for the taxation of the 'social' element as an extension of this argument.[225] Many of his examples, such as the claim that
'the value of a site in London is something essentially due to London,
not to the landlord', or his attack on the gains of financial speculators
as 'a tax which astute or fortunate individuals are able to levy on the
producer [rather than] the reward which they obtain for a definite
contribution on their own part to production', exploited conventional
liberal prejudices against 'inherited' as opposed to 'acquired' wealth

without stretching them too far.[226] Where the new liberalism definitely parted company with the old, was in treating the profits of industrial capitalists in analogous terms. Hobhouse claimed employers were only entitled to a remuneration reflecting their own personal contribution. For excessive profits were not only unfair, they reduced the available capital for the stimulation of the economy by consumption. No one individual could either produce or consume more than a limited amount. Overly large incomes, therefore, exceeded the sum any single person deserved and formed an 'unproductive surplus'. Hobson's 'underconsumptionist' economics, on which Hobhouse freely drew, creatively reworked the Ricardian model examined earlier in this chapter, with saving replaced by spending as the driving force of the economic system. Taxation served to ensure that the social portion of wealth (including spending power) was shared equally, and that differences of income only reflected the variations in ability and effort between individual citizens.

The coherence of Hobhouse's theory depended on finding a practical means for separating out the 'individual' from the 'social' elements, and quantifying them in monetary terms. Faced with the impossibility of calculating in this fashion our debt to a Shakespeare or a Newton,[227] he promptly switched tack to argue:

> Economic justice is to render what is due not only to each individual but to each function, social and personal, that is engaged in the performance of useful service, and this due is measured by the amount necessary to stimulate and maintain the efficient exercise of that useful function.[228]

Arguably, the market performs just this task. However, the recurrent economic crises and chronic unemployment of the period had convinced Hobhouse, in common with many other liberal thinkers and politicians, that it did so in a highly inefficient manner and at an unacceptable cost in terms of human misery. Yet once the assignment of rewards becomes a matter of conscious government planning, then the assumption that the scale of rewards reflects a natural order of individual abilities rather than being a socially determined matter cannot be easily sustained. He provided no justification for his choice of the figure of £5,000 as 'the limit of the industrial value of the individual' beyond the pragmatic considerations that led Lloyd George to introduce super tax on incomes above that amount. As he acknowledged, if all one could expect to obtain for one's services was £5,000, then no doubt people would make the same efforts for that sum as they currently made for £50,000.[229]

Further disturbing ambiguities revealed themselves when Hobhouse considered the problem of poverty, which had led him to formulate his conception of economic justice in the first place. When taxing the rich, he had argued that any payment above a certain maximum level of remuneration was both counterproductive and undeserved. Turning to the poor, he maintained that a minimum also existed below which one could not expect ordinary men and women to fulfil their functions adequately. The state had a duty to assure the mass of people 'the means of a decent livelihood' either by 'continuous employment at a living wage' or by 'public assistance'. Hobhouse denied that this meant feeding, clothing and housing the people by state action. Rather, 'it is for the State to take care that the economic conditions are such that the normal man who is not defective in mind or body can by useful labour feed, house, and clothe himself and his family.'[230] The 'right to a living wage' rested on 'the equation of social service and reward'. Need did not replace desert in Hobhouse's conception of social justice. Indeed, the worker's right to a minimum brought with it a correlative duty 'to make the best use of his opportunity, and if he fails he may fairly suffer the penalty of being treated as a pauper or even, in an extreme case, as a criminal'.[231] Thus, by a mixture of carrot and stick, each was brought to perform his or her station and its duties. If the mentally or physically unfit were entitled to our humanitarian concern and help, 'punitive discipline' was the only way to deal with the 'morally uncontrolled'.[232]

Although Hobhouse denied some of the more illiberal implications of this functionalist view of rights, it illustrated how his revised liberalism did not extend beyond a moralization of capitalist relations. It also revealed the degree to which new liberal discourse continued to mix ethical and economic arguments, treating the free person, the rational moral agent and the productive worker as one and the same. A basic ambiguity persisted throughout his discussion as to whether economic justice consisted in giving to each what was necessary according to some sort of marginalist calculation of the costs of labour to make them work, or in rewarding everyone according to some criterion of desert. This confusion reflected in turn the identification of the common good with social efficiency which ran through his discussion. Once more, his argument depended upon the assumption that, to paraphrase only very slightly, the self-development of each was the condition for the self-development of all, that each person's 'rational' self-realisation enhanced that of everyone else. The thought that some individuals might be unfortunate enough to possess talents that a given society did not require or undervalued, for example, seems not to have bothered him. Like the clash of incompatible individual freedoms, it could be explained away as the result of the immorality and irrationality of the agents involved.

Liberals had been galvanized into action on the social question by Chamberlain's social imperialist policies.[233] For a number of Liberal businessmen, such as Sir John Brunner, the recognition of the commercial cost of unemployment combined with the belief that by aping Teutonic methods they could counter German competition, had provided the spur for their espousal of social reform. As we saw, whereas orthodox Ricardian political economy had regarded unemployment as the product of overpopulation or of labour pricing itself out of the market by putting an excessive strain on the wages fund, the new economics associated with Alfred Marshall argued that raising wages would have the beneficial effects of improving the education, earning capacity and character of the working classes, the enhanced 'personal efficiency' of the workers benefiting the nation as a whole. Far from discouraging thrift and promoting reckless procreation, securing a minimum standard of living would encourage self-help by rendering it a genuine possibility. The much vaunted Old Age Pensions scheme, for example, being in large part contributory, was designed to help those who helped themselves. The destitute, the so-called 'unemployable', and the casual labourers, whose plight formed the vast bulk of the social problem, were largely neglected by the New Liberal legislation. The new labour exchanges failed to address their needs, and the unemployment insurance scheme referred predominantly to those groups of skilled and organized workers most able to make provision for themselves in any case. The line between the 'residuum' and the rest became drawn more tightly. The 'ideal', according to Beveridge writing in 1906:

> should not be an industrial system arranged with a view to finding room in it for everyone who desired to enter, but an industrial system in which everyone who did find a place at all should obtain average earnings at least up to the standard of healthy subsistence...The line between independence and dependence, between the efficient and the unemployable has to be made clearer and broader...Those men who through general defects are unable to fill such a 'whole' place in industry, are to be recognised as unemployable. They must become the acknowledged dependents of the state, removed from free industry, with the complete and permanent loss of all citizen rights – including not only the franchise but civil freedom and fatherhood. To those, moreover, if any, who may be born personally efficient, but in excess of the number for whom the country can provide, a clear choice will be offered: loss of independence by entering a public institution, emigration or immediate starvation. The slow starvation of the casual labourer, like that of the 'sweated' worker, must become impossible.[234]

This passage exemplified the dangers implicit in many New Liberal arguments. Indeed, fear that the propagation of the unfit might lead to the degeneration of the race, resulted in a number of liberals considering eugenic policies in addition to labour colonies to purge the community of unsuitable citizens.[235]

Fortunately neither of these measures ever reached the statute book, although traces of such thinking can be found in some reforms, such as the Mental Deficiency Bill (1912), which did. Hobhouse generally steered clear of such conclusions. A staunch anti-imperialist and supporter of Campbell-Bannerman, he opposed the leanings towards

'national efficency' within the Liberal Party and the Fabians.[236] Unlike
Hobson, eugenics similarly repelled him as illiberal.[237] Yet, his theory
shared an undeniable family resemblance to these rejected alternatives.
He only avoided such pitfalls by preserving a Millian faith in the
progressive outcome of allowing as much diversity as possible, believing that 'liberty, equality of opportunity, and the social atmosphere of
justice and considerateness are the most eugenic of agencies.'[238] As it
was, he still advocated punitive labour camps for 'idlers'.[239] Thus the
New Liberals' expansion of the notion of citizenship to include social
rights only extended to those individuals capable and willing to fulfil
their obligations to society. Those who could or would not contribute to
the common good were not eligible.

If the democratic and liberal intentions of Hobhouse cannot be
doubted, the same cannot be said of the coherence of the underlying
teleology which enabled him to remain true to them. Provided his thesis
concerning human moral progress appeared plausible, he was spared
the potentially authoritarian conclusions to which it could give rise
when in competition with other conceptions of the good life. Liberal
politicians were not so fortunate. Forced to make practical decisions,
it was harder for them to maintain their theoretical integrity. The
identification of the free agent with the rational, moral and efficient
worker meant that the policy of social reform could be easily subsumed
into the technical matter of making society more productive.[240] So long
as the prospect of continued economic growth existed, it was possible
to avoid compelling recalcitrant individuals into performing 'useful
services' in the name of freedom, and their measures could seem genuinely progressive. In less prosperous times, however, economic and
ethical liberalism came into conflict. The First World War revealed to
Hobhouse, amongst others, the tremendous coercive power possessed
by the state, and shook his faith in the historical immanence of the
liberal moral community. The tension between the Gladstonian view of
the state as a moral force, an agency for the maintenance of ethical
values between itself, its citizens and other states, and the economic
notion of the state as a material force, a power entitled actively to
pursue the prosperity of its citizens, if necessary in conflict with other
states, became increasingly manifest. The crisis of the 1930s divided the
remaining liberals between those wedded to their ethical ideals and
those who opted for the protection of certain economic interests.[241]
Thus, new liberal values survived to the extent that prevailing economic
conditions rendered them a viable 'business proposition'.[242] In saying
this, I do not mean that the values of the new liberalism were entirely
congruent with the fortunes and mores of turn-of-the-century capitalism. Rather, that it was only capable of surviving as an important ideology so long as its fair-weather political supporters, such as Lloyd
George and Winston Churchill, held this view. After the war, Hobhouse
and Hobson attempted to keep their ideals intact, the one going into

dignified independent opposition, the other joining the Labour movement. Yet they continued to base their hopes on the increasingly unlikely prospect of both worker and capitalist embracing their somewhat narrow ethical standpoint, and remained wilfully blind to the real causes of tension within modern industrial societies stemming from conflicts of class and other material and moral interests.

The salient weakness of British liberalism sprang from a tendency to equate individual with social morality. Whereas continental thinkers appreciated the role played by institutional and economic forces in shaping individual lives, British theorists reversed this perspective and maintained that the social order reflected the character of the participants alone. Even Mill, who should have known his Guizot and de Tocqueville better, based his championing of suffrage reform on the British having reached that 'point of character which beyond any other fits the people of this country for representative government'.[243] The basic structure of British society was interpreted as the natural product of human development. In consequence, it became increasingly difficult for British liberals to question the practices of the liberal order itself. For the autonomous person was identified with the liberal citizen who had so internalized the norms of liberalism that they commanded his or her unreflective allegiance. Such an individual may spontaneously choose this way of life, but only by virtue of having been socialized into accepting it. This Foucaultian dimension of power, produced by the identification of agents with the available options of the society which disciplines their wants and desires, remained a blind spot of the Anglo-American liberal tradition.[244] Elsewhere in Europe, liberals could not take the basic structure of their societies for granted, nor be so sanguine about seeing the liberal order as the inevitable product of the evolutionary process. The British model may frequently have appeared to them as the natural form of social development, but in their cases the liberal social fabric and citizenry had to be consciously created and moulded, in Germany and Italy at the same time as constructing a national state and people out of a hotchpotch of local communities. Whereas in Britain the influence of social forces were so pervasive they went practically unnoticed, elsewhere they were so feeble they became the central focus of attention.[245] To a considerable extent, the degree to which liberal values and practices became subjected to debate and criticism mirrored the difficulty involved in making them the basis of a given society. Since France was the second most stable state in Europe at this time, French liberals came nearest to sharing the concerns and shortcomings of British liberalism. Yet even here, the prospects of liberalism seemed far more precarious than their colleagues across the Channel generally recognized, and their analysis correspondingly more questioning.

2

France: Liberalism Socialized

The antinomy confronting British liberals, between individual autonomy and the need for social institutions and a collective morality capable of fostering its development, stood at the centre of Emile Durkheim's (1858–1917) sociology. As he phrased it in the preface to his first major work, *The Division of Labour in Society*:

> How does it come about that the individual, whilst becoming more autonomous, depends ever more closely on society? How can he become at the same time more of an individual and yet more linked to society? For it is indisputable that these two movements, however contradictory they appear to be, are carried on in tandem. Such is the nature of the problem we have set ourselves.[1]

In attempting to resolve this dilemma, Durkheim engaged in an investigation into the nature of the social bonds within modern societies of a more sophisticated kind than that of his British counterparts. The first section of this chapter will relate this endeavour to the parallel projects of his French contemporaries to provide a solution to the social conflicts confronting the Third Republic. It is hoped that this context will resolve the scholarly dispute over the precise ideological ramifications of Durkheim's theory as either conservative, socialist or, as I maintain, liberal, when we turn to its examination in subsequent sections.[2] Indeed, I shall argue that the relationship Durkheim postulated between 'individual personality and social solidarity' rested less upon any empirical fact discovered through his sociological studies, than upon certain conventional liberal assumptions concerning the moral basis of the social order of Republican France.

SOLIDARISM, SOCIAL SCIENCE AND THE 'SOCIAL QUESTION' IN THE THIRD REPUBLIC

If few historians today regard the French Revolution as the product of the rise of the bourgeoisie,[3] most agree that it served as the midwife for a bourgeois social and political order.[4] The restoration in 1814 brought a return not to the *ancien régime* so much as the gradual establishment of the liberal regime sketched out during the period 1789–91, and which had come to an abrupt end with the Terror. This liberal settlement involved a constitutional government incorporating the separation of powers, some form of representative democracy and the entrenchment of the declaration of the Rights of Man and Citizen.[5] French liberals based their programme on an historically informed belief that this system was the best suited to a modern commercial world characterized by private property and the free exchange of goods and services between legally equal individuals, rather than on certain ideal principles of justice. Although their ideas were loosely modelled on an idealized view of the British Constitution, French liberals from Montesquieu onwards qualified their admiration with a recognition of the rootedness of British political institutions within a peculiar social and cultural context which they sought to promote in France.[6] The Abbé Sieyes (1748–1836), Benjamin Constant (1767–1830) and François Guizot (1787–1874), in particular, linked liberalism explicitly to the value system of the commercial and manufacturing middle class, and they considered the chief aim of social institutions to consist in raising progressively more and more people into the ranks of the bourgeoisie by removing the legal barriers to social advancement through hard work and enterprise. They believed this goal to be best achieved through a free market society regulated by the rule of law which guaranteed equal opportunities for all to enrich themselves and, in the process, society as well. They firmly opposed the redistribution of wealth by the state for the usual moralistic reasons, claiming that it 'abolish[ed] the responsibility inherent in human liberty' and 'excit[ed] bad passions through false hopes'.[7]

As in Britain, French liberals feared the degeneration of their doctrine into a crude economic individualism.[8] Alexis de Tocqueville (1805–59), especially, expressed concern at the tendency of the middle classes to give their private business and family priority over public affairs, and he worried that such attitudes would ultimately degenerate into a destructive egoism.[9] To a greater degree than their British counterparts, French liberals stressed the importance of continued political participation to maintain a minimum of public spiritedness. They saw the need to foster a general awareness that the liberties available to the individual resulted from a social framework which it was a matter of common concern to uphold against the incursions of particular self-interested persons.[10] If this consideration expressed itself mainly in a restriction of the franchise to those groups with property and an interest in the prevailing economic system, they were not unaware that 'the middle classes have their faults, their illusions, their share in lacking foresight and in showing obstinacy, vanity and egoism.'[11] Thus, Durkheim's sociological understanding of liberalism and his antipathy towards vulgar forms of economic egoism were entirely at one with the French liberal tradition.[12]

From their first attempt to achieve a constitutional settlement prior to the onset of Jacobin rule in 1792 until their eventual success in 1871, French liberals were caught between conservatives seeking to restore the hierarchical social order and those inspired by revolutionary Jacobinism. The first they regarded as attempting anachronistically to return to a political system which no longer had any foundation in society, the second they accused of seeking to fashion society anew on the basis of abstract principles with no basis in human nature or social conditions. They thought both projects doomed to failure and inevitably leading to despotism. Nevertheless, political isolation forced them at different times to make alliances with one or other camp. As a result, French liberalism spanned the ideological spectrum. It ranged from figures such as Guizot and the group known as the *doctrinaires*, who sided with the conservative camp during both the July Monarchy and in the later stages of the Second Empire, through more centrist figures such as Constant and de Tocqueville, who at various times expressed sympathy with both groups, to the radical supporters of the Second Republic of 1848 such as Léon Gambetta (1838–82). The Third Republic marked the belated triumph of bourgeois liberal values. It emerged from the temporary disarray of conservatives and revolutionaries alike resulting from the collapse of the Second Empire following the military defeat of 1870–1 by Prussia and the ensuing suppression of the Paris Commune respectively. The new regime gained its stability from an alliance between the two classes to benefit most from the post-revolutionary period – the capitalist bourgeoisie and the petty urban and rural producers, united in their joint fear of the return of a feudal-clerical aristocracy on the one hand and of an emergent working class on the other. The momentary defeat of both these elements provided the possibility for the construction of a lasting liberal social and political order.

Crudely put, the republicans aimed at the institutionalization of the ideals of 1789; a project entailing, to paraphrase the rhetoric of the day, an end to the privileges of the aristocracy and the power of the Catholic Church, which provided their endorsement, and the opening up of society to the satisfaction of the aspirations of both the industrialists and the *nouvelles couches sociales* of lawyers, doctors, teachers and small entrepreneurs by providing equal opportunities for all citizens to exercise their natural talents, acquire property, and ascend the social ladder. As with earlier liberals, this goal entailed rather more than *laissez-faire*, a creed in any case tainted in republican eyes by its association with the Second Empire. Moreover, the predominant *petit bourgeois* element was generally inimical to the interests of big business and finance, which continued in consequence to be partly tied to royalist politics. Liberty implied the economic independence and rational self-direction of the individual producer, rather than the conspicuous consumption and profit-making of the major capitalist.[13]

A brief initial attempt in 1876–7, led by Marshal MacMahon, to reassert traditionalist conservative values, helped damp down the likely tensions within the alliance of the 'populist' republicanism of the petty producers, linked to Léon Gambetta, and the provincial capitalists, represented by Jules Ferry (1832–97), by giving substance to their attacks on the feudal-clerical elites. The period 1879–85 saw the implementation of the essentials of a liberal regime. Despite the constitution's creation of a theoretically strong Presidency and Senate, the abortive use of these powers by MacMahon effectively rendered the Chamber of Deputies sovereign. The bureaucracy and judiciary were 'purged' of the more notorious anti-Republicans, and legislation was passed protecting individual civil liberties, such as the freedoms of speech, contract and combination, and re-instituting the right of divorce. Next, starting with the 'Freycinet plan' of 1878, schemes for the expansion of the economic infrastructure were set in motion, aimed above all at the provision of a modernized system of communications, notably a national railway system. The cornerstone of Republican policy, however, was the educational system. A series of laws, largely associated with Ferry, established free compulsory primary schooling and excluded religious teaching in favour of civic instruction, banning members of holy orders from holding posts in state schools. Ferry believed it was necessary to maintain 'certain doctrines of the state which are important for its conservation'. Since 'the principles of 1789 are the basis of modern French society: the teaching of them must be ensured.'[14] This conviction remained an article of faith of Republican policy throughout this period and formed the keystone of Durkheim's political sociology. Finally, abortive attempts at colonialism emanated from the mixture of economic and populist motives which underpinned the regime and epitomised the 'civilizing mission' of liberal republicanism. Taken together these measures seemed to secure the liberal ideal of an uncoerced, independent and rational citizenry, secure in the possession of their property and able freely to enter into exchange relationships with each other and to make full use of their abilities, whilst a parliamentary system satisfied the desire for participation and allowed conflicts of interest to take place without questioning the basis of society.

Durkheim, then a student at the Ecole Normale Supérieure, passionately supported the reforms of Gambetta and Ferry, seeing in them the creation of a new era. As he remarked twenty years later:

The men of my generation recall how great was our enthusiasm when...
we finally succeeded in toppling the last barriers which we impatiently
confronted. But alas! disenchantment came quickly; for we had to admit
that no one knew what to do with this liberty that had been so laboriously
achieved. Those to whom we owed it only made use of it in internecine
strife. And it was from that moment that one felt the growth in the
country of this current of gloom and despondency..., the ultimate result
of which must inevitably be to break the spirit of those least able to resist.[15]

The late 1880s and 1890s witnessed two conspicuous changes in the
political life of the Third Republic, to which Durkheim was referring.
First, without the stimulus provided by conservative attacks upon the
regime, Republicanism had a tendency to degenerate into clientalism,
and politics seemed dominated by local interests to the detriment of
national issues. The Wilson and Panama scandals, of 1887 and 1893
respectively, offended the populist Republicanism of the *nouvelles
couches*, for they appeared to reveal the corruption at the heart of the
'Opportunist Republic' and to show the unacceptable face of liberal capitalism as represented by the 'unproductive' world of finance. Second,
the stability of the regime was threatened by structural changes affecting
its social base. Although some historians have regarded the pace of economic change and industrial growth in France as laggardly compared to
Britain and Germany, a profound transformation in the direction of a
greater concentration of both capital and labour characterised the major
industries during the 1890s. Despite the depression of the 1880s, the
workforce of the manufacturing industries increased by 50 per cent
between 1886 and 1896, for example.[16] This development placed the class
alliance of industrial capitalists and petty producers under a certain
strain. The ideal of the latter of a community of independent property
owners, appeared threatened by the dual challenge posed by corporate
capitalism and organized labour. An unprecedented wave of strikes,
such as the miners' at Anzin in 1884 (the inspiration for Emile Zola's
novel *Germinal*) and at Carmaux in 1892, which turned Durkheim's
fellow *Normalien* Jean Jaurès to socialism, disturbed the peace of the
regime.

The 'social question' came to head the political agenda of the 1890s,
prompting a refinement of liberal ideology. For, as the quotation from
Durkheim cited above illustrates, these disturbances seemed to the
liberal republicans to indicate a perversion of the individual liberty they
stood for, whereby freedom had given way to licence. They attributed
this attitude on the part of corporate capitalists and socialists alike to the
prevalence of purely economic motives within their thinking. Both political economy and Marxism were criticised as doctrines based on
self-interest, possessing an inherent tendency to destroy the social fabric
of the community. In spite of the economic and social changes just
described, the parallel growth of a large tertiary sector of salaried and
self-employed and the continued existence of a substantial group of

craftsmen and small peasant proprietors meant that the bourgeois virtues of thrift and self-improvement had lost none of their relevance to a large percentage of the population. Thus the liberal intelligentsia was faced with the task of adapting these values to the industrial age and in particular of demonstrating their worth to the new forces of capital and labour in order to mediate between them. This project gained even greater urgency because the Boulanger (1888–9)[17] and Dreyfus (1898–9)[18] affairs revealed that popular discontent at social and political unrest could be channelled in a conservative direction by feeding the desire for a return to the authoritarian order of the past.

Confronted by such threats, Republicanism acquired a social dimension. The Radicals came to the fore, their share of the parliamentary seats increasing from 19 per cent in 1885 to 25 per cent in 1898 to become *the* republican party. If anticlericalism and secular education still formed the main plank of their programme, they also gave attention to social reforms aimed at integrating the workers into the republic. They directed their programme equally against unbridled *laissez-faire* and collectivism of both socialist and capitalist varieties. The new doctrine of solidarism was intended to harmonize individualism, corporatism and morality within an essentially liberal framework. In this manner the Radical republicans hoped to meet the triple dangers of monopoly capitalism, socialism and traditionalism.[19] This current of thought provides the ideological context of Durkheim's sociology, elaborated largely during the period of Radical ascendency and recognised and appropriately rewarded as a justification of its main tenets.

Durkheim's criticism of egoism, or self-interested individualism, his appeal to the importance of communal values, and his advocacy of a revived form of corporatism have led a number of commentators to accuse him of conservatism. Nisbet, in particular, has associated him with the superficially similar ideas of the reactionary Catholic social scientist Le Play. As critics of this interpretation have pointed out, a corresponding desire to find a scientific basis for morality, whereby social order could be restored to commercial society, ran through the whole French sociological tradition, and Durkheim's debts to its founding fathers, such as Montesquieu, de Tocqueville, Saint-Simon and Comte, were far more conspicuous. Moreover, in the course of the Dreyfus affair he explicitly denounced the traditionalist view of the crisis of contemporary mores. Yet if his intentions were not reactionary, they were definitely counter-revolutionary. Those commentators who rightly label Durkheim a social liberal, rarely submit this ethos itself to critical examination, regarding it as a positive extension of liberalism to the needs of the newly enfranchised industrial classes. 'Liberal', far from being a neutral description of Durkheim's political views, becomes a term of tacit approval. Usually such writers offer no reasons for this approbation beyond an assumed progressive consensus on the part of their readers. I shall attempt a partial remedy of such accounts below, by giving a brief examination of the dominant elements within contemporary French Radical ideas and policies in order to provide a benchmark against which Durkheim's theory can then be evaluated.

The most sophisticated analysis and defence of republican values was provided by the neo-Kantian philosopher Charles Renouvier (1815–1903).[20] A follower of Saint-Simon, he earned his liberal credentials during the Second Republic, for which he composed a popular guide to civic ethics – the *Manuel républicain* (1848). Renouvier assimilated the liberal virtues to the Kantian doctrine of autonomy, that is the exercise of free will in the rational pursuit of the dictates of the moral conscience. The ruling principle of social and political conduct consisted in the obligation to accord respect for the autonomy of others. Renouvier rendered this precept as a rephrasing of the Kantian categorical imperative, according to which the good citizen ought to 'recognize the person of others as your equal by nature and in dignity – as an end in itself, and as a consequence never use it as a simple means to reach your own ends'.[21] However, he criticised Kant for having located ethics and the fixed set of categories of the Understanding in the noumenal world, rather than seeing them as practical tools of our phenomenal experience. Invoking a thesis later adopted by Durkheim, he regarded the good as an object not just of duty but of desire. As such, the good represented a goal to be achieved through the creation of a suitable social and political environment, rather than a transcendent realm beyond human reach. According to Renouvier, the ideal world of harmoniously coexisting autonomous individuals coincided with a 'state of peace', at variance with the existing reality of a 'state of war'.[22] The task of politics was 'the establishment of legitimate social relations' consistent with his model of free rational human agency. Ideally, this society would approximate a community of freely contracting individuals. Practically, Renouvier contended that this state of affairs depended upon everyone possessing a minimum of private property guaranteeing their independence, so that maximising autonomy became linked to expanding property ownership.[23] Although moral autonomy would never be fully attainable, we had a 'right of defence' which enabled us to preserve as much of it as possible. He criticised the utilitarian and egoistic views of political economists for neglecting the way the untrammelled pursuit of individual self-satisfaction potentially undermined the autonomy of others by denying them similar opportunities for self-advancement.[24] Summing up his social philosophy, he maintained that the 'guiding idea of a society of rational beings consists in each being an end in himself and in having the means to pursue this end, with the aid of others if need be and if it is possible'. Apart from limited redistributional measures, such as a progressive income tax, Renouvier favoured the formation of voluntary associations such as producers' co-operatives, which would gradually substitute the collaborative spirit of the 'state of peace' for the present warlike competitiveness in the economic sphere.[25] Finally, republican education in state schools would promote the new religion of *personalisme*, fostering a collective commitment to the promotion of individual liberty and dignity.

Renouvier not only supplied a philosophical basis for the conventional nostrums of contemporary liberalism, his subordination of theoretical to practical reason served as a bridge between the liberal morality of autonomy and the sociological theories of Saint-Simon and Comte, who had argued, admittedly in divergent ways, that the norms regulating individual behaviour arose from the organization of social life itself. A number of later thinkers, of which Durkheim was the most conspicuous, were to develop this line of argument. It drew additional support from the biological analogy of a progressive evolution within social organisms from a simple homogeneity towards a complex heterogeneity popularised by Spencer and Maine. Industrial society came to be conceived as a complex organism of co-operating individuals whose relations were regulated by a just social contract ensuring the conditions of autonomy for all, notably in regard to the distribution of property. However, such theorists as Espinas and Fouillée differed from Spencer in having substituted the collective pursuit of individuality for the competitive individualism of the free market. As the Spencerian sociologist, Réne Worms, observed: 'In France, organicism had the good fortune to be linked to solidarism'.

The shift from philosophy to sociology amongst Republican thinkers was directly related to their concern to find a formula for regulating the relations between capital and labour capable of removing their conflictual tendencies. The emergent social science aimed to show that the morality of co-operation inhered in the organisation of production itself. The functions of worker and of capitalist, like those of the different organs of the body, were said to be complementary to the working of the system as a whole. Sociology purportedly provided a scientific basis for asserting that solidarity rather than conflict naturally existed between different classes. The current disorders arose from a disregard of the norms of mutual respect deriving from the ties of reciprocity uniting individuals in a well-ordered community. Politically the Radicals hoped to demonstrate a middle way between various forms of collectivism, be they socialist or monopoly capitalist in kind, and economic individualism, as found either in *laissez-faire* doctrines or the bargaining of trade unions. As Sanford Elwitt has observed, their own schemes for a form of corporatism reflecting the organic nature of the industrial world risked simply validating the production relations of the factory and extending them to social life as a whole.[26] Le Play's utopia of a hierarchically ordered corporate society certainly conformed to this pattern. However, even if the Radicals wished to alleviate the iniquities of capitalism rather than to change the system which produced them, the progressive nature of the reforms they proposed should not be denied.

The clearest statement of the Radicals' proposals was provided by the aptly named Léon Bourgeois (1851–1925), whose *Solidarité* (1895) became the most popular exposition of their ideas.[27] A powerful figure within the party during the period of its greatest ascendency, and leading the only all-Radical government from 1 November 1895 to 21 April 1896, he established solidarism as the official doctrine of the Third Republic. The Radicals wished to reconcile the emergent working classes to the Republic by committing themselves to social as well as to political reform. Georges Clemençeau, Bourgeois's predecessor in the role of Radical leader, expressed the essentials of their programme as early as 1876. 'We, the *radical* republicans', he wrote, 'want the Republic because of its results: the great and fundamental social reforms to which it leads. Our proposed aim is the fulfilment of the great metamorphosis of 1789, launched by the French bourgeoisie, but abandoned before it had been completed.'[28] Their claim was that the values of liberty, equality and fraternity could form the basis of a new social and moral order. In this respect, they self-consciously continued the radical republican tradition of Fourier, Proudon and Louis Blanc.

Bourgeois's famous tract summarized many of the themes discussed above. It began by criticising the opposing views of 'economists' and 'socialists' respectively, attacking the first for neglecting the individual's debt to society and the second for denying each person's distinct individuality.[29] Bourgeois argued that both elements played a part in the functioning of society, it being an association of individuals bound together by ties of reciprocal dependence as evinced in the division of labour. Thus the individual both relied upon and was vital to society. Bourgeois looked upon solidarity as the 'natural law' of both animal and social organisms. However, this circumstance did not entail that the system was self-regulating, as *laissez-faire* economists supposed. Unlike animals, human beings were not governed solely by instinct. The philosopher Alfred Fouillée (1838–1912) had developed Renouvier's view of practical reason and argued that human ideals and concepts, *idées forces* in his terminology, determined action as much as material forces. Reconciling determinism and voluntarism, Fouillée opined that if all action conformed to material laws, these could nevertheless be directed to moral ends. Drawing on this thesis, Bourgeois maintained that the fact of interdependence was in itself amoral, only rational intervention rendered it just. Adopting a characteristically metaphorical line of argument, he contended that much as bridges did not spontaneously appear, but had to be built (albeit in conformity with the laws of mechanics), so a just society had to be constructed consciously in accordance with social laws. Just as:

we seek the means to establish the equilibrium of our material edifices in the law of gravity; it is in the law of solidarity that we must find the means to establish an equilibrium between moral and social facts, that is to say justice.[30]

So stated, Bourgeois's theory appeared to stem from a fundamental critique of existing social arrangements for failing to meet certain moral standards, and arguably this was precisely what he was doing. However, the basis he chose to adopt for his argument was both less straightforward and less radical. For on Bourgeois's understanding of morality, those standards were provided by society itself. Ethics complemented the findings of social science by directing the actions of citizens and maintaining the character of their relations. A society only endured so long as its moral code conformed to its nature as revealed by scientific study. Possessing no transcendent property, the purpose of morality ceased to consist in the evaluation of existing social relations and served instead to conserve them by maintaining an 'equilibrium', itself a product of existing social forces, between the various classes in society. As he approvingly quoted from Fouillée, 'the moral laws which the individual prescribes himself are nothing but the general conditions of society'.[31] However, such reasoning would allow one to call moral any system of beliefs, regardless of its truth, which managed to reconcile individuals to their place in the community. Presumably if everyone agreed that society ought to be arranged in a particular way, then such arrangements would prove both harmonious and workable. But this consensus would not signify that they were either the most suitable way of doing things or the way things ought to be done. It may mean that its members have been socialized into accepting a system which enables the oppression of some individuals by others without their realising it.

Bourgeois, like Durkheim after him, side-stepped such disturbing conclusions by assuming that societies were naturally harmonious, that they could only sustain one code of behaviour, and that we were best served by maintaining them rather than seeking to change them. He employed such arguments to 'prove' Republican ideology was the sole morality capable of obtaining the rational assent of the French people. Three practical consequences resulted from this thesis. First, all deviations from solidarist orthodoxy, particularly the criticisms of conservatives and socialists which identified permanent sources of conflict and unrest in the Republican settlement, could be condemned as 'unscientific' and contributory to the very tensions they denounced. Second, political action became directed not at social change *per se*, so much as at the realization of an ethical order inherent to the social structure of modern France by raising the moral consciousness of the populace. Finally, Bourgeois's argument was somewhat paradoxical. On the one hand, he regarded this new ethos as being intrinsic to the industrial economy. This view suggested a concern simply to preserve the status quo. On the other hand, he maintained that the desired social order required the prior adoption of the norms essential to its operation in order to come into being. Like Durkheim after him, he resolved the paradox by arguing that 'our social and moral malaise' arose from social change being out of synchronization with moral change as a result of the one outstripping the other.[32] In an analogous way to Mill in the Britain of the 1840s, Bourgeois borrowed the Comtean notion of a 'transitional' epoch to express his mixed feelings at the transformations affecting his society. The resulting amalgam of descriptive and prescriptive elements within his theory attested to the incomplete hegemony of Radical values within French civil society. Similar reasons accounted for the curious mixture of libertarian and authoritarian measures adopted by the Radical party during these years, whereby the broadening of equal opportunities gave way to indoctrination concerning the merits of each station and its duties and the use of coercion to retain each citizen in his or her duly appointed place.

The solidarist ethos consisted of little more than a rehash of Renouvier's *personalisme*. Like Fouillée, Bourgeois believed that as humankind evolved so our acts became increasingly motivated by will rather than instinct; a development 'demonstrated' by the growing importance of contract over custom in the regulation of social relations. This circumstance reflected changes in the material basis of society itself, notably the more individualistic and artificial nature of industrial production compared with the very different organization of agricultural communities.[33] Bourgeois ascribed the recent social unrest to a failure on the part of both workers and capitalists to appreciate that despite this change, they continued to rely the one upon the other. He contended that by explicating the precise nature of these bonds, he would be able to elucidate the rights and duties of the modern citizen.[34]

Bourgeois did not challenge the traditional liberal opinion that the efforts of individuals underpinned social progress. However, he maintained that the available opportunities and resources employed by each one of us had been provided by the accumulated efforts of other people. Hence, each person both relied upon and contributed towards the collective product of society when engaged in their various separate pursuits. Moreover, as these occupations became more specialized, so our reliance upon other people to perform the multifarious tasks upon which our general quality of life depended increased. In consequence, he concluded, 'man is born in debt to society.'[35] In Bourgeois's terms, each citizen entered into a 'quasi-contract' with every other member of the community, past, present and future. Although no person explicitly consented to this arrangement, hence its 'quasi' status, it expressed our permanent indebtedness to society and our obligation both to offer a fair exchange for the services rendered us by our fellow citizens and to renew the common legacy for the use of future generations in return for the benefits we had received from the efforts of our predecessors. Bourgeois believed that he had found a formula whereby the rights of the individual could be harmonized with the duties owed to society without detracting from personal autonomy.[36] Once we had settled our debts, then we would be free to exercise our talents on our own account.

Bourgeois's theory paralleled that of the new liberals in attempting to discriminate 'individual' and 'social' elements in the creation of wealth in order to justify a policy of limited redistribution.[37] His effort to harmonize liberal and socialist sentiments had similar political reasons to theirs. Like the new liberalism, solidarism reflected an analogous bid by the Radical Party to woo working-class support without alienating its traditional middle-class constituency by appearing to license a general attack on property by denigrating the rewards due to individual merit. Deriving practical legislative proposals from this notion proved difficult. Ideally, Bourgeois believed each individual's contribution could be subjected to some sort of cost-benefit analysis, and the credits and debits assessed to arrive at the 'social debt' each person would have to work off. In practice, he recognized the impossibility of such an exercise. Instead, he suggested that we must *mutualiser* the benefits and disadvantages of society, by regarding us all as joint-stock holders in the human association in which all the risks and profits were shared.[38] As a number of contemporary commentators pointed out, the measures Bourgeois deduced from this arrangement owed more to the dictates of political prudence than the rigours of logic.[39] 'Social risks', in Bourgeois's opinion, included war, internal disorder and economic crises. They threatened the existence of the social system, and so all its members should bear the costs of insuring against them. Societies not only had to provide an army, police force and judiciary to protect the bodily integrity of its citizens, any association had a 'social duty' to guarantee a minimum level of subsistence as well, to protect those who contributed to the collective welfare against misfortunes such as accidents, sickness and involuntary unemployment which prevented them from supporting themselves.[40] Note that no provision was made for the habitually sick and incapable, who never rendered any service to the group. Society owed them no debt, and helping such persons to perpetuate themselves would only lower the moral and physical level of the race. Bourgeois envisaged that his proposed measures would be paid for by a mixture of contributory insurance schemes and progressive taxation, which gave everyone access to the 'social capital' of society, for the resources of the association had to be divided as well, so as to allow each individual to exercise his or her natural aptitudes to the full. Bourgeois insisted that 'natural' inequalities reflecting differences in physical or mental ability could never be eradicated, but justice required that these inequalities should not be increased by others of social origin, such as education and inherited wealth. He advocated a free system of state education, available not just at primary school level, but at the highest level achievable by the student, in order to ensure equal access to the 'intellectual capital' of society. The Ferry reforms had left higher education the preserve of the elite, a year at a *lycée* costing around 1,000 francs or approximately the annual wage of an industrial worker. Deciding on the just division of the 'material capital' of society required rather fancier intellectual footwork to avoid the various political pitfalls. Defending himself against the accusation of excessive socialist sympathies, Bourgeois remarked:

> My socialism tends toward the realisation of the conditions within which the individual, any individual, will develop himself fully, will reach the total potential of all his energies and all his faculties, will possess true freedom. I am, for that reason, absolutely opposed to collectivism, to communism, which invokes the power of the state and which tends inevitably to the destruction of freedom. Individual property appears to me to constitute the extension and the foundation of freedom…The development of individual property not its suppression is my goal, and my social ideal is that in which each person would obtain private property in just measure.[41]

All human labour employed the accumulated machinery and resources of society. Whilst individual effort and aptitude deserved their reward, many started with a totally 'unearned' advantage arising from inherited wealth. Taxation existed not for the purpose of levelling incomes but to support common goods and services. However, it was only right that those who had benefited from the unfairness of the initial distribution of wealth should pay more for their use.[42] He attacked all arrangements which gave certain individuals 'artificial' privileges other than their personal attainments. Trusts and monopolies significantly joined distinctions of birth as inadmissible practices which hindered the working of a just society based on the fair exchange of services.[43] Bourgeois even adopted Fouillée's notion of 'social property' to justify the leasing of all landed property by the state, on the grounds that rent increased because of social forces rather than as a result of individual improvements.[44] Once they had acquitted their 'social debt', individuals were free to make their own way, and the inequalities which resulted from their efforts were perfectly acceptable.

Bourgeois's distinction between the injustices of the 'natural' solidarity advocated by *laissez-faire* liberals and political economists and his own moral version based on reason might appear to justify widespread state intervention to secure its realization. Yet such measures were conspicuously lacking from his programme. True, he supported the introduction of a progressive income tax to secure a more equitable division of the 'material capital' of society and pay for certain social policies, but this proposal foundered when he capitulated to its rejection by the Senate in 1896. However, subsequent failures to press the issue did not reflect a weakness of political nerve or a lack of favourable circumstances alone. It also attested to an aversion to direct state interference of this kind intrinsic to his theory, for Bourgeois regarded social and political change as following from an alteration in the moral perceptions of individuals in accordance with society's needs. The state's function, therefore, did not consist of promoting social reforms directly, so much as designing schemes which facilitated their voluntary adoption as part of the general moral self-regulation of society by its members.[45] Indeed, his contention that this ethos accorded with the efficient running of the community provided a motivation for the collectivity, if not for each individual alone, to enter into such programmes.

Apart from education, the prime instruments of this moral transformation were to be the mutual benefit societies (*sociétés de secours mutuels*). Possessing a long history in France, the Radicals gave the movement a significant boost with a law of 1898 legalising such societies and promising state subsidies proportionate to the benefits they offered and the money they raised. They hoped that the whole range of social services – from employment exchanges to medical attention and pensions – would devolve upon them with little cost to the state. They urged their amalgamation in the belief that this would spread the habit of mutual aid throughout the land, making 'the French Republic...a vast mutual benefit society'.[46] In fact they met with little success. In 1902 71 per cent had fewer than 100 members. Unlike British friendly societies, they were not a focus of working-class culture, but included local notables and employers as honorary members. Indeed, their low membership made the contributions of these groups and of the government vital to their financial solvency. As a result, they ended up part of the network of state and employer paternalism. State endeavours to supplement these schemes tended to be inadequate due to lack of funds. For example, in 1910 only 10 per cent of the working class had insured against old age. The government had acknowledged this failure of mutualism in 1901 and attempted to pass a bill giving workers a right to a pension. It took nine years to get on the statute book due to protests from the Senate. Even then, its restriction to those aged sixty-five and above at a time when the average life expectancy was fifty rightly led socialists to ridicule them for giving 'pensions to the dead'. Whilst the Radicals had some success with provisions for the sick, infirm, women and children, those improving working hours and conditions were rarely effectively implemented due to a lack of efficient machinery for their enforcement and the resistance of employers.

As with social insurance, the Solidarists regarded voluntary schemes as the best means of reforming working conditions, and co-operatives were legalised in 1899. However, if mutualism proved a disappointment, the co-operatives were a definite failure, involving only about 500 firms. In any case, their potential as instruments of social change was decidedly limited, since they were premised upon the acceptance of the division between capital and labour as necessary and essentially complementary functions, rather than as antagonistic forces within the productive process. As one of the movement's principal popularists,

Edouard de Boyve, stressed, co-operation strengthened national solidarity by effecting the 'harmony of capital and labour'. It advanced 'the
union of workers...without weakening the creative power of capital'.[47]
Their main aim was to encourage habits of self-help and class collabora-
tion, opposing a divisive socialism based on the antagonism of classes
with a 'healthy socialism' which would resolve the social question, 'the
struggle between capital and labour having lost its justification once
capital and labour become closely allied by their common interest'.[48]
Significantly, the thrust of the co-operative movement was eventually
away from production to associations of consumers, supposedly capable
of taking on the 'formidable capitalist coalitions' and reducing capital to
'its proper role...as a factor in production and remunerated as such'.
Charles Gide, the prime mover of the co-operative idea in solidarist
circles, argued that profit arose from the price of commodities in the
market, rather than the extraction of surplus value on unpaid labour.
Typically, he located the relations of capital and labour in the realm of
exchange, not production which he left unaltered.[49]

Bourgeois's misplaced faith in the power of the voluntary movements
to foster an awareness and practice of solidarity within French society
revealed the respective weaknesses both of his theory and of the reforms
he believed flowed from it. Whilst Bourgeois wished to curtail certain
'artificial' inequalities arising from the advantages of initial differences
in wealth and background, he failed to develop fully the egalitarian
potential of this view, and hence to recognise the difficulties of implementing it. His position amounted to little more than a characteristic
liberal attack on the inherited privileges of the aristocracy and the
power of corporate capitalism on behalf of a bourgeois meritocracy.
His tendentious category of 'natural' inequality led him to leave un-
addressed a whole range of problems concerning the fickle way different abilities get rewarded by market mechanisms. The grievances of the
less well-off lost their legitimacy. The less successful deserved their fate.
Not surprisingly, those who possessed nothing looked on Solidarism as
merely a new and more ingenious justification of inequality, rather than
a means for attenuating its injustices.

'The most liberal of socialists',[50] Bourgeois opposed all forms of
collectivism which entailed an increase in state power. Since he linked
the individual's ability for self-development to the possession of property, he stood for the extension of private ownership rather than its
curtailment. Although he acknowledged that disparities of wealth
exacerbated class struggle, he did not challenge the capitalist's right
of appropriation. Thus the campaign for social justice left capitalist
relations untouched. Instead he sought to further working-class collab-
oration in the economic system by encouraging the workers' transformation into small capitalists themselves. As with the British New
Liberals, structural reforms became subordinated to the moralizing of
existing social relations. For Bourgeois 'the social question is, in the last

instance, a problem of education.'[51] Writing in 1891 at the height of the industrial unrest occasioned by the Great Depression of 1873–96, Alfred Fouillée spoke for the Solidarist movement generally. He located the 'chief cause of [France's] current malaise', in the 'conflict of ideas and purposes both between different social classes and between political parties; the solution lies in all forms of social education that shape ideas according to a conception of absolute harmony.' A 'scientific' under-standing of social solidarity 'will replace the intellectual and moral anarchy that threatens to split us up' with 'national unity'.[52] Numer-ous educational associations, such as the *Ligue de l'enseignement*, the *univérsités populaires*, and the *Société pour l'éducation sociale*, of which Bourgeois was the president, were formed to translate this doctrine into practice. 'Social education', according to the Radical educationalist and politician Férdinand Buisson, comprised 'that part of education which creates within us a consciousness of our social existence'; its purpose, to establish the habits of 'solidarity...in which each individual freely subordinates his activities to the interests of the collectivity'.[53] This 'common consciousness', as Bourgeois termed it, consisted in a recog-nition of the respective rights and duties of each station in life, whilst allowing for the hardworking and intelligent individual to change his or her position.[54] Since 'moral' and 'rational' social relations derived from the 'social facts' of interdependence observed in the workplace, their theory tended to legitimize the new forms of industrial organization rather than to challenge them. However progressive in intention, solid-arism quickly became a recipe for social conservatism, since it ruled out any change to the existing organization of society beyond measures designed to assist its efficient and 'moral' functioning. We have already cast doubt upon the theoretical coherence of its moral position, and will develop these arguments in relation to Durkheim's sociology of morals. In practice, the Solidarists' position meant that reform became linked to the disciplining of the worker, for example in the way schemes for 'social hygiene' included not only improved housing conditions but equally the encouragement of sobriety amongst the masses. Even baths were championed because, in Férdinand Faure's words, 'when French-men come to have two baths a week, the moral, intellectual and political condition of our country will be transformed'.[55]

Thus solidarism simultaneously served the purposes of progressive reform and counter-revolution by integrating the labour force into the new forms of industrial organization. After 1900 Radicalism began to change, moving from Centre-Left coalitions to a realignment with the Right. Between 1906 and 1914 the Radicals gained 40 per cent of parlia-mentary seats, becoming the establishment party. The *univérsités populaires* failed to attract sufficient support and *Libre pensée* groups fractured along class lines. Anticlericalism still enabled them to maintain a populist appeal, but after the resolution of the Dreyfus affair this in itself proved insufficient to paliate the Left. Radicalism began to be outflanked by the growing socialist movement, especially in industrial areas and in Paris. The Right, under Poincare, also began to shift its ground towards a populist conservative nationalism. Clemençeau, who had once defended the right to strike and attacked the brutality of the police in smashing workers' protests, as Prime Minister from 1906 to 1909 made full use of the unreformed police powers to crush proletarian unrest. With the ascendency of Briand, who led four cabinets from 1910 to 1914, Radicalism turned decisively to the Right, smashing the 1910 rail strike, securing Poincare's election as President, supporting renewed colonial adventures and taking a firm stance against socialism and income tax. Conscription and the financial burden of rearmaments in the run-up to 1914 kept alive a rump of leftist Radicals, prepared to deal with socialists, around Caillaux and Viviani, a group to which Durkheim was aligned. But if they advocated a reform of income tax, they remained decidedly wary of recognizing the rights of trade unions, even if they deplored the punitive measures used against them.

The mixture of progressive and conservative elements within French Radicalism renders the divergent ideological positions which have been attributed to Durkheim comprehensible. As I shall show in the next sections, an ambivalence did exist in his sociological and political ideas, largely reflecting that of French radical liberalism. Of course, it would be mistaken to assimilate Durkheim completely to the Solidarist tradition. He disputed the workability of a number of their redistributive schemes, and thought that their political reforms too often took an awareness of the organic solidarity of society for granted.[56] Yet, analogous criticisms could easily be made of his own ideas, for he fashioned his own distinctive thesis in the context of their debates, sharing their strengths and, more especially, lacunas.

EMILE DURKHEIM, THE DIVISION OF LABOUR AND THE SOURCES OF ORGANIC SOLIDARITY

In 1887 Durkheim was appointed *chargé de cours* of social science and pedagogy at the university of Bordeaux. The post had been specially created for him at the joint instigation of the pioneering sociologist Alfred Espinas, then Rector at that university, and Louis Liard, a disciple of Renouvier and director of higher education in France. The linking of the teaching of education and sociology in Durkheim's new position was highly significant. If the Catholic Church had disseminated the feudal ethos, the Republicans regarded the state school system as the main vehicle for spreading the new religion of liberalism. This secular morality had to reflect the requirements of modern societies just as effectively as Catholicism had met the needs of former times. Sociology played a vital role in this endeavour through its promise of placing morality on a scientific basis by relating it to the demands of the social system, rather than seeing it 'philosophically' in terms of deductions from a priori principles. It discovered and clarified the beliefs uniquely capable of assuring the social integration of contemporary France. Durkheim's claim to provide an authoritative endorsement of republican ideology by this means was a far from negligible factor in the rise of Durkheimian social science to establishment status, and its becoming a major component of the curriculum in French teacher training schools.

Durkheim's sociology not only served an overt political purpose in seeking to form public opinion, it was inherently political in conception. For the very way in which he treated society as providing the norms for the regulation of individual behaviour effectively delegitimized and condemned as 'unscientific' and abnormal those who struggled against the republican order. He stressed these 'salutary' practical aspects of social science in his inaugural lecture. Remarking on the atomism and consequent loss of the collective spirit within French society, he insisted:

> Our society must regain consciousness of its organic unity; so that the individual feels this social mass which envelops and penetrates him...and this sentiment always governs his conduct; for it is not enough that he should merely be inspired by it from time to time in particularly crucial circumstances...Messieurs, I believe sociology, more than any other science, is in a position to restore these ideas. It will make the individual understand what society is, how it completes him and what a little thing he is when left to his own devices. It will teach him that he is not an empire within another empire, but the organ of an organism, and will show him how good it is conscientiously to perform his role as an organ. It will make him feel that there is no loss of standing to be linked [*solidaire*] with others and to depend upon them, rather than belonging entirely to himself. Without doubt these ideas will not become truly efficacious until they are diffused amongst the lower strata [*couches*] of the population; but for that to occur, we must first elaborate them at a scientific level at the University. It will be my principal concern to contribute to the attainment of such a result as much as I am capable and I could have no greater happiness than to succeed a little in that goal.[57]

Like his fellow republicans, Durkheim wished to stem the individualist attitudes associated with the modern economy without advocating a return to traditionalist communitarian values based on outmoded conventions and beliefs of a metaphysical nature, which totally subordinated the individual to the collectivity. This project entailed showing that the relationships between the members of the industrial world involved more than mere rational self-interest, as he believed utilitarian theorists and political economists argued, and that individual development was in some sense dependent upon society.

These concerns dominated his first major work, *De la division du travail social*, of 1893. Durkheim's hopes for the sociology of morals rested on assumptions akin to those we observed in Bourgeois's writings. At the heart of his work was the thesis that value systems reflected a determinate social order. Morality, in Durkheim's view, did not consist in a set of universal criteria to be applied to individual actions in all circumstances, as philosophers supposed. Nor did it derive from certain innate traits of human nature, as psychologists argued. It denoted those rules of conduct regulating individual behaviour necessary for the stability of a particular society at a given stage of its development. The sociologist of morals, therefore, sought to show how changes in social organization effected transformations in the character of moral norms which enabled the system to achieve a harmonious equilibrium between its constituent parts. Durkheim insisted on the scientific credentials of this enterprise. 'Moral facts', he asserted, were 'phenomena like any others' consisting 'of rules for action recognizable by certain characteristics capable of classification and assimilable to certain general laws'. He surmised that if one could determine the tendencies present within society, it would be possible to deduce the appropriate moral rules required for its 'healthy' functioning.[58]

Unlike the contemporary French sociologists Espinas and Izoulet, Durkheim believed that biological concepts only served as useful metaphors for the understanding of human association. For whilst animal organisms operated 'mechanically', human societies were united 'not by a material relation, but by ties of ideas'. Although these norms could be attributed ultimately to 'individual minds', the composite *conscience collective* constituted a whole greater than the sum of its parts, with *sui generis* characteristics of its own reflecting the practical requirements of the collectivity at a given time and place. In spite of borrowing his terminology, Durkheim did not follow Espinas in regarding this entity as a 'social brain' created by the 'mind' of society, the intellectual elite.[59] Nor did his view imply any denial of individual agency, like certain German idealist doctrines which reduced people to being cyphers of a metaphysical demiurge such as *Geist*. He contended 'merely that we are at the same time actors and acted upon, and each of us contributes to forming this irresistible current which sweeps him along' much as 'each of us speaks a language he did not create.'[60]

Durkheim claimed to have rendered the study of morality truly scientific by discovering within the set of observable moral facts an 'objective element which is capable of precise determination and, if possible, measurement'. Durkheim found this index in law, which, as Steven Lukes has pointed out, the French term *droit* links both conceptually and linguistically with notions of justice, fairness, rights and obligation in a manner unfamiliar to English jurists. By noting changing features of the law, he hoped to penetrate to the underlying alterations in morality and hence to arrive at a typology of the forms of social solidarity.[61] On this basis, Durkheim identified two main types: 'mechanical' solidarity, found in pre-industrial societies, and the 'organic' solidarity of the present. 'Mechanical' solidarity belonged to 'segmental' small-scale tribal societies, lacking any significant degree of specialization amongst their members and characterised by a low density of population and the virtual communal ownership of property. Such communities needed generalists, capable of performing the same broad set of tasks in concert with others, rather than experts. The efficient functioning of these societies required a high degree of social conformity of their members, so that 'this solidarity can therefore only increase in inverse relationship to the personality.'[62] The individual's thoughts were 'enveloped' within the 'collective consciousness', or shared norms, of society. In primitive societies it consisted of an extensive set of uniform beliefs and practices of a largely religious nature, which led the individual to identify completely with the life of the community.[63] According to Durkheim, one could measure the intensity and pervasiveness of these common sentiments by the incidence of repressive rules, which reflected a social system based upon the enforcement of uniform behaviour.

'Organic' solidarity developed with the advent of the division of labour. He attributed this innovation to population growth and the improvement of the methods of communication and transport, which increased the 'volume' and 'density' of societies and heightened social interaction.[64] Adopting a variant of Social Darwinism, Durkheim argued that the impetus towards specialization resulted from the heightened struggle for existence as competition over resources became more accute. Darwin, he believed, had revealed that conflict was most intense between organisms of the same type. Differentiation enabled their co-existence, since once they ceased to go after the same objects the survival of the one no longer jeopardized that of the others.

Durkheim contrasted his own 'sociological' explanation of this transformation with Spencer's and the utilitarian's reliance on psychological factors. He thought they accounted for social change by the refinement and evolution of human desires as individuals sought after increasingly complex forms of happiness. He countered that our capacity for pleasure, however sophisticated, was finite and could not motivate such momentous developments.[65] Durkheim's approach neatly inverted that of the British liberals, who habitually attributed social change to the evolution of morals rather than vice versa. This procedure had important consequences for his understanding of 'organic' solidarity. Whereas Spencer had attributed functional specialisation to the prior development of individualism and the increasing heterogeneity of interests, Durkheim contended that this diversity derived from, and was regulated by, the division of labour itself, as it progressed in response to social requirements:

> Work is not shared out between independent individuals who are already differentiated from one another, who meet and associate together in order to pool their different abilities. It would be a miracle if these differences, arising from chance circumstances, could be so accurately harmonised as to form a coherent whole. Far from preceding collective life, they derive

from it. They can only occur within a society, under the pressure of social sentiments and needs. This is what makes them essentially capable of being harmonised.[66]

Spencer had made the grave mistake 'of deducing society from the individual'. However, 'collective life did not arise from individual life; on the contrary, it is the latter that emerged from the former.' Durkheim maintained that co-operation could never have resulted from the agreements of pre-social individuals, since it was permeated with moral notions that could only originate from the experience of society. Indeed the very individualism Spencer praised arose from alterations in the social structure. 'On this condition alone', he wrote, 'can we explain how the personal individuality of social units was able to form and grow without causing society to disintegrate.'[67]

He accepted the common contention of Spencer, Maine, Saint-Simon, Comte and Tonnies that occupational specialisation had rendered the structure and sentiments of modern societies more heterogeneous than the simple homogeneous agararian communities of the past, but he disputed the conclusions they drew from this change. Like these other theorists, he associated this general trend with a decline of societal regulation based on status and convention and the emergence of more individualistic forms linked to contract. However, at least on Durkheim's reading, Spencer in particular, and also Maine, Saint-Simon and the general run of political economists, had made the mistake of regarding the harmony of contractual relations as amoral, the spontaneous and unintended consequence of each individual following his 'best interest'. He countered that a society truly based on egoism would rapidly degenerate into a highly discordant anarchy:

> For where interest alone reigns, as nothing arises to check the egoisms confronting one another, each self finds itself in relation to the other on a war footing, and any truce in this perpetual antagonism cannot be of long duration.[68]

Of itself, a contract merely signified a temporary cessation of hostilities, reflecting the balance of power between the parties at a given moment, and hence continually open to renegotiation when circumstances altered to the advantage of either of them. To be stable, Durkheim argued, 'a contract is not sufficient in itself, but supposes a regulatory system that extends and grows more complicated just as does contractual life itself.'[69]

In some respects, Tonnies (and Comte) had adopted a similar argument. They observed that the communitarian cohesion of the primitive *Gemeinschaft* had given way to the atomistic relations of the modern *Gesellschaft*, in which the remnants of collective life 'result, not from an internal spontaneity, but from the wholly external stimulus of the state'. However, Durkheim rejected this theory also, attacking it for failing to appreciate 'that the life of large social agglomerations is just as natural as that of small groupings. It is no less organic and no less internal.'[70] True, the need for greater specialization had weakened the pervasiveness of the *conscience collective*, which 'comes increasingly to be made up of highly generalized and indeterminate modes of thought and sentiment, which leave room open for an increasing multitude of individual differences'. As such, it could no longer 'engender the same results as that multiplicity of extinct beliefs'. For 'if the faith is common because it is shared by the community, it is individual in object. If it impels every will towards the same end, that end is not a social one.'[71] However, he did not fear the descent into the war of individual appetites predicted by Tonnies because the division of labour increasingly took over this regulatory role itself:

> Through it the individual is once more made aware of his dependent state *vis-à-vis* society. It is from society that proceed those forces that hold him in check and keep him within bounds. In short, since the division of labour becomes the predominant source of social solidarity, at the same time it becomes the foundation of the moral order.[72]

The division of labour did not produce social solidarity 'only because it makes each individual an agent of exchange...It is because it creates between men a whole system of rights and duties joining them in a lasting way to one another.'[73] The 'cult of the individual' replaced the veneration of society *per se* as the source of social solidarity.[74] The need constantly to deal with others, which the division of labour entailed, produced ways of acting and habits which with time became rules of conduct. These norms enjoined a mutual respect for each person's individuality and particular function within the social system, a change symbolized by the shift from the repressive laws of primitive communities to the increasing preponderance of restitutive law in the present. Moreover, if the quality of law had changed, *pace* Spencer, it had greatly increased in bulk since social life had grown immensely in complexity and necessitated greater regulation. Thus the influence of the state had grown, but not in order to retain its punitive and constraining role of the past, as Tonnies and Comte had believed. Rather, its administrative and organizational activities had increased. Hence the apparent paradox he noted at the start of the book seemed resolved, for the individual owed his or her autonomy to the introduction of the division of labour, which in turn augmented our dependence on society and increased governmental functions.[75]

At this point, Durkheim faced an obvious difficulty. If the division of labour was self-regulating, how could he explain the class conflict and economic disruptions which rocked contemporary France? Durkheim's theory relied upon the natural evolution from 'mechanical' to 'organic' solidarity as society progressively developed from a simple to a complex and differentiated state. He got around the apparent falsification of this hypothesis by maintaining that France's problems arose from the country being in a transitional stage, in which the spread of the division of labour had temporarily outstripped the diffusion of the moral norms that governed it. Commercial crises, bankruptcies, the hostility between labour and capital, testified to a lack of regulation between the organs of the social body: a normless condition Durkheim dubbed anomie. However, given sufficient time, rules would spontaneously establish themselves between the different social functions, determining fair contracts for the hiring and exchange of services, and co-ordinating the market in such a way that supply no longer surpassed demand. Durkheim had yet to elaborate upon the institutional framework necessary to attain the requisite communication between the various sectors of the economy, a development examined here in the final section. For the moment, he remained content to assert that 'we may say a priori that a state of anomie is impossible wherever organs linked solidly to one another are in...sufficiently lengthy contact.'[76] He disputed the view that one of the consequences of the division of labour had been to diffuse social bonds by dividing people from each other, reducing the individual to a 'lifeless cog' in an impersonal machine. This only occurred 'in exceptional and abnormal circumstances'. Normally:

> The division of labour supposes that the worker, far from remaining bent over his task, does not lose sight of those cooperating with him, but acts upon them and is acted upon by them. He is not therefore a machine who repeats movements the sense of which he does not perceive, but he knows that they are tending in a certain direction, towards a goal that he can conceive of more or less distinctly. He feels that he is of some use.[77]

In spite of the implausibility of this picture of industrial production, an image heavily dependent on the organic analogy, Durkheim never abandoned it. Nevertheless, he admitted that not any set of rules would provide the sort of harmonious equilibrium between capital and labour he had described. The wrong sort of moral regulation caused social upheaval instead of preventing it. Turning to the current crisis in France, he argued 'class war' flared up because the exchange of services was being regulated by an inappropriate set of rules, those based on rank and inherited privilege.[78] Frustrated in their ambitions, the lower orders turned to revolution:

> If one class in society is obliged, in order to live, to secure the acceptance by others of its services, whilst another class can do without them, because of the resources already at its disposal, resources that, however, are not necessarily the result of some social superiority, the latter group can lord it over the former. In other words, there can be no rich and poor by birth without there being unjust contracts.[79]

Characteristically, Durkheim skirted around the problem of how to persuade the rich to give up their privileges. He merely contended that the
conditions which had given rise to them had been superseded. The new
social order required a meritocratic ethos for it to function without strife.

Durkheim contrasted the 'forced division of labour' to the equitable
concord which would result when the distribution of jobs and rewards
really reflected the capacities and merit of their recipients. He assumed
that so long as the functional differentiation occurred 'naturally', as part
of a general process of adaptation to changing structural circumstances,
then the 'normal' division of labour would be non-conflictual. When
the allocation of functions occurred 'spontaneously', without external
hindrances of any kind, then 'inevitably only those most fitted for each
type of activity will succeed in obtaining it', ensuring a perfect fit
'between the constitution of each individual and his condition'.[80]
Furthermore, equality of opportunity not only sufficed 'to secure each
individual to his function, but also to to link these functions with one
another'.[81] Each service had a 'fixed' 'social value' representing 'the
amount of useful work intrinsic to it'. Durkheim surmised that, provided
services were exchanged according to their true worth, an 'equilibrium
of wants' equivalent to the 'equilibrium of things' would result. Thus,
'normality' entailed that both selection for employment and market
transactions were 'just' in the sense of being in accordance with a
presumed 'natural' order.[82]

Durkheim dismissed the possibility of individual frustration through
having to perform a demeaning or insufficiently demanding job as but
another 'abnormal' form. A 'healthy' system matched the increase and
nature of specialisation to the available needs and capacities of its
members. Unemployment and lack of fulfilment in one's work derived
from the imperfect co-ordination of functions caused by a lack of solidarity. Durkheim maintained that increased efficiency led to more
specialisation without provoking either crises of overproduction or
deskilling jobs and rendering them monotonous or even redundant.
Quite the reverse, people had to work harder and their tasks became
more interesting as 'useless' jobs were suppressed. Since he denied that
human needs were infinitely elastic, he must have attributed this expansion and change in the quality of production to factors internal to the
division of labour, notably technological innovation.[83] Provided all the
parts of the social organism remained in sufficient contact with each
other to respond to the needs of society as a whole, then economic crises
and strikes would become things of the past. Durkheim's optimistic
interpretation of factory production saved him from confronting either
Beveridge's cynical picture of an efficient industrial society rejecting the
'unfit', cited in the previous chapter, or the managerial nightmare of
Taylorism, in which workers were reduced to automatons. In a similar
manner to the new liberals, he optimistically believed that justice and

national efficiency went hand in hand, so that 'to inject an ever greater
equity into our social relationships' was 'to ensure the free deployment
of all those forces which are socially useful'.[84]

When one considers that the threat posed by machinery to a predominantly craft-based, skilled labour force formed a prime source of social
unrest in France at this time, Durkheim's theory seems curiously out of
touch with the practical reality of the processes it supposedly described.
Semi-skilled machine minders (*ouvriers spécialisés*) had increased to a
third of all industrial workers by 1900, and their growing predominance
within the new factories, where skilled operatives accounted for less
than 20 per cent of those employed on the shop-floor, provided a major
cause of workplace disputes. The division of labour had certainly
advanced apace, an industrial dictionary of 1896 listing 858 trades
compared to the 15,000 documented by one of 1909, but for many of
those directly affected by the change it seemed less liberating or
progressive than its theoretical champion made out. Since those workers
most adversely affected tended to be the most articulate and best
organized as well, the bulk of the syndicalist movement coming from
their ranks, the ensuing conflicts tended to be particularly bitter and
protracted. Whereas during the period 1885–9 12 per cent of strikes
involved job control issues, this figure had risen to 25 per cent by 1910–
14, and strikes generally increased from 100 to more than 1,000 a year
over the same period. These various actions came to a symbolic head
with the 1913 Renault strike, which ended with the sacking of 436
workers as the result of the introduction of Ford-style rationalization.
Little wonder then, that the leaders of the labour movement should look
upon Durkheim's project with distrust. As Lafargue commented, 'it is
no longer religion which condemns the workers to misery, it is science.'[85]

Durkheim's blending of moral and economic arguments led him to
idealize the emergent liberal order. In a similar manner to Hobhouse, he
had a tendency to equate the individual's self-development with that of
society as a whole. Like the Solidarists examined in the previous section,
Durkheim argued that 'organic' solidarity followed from the citizens'
recognition of the juridical and moral implications of their interdependence stemming from the division of labour. The full economic benefits
of these relations only obtained when they were arranged in a moral
manner, for the morality he advocated was an aspect of the system itself
rather than a collection of abstract principles. This new ethos demanded
that 'no obstacle whatsoever prevents [all individuals] from occupying
within the ranks of society a position commensurate to their abilities.' A
just society enabled each person to perform the duties and enjoy the
rewards appropriate to the station to which he or she was best suited.
It must be 'constituted in such a way that social inequalities express
precisely natural inequalities'.[86] Durkheim meant by this the destruction
of the privileges of hereditary wealth and the institution of the principle
of equal opportunities and rewards for equal services and merits. How-

ever, he also presumed that the 'spontaneous' distinctions arising out of the capitalist system were fair and complementary. The division of labour enabled each person to express his or her individuality by finding an appropriate niche in life and earning the respect of others through contributing to the ever increasing manifold requirements of society. Durkheim's vision of moralized capitalist relations bore a close resemblance to those of the British liberals examined in the previous chapter. More than theirs, his model of society suffered from many of the defects of 'organic' social theories, which treat individuals as functional units of a greater whole. The individual was pigeon-holed with his or her role in the productive process with little or no account given of its relation to other aspects of human life. Nor, for reasons explored more fully in the next section, did he contemplate the likely result of a greater awareness of social reality amongst factory operatives – namely, increased dissatisfaction with industrial labour. A boring and repetitive job remains such, no matter what the ultimate purpose might be. By such poor arguments, he alleged to have given scientific proof that the bourgeois meritocracy advocated by the Radicals was vital to the well-being of the Republic, providing the answer to the economic and social crises which assailed it. Once adopted, peace and prosperity would ensue.

Durkheim offered precious few indications as to how to bridge the undeniable gap between his ideal and the reality of contemporary French capitalism. For example, his view that property should be linked to 'the services individuals have rendered society'[87] implied the need for fairly drastic changes in the current distributional arrangements, notably the abolition of inherited wealth. He acknowledged that whilst disparities in riches existed between citizens which owed nothing to 'social merit', then the whole contractual system as he conceived it was undermined at its very foundations. So long as people were born rich or poor, the former would always make use of their unfair advantage to impose an inequitable contract upon the latter. All reforms short of the removal of this division of society into two great classes were mere 'palliatives', since the community would continue to be based on a principle which did 'not allow it to be just'.[88] Yet he denied equally that a 'miraculous' transformation of property relations, which placed all resources, including the means of production, under common ownership, would resolve the problem of injustice either, for it was essentially a question of moral regulation.[89] If Durkheim accepted that clashes between interests occurred, he refused to admit that it could ever be the 'natural' state of society.[90] The Marxist contention that capitalist social relations consisted of just such a state of war, engendered by the existence of inequalities inherent to capitalism's very functioning, was totally foreign to his theory. Instead, Durkheim argued that the present conflicts derived from a failure to appreciate and abide by the moral code intrinsic to the industrial world. However, even though he objected to the class analysis underlying the Marxian strategy of social revolution, his own view that reform must involve a 're-casting of the morals of property' had almost as revolutionary consequences for the present organization of society, and had to face the same practical question of how to overcome those vested interests which would oppose such a fundamental alteration in their fortunes. Although Durkheim briefly raised this difficulty, he relied entirely upon the hypothesis of a progressive evolution of human sentiments congruent with the enlarged horizons of the unfolding modern social order to account for this hoped for change. The family, he claimed, was losing its centrality as the natural locus of our affections, removing the presumption in favour of kith and kin which gave inheritance its rationale. He maintained that as we became increasingly dependent upon society, and our affections and understanding expanded to include a sympathy for the community as a whole, we came to see the value and justice of rewarding the most capable and useful citizens. The economic corporation, as the body most commanding our allegiance in contemporary conditions, would replace our relations as the natural beneficiary of our accumulated efforts, except for a few personal belongings of negligible worth.[91] His explanation relied on an evolutionary optimism akin to the British liberals', only differing from theirs in its dependence on the prior development of the social structure for the change in human character rather than the other way around. However, he went on to admit that social utility could not be decided on objective criteria alone, such judgements contained 'a subjective factor which cannot be eliminated'.[92] Indeed, he anticipated a time when people's attitudes would be so transformed that all advantages of birth, such as intelligence, would be regarded as 'unmerited', and even those who did deserve high rewards would no longer require them as necessary incentives to stimulate their efforts.[93] This image of a perfectly altruistic and egalitarian future brought to the fore an ambivalence underlying the whole of Durkheim's thesis, namely the degree to which morality derived from or constituted social relations.

This ambivalence became increasingly apparent in Durkheim's later work. In the *Division of Labour* Durkheim had been content to treat this condition of anomie or normlessness as a passing phase of a transitional period. Once the modern patterns of production were fully established the crisis would recede. The resurgence of political and economic cleavages in the 1890s provoked him to investigate the phenomena in depth in his study of *Suicide* (1897). Durkheim's interpretation of this most personal of acts as a product of the moral malaise of contemporary life was intended to vindicate his sociological method. Instead, it highlighted certain key and contentious presuppositions concerning the relations between the individual and society and the character of human nature, which ran through his theory and vitiated much of his project.

ANOMIE, EGOISM AND THE MODERN MORAL MALAISE

Durkheim echoed a common opinion in treating the rising incidence of suicide as an index of 'the general malaise currently being undergone by European societies'.[94] The liberal faith in progress had as its obverse the fear of degeneration and moral decline.[95] Suicide rates had steadily increased during the nineteenth century, and the phenomenon was widely associated with the crisis of traditional values under the impact of industrialization.[96] However, Durkheim's analysis had two distinctive features. First, he eschewed the racial and the psychological approaches dominant at the time, for a self-conscious sociological consideration of the problem. Second, whilst he shared the view of many contemporary socialists and conservatives that suicide could be related to the disorientation arising from the differentiation and fragmentation of capitalist economies, he differed from them in maintaining that this new social order contained a distinctive regulatory moral code capable of curing this 'collective malady'.[97]

Durkheim identified four categories of suicide, each of which reflected an inadequacy in the individual's relationship to society. Egoistic and altruistic suicide arose from the manner in which individuals related to social ideals and purposes. Anomie and fatalistic suicide depended on the way in which society regulated individual desires and aspirations. In the case of egoism, individuals felt isolated as a result of being inadequately integrated into society. Life seemed pointless to them, because they could not identify with the goals stemming from their social context. Altruistic suicide, in contrast, arose when people were so integrated into society that they lost all sense of individual autonomy and hence any personal reason for living. Anomic suicide resulted from the absence of any curb on the individual's passions, fatalistic suicide from their oppressive repression. Without moral discipline, we became a prey to insatiable and unrealistic desires, the inevitable disappointment and unsatisfactory nature of which drove us to despair. Yet if our passions were habitually frustrated, we felt equally despondent. Durkheim maintained that the 'excessive individuation' and conspicuous production and consumption, characteristic of modern societies, rendered egoism and anomie the main present dangers. Both resulted from 'society's insuffecient presence in individuals'.[98]

A particular view of human nature ran through Durkheim's account. The egoism–altruism and the anomie–fatalism polarities corresponded to what he regarded as the two essential human moral requirements: the one to our need for an 'object and meaning' to justify our life, the other to our need for a check on the 'sensory appetites' which were 'rooted in our organisms'.[99] Egoism and anomie testified to the absence of a sense of belonging and of discipline respectively, both of which were produced by social bonds, for, according to Durkheim, 'the intellectual

and moral life' was 'nothing but an extension of society'.[100] Some commentators have argued that egoism and anomie cannot be meaningfully distinguished.[101] This conflation arises from confusing Durkheim's
technical conception of egoism with our common understanding of the
term, which is indeed similar to what he called anomie. For Durkheim,
egoism reflected an individual's alienation from those social groups,
such as the Church, family and community, which provided our lives
with a focus. Cut off from such centres, he claimed the individual fell
into despair, becoming 'a mystery to himself, unable to escape the exasperating and agonising question: to what purpose?'[102] Egoistic suicide
was particulary common amongst disaffected intellectuals. However,
this sense of detachment 'almost inevitably' gave rise to the deregulation characteristic of anomie – the absence of social norms to control our
behaviour.[103] Durkheim reasoned that the appetites of animals were
defined by their physical make-up, so that they consumed no more than
they required for a healthy existence. Humans, in contrast, possessed
the power of reflection which enabled them to aspire 'beyond the
indispensable minimum which satisfies nature when it is governed by
instinct'. Durkheim maintained that 'nothing appears in man's organic
nor in his psychological constitution which sets limits to such tendencies
...Irrespective of any external regulatory force, our capacity for feeling is
in itself an insatiable and bottomless abyss.' This proneness to unlimited
base desires proved a potential source of human misery, for to pursue
infinity took away any sense of achievement or progress from our
activity. We were saved from 'perpetual unhappiness' either by
self-delusion or by the 'moral power' of society, for societies, like
animals, were homeostatic self-regulating organisms. Durkheim offered
no explanation for this. He simply asserted that societies by definition
throw up moral codes establishing 'a genuine regimen...which fixes
with relative precision the maximum degree of ease of living to which
each social class may aspire'.[104] Thus, anomie occurred whenever some
major upheaval in the social structure overturned the existing scale
without leaving any time for a new one to take its place. He pointed to
the correlation between an increase in suicides and the incidence of
periods of economic boom or slump as confirmation of his hypothesis.[105]

Egoism and anomie were distinct but related states, therefore: the first
fuelled the second. The differentiation of industrial societies had given
an especially strong impetus to these morally morbid tendencies, for
initially at least this process appeared to separate individuals from each
other and from the influence of society. Employers suffered from the
resulting sense of social isolation even more than workers, whose
horizon was 'limited by those above them', or the poor, since 'poverty...
is a restraint in itself.'[106] The present social crises arose from the way the
'very development of industry and the almost infinite extension of the
market' had rendered the anomic and egoistic dispositions 'so inbred
that society...is accustomed to think them normal'.[107] Employers became

locked into a never-ending pursuit of profit which worked against their co-ordinating their activities with their fellows, leading to crises of overproduction, excessive speculation, and ultimately commercial and financial collapse – with all their attendant social disruption. As a result, 'all classes are set against one another because there is no longer any established classification.'[108]

Durkheim's argument bore some resemblance to certain aspects of the socialist critique of capitalism, with which he sympathised. However, he disputed what he regarded as the socialist goal of so organising the relations of production as to fulfil all our appetites. Durkheim thought socialist criticism of the current lack of co-ordination between production and consumption, the oppressiveness of factory conditions, and the inequity of their contracts was fully justified.[109] But he believed socialists failed to realise that 'the malaise from which we suffer is…not simply a question of diminishing the share of some so as to increase that of others, but rather of remaking the moral constitution of society.' The pay-off came in his conclusion: 'this way of putting the problem is not only truer to the facts: it should have the advantage of divesting socialism of its aggressive and malevolent character with which it has often, and rightly, been reproached.'[110] Socialist doctrines were themselves a symptom rather than a cure of a diseased society.[111] Class conflict was not endemic to capitalism but 'secondary and derived' and 'in no way requir[ed] the overtoppling and entire renewal of the whole social order'.[112] The solution lay in providing 'a curb from above which checks appetites and so sets a limit on the state of disarrangement, excitement, frenzied agitation'. Posed this way, the 'social question…is not a question of money or force; it is a question of moral agents. What dominates is not the state of our economy but, much more, the state of our morality.'[113]

Durkheim shared common cause with that strand of socialism concerned to eradicate the unfair exploitation of labour by capital. His related proposals for the restructuring of property ownership, examined in the previous section, were particularly radical. In this respect, Durkheim's ideas bore a certain similarity to those of a number of other liberals on this issue: the early Spencer, J. S. Mill in his later writings and Lockean socialists such as Henry George have all adopted analogous arguments. However, he was fiercely critical of those socialists committed to the alleviation of human needs. Durkheim's theory of social justice remained essentially liberal in being based on desert. In his view, we were only entitled to a fair recompense for our contribution to the general utility of society. His structural reforms were designed solely to remove those sources of privilege which gave certain individuals an unfair advantage over others, not to provide welfare relief for those lacking marketable skills or to help people suffering from other disadvantages which might hinder their ability to make a living. He maintained that a completely just free market economy offered the only means whereby the necessary restraint of society on human excesses could make itself felt, since market mechanisms would oblige people to act in accordance with social requirements. He denied that class divisions were inherent in such a system. Because everyone would receive what they truly merited, society would cease to be split into two antagonistic camps of exploiters and exploited. Production for need, in contrast, was an incoherent notion: for 'how fix the quantity of well-being, comfort, luxury, that a human being ought to possess?' The 'most productive economic organization possible and a distribution of wealth which assures abundance to even the humblest', he wrote, would only satisfy everyone 'at the very moment it was constituted... For desires, though calmed for an instant, will quickly acquire new exigencies...for the very reason that they have nothing before them which stops them.'[114] Durkheim's remarks partly prefigure recent criticisms of Marxism's traditional hostility to theories of justice and morality.[115] At the most general level, his contention that all societies will require some rules which regulate our interactions with other people and set limits to the legitimate satisfaction of desires seems, to the present writer at least, indisputable. However, those non-Marxian socialists and Marxist 'revisionists' who seek to recruit him to the socialist camp clearly face certain interpretative obstacles. For Durkheim's view of the moral and just society was unequivocally liberal in nature.[116]

Seen from a different standpoint, Durkheim's thesis also had certain similarities with the conservative critique of capitalism. He divided their concern with the lack of moral cohesion within modern societies arising from the fragmentation of traditional communal bonds and the loss of a common faith. However, as he made clear in his Dreyfusard pamphlet 'Individualism and the Intellectuals' (1898), he believed that the nature of our attachment to society, and hence of the norms governing our relationship with others, had radically altered. The anti-Dreyfusards had accused the 'band of arrogant madmen', the 'intellectuals', to which Durkheim belonged, of undermining the moral fabric of French society through their treatment of 'our generals as idiots, our social institutions as absurd and our traditions as unhealthy...'[117] In his reply, Durkheim coolly agreed with the conservative claim that 'all societies require in order to hold together is that their members fix their eyes on the same end and come together in a single faith.' However, he observed that, being a 'social product', this creed necessarily changed in step with society. As a result, 'yesterday's religion could not be that of tomorrow.'[118] On the contrary, he contended that 'all the evidence points to the conclusion that...as a consequence of the division of labour... [o]ne is...gradually proceeding towards a state of affairs...in which the members of a single social group will no longer have anything in common other than their humanity, that is the characteristics which constitute the human person in general.'[119] In conventional terms, Durkheim equated this new 'religion of humanity' with 'the individualism of Kant and Rousseau…which the Declaration of Rights sought, more or less successfully, to translate into formula, [and] which is currently taught in our schools and has become the basis of our moral catechism'.[120] He thereby turned the tables on the anti-Dreyfusards. He now accused them of threatening society's moral basis through their attack on individual rights. Such assaults could not 'be freely allowed to occur without weakening the sentiments they violate: and as these sentiments are all we have in common, they cannot be weakened without disturbing the cohesion of society'.[121] Conservatism, in other words, had had its day with the passing of feudalism. In the current context, its revival would prove disruptive and oppressive, and provoke an understandable social reaction. Only liberalism could provide the moral regulation appropriate to a modern industrial society.

Durkheim carefully distinguished this liberal 'cult of the individual' from the 'egoistic cult of the self for which utilitarian individualism has justly been reproached'. Although both stemmed from modern conditions, only the former was capable of restoring contemporary societies to a healthy moral equilibrium. For whilst it united individuals through 'sympathy for all that is human', the latter divided them by their pursuit of self-interest.[122] Durkheim was nevertheless very imprecise as to what the 'cult of the individual' required from its devotees. In Kantian manner, it seemed to consist of a set of formal rules about how moral arguments should be conducted and a set of assumptions about what a moral community presupposed: namely, autonomous agents, living by universalizable moral rules and treating each other as ends rather than as means. Even his view of social justice, summed up in the precept 'to each according to his works', included no criteria as to how we were to measure the worth of each person's efforts. Durkheim talked of the need 'to alleviate the functioning of the social machine, still so harsh to individuals, in order to put at their disposal all possible means for developing their faculties unhindered', yet condemned the 'negative ideal' of political liberty as 'dangerous'.[123] This caveat suggested that he believed a collective commitment to self-development differed from simply maximizing individual freedom, although he never described exactly how. The somewhat procedural picture of human rights upon which he relied posed two main additional problems. First, the Kantian doctrine that we should never use another (or ourselves) as a means for furthering a project of our own or of someone else, potentially treats all service relationships as immoral, rather than regulating them as Durkheim and the Solidarists supposed. Kant thought that to 'give away or sell a tooth' or even hair, or 'to submit oneself to castration in order to gain an easier livelihood as a singer' involved abusing oneself to serve others.[124] Any work which was not done for its intrinsic worth, for example doing a labouring job to get money to pay for the rest of one's activities as opposed to doing it for the joy of physical exertion, could plausibly infringe Kant's injunction. Durkheim and Bourgeois never saw this paradox, because they never acknowledged that clashes within capitalist relations between different types of self-development was anything but an abnormal phenomenon. Yet even individuals are forced into making hard choices between incompatible and equally worthy options, such as when deciding upon a career. Durkheim did at least recognize the second, and related, problem: the 'great objection', as he called it, that 'if all opinions are free, by what miracle will they then be harmonious.' His solution laid bare the somewhat shakey foundations on which his claims for sociology relied. He retorted that freedom of thought 'does not sanction an unlimited right to incompetence'. When one had to decide upon a question in an area where one lacked 'expert knowledge', it was perfectly rational to defer to the authority of those who did. Durkheim, of course, maintained that sociology offered just such professional guidance in matters of social morality. However, it is one thing to show that a given means provides the best method for attaining a certain end, and quite another to seek to adjudicate 'scientifically' between ends. In fact, Durkheim conspicuously failed to do this. At most he established the existence of certain rights. Wisely, he shrank from specifying to what purposes they should be exercised. Many of his arguments, though, suggested that he believed he could, and implied a teleological view of human nature which regarded certain ends as contributing more to our 'individuality' than others.

Durkheim believed his sociology had removed all legitimacy from the ideologies of socialists, conservatives, and *laissez-faire* capitalists alike. However, he only achieved this result because the categories essential to his social theory were premised upon what they purported to prove, namely the justice of the Republican order. As the contemporary critic Gabriel Tarde remarked,[125] Durkheim's argument for a transformation of the nature of social solidarity presupposed that some form of social cohesion based on a moral authority had to persist. Yet he had offered no reason why this should be so. He had declared that because individualism was widespread it necessarily attested to a social fact capable of forming a common bond. However, this inference rested upon an a priori argument about the pathology of normless egoism, the complementary character of different individual tastes and abilities, and the regulative capacities of the social system. He had not shown that anomie and egoism were not normal within capitalist relations, merely defined such behaviour as always abnormal. Both Marxists and libertarians deny this, arguing, albeit with different emphases, that the system relies upon and encourages these attitudes.[126]

If Durkheim's condemnation of conspicuous consumption and the acquisitive society had its progressive side, it also contained a repressive aspect that blocked radical forms of social criticism by blinding him to some of the mechanisms inherent to the working of the society he was describing. He could not talk about the stultifying effects of a given social order upon human potential, because the individual's submission to society was 'the condition of his liberation'. Freedom, according to Durkheim, 'consists in the deliverance from blind, unthinking physical forces' which we achieved 'by opposing against them the great and intelligent force which is society'.[127] As I argued in the previous chapter, self-mastery undeniably forms part of our liberty. But it does not follow that there are no competing ends which we can rationally pursue, or that we are each suited for a particular station in life which renders us truly free. In supposing that this was the case, Durkheim could make a virtue of those very features of the division of labour that radical, particularly Marxist, critics find oppressive. According to the French theorist, our restriction to roles and forms of behaviour which are not the result of our own choice only prove alienating to the anomic individual who desires too much, for these 'limited horizons' and 'definite and specific tasks' were essential to the health of both the individual and society.[128] The desire for the many-sided development of the individual constituted a pernicious socialist utopia, which aroused unfulfillable expectations and therefore unnecessary misery and opposition to the natural order.

As Anthony Giddens has stressed, Durkheim's analysis of moral norms escaped degenerating into an authoritarian justification of the status quo because it was underpinned by an acceptance of their historical specificity.[129] Sociologists not only brought their fellow citizens' attention to the values necessary to hold the community together, they also made them aware of 'new tendencies' related to recent changes in their collective existence which subverted traditional opinions.[130] Both stances could put the social scientist at odds with the dominant views of his or her age, as the Dreyfus affair had demonstrated. Moreover, Durkheim insisted that morality in the the modern world had to command our rational respect and could not be imposed by a dominant group without arousing widespread dissent. However, the very nature of Durkheim's project prevented him from developing to the full what critical import his theory possessed. Durkheim regarded the 'state of society' as providing 'an objective standard to which our evaluations must always be brought back'. 'If', he wrote, 'we find an objective criterion inherent in the facts themselves to allow us to distinguish scientifically health from sickness in the various modes of social phenomena, science' will be in a position to throw light on practical matters while remaining true to its own method.' The statesman would become a doctor rather than a visionary, forestalling 'the outbreak of sickness by maintaining good hygiene' and re-establishing 'normality' should it occur.[131] No aspect of Durkheim's work has come under more attack than his distinction between the 'normal' and the 'pathological'. The identification of a single moral norm as essential to social stability was in itself a dubious exercise. Empirical evidence may well show that the reasons for someone holding a particular belief are unfounded, that it has unforeseen consequences or is based on misleading or incorrect information about what it seeks to explain. But it is of the nature of moral convictions that they reflect different preferences which affect our evaluation of the costs entailed by pursuing them. Empirical knowledge alone will not be able, therefore, to adjudicate between the rationality or desirability of pursuing a wide variety of moral ends, all of which are grounded on correct information about what is required to attain them. Durkheim could only avoid the problem of moral relativism by virtue of his insistence that all our concepts could be related to the 'objective' reality of society without reference to the subjective meanings of individual actors. Even so, he was forced into ethical naturalism in order to maintain that the norms functionally necessary to society were *ipso facto* those we ought to pursue.

A further difficulty arises from Durkheim's identification of society with morality, namely that it becomes hard to say what distinguishes the two. This feature was compounded by the way Durkheim's analysis of contemporary society more often than not turned into a description of its as yet to be realized 'normal' state. What he took as vital to its 'healthy' operation rested on a view of how it ought to be organised rather than an account of how it was actually arranged. Although this tension existed in all his major writings, a decided alteration occurred during his career from inferring morality from the 'morphological' features of the social structure to constructing a society in tune with the dictates of his moral ideals. Indeed, he came to conceptualise society largely in terms of a particular social consciousness or 'collective representation', going so far as to state that 'it is thought which creates reality, and the pre-eminent role of collective representations is to "make" that superior reality which is *society* itself.'[132]

His study of suicide had revealed that 'our very egoism is in large part a product of society', and could not be attributed solely to passional drives 'rooted in our organisms'.[133] Modern societies evinced conflicting moral ideals, 'the utilitarian egoism of Spencer and of the economists' and 'rationalist individualism'. In order to make his case for the latter, Durkheim had to insist that it was the more 'natural' form of human development. This move in his argument resulted in him adopting a theory of human agency and its relation to social change akin to that of T. H. Green. Like the British idealist, he identified self-realisation with self-determination, and both with self-abnegation. Autonomous action entailed sublimating one's base instincts and willing a superior good stemming from a 'higher source' present within each person's consciousness.[134] Adopting a similar neo-Kantian position to Green's, he considered the fundamental categories of the human mind (space, time, causality, etc.) to be not simply presuppositions of knowledge, but actually grounded in reality.[135] However, whilst Green attributed this circumstance to the omnipresence of the divine consciousness, Durkheim linked it to society. As he saw it, 'one must choose between

God and society…I myself am quite indifferent to this choice, since I see in the Divinity only society transfigured and symbolically expressed'[136] – a view, in practice, little different from Green's. To a large extent, his later writings treat the social world as a product of the collective morality of its members. Durkheim even came to share Green's belief that social relations were transformed through an evolving consciousness amongst humankind of the common nature of the good involved in each citizen's self-fulfilment. For when 'the moral value of the individual…looms large in the public estimation, we apply this social judgement to others as well as to ourselves; their persons, as well as our own, assume more value in our eyes, and we become more sensitive to whatever concerns each of them individually as well as to what concerns us particularly.'[137] This enlarged sympathy with our fellow human beings underlay and justified Durkheim's advocacy of state intervention in economic life in order to make it more just, and enabled him to believe that workers might conceive themselves to be contributing to the common good. Even so, Durkheim realised political changes would be necessary to work such a momentous alteration in people's perceptions. In the main, British liberals had taken the emergence of this common morality for granted. Durkheim, in contrast, devoted considerable attention to devising an institutional framework capable of facilitating the social integration and discipline necessary for it to come into being. If the bonds of family, Church and community had been eroded, then new social ties would have to be created. This was the task of the political system.

POLITICS, POWER AND COMMUNICATION

Nothing reveals better the ambiguities, strengths and weaknesses of Durkheim's sociology than his theory of politics. For it was constrained by his conception of social science so as to exclude many of the most important components of political life. Durkheim's sociology focused consistently on the relationship of the individual to society and the bonds attaching us to society. The exercise of power by some individuals over others, and the conflicts of interests, values, ideologies and self-definitions between different social groups, were largely relegated to the category of pathological phenomena. The object of Durkheim's political thought was not the recent liberal concern with the problem of obligation in a polity founded on the subjective consent of a citizenry committed to a plurality of values.[138] He was preoccupied with making the members of society aware of the communal values he posited as naturally uniting them. Since these norms belonged to the system itself, the chief task of politics was not conflict resolution *per se* but communication.

Durkheim's political theory reflected the increased importance given to moral regulation we have observed within his general sociology. In the *Division of Labour*, he had assumed that although the functions of the state increased with the progress of society, it lost its coercive character. Instead of repressing the individual by forcing its citizens into a uniform pattern of behaviour, the modern state mediated between the different sections of society, and upheld the individual's rights and integrity against the incursions of others. During the late 1890s, Durkheim qualified this view in a number of respects. Now he believed 'that the degree to which a government possesses an absolutist character is not linked to any particular social type', its coercive power depended upon 'the degree to which all counterweights organized with a view to restraining it are missing'.[139] Unlike Spencer, he did not equate the growth of state absolutism with the range of activities in which it was engaged. In primitive communities these were relatively few but their governments were invariably despotic. Durkheim still maintained that in undifferentiated societies law was likely to be more repressive, for such societies required greater uniformity from their members. Crimes were treated as blasphemous acts that infringed the religious code binding the collectivity together. Potentially, the division of labour altered this situation. Greater respect for the individual meant that punishment was less cruel and placed more emphasis on the responsibility of the offender, rather than seeking reparation from the whole group. However, if the state continued to constitute the sole authority, it became distanced from its subjects and retained its 'religious' aura. 'Offences directed against a being so palpably superior to all its offenders will not be considered as ordinary crimes, but as sacriligious acts and, by virtue of this, will be violently repressed.'[140]

Durkheim's heightened awareness of the relative autonomy of the political structure from the stage of development of a given society, formed part of a broader rethinking of the relationship between the state and civil society. He had originally regarded the division of labour to be essentially self-regulating, with the state taking on a co-ordinating role. However, he soon expressed doubts about the capacity of both these agencies to fulfil the purpose he had assigned to them. The expansion of markets and increased specialization had dissolved the older social forms of organization, such as the family, the neighbourhood or organized religion, without putting anything in their place. The spontaneous harmony which he had expected to arise from the contractual system had not occurred. Instead, the lack of a suitable moralizing environment had produced the anomic anarchy he had diagnosed in his study of *Suicide*. The state alone 'survived the tempest'. Confronted by 'an unstable flux of individuals', it was forced to assume functions for which it was unsuited. It was 'too remote from individuals, its connections with them too superficial and irregular, to be able to penetrate the depths of their consciousness and socialise them from within'. Unable to adapt to the 'infinite variety of special circumstances', the state's cumbersome attempts at controlling the economy were necessarily 'compressive and levelling'. Without the moderating influence of intermediary bodies, the modern state seemed condemned to oscillate 'from authoritarian regulation made impotent by its excessive rigidity, to systematic abstention which cannot last because it breeds anarchy'.[141] Without the prior organization of society, therefore, the state was bound to gravitate towards absolutism in a feeble effort to contain it. He condemned this state of affairs, in a revealing remark, as a 'sociological monstrosity': presumably it was most monstrous in offending the canons of his ideal of a well-ordered society.[142]

New forms of political organization were needed to resolve this crisis. The changed conditions and requirements of modern societies, brought about by the division of labour, called for new mechanisms of social involvement and restraint. Only then could the political system effectively curb anomic and egoistic behaviour without adopting despotic methods. Durkheim advocated reviving the old guilds or corporations for this purpose, and making them 'the elementary division of the state, the basic political unit'.[143] He claimed people no longer felt particularly strong attachments to a given geographically located community, such as the commune or *département*. Increasingly, individuals identified with their peers at work, and thought of themselves as professors, manufacturers or engineers rather than as Parisians or Alsatians.[144] Occupational groups, in consequence, offered a natural focus for the formation of a common moral schema suited to the regulation of the activities of their members. Through them the different professions could fix upon a code of practice appropriate to their distinctive needs. The corporation might even provide the principal centre of social life, bonding its participants together through forms of entertainment and mutual aid, as well as many educational activities.[145] As work dominated the greater part of our lives, the functional community could fill the lacuna left by the family, the nation and organized religion as the source of our values and sense of personal identity. Durkheim distinguished these proposed new bodies from trade unions, which he regarded as 'private associations' that sought to promote egoistic interests. The corporation was supposed to include both employees and employers within a given trade or industry. Unions were generally more restricted in scope, representing only a part of the workforce within a given sector, and had a correspondingly narrower view of their purpose. In general, they aimed to attain the best wages and conditions possible for their membership, regardless of the cost to other relevant parties. Durkheim not only opposed the revolutionary class-based syndicalism prominent at the time, he found the middle-class unions forming within the civil service to be an equally 'retrograde move', disorganizing social life by creating powerful coalitions of 'special interests'.[146] The corporation should be a public body, providing an important link between each occupational group and the state.

A 'vast system of national corporations' offered a practical solution to the anomic sickness afflicting the social organism. According to Durkheim's thesis, economic crises occurred because of a shortfall or surplus of a given commodity due to a lack of co-ordination between the different sectors of the economy. This industrial anarchy resulted from producers seeking excessive profits, itself a sign of the absence of any set limits to the contemporary citizen's desires.[147] The corporative network would put an end to this situation by drawing individuals out of their 'moral isolation'. It would furnish a near total regulation of economic life, intervening 'whenever excited passions tended to exceed all limits'. He envisaged the drawing up of a set of rules for each profession and industry, 'fixing the amount of labour required, the just reward for the various people engaged in it, and their duties towards the community and towards one another etc....'[148] By giving employers and employees a 'sense of their reciprocal duties and the general interest', so that their passions did not degenerate into a 'morbid fever', a new sort of 'moral discipline' would be established. The present Hobbesian competition would be replaced by novel and complex forms of co-operation which exploited the division of labour to the full. Durkheim imagined even the 'most inferior aptitudes' would find a useful place in society, whilst the 'more intense production' would raise everyone's living standards and eliminate poverty.[149]

The corporations served a dual purpose within Durkheim's scheme. First, they exerted a far more flexible and closer moral surveillance of the affairs of each occupation than a single central authority ever could. They decided upon all questions of hours of work, health and safety, wages, social assurance and assistance, and settled all disputes, etc., for their respective groups.[150] Second, they provided the missing countervailing force needed to restrain the state from dominating the individual. However, they did not replace the state. Unlike Marx or certain British liberals such as Mill and Spencer, Durkheim did not anticipate the absorption of the state by a society which administered itself. All small-scale organizations tended to manifest the repressive attributes associated with the 'mechanical solidarity' of earlier segmental societies, and the corporations were no exception. Like the medieval guilds, they ran the risk of degenerating into oppressive institutions, which hindered individual initiative and innovation with their monopolistic and restrictive practices. These deleterious dispositions had to be countered in their turn by the state, for 'it alone can oppose the sentiment of general utility and the need for organic equilibrium to the particularism of each corporation.'[151]

Durkheim's corporatist system culminated in a reconceptualization of the nature of democracy. He disputed the traditional classification of forms of government according to the number of persons actually ruling (that is, one, a few, or many, corresponding to monarchy, aristocracy and democracy respectively). Government, by definition, must be exercised by a minority. It owed its character to the degree of communication existing between the state and the mass of citizens, and the 'extent' and 'range' of its 'consciousness' of their activities.[152] By this somewhat obscure definition, Durkheim appeared to mean that democracy involved responsive and open government, free from the *arcana imperii* and 'invisible powers' found in primitive societies or under absolutist regimes, where authority was upheld by taboo.[153] A democracy's laws were clear and specific, extending over all the doings of society, and applying equally to all. Whilst he no longer believed that the division of labour was a sufficient condition for the appearance of democratic government, it remained a necessary one, for democracy implied the enhanced status of the individual and the diversity of opinions found in modern societies. In spite of the enlarged regulative role of the democratic state, there was no mystique about the framing or operation of its legislation. By being in closer contact with the people, it could respond to their needs rather better and with more flexibility than a despotic government which shut itself off from its citizens, and because it obtained their rational assent to its injunctions a democracy was much more stable than other forms of government as well. Only democracies, therefore, could exercise the degree of control essential to the healthy running of the industrial economy.

Although democracy owed its 'moral superiority' to the way 'it allows the citizen to accept the laws of the country with more intelligence and thus less passively',[154] Durkheim did not regard democratic procedures as a means of self-government. He dissented strongly from such 'Rousseauean' notions.[155] Autonomy, as he defined it, involved self-control rather than self-determination:

> The autonomy an individual can enjoy does not consist in rebelling against nature; such a revolt is absurd, sterile, whether directed against the forces of the material world or those of the social world. To be autonomous means, for man, to understand the necessities to which he has to bow and to accept them in full knowledge of their cause. We cannot make the laws of things other than they are; but we can free ourselves from them in thinking them; that is to say by making them ours via thought.[156]

The moral basis of society was not to be decided upon by the citizens themselves, it already existed as an 'objective' fact embodied within their social relations. He thought the idea, common to proponents of direct or participatory democracy, that governments should merely 'translate as faithfully as possible,... the sentiments of the collectivity' was fundamentally flawed. In any complex society, this type of regime would quickly degenerate into anarchy as the social malaise infected the political sphere. The role of the state, he countered, was 'not to express, to sum up, the unreflective thought of the crowd, but to superimpose on this unreflective thought a more considered thought, which, in consequence, cannot be other than different.'[157] Even the democratic state had to retain its dominant role *vis-à-vis* civil society, drawing the attention of its subjects to the public interest. If it noted the information and demands emanating from the various subgroups when formulating its policies, its point of view remained qualitatively different from theirs. Thus, democratic mechanisms were not required to legitimate the state's decisions, but to inform them. They gained their authority from being 'correct', in Durkheim's terms appropriate to the 'normal' functioning of the social system, rather than because they had been formally assented to.

The central issue of politics, therefore, was to design an institutional framework capable of ensuring the responsiveness of the state to the requirements of society, without submerging it beneath the subjective and particularistic wills of its citizens. Durkheim held the common opinion that it was the excessive subordination of deputies to the interests of the electorate which accounted for the current parlous condition of the Third Republic. Parliament was paralysed by the influence of particularist sentiments from passing effective national legislation, with the result that an unrepresentative bureaucracy took effective charge of the country. Lacking any real contact with the electorate, its attempts at control had been as inept as they were intrusive. Thus, the Republican regime had vacillated between periods of social unrest and administrative repression.[158] No better illustration could be given of the relationship between Durkheim's social theory and his perception of the problems facing contemporary France.

Durkheim advocated the creation of intermediary bodies based on his proposed occupational groups to remedy the defective operation of French parliamentary democracy. They would prevent society from engulfing the state and vice versa. He envisaged a two-tier electoral system, with individuals voting directly for their representatives within each corporation, who in turn sent delegates from amongst their number to a national assembly. Two benefits accrued from this scheme. First, by replacing the locality with the professional associations as the main secondary organ, government assemblies would better reflect the underlying structure of society. Second, the sheer size and complexity of economically developed nations removed the face-to-face relations and shared goals necessary for a general will to emerge, and led everyone to act egoistically. The two-tier system restored the sense of community essential to consensual collective decision-making. Since everyone could competently decide upon the needs of their profession, the general regulations covering their particular guild were best framed directly by them or their representatives. However, not everyone possessed the same competence in national matters. Indirect election to the central assembly rectified this situation. Instead of being bound by a mandate to vote according to the narrow interests of their constituents, delegates would be allowed to deliberate freely on inter-professional relations and to consider only the common interests uniting them. Because they operated at a higher degree of abstraction than the rest of the population, who remained tied to their everyday and largely personal concerns, Durkheim held the general will would prevail over the will of all:

> The councils of government would then be genuinely what the brain is to the human organism – a reflexion of the social body. All the living forces, all the vital organs would be represented there according to their relative importance. And in the group thus formed, society would truly become conscious of itself and of its unity; this unity would result naturally from the relations which would establish themselves between the representatives of the different professions so placed in such close contact.[159]

Durkheim's state acted as the organising mental centre of the secondary groups, which brought their goals together into a higher synthesis reflecting the aims of the collectivity. Consisting of both 'government' and 'parliament', its function was 'deliberative' rather than 'executive', as was commonly supposed, since the execution of legislation belonged to the bureaucracy. The state legislated at a more general level than the occupational associations, formulating the norms and ethos of the whole of society. Durkheim identified these values with the rights and duties encapsulated in the 'cult of the individual'. As we have seen, Durkheim regarded a particular type of meritocratic individualism to be essential to the maintenance of 'normal' social relations in advanced economies. However, he now argued that it was the state, rather than societal evolution *per se*, which brought this about by:

> planning the social environment so that the individual may realise himself more fully, controlling the social machine so that it will bear less heavily on individuals, guaranteeing the peaceful exchange of services and the co-operation of all men of good will aiming at an ideal which they pursue peacefully and in common...[160]

Once more the terms of Durkheim's argument resemble those of T. H. Green, particularly the belief that self-development could become a non-competitive ideal only capable of being achieved co-operatively. His conception seems similarly flawed as a characterisation of factory production, even if it has some plausibility for certain activities such as football. Like Green, Durkheim identified the cultivation of individuality with an attitude of mind rather than material well-being. The moral regulation of society did not involve 'simply ensuring everyone had access to enough food and drink, but that each is treated as he deserves, that he is freed of all unjust and humiliating dependence, that he is joined to his fellows and to the group without abandoning his personality to them'. Durkheim appeared to go beyond the British new liberals in recognizing that securing these conditions involved freeing the individual from the coercive power of others. In particular, he argued that both the state and the secondary bodies must check the other from exerting too repressive an influence. A confusion entered Durkheim's account at this point. On the one hand, he stated that 'it is from this conflict of social forces that individual liberties are born.'[161] On the other, he talked of the state liberating the individual from the oppressive parochialism and domination of lesser local, professional or domestic associations, by opposing a more universal morality, that of the 'cult of the individual', to their more particularist ethos.[162] The latter explanation, which predominated, treated the ideals upheld by the state as superior, reflecting the rights and duties of all individuals rather than simply those of the member of a given profession. The former, in contrast, acknowledged that the very generality of the state's law could make the state in turn 'a leveller and oppressive'. Indeed, its 'oppression was even more unbearable than that of smaller groups. The state, in our large-scale societies, is so distant from particular interests...that when it attempts to regulate them, it can do so only by denaturing and doing violence to them.' To be 'the liberator of the individual, it has itself need of counterweights; it must be contained by other collective forces,...the secondary groups.'[163] Durkheim failed to incorporate these insights fully into his theory, for the dominant tendencies of his thought went against any recognition of conflict or a genuine value pluralism as 'normal' phenomena. He offered no explanation of how the two institutions would balance each other out.

Recent pluralist conceptions of politics, which stress the 'polyarchal' nature of modern society, have seen the competitive party system as the best means for translating this diversity into policy. When different parties vie for the people's vote, they are forced to construct coalitions between various interest groups in order to gain a majority. However, Durkheim rejected any suggestion of popular participation in the formation of government policy. Electoral politics received no extensive treatment, for he regarded the difference between a system in which 'the governing minority [is] established once and for all', and one in which 'the minority that carries the day may be beaten tomorrow and replaced by another' as 'only slight'. The legitimacy of the state and respect for its laws derived from its clearly expressing 'the natural inter-relation of things'. According to Durkheim:

> It is not because we have made a certain law or because it has been willed by so many votes, that we may submit to it; it is because it is a good one – that is, appropriate to the nature of the facts, because it is all it ought to be and because we have confidence in it.

Democracy ensured that the state and civil society were in sufficient communication with each other for such good laws to be passed. Voting of any kind was destined to disappear, when in 'some vague future and in societies better organized than our own,...the appointments necessary to control political organs may come about, as it were, automatically, by the pressure of public opinion, and without, properly speaking, any definite reference to the electorate.'[164]

Although Durkheim praised diversity, he believed that it must eventually be reintegrated into a more fundamental unity. Arguably, Durkheim was led to this conclusion by concentrating almost exclusively on the division of labour and the differentiation of economic functions, since the exchange economy could be said to reunite them into some sort of higher social harmony. He may have accepted that in certain circumstances these relationships were unjust or discordant, and would not rectify themselves spontaneously, but he remained convinced that agreement on a shared moral code would correct these 'abnormalities'. Political institutions were supposed to make us aware of the bonds 'naturally' tying us to our fellows. He acknowledged only fleetingly the difficulty of overcoming class divisions and existing inequalities of social and economic power. The corporations had to contain both employers and employees to perform their moralising function, for example, yet even Durkheim wondered 'whether a distinction would not have to be made at the base of the structure…when their respective interests were manifestly in conflict'.[165] The topic, so tantalizingly raised, characteristically sank once more without trace. Far more intractable, though, were the sources of social tension Durkheim never considered, those between people holding different scales of values, or even the hard decisions we all face when two equally important aspects of our own ethical code seem incompatible. Genuine moral dilemmas give rise to many of the most important contemporary political struggles, such as whether to prioritize the protection of the environment or economic growth, the rights of unborn children or those of the mother, and the sectarian strife between religious or ethnic groups. Durkheim's naturally consensual society avoided such disputes, for it was premised on their absence. Instead, everyone would agree on the values inherent to the 'cult of the individual'. Yet this ethos was inadequate to its task. Where deep differences exist, it may be true that the only common code likely to be preserved would consist of a recognition of the equality and right to mutual respect of persons, as Durkheim, like certain recent liberal theorists,[166] claimed. However, this 'thin' conception of the good will not eliminate conflicts between 'thicker' notions, at most it entails that they are resolved in as fair a manner as possible, without the use of physical force. The necessity for compromises and trade-offs between the various parties still remains. Durkheim's institutional model provided no mechanisms for resolving such differences. Its narrow occupational focus underestimated our continued membership of other groups, reflecting our sex, race, religion, age group, background, where we live, etc., so that many of these problems never even arrived on the agenda. More important, he assumed that a smooth-running economy would provide a suitable niche for the talents of each and every person. However, not only is it highly contentious that all of our abilities complement those of everyone else, it is also highly doubtful that they find complete fulfilment in any one job. Durkheim never tackled the constraining aspect of the division of labour, the enervating effects of boring tasks, the constrictions of working to an imposed routine. Within a true meritocracy, he believed all candidates would get the position they deserved, and that dissatisfaction could only result from unrealistic aspirations. His theory of human nature made such limitations necessary to our mental equilibrium. In spite of his criticisms of political economists, maximal self-development for all became subtly equated with the maximum efficiency of the industrial economy. Leaving aside the question of whether the means to achieve this could easily be agreed upon, the real weakness of Durkheim's theory rested on his supposition that the goal itself was an 'objective' and uncontentious matter.

The central premises of Durkheim's sociology led him grossly to underestimate the opportunities for coercion and conflict within modern social and political life. His theoretical emphasis on the link between morality and social structure also resulted in him neglecting the effective gap existing between the two, mistaking the normative for the normal. In making the state the organ of 'moral discipline', he appreciated the danger of it abusing this position. However, he never examined why this might happen. The state remained a largely impersonal entity within his discussion, he did not identify it with the interests of a dominant class who might seek to abuse it for their ends. He saw the state as expressing the implicit moral code of its surrounding society, without exploring the possibility that it could be upholding no more than the ideology of the ruling elite. Yet as his theory moved from the descriptive to the prescriptive, this hazard became ever more real, with the state socialising its citizens into an acceptance of a social structure yet to come into existence. Like the Solidarists, Durkheim argued that moral reform, the internal transformation of the citizen, must precede political change, and he joined them in their work in the *Société pour l'éducation sociale*. In 1912 he finally made it to Paris becoming *chargé d'un cours* in the Science of Education at the Sorbonne. He replaced Férdinand Buisson, the former Director of Primary Education at the Ministry of Public Instruction who between 1879 and 1896 was responsible for the implementation of the Ferry Laws. In addition, from 1904 to 1913 he lectured on the functions of the teacher to the elite of the French educational system at the Ecole Normale Supérieure. It was a fitting apogee to his career, for Durkheim had become the apostle of the civic religion of Republican France, whose secular 'priests' were the school teachers.[167]

The First World War definitively undermined the evolutionary optimism on which so much of Durkheim's theory rested. He had endorsed Spencer's view that militarism belonged to a non-industrial type of society, although he accounted for its disappearance somewhat differently as the result of the merging of the national into the human ideal:

If every state had as its essential task, not to expand or to extend its borders, but to...call the largest number of its members to an ever higher moral life, then every contradiction would disappear between national morality and human morality. If the state had no other aim than to make its citizens men, in the full meaning of the word, then civic duties would be but a particular form of the general obligations of humanity. Now, we have seen that evolution takes this direction.[168]

A second apparent 'antinomy' was thereby resolved. The growth in the power and internal organisation of nation states promoted rather than disturbed international peace, as 'patriotism tended to become a small part of cosmopolitanism'. States would no longer compete in order to become the 'largest' or the 'wealthiest', but to show which was 'the most just, the best organized, to have the best moral constitution'. The very universality of the 'cult of the individual' made it a world religion capable of forming the basis of a cosmopolitan order.

In a pamphlet written during the war, Durkheim attempted to salvage his thesis by characterising Germany's development as 'abnormal'. He attributed this to the 'German mentality', 'a system of ideas...made for war' resulting from a 'morbid hypertrophy of the will, a kind of will mania'. The German state, in sum, suffered from anomie on a national scale. However, he believed this sickness could not last:

There is no state so great that it can govern itself externally against the wishes of its subjects and force them by purely external coercion, to submit to its will. There is no state so great that it is not merged within the vaster system of other states, that does not, in other words, form part of the greater human community, that owes nothing to this. There is a universal conscience and a universal opinion, and it is no more possible to escape the empire of these than to escape the empire of physical laws, for they are forces which, when violated, react against those who offend against them. A state cannot survive that has humanity arrayed against it.[169]

Such attitudes exonerate Durkheim from the charge of having justified a blind nationalism,[170] or of having espoused a sort of moral relativism which treated all ethical codes as equally valid. He clearly imagined the appearance of a morality of universal application to all advanced societies, by which the conduct of all nations could be measured and criticised. Durkheim's faith in the inevitable triumph of these humanitarian sentiments proved unfounded. Instead, modern states have had far greater means for oppressing their citizens and destroying their neighbours than ever before, and have not shrunk from using them. Overwork, and profound sadness at the loss of his only son in the war, saved Durkheim from having to explain away the totalitarian regimes of the twentieth century. He died at the early age of fifty-nine on 15 November 1917.

In common with the Solidarists, albeit with certain differences of detail, Durkheim saw society as tending towards a liberal utopia: a socially just meritocracy. His complacency in this regard no doubt owed a great deal to the staggered and relatively smooth course in France of the economic and social transformations associated with the process of industrialisation and the establishment of bourgeois hegemony. If the early crisis points were far more traumatic than in Britain, the most severe threats to the liberal order had been overcome by 1870 and they remained thereafter within tolerable limits. Italy and Germany offered a considerable contrast. The pace of change was far swifter and produced correspondingly greater social unrest. The liberal classes were conspicuously smaller and found it harder to identify their ascendency with the progress of society at large. The state seemed not only distinct from society, it dominated it. The problems of legitimising and controlling the exercise of power took centre stage as liberals were forced to create the new social order from above.

3

Italy: Liberalism Transformed

Italian liberalism contrasted sharply with that of Britain and France. The Italian liberal elite were progressive landlords rather than an entrepreneurial bourgeoisie, who sought to modernize the rural economy without disturbing traditional hierarchical social relations. As a result, in Italy liberal ideas and institutions were compromised in decisive ways by the constraints of a predominantly agrarian society.[1] In spite of rapid industrial growth at the turn of the century, the new class of industrialists remained secondary, both economically and politically, to the landowners. Rather than challenging the morality and privileges of the pre-industrial elites, the Italian bourgeoisie adapted them to their own interests and continued to uphold the old order.[2] Moreover, the very backwardness of Italian society made it harder than in Britain and France to regard the creation of a liberal economic order as the unharnessing of natural social forces. More obviously than in any other of the major European nations, the new relations of production had to be artificially imposed by an increasingly intrusive state. Not surprisingly, both the theory and practice of Italian liberalism involved a number of inconsistencies and internal contradictions. The tensions between liberal ideals and social realities, ethical and economic liberalism, present to some degree in all the liberal regimes, were all too clear in Italy. Yet, in many respects, the very failings of liberal politics produced a more robust and revealing theorisation of liberalism in Italy than in either Britain or France.

TRASFORMISMO: THE DIALECTIC OF FORCE AND CONSENT FROM CAVOUR TO GIOLITTI

The thinkers of the Risorgimento had seen the resurgence of Italy as part of a European movement towards liberty and self-government. Both the

Giobertian Catholic-liberal school and the radical democrats inspired by Mazzini had professed essentially eschatological ideologies, in which the unification of Italy was seen as the realization of a national destiny. Both movements placed great emphasis on the role of the people as carriers of this national consciousness – they constituted the 'real' nation in contrast to the merely 'legal' foreign-backed governments then ruling the various provinces of the country. The failure of the revolutions of 1848 dashed their hopes of building a new nation via a spontaneous uprising of the people. United by Piedmontese annexation rather than the popular will, the nature of Italy's liberal institutions largely derived from Piedmont and took on a decidedly statist character as a result.

The liberalism of the northern aristocratic landowners grouped around the Piedmontese statesman Count Camillo di Cavour originated from the desire to abolish economic restrictions hindering the development of a competitive commercial agriculture. This programme involved securing property rights in land by ending feudal tenure and the customary use-rights of peasants and tenants, selling off Church and communal lands, creating a free market in land by curtailing entails, trusts and primogeniture, and the removal of administrative and protectionist barriers to free trade in agricultural goods. Admirers of the British system of *laissez-faire*, their proposals hinged on a belief in the complementary interests of Italian exporters of primary goods and the industry of the more developed nations.[3] They hoped that a liberal community might be created simply by unleashing the dynamic forces of society by removing obstacles to economic initiative, such as internal trade barriers. Although their liberalism was of a more pragmatic kind, they shared the faith in human progress and the confidence in individual enterprise of the British liberals, such as Gladstone, Cobden, Mill and Spencer, whose views inspired them. In practice, however, it became necessary to impose the requisite changes from above through state action. It did not take long for them to become as uncomfortably conscious as their more idealistic contemporaries that the liberal ideal had precious few roots in popular feeling.

The Cavourian liberals' economic programme had important political implications.[4] It involved taking on the reactionary forces of the Church and *rentier* landlords gathered around the monarchy, the creation of a more rational bureaucracy, extensive revision of the legal system, and state financial help in getting investment for roads, canals, railways, irrigation, etc. The eventual success owed as much to the weakness of the Piedmontese monarchy as it did to the astuteness and commitment of Cavour. The carrot of dynastic expansion combined with fears of revolution to win the crown to the cause of modernisation, for only a sound economy could finance a strong army and provide the prosperity necessary to stave off social unrest. The threat of a democratic alternative offered by the Mazzinians and other groups during the upheavals of 1848–9 further encouraged dynastic ambitions and the policies of the liberal elites to converge. The winning of constitutional concessions from the King in 1848, for example, derived as much from Cavour's desire to pre-empt a broader social revolution as from his devotion to the liberal ideal. By carrying through a political reform offering civil guarantees and political representation to the wealthy, he hoped to link the interests of the monarchy and elites and 'bring together the elements of order, force and stability'.[5]

The numerical weakness of the progressive elites, caught as they were between reactionary and radical opponents, added to their aristocratic turn of mind, led them to favour liberal reform being carried through from above. Establishing a model of government that was to endure into the new Italian state, Cavour increased his support in Parliament through the creation of a cross-bench majority known as the *connubio*. The power of the executive was promoted further by gaining ministerial control of the bureaucracy, providing them with a more effective instrument of change than the legislature and a useful source of patronage for their supporters. Even so, the reform programme would have been halted by the resistance of the Church were it not for the emergency powers granted to the government after the declaration of war on Austria in 1859. Most of the principal innovations, from the reorganization of the magistracy and education system to the new penal code, were carried out under these regulations. The decidedly authoritarian manner in which the liberal regime came into being enhanced the appeal of the Piedmontese state to the landowning elites of Lombardy and central Italy, convincing them of the practicality of the Cavourian formula for combining economic liberalism with social conservatism through a strong administrative state. If these features aided the process of unification, they also gave an ominous form to the new nation.

Cavour had only envisaged uniting northern Italy. The unexpected success of Garibaldi's volunteer army in toppling the Bourbons in the south renewed the danger posed to the liberal settlement by both radicals and reactionaries. Garibaldi's awakening of peasant discontent threatened to erupt into a general *jacquerie*, reviving the fears of revolution of 1848–9. The annexation of the Papal territories strengthened the opposition of the Church and potentially provided a populist base for legitimist forces seeking to restore the Bourbons. Alienation of the Vatican certainly limited peasant political support for the liberals, increasing their isolation within the country and making extension of the franchize difficult. Finally, the semi-feudal landowners of the south proved far harder to win to the liberal side than their more economically progressive northern counterparts.

The confrontation with the south had the effect of increasing the authoritarian and centralizing tendencies of Piedmontese liberalism. Cavour and the liberal moderate party had always paid lip-service at least to the British pattern of local self-government, and had initially favoured a certain degree of regional autonomy. The prospect of putting power into the hands of a corrupt southern nobility and the need to crush the peasant revolt forced them to abandon these ideals. Piedmontese institutions were extended to the whole of Italy instead. The emergency powers of 1859 remained in force and were added to, thus providing the framework for the administration of justice and policing which lasted until the First World War.[6] As peasant unrest erupted in an outbreak of brigandage, martial law was declared. Acting through the army and a purged bureaucracy organized along the prefectorial lines instituted earlier in Piedmont, the government tried to impose the liberal settlement upon the recalcitrant south. For the first five years of the Kingdom, 1861–6, 'troops, troops and more troops' were poured into the region and the brigand rebellion brutally suppressed.[7]

Although the authorities recognized the social origins of the disturbances in the wretched poverty of the peasants, the measures they took tended to exacerbate the situation. Cavour's successors, following his premature death in 1861, shared his faith in the forces of economic progress. The classical myth of a naturally fertile south gave credence to the idea that a policy of *laissez-faire* would unleash those productive energies currently repressed by feudal ties. In fact, the removal of the high Bourbon tariffs and attempts to abolish feudal residues tended to worsen the lot of the peasants without weakening the position of the landowners. In many ways the liberals' concern with the rights of private property and the loosening of feudal obligations even strengthened the standing of the old landlords. Most important, the weight of its bureaucratic and military machine notwithstanding, the new state utimately proved too weak to govern without the aid of influential local factions. It became increasingly obvious that the breakdown in law and order drew sustenance from the resistance of the agrarian elites to the government's attempts to displace them from the civil administration. Forced to choose between the landowners and the peasants, the state ended up underwriting the power of the southern notables with its patronage and coercive apparatus.

The legacy of these post-unification years of virtual civil war was twofold and had a decisive impact on the subsequent evolution of the Italian political system.[8] First, the various 'preventative' measures not only produced a legal code severe in the extreme against all crimes against property, they also gave the administration wide-ranging police powers which, under the blanket term of subversion, effectively allowed the criminalisation of all criticism of the regime. Many of the civil liberties granted by the constitution came in this manner to be either revoked or made discretional by the criminal law and public security regulations. The general tendency of Italian liberals to sacrifice freedom and the rule of law to the claims of order and authority was therefore considerably reinforced. Second, the inability of the government to oust the local elites from their entrenched positions meant that their compliance had to be won by favours. This encouraged clientalism, the practice of building up parliamentary majorities by wooing local interests with the skilful manipulation of state patronage – a phenomenon further aided by the system of single-member constituencies. In many areas the personal influence of the candidate was of greater importance than party allegiance, and amongst the ruling elites true parties, organized along ideological lines with an organisational and popular base, failed to emerge. Instead, parliament was dominated by informal groupings gathered around influential statesmen. Both these factors served to free the executive from the control of the legislature and hence the electorate. Through the Prefects, the Minister of the Interior channelled state patronage and managed the police, making this the key post in any ministry. By judiciously rewarding friends and punishing enemies, the mass of deputies could be kept on the government's side. Liberal Italy came to be governed by the Machiavellian manipulation of force and consensus, and the reinterpretation of these two key concepts of the Florentine writer forms a subtheme in the work of Italian political theorists of this period. The ultimate failure of Italian liberalism and the rise of fascism stemmed from the inability and unwillingness of the ruling class to adapt the arts of consent to the circumstances of democratic politics. As the extension of the suffrage and the advent of mass parties began to undermine the importance of the clienteles, they came increasingly to rely on force alone.[9]

The centralizing turn of Italian liberalism has often been associated with the southern intellectuals who came to play an important part in the formulation of the official doctrine of the Historical Right, the name used to designate the Cavourian moderate party after unification on account of the part of the parliamentary chamber in which they took their seats. Some historians have credited the Hegelian doctrines of Silvio and Bertrando Spaventa and, to a lesser extent, Francesco De Sanctis, with the emphasis placed on the role of the state rather than civil society in the creation of the liberal order.[10] The use made of Bertrando Spaventa's work by the fascist philosopher Giovanni Gentile further served to discredit their ideas. At most, however, they gave voice to trends which we have seen were already firmly entrenched in the practices of northern liberals long before their encounter with the political traditions of the south. Although the influence of the Neapolitan Hegelians should not be overstated, they provided a theoretical justification of the liberals' programme which accurately captures their ideals.[11] During the Risorgimento, they had adopted the Hegelian theory of the 'national spirit' or *Volkgeist* as the basis of their demands. 'The ideal of nationality', according to Silvio Spaventa, 'has been either the express subject or the intimate and vital material of the Italian movement.' It constituted the 'living consciousness of the state, because it is the intimate reflection of its own material in which human association is brought about'.[12] Once in government, however, Spaventa was faced with the awesome task of reversing the Hegelian formula and having the state create the nation. 'The modern state', he now wrote, had a tutelary function, it 'directs a people towards civilization' and hence did not 'restrict itself solely to the administration of justice and the defence of society, but wants to conduct them by those paths which lead to the highest ends of humanity'.[13] For these southern liberals *laissez-faire* was, in De Sanctis's words, a 'commercial formula...liberty without content, which does not render men worthy to call themselves liberals', whereas there was 'a second liberty, a liberty which has a content, which has a programme, which wishes to attain certain ends, certain social goals; and this is the liberty which constitutes the liberal party'.[14] Such statements should not be interpreted as indicating a sympathy for some form of state socialism, however, for the southern Hegelians remained wedded to the ideals of liberal economics. They regarded themselves as an enlightened minority who had to use the state in a benevolently paternalistic fashion to build the infrastructure and legal framework required for capitalist relations of production and exchange, and to educate the populace into an acceptance of the associated liberal social values of thrift, hardwork, etc. This project involved measures to improve communications – notably a national railway network, the establishment of a single internal market and the standardisation of currency, patent laws and weights and measures, the securing of financial stability and sound money with a balanced budget, a secular education system – with particular emphasis on primary schools, and of course laws securing property against social threats from below. Although no democrats, they stood for the rule of law and a strong constitutional regime, what the German jurists called the *Rechtsstaat*, and so placed more emphasis on civil liberties than their reputation has often allowed. However, whilst they strongly condemned the growing political interference with the independence of the administration and judiciary, they fully endorsed the draconian measures used against those who they regarded as enemies of the liberal social and legal system.[15] Bertrando Spaventa had argued that the 'ethical state' was not a '*force* which draws to itself all the individuals and remains external to those who it draws' but 'unites them to the extent it is *immanent* in the *whole* understanding, in *all* the activity of the individual'.[16] The people's voluntary identification with the liberal state proved impossible to achieve, though, and the Right found themselves resorting to external compulsion.

The high moral tone adopted by the Right, whereby they saw themselves as the agents of progress, was both their strength and the cause of their downfall. On the one hand, it made them less susceptible to the corruption which engulfed Italian politics, though not as much as they later made out. On the other hand, it led them to treat all opposition, particularly from the lower orders, with contempt – seeing it as an indication of Italy's relative backwardness. Such attitudes cannot be laid at the door of philosophical idealism, as many commentators maintain.[17] Rather, they mirrored the aristocratic liberalism of the ruling class as a whole. Indeed, until Croce's revival of idealism at the turn of the century, positivism represented the official ideology of the liberal regime, offering supposedly scientific laws whereby the social organism might be controlled and the integration of the individual parts of the political 'body' obtained.[18] After all, it was the northern positivist criminologist Cesare Lombroso who was to provide the cruel repression of 'subversives' with a spurious 'scientific' basis by identifying criminal and rebellious minds with certain atavistic psychological types.[19]

The Right's ousting from office in 1876 illustrates the ambivalent nature of their approach. The obsession with balancing the budget and paying off the debts incurred in fighting the Austrians produced a regime of financial rigour which narrowed the scope for patronage. It also led to the imposition of a grist tax which not surprisingly was deeply resented and sporadically resisted by the lower classes. The opposition party, known as the Left, became the focus not just of radicals, democrats and others concerned at the poverty and repression of the south but, more important, of particular interests who disliked the centralising aspects of the state which they saw as a potential threat to their local influence. Significantly, the Right fell on the issue of the nationalisation of the railways. Some historians, influenced by contemporary polemics, have seen this act as an illustration of the Right's illiberal statism. However, Spaventa justified the measure on the traditional liberal grounds that private concerns should not control monopoly services, especially when they were joint-stock companies in which the separation of ownership from management reduced the incentive of directors to act in an entrepreneurial fashion.[20] Much of the antagonism provoked by the Right arose from their attempts to prevent the state being used as a source of corruption – an objective which ironically required increased state intervention. Their departure, far from producing a more democratic regime, was to open the way for the speculators and various industrial and agrarian elites to consolidate their control of the bureaucratic machine.

The Right's difficulties stemmed from their isolation within the country. In 1861 only 1.92 per cent of the population had the right to vote. Although, as Acquarone has pointed out, this was not so different from liberal regimes elsewhere in Europe – the British Reform Act of 1867 only extending the franchise to a mere 10 per cent of adults,[21] in the Italian case the figure accurately reflected the narrowness of the interests represented in the country. As the moderate politician Massimo D'Azeglio famously remarked, having 'made Italy' it was necessary to 'make Italians' and unify socially and culturally the inhabitants of the different regions formally united by Piedmontese arms and institutions. The obstacles in the way of this were clearly formidable. For a start the preponderance of regional dialects meant that only 2.5 per cent of the population, and only 0.6 per cent outside Rome and Tuscany, even knew Italian. Illiteracy rates were similarly impressive – 74 per cent in Italy as a whole, and between 85 and 90 per cent in southern regions.[22] However, such facts do not get to the heart of the matter. For Cavour and his successors the political and cultural unification of the country formed part of a more general process of economic and social modernization. The chief barriers to the creation of a national spirit and broader political participation arose from the economic backwardness of large parts of the country and the strength of resistance at all levels of society to the liberal project. They tended to blame this opposition on the Italian character and the lack of civic virtue.[23] The roots of mass political alienation stemmed less from biology, though, than the exclusiveness of Italian politics and the liberals' ultimate reliance on the reactionary local factions of the south. The problem facing the liberal elite was how to expand their support without undermining their own power. As we noted above, the rift with the Church had cut off the possibility of exploiting peasant conservatism along the lines of Bismarck and Napoleon III. Attempts to widen the electorate in the hope of strengthening the regime, namely Depretis's small reform of 1882 increasing the voters to 7 per cent of the population and Giolitti's intro- duction of universal manhood suffrage in 1912, usually rebounded and destabilized it by loosening the notables' grip on politics without bring- ing them new adherents from the middle and working classes.

Contemporaries criticized the resulting gaps between 'legal' and 'real' Italy,[24] 'rulers' and 'ruled',[25] North and South[26] – themes which have dominated much later historical analysis of the period.[27] However, the dilemma facing the liberals becomes even clearer when one realises that most of these critics were conservatives, who blamed the absence of a civic culture and the poverty and rebelliousness of the south on the destruction of traditional social bonds by the abstract individualism of liberal doctrines, the commercialism associated with *laissez-faire*, and the impersonal and coercive power of the centralized state.[28] Naturally the 'real' Italy of harmonious feudal relations invoked by these writers was largely fictitious, but so was the 'legal' Italy they attacked. The state's weakness was more in evidence than its strength. Nevertheless, these criticisms reflected the paradox confronting Italian liberalism – namely, the impossibility of broadening the acceptance of liberal political and economic values without a commensurate alteration in social relations.

The nearest contemporary commentators came to recognizing this problem was in the studies of southern poverty by predominantly northern liberal *meridionalisti* such as Pasquale Villari and Sidney Sonnino. They argued that the solution to the 'social problem' lay in the creation of a class of small proprietors and tenants who would have the incentives for moral and economic self-improvement. However, these proposals, which drew on Mill's ideas for land redistribution in Ireland and the similar schemes of the Lombard thinker Carlo Cattaneo,[29] tended to involve an idealization of the share-cropping system (*mezzadria*) of Tuscany and to stress its efficacy as a means of social control more than its ambiguous economic merits.[30] Alongside genuine humanitarian concern at the plight of the southern poor, went a far less altruistic fear of 'the spectre of socialism'.[31] Significantly, the emphasis was on the paternalistic side of Mill's thought rather than on its libertarian aspects.[32] These preoccupations were shared by various members of the Right, and reflected the worries of a mainly landed ruling class. Disturbed by what they regarded as the deleterious moral effects of the division of labour and industrial society, the Right had hoped for an alternative in a competitive agriculture which preserved traditional hierarchical values. As we have seen, British and French liberals voiced similar doubts about modern society, but they were able to rethink industrial production in ways which aimed to create distinctively liberal patterns of social cohesion and offer some kind of opening for the emerging working classes. The path of institutional and social reform adopted by liberals in Britain and France, whereby opposition was diffused by incorporation within the liberal framework, proved difficult to emulate in Italy. The determining factor of this failure ultimately stemmed from the continued predominance of the agrarian elites.[33]

A crucial issue to be addressed, therefore, concerns why the industrial bourgeoisie failed to take the political initiative. Undoubtedly a large part of the answer lies in the fact that Italy remained a mainly agricultural country right up to the fascist seizure of power. The considerable expansion of the industrial sectors after unification occurred mostly within the northern triangle of Genoa, Turin and Milan. However, the chief reason lies with the successful incorporation of the Italian capitalist bourgeoisie into the clientalistic Italian political system.

After the fall of the Right in 1876, the various groupings within the Left began to splinter. Agostino Depretis, who led most subsequent administrations until his death in 1887, set in motion the process of forging parliamentary majorities by purchasing individual deputies with public funds and favours, including the aid of the local administration at election time if necessary. Small though it was, the franchise reform of 1882 appeared to threaten these arrangements with the election of the first socialist deputy and the increased representation of members with democratic sympathies. Depretis managed to stay in power through the connivance of a large part of the old Right led by Marco Minghetti. Ironically, Minghetti had written one of the most incisive critiques of Depretis's methods, in which the means whereby his own party was 'transformed' into loyal supporters was clearly described:

When a deputy is no longer a representative of principles, when he ceases to be urged on by the general interests of the country, and becomes an agent for local interests, when he is the patron, the protector, and the solicitor of his electors, this is an evident sign that corruption is rife. On

the other hand, a Minister who cannot surround himself with a majority to
sustain his ideas is forced to make up the deficiency by enticing to his
side, one by one, the Opposition deputies, and this he does by distributing
among them honours and favours of all kinds.[34]

Fear of the apparent threat from below ultimately proved stronger than
his own moral principles. The process of *trasformismo*, whereby successive governments maintained themselves in office, was inaugurated, and
the old party distinctions of Left and Right disappeared. Policies became
based more on what was necessary to keep the various factions happy
than on any coherent programme. Although ministries changed frequently as favours were spread around, the same groups reappeared
time and again and elections were rarely called. Significantly, the
'remedies' for parliamentary corruption put forward by Minghetti,
Spaventa and other members of the Right steered clear of democratic
solutions. Indeed, they blamed the decline in standards on Italy's parliamentary institutions. They advocated the old constitutional means of
securing a balance of power between the executive, the judiciary and
administration and the localities.

This period of political change coincided with the onset of a European
economic recession which began to hit Italian cereal production and
the textile industries around 1881. Although Italy lacked the natural
resources for heavy industry, it had been argued that for military
reasons it was necessary to have an independent manufacturing base.
Massive state subsidies were poured into building up a navy and a railway network, and during the 1880s iron, steel and shipbuilding enjoyed
a mini boom. The impact of foreign competition and a general downturn in trade produced increasingly vociforous calls – most notably from
the wheat producers and cotton and wool manufacturers – for state
protection to be extended to other areas in the form of tariffs on imports.
This pressure culminated in the imposition of a 'general tariff' in 1887
and a tariff war with France, with whom Italy had previously had a
special treaty accounting for two-fifths of Italian foreign trade.
Historians have differed in their evaluation of the economic consequences of these protectionist measures.[35] Generally speaking, the
verdict would appear to be that although state support of heavy industry proved beneficial at first, the new tariffs probably did more harm
than good, damaging the prospects of the engineering industries by
denying them cheaper supplies and cutting off the export trade, hitting
agricultural products, such as wine, destined for foreign markets, and
increasing the cost of living for ordinary Italians – especially staple food
prices. The political consequences, however, are the focus of our attention. The tariff campaign forged important links between certain industrial and agrarian interests and the state, which created a powerful block
to the emergence of democracy. The alliance was essentially a northern
one – the southern *latifondisti* gaining surprisingly little from these

measures, as the massive emigration of peasants indicated – and chiefly involved heavy industry, textiles and the large landowners.[36] Its effect was to satisfy influential sectors of the Italian business community that their best interests were served in upholding the narrowly based state rather than with allying with those groups seeking to reform it. As long as profits could be obtained by winning state contracts and indulging in financial speculations which owed their success more to political influence than economic acumen, then there was no incentive to challenge the prevailing social and political values and institutions.

Leading industrialists, such as the wool manufacturer Alessandro Rossi, joined the attack of conservative landowners on the evils of *laissez-faire* liberalism to argue in favour of a Catholic paternalism. Rossi labelled British entrepreneurs the 'vampires of capital', whose 'egoism' and 'materialism' had destroyed the moral bonds binding the social order together and 'sown the seeds of socialism'. His model factory at Schio in the Vincenza countryside was a deliberate attempt to adapt advanced industrial processes to the semi-feudal patterns of rural life.[37] The development of the textile industry, the main Italian manufacturing sector, remained integrated into the rural economy by organizing production in small-scale workshops using peasant labour rather than in large urban factories. The sort of middle-class radicalism which characterised British liberalism remained peripheral to Italian bourgeois culture, although exceptions existed – especially amongst sections of the 'labour aristocracy'.[38] Protectionism, therefore, cannot be seen as a purely economic policy. Rather, it fed into a political practice and philosophy advocating a route to industrialisation which kept established social structures intact.[39]

This project gained in coherence under Depretis's successor Francesco Crispi. A former radical and supporter of Garibaldi, Crispi had become the focus of opposition within the Left to the politics of *trasformismo*. An admirer of Bismarck, he aimed to restore the initiative to the state through a policy of social imperialism along the lines advanced by contemporary radical liberals such as Clemençeau and Chamberlain. This project sought to provide the ruling classes with a populist base by forging together the different elements of Italian society with a combination of protectionist measures, colonialism, patriotic sentiment and social reform. Yet the policy was to prove a failure, for whilst the landowners and industrialists fully endorsed those items which supported their interests, they fiercely resisted any measures which threatened their autonomy and control of the labour force.[40] Social reforms were consistently blocked, and the new powers given to local bureaucrats in matters of health and welfare were frustrated by the antagonism of the Church, employers and landowners, whose paternalistic functions Crispi had sought to usurp. He introduced many of the proposals advocated by the Right for reducing state corruption, setting up a group of ombudsmen to overlook administrative abuses and strengthening local government. However, the collapse of numerous small banks with the withdrawal of French finance, including two of Italy's largest credit institutions, revealed that financial corruption on a massive scale continued to be rife amongst Italy's politicians. The efforts of the finance minister Sonnino to prevent speculation at the expense of the state and to revise the taxation system in a progressive direction predictably came to nothing. The weakness of the state was shown further when Crispi's bids for populist success with colonial adventures ended in disaster, Italy's defeat by the Abyssinians at Adowa in 1896 making her the first Western nation to be defeated in a battle with an African army. The one measure to broaden popular involvement, the extension of the electorate at local elections to all literate males over twenty-one who paid local taxes of at least five lira per annum, only brought the regime fresh difficulties. Hopes that the power of local notables would still have a decisive influence on the new voters proved illusory, with the reforms aiding the growth of the Catholic and Socialist opposition, now beginning to develop into mass parties.

If the various interests grouped around the state resented any interference which threatened their position, they demanded its protection against foreign competition and labour conspiracies. These two demands became increasingly interconnected as the economic problems of the 1890s produced sporadic rioting and unrest. Two episodes were of particular importance – the disturbances of the Sicilian *fasci* in 1893–4 and the food riots in Milan in 1898. Both events illustrate how repression was the only form of state interference likely to be tolerated by the government's supporters, and how it was not even strong enough always to manage this successfully. Although Crispi had tried to clear up a number of the more glaring anomalies of the Italian legal system with a revised penal code and public security law, recognizing for example the right to strike, plenty of coercive potential still remained. The Sicilian *fasci*, a movement of peasant demonstrations and land seizures, were a curious phenomena, combining anarchist and socialist ideas with the traditional feuding of *mafiosi* and peasant millenarianism. Ignoring the roots of their protest in the damage done to southern agriculture by the loss of the export trade, Crispi fixed on the fact that a number of radical intellectuals figured prominently in the movement, providing it with a leadership and organization lacking from ordinary peasant riots. His response was one of brutal suppression. A State of Emergency was declared, the *fasci* disbanded and their leaders given harsh sentences by military tribunals. Over 1,000 people were deported to penal islands without trial. 'Anti-anarchist' laws were passed curtailing political liberties, the Socialist Party dissolved and its deputies arrested, and southern electoral registers 'revised' to exclude troublesome voters. However, his feeble attempt to palliate the wave of protest which arose from these actions with a bill to take over the large estates and uncultivated land and lease them out in medium-sized holdings, was successfully resisted. Appropriately it was the leader of the southern landowners, the Marchese di Rudini, who was responsible for the next high point of government reaction. The rising food prices associated with the poor harvest of 1897 produced a wave of strikes, demonstrations and riots throughout Italy in 1898 and 15 seats for the Socialists in general elections. Faced with calls to abolish the wheat tariffs and taxes on bread, di Rudini reacted with too little too late and ended up by employing the time-honoured methods of declaring martial law and using brute force to quell the unrest. Events came to a head in Milan in May when a mass protest against police attempts to suppress socialist pamphleteers was squashed at the cost of over a hundred deaths and several hundred wounded.

Di Rudini's actions proved to be the climax of the authoritarian policies of 1893–1900. His laws to restrict the freedoms of speech and association failed to get through parliament and he was forced to resign. Similar proposals by his successor General Pelloux also met with obstruction. In a famous article of 1897 Sonnino had advocated a return to the letter of the constitution of 1848, whereby ministers were responsible to the King rather than parliament and laws could be passed by royal decree.[41] His suggestion had met with little support at the time even from the King, and Pelloux's attempt to use these methods led to an uproar and caused a group of 'constitutional liberals' under Zanardelli and Giolitti to go into opposition. His emergency legislation was declared illegal by the Court of Cassation and Pelloux was forced to go to the country. Ensuing elections produced fresh victories for the socialists and radicals, who by siding with the 'constitutional liberals' forced Pelloux's resignation. It was clear that the writing was on the wall for the conservative liberals, and a further reactionary ministery under Giuseppe Saracco soon gave way to the progressive grouping led by Zanardelli and Giolitti.

The crisis of the 1890s revealed the disunity of Italy's ruling class and the growing power of the opposition. Rather than forging together a new political axis between landowners, industrialists and the new working classes, protectionism had exacerbated the divisions within Italy's elites and offered a focal point for a heterogeneous set of opposition groups – from free-trading liberals to socialists, anarchists and Catholics. The regime's own adherents had prevented it from increasing the effectiveness of its administration, forcing it to rely on ever more arbitrary and coercive measures. The successful defence of the rule of law and parliamentary procedure seemed to offer the opportunity for Italian liberalism to take a democratic and reformist direction.[42]

The statesman most identified with the new era was Giovanni Giolitti, who dominated Italian politics until the rise of fascism. From 1898 to 1908 Italy enjoyed a period of relative economic prosperity. Industrial production almost doubled and the national income grew by about 50 per cent. Although these improvements were restricted largely to the north, so that the disparity between north and south became even more pronounced, and Italy remained a mainly agricultural nation, economic changes were beginning to alter the character of Italian society. At first the signs that the liberals would adapt to meet these new circumstances were auspicious. In a famous speech outlining the fresh direction of liberal politics, Giolitti insisted that the state must cease to regard the labour movement as inherently subversive and recognize strikes as a legitimate way for workers to better their condition. The state should remain neutral in disputes, rather than automatically siding with the employers. The 'failure of reactionary politics', he declared, 'had opened up a new historical period'. The rise of the working classes was 'an irresistible movement, because common to all civilised countries and grounded in the principle of equality of all men. He concluded:

> Nobody could delude themselves that it would be possible to prevent the popular classes conquering their share of economic and political influence, and friends of institutions have one duty above all: to persuade these classes, and persuade them with deeds rather than talk, that they can hope for far more from existing institutions than from dreams of the future.[43]

The reformist turn of the Italian socialist party under Turati augured well for Giolitti's policy and suggested the possible emergence of a centre-left liberalism. This early promise failed to materialise. The economic crisis of 1907–8 and the ensuing recession undoubtedly made Giolitti's task of conciliating capital and labour harder. The reluctance of the socialists and Catholics to co-operate at crucial moments created further difficulties for him; but the chief factor in the liberal failure to move in a democratic direction arose from his control of parliament. The special powers which had been at the centre of the political storm of the 1890s remained in force, even though they were applied with more subtlety. Election rigging continued, as did protectionism, and his resulting guaranteed majority provided by the southern deputies rendered parliament a farce. His moves to conciliate the rising forces of mass politics represented not so much a new departure as a return to the practices of *trasformismo* by extending the patronage network to previously excluded groups. The tariff and tax structure remained unreformed, Giolitti preferring to employ increased government spending. Protection was maintained for grain and a whole range of commodities from sugar beet to sulphur, and the subsidy on steel was increased. Prosperity helped these policies and enabled him to put a certain degree of pressure on employers to accede to his concessions to the workers.

However, deep dissatisfaction and resentment began to build up. Both left and right attacked the way in which he had demeaned parliament and abused government control of the bureaucracy. Nationalist and anarcho-syndicalist groups in particular began to explore extra-parliamentary forms of opposition and to call for a new kind of state.[44]

Even amongst democrats, such as the reformist socialist Salvemini, disgust with Giolittian corruption came close to bringing the very notion of parliamentary government into disrepute.[45] The limits of Giolitti's methods became clear once the downturn in the economy made more substantial political concessions necessary. In an amazing balancing act after 1911, he offered universal suffrage and the nationalization of life insurance to the socialists, the invasion of Libya to the nationalists and the 'Gentilone Pact', a pre-election agreement with the Catholic electoral union, to the clericals. For the principled politicians within each 'block' such blatantly transformist tactics proved unpalatable and Giolitti's measures merely served to make the opposition all the more intransigent.

As Giolitti followed his usual practice of retiring from office whenever the going got tough, the liberal ruling class went back to its habitual alternative – an attempt at authoritarian populism. The traditional landowning group returned under Salandra and Sonnino, as did the old policies of repression. Anti-socialism was used in a bid to gather nationalist and Catholic support for the existing social order, a strategy aided by the mounting violence on the left, culminating in the 'red week' of June 1914. Hoping to restore the prestige of the monarchy and army, and have an excuse for resorting to emergency executive powers which would free him from Giolitti's hold on parliament, Salandra took Italy into the First World War in 1915. As most responsible opinion on all sides had foreseen, the decision had disastrous consequences. The army and economy were unequal to the engagement, as the massive defeat at Caporetto in which Italy lost 300,000 prisoners and most of the Veneto to Austria amply demonstrated. Far from uniting the people behind the government with patriotic feeling, the war raised the political consciousness of workers, peasants and *petit bougeoisie* and confirmed their antagonism to the liberal regime. Frustrated in its hopes of territorial gains by the US President Woodrow Wilson's policy of national self-determination, the Italian state emerged from the war with its prestige and resources at the lowest point in its history.

The post-war years witnessed greater social and political agitation than ever before, both in industrial centres such as Turin – where Gramsci's 'new order' movement organized the occupation of the factories[46] – and in the countryside, particularly Emilia, the Po Valley, Tuscany, Umbria and the Veneto. The introduction of proportional representation and universal manhood suffrage in the elections of 1919 further reduced the ability of the liberal elites to cope with the situation with their usual methods of parliamentary management. The Socialist Party and the Catholic *Popolari* won over half the seats in parliament and only their own divisions allowed in a liberal government. Returning briefly to office, Giolitti discovered that the old techniques would not work. The stress of the times combined with a tradition of mere fixing reduced greatly the ability and will of Italy's liberal politicians to institutionalize political conflict within the parliamentary framework and by now most of the opposition had abandoned it too. The experience of the 'two red years' (*biennio rosso*) of 1919–20 convinced the industrialists and especially the landowners that the advent of mass politics prevented the containment of the new social forces within the liberal political system and threw them into the hands of the fascists.

The rise of fascism cannot be disassociated from the failure of the liberal state. Without the active connivance of the authorities, fascist violence could easily have been stopped – as indeed it was whenever officials showed firmness, as at Sarzana in 1921 when police shot at and scattered a fascist force.[47] In general, however, the army, police and local bureaucracy actively helped the employers use the fascist squads to regain the ground lost in government-imposed concessions to the labour organizations after the war. For most of 1921 *squadristi* were engaged in waging a systematic offensive against the socialists and their local institutions, particularly in the countryside. Unable to reach agreement with the Catholics, who often took as prominant a part in rural agitation as the socialists, or to convince reformist socialists to collaborate in government, the liberal politicians began to look for a solution to the crisis outside parliament. For the liberals, fascism was simply an adaptation to the age of organized labour of their time-honoured policy of imposing order. Their own reliance on emergency powers and arbitrary force in the past had so blurred the issue of legality, that conservative liberals such as Salandra could openly advocate fascist violence as the only way to restore the authority of the law against the 'subversion' and 'anarchism' of the left.[48] By the time of the March on Rome in October 1922, liberal leaders were racing to gain Mussolini's support for their own coalition. Had they made a united stand against him, the fascist seizure of power would never have taken place. Instead, they fell over themselves to legitimate it with electoral pacts. By 1925 most of them had happily given up all semblance of the liberal parliamentary constitution in return for the effective guarding of their interests by a fascist state. After all, as one of their number put it, 'Democracy has no other purpose than that of tying together liberalism and its natural enemy socialism.'[49] Nothing had been lost by abandoning it altogether.

The following sketch of the language and politics of Italian liberalism c.1860–1922 provides the all-important context for discussing the liberal theories of Vilfredo Pareto (1848–1923) and Benedetto Croce (1866–1952), the two thinkers singled out for especial attention in this chapter. To a striking degree, the elaboration of their respective doctrines reflected the evolution of the Italian political system in this period. In particular, both their conceptualization of the nature of politics and the changes they periodically introduced into their theories reflected the dialectic of force and consent within Italian liberal thought and practice outlined in this section. In spite of certain pronounced tendencies within Italian liberalism, it would be wrong to regard the course it took as in any way inevitable. On several occasions, most particularly during the

Giolittian heyday of 1903–8, the possibility for a move in a democratic direction existed. Their ideological and epistemological differences notwithstanding – Pareto being a free market liberal and a positivist and Croce a conservative liberal in the tradition of his uncle Silvio Spaventa and the Historical Right, who sought to revive the Italian idealist tradition – both theorists reveal in different ways the conceptual as well as practical obstacles which blocked the reformist path. Rather than being regarded as an instance of Italian perversity, however, this failure shows up the contingent and limited aspects of much of the Anglo-French liberal tradition – weaknesses which Pareto and Croce sought to transcend.

A FRUSTRATED LIBERAL: VILFREDO PARETO AND THE FAILURE OF ETHICAL LIBERALISM

Born in 1848, the year of liberal revolutions, and dying only one year after the March on Rome in 1923, the evolution of Pareto's thought mirrored in exemplary fashion the changing fortunes of Italian liberalism during this crucial period. The son of a Mazzinian exile, he initially held liberal democratic opinions and was a free marketeer all his life. However, he grew cynical about democracy and ended up lending qualified support to fascism. This alteration in his political allegiances was paralleled by his switch from economics to sociology and has given rise to various interpretations. Many have attributed the change to disillusionment at the frustration of his early hopes and have regarded the later phase as marking a complete rejection of his former beliefs.[50] When events led him to lose his faith in the forms of human rationality assumed by his economic theory, he ended up searching for a sociological explanation of humanity's irrational impulses. Others have argued that his early economic liberalism was so extreme that it easily led to fascism. According to Joseph Schumpeter:

> There was something in that ultraliberalism of his that points in a direction exactly opposite to the creeds and slogans of official liberalism...He did not fight against government interference *per se* but against the governments of parliamentary democracy...Viewed from this angle, his type of *laissez-faire* acquires a connotation that is entirely at variance with the *laissez-faire* of the English type. And once we realise this, the rest is easy to understand.[51]

The approach presented here rejects both these views.[52] The first underestimates the degree of continuity between the two periods of Pareto's life, for the sociology remained conditioned by the presuppositions of his economics, the former presenting a virtual mirror-image of the latter. *Pace* Schumpeter and other adherents of the second view, the frustrations of the young free marketeer arose precisely because Italy refused to live up to the ideals of British liberals, whose writings Pareto so admired. As a result, he came to question the moral framework which we have seen governed British liberalism. However, in dropping the ethical aspect of liberalism he accentuated even further its economic elements. The sociology reflected an attempt to provide a less moralistic account of human behaviour which explained divergences from the rational pursuit of our true interests as given by classical economics. The result of this process was a reformulation of liberalism by way of a powerful autocritique of many of the more dubious ethical presuppositions to be found in the British tradition.

Pareto began by following his father's career and becoming an engineer, graduating in 1869. He was appointed a director of the Florence branch of the Rome Railway Company in 1870 and held this post until 1874 when he became managing director of the Società Ferriere d'Italia, also based near Florence. During this time Pareto became involved with the Tuscan landlords' technical and agronomical society, the Accademia dei Georgofili. The association consisted of the progressive landowners of the region; it was at the forefront of campaigns for a more commercial agriculture and was committed to *laissez-faire*. Under the influence of a leading member of this group, Ubaldino Peruzzi, Pareto entered political activity.

Far from reneging on the democratic ideals of his parents as Stuart Hughes and Schumpeter affirmed, he actively campaigned for them. His very first writings involved a defence of the Millian scheme for proportional representation. Like Mill he declared himself a believer in human progress and regarded the vote as an important instrument for training the populace in their civic responsibilities. Pareto contended that the opposition of the ruling classes to universal suffrage was motivated by the desire to protect their privileges, rather than a principled defence of freedom as they maintained. They argued that the franchise must remain limited because only those who paid taxes had a stake in the nation, the illiterate masses being unable to make reasoned decisions in any case. Pareto retorted that responsible government would only result when all, through elections, were involved in it. The vote was not a right, he wrote, but 'the exercise of a necessary function for the good working of civil society'. Only by having everyone represented could the country avoid falling a prey to the particular interests of powerful minorities. Whilst he conceded that the voter required, as a 'first and indispensable quality', the possession of 'the culture and the necessary knowledge to fulfil adequately his task', he advocated compulsory education to remedy this deficiency rather than disenfranchizement of most of the population. In the meantime, he supported the adoption of Mill's system of 'fancy franchises' which counterbalanced the adverse effects of universal suffrage by giving more votes to the better educated.[53]

Again following Mill, he defined liberty as 'the faculty of doing everything which in a direct and immediate way does not harm others'.[54] On these grounds he stoutly defended freedom of speech and association, including the workers' right to combine and strike. However, he did not believe any more than Mill that this principle implied that all state intervention was wrong. Sometimes not to interfere could cause harm. For example, he argued 'that compulsory education should rather be called freedom of education, since the parent who does not educate his son harms him greatly and in a direct way'.[55] He also accepted that analogous reasons lay behind legislation such as the British Employers' Liability Act of 1880, although he believed that workers were often more responsible for the harm done to them as a result of their own carelessness than this bill recognized.[56] Since trade was a social act, and hence other-regarding, he justified *laissez-faire* mainly on the practical grounds of economic efficiency. The connection with the issue of liberty was an indirect one. He maintained that the economy functioned better when, as much as possible, left up to private initiative. As with Mill, this belief derived from a faith in the inventiveness of the individual and the fear that a planned economy would stultify this capacity and give excessive power to whichever group controlled the state. In any case, economic freedom certainly did not entail allowing monopolists and other materially powerful groups to exploit their workforce and cheat the consumer, and it was the state's duty to ensure this did not happen.[57]

Pareto generally opposed social legislation, such as the introduction of a minimum wage or employment insurance schemes, plans for which emerged in Italy as elsewhere in the 1880s. He argued that in Italy the social problem could only be solved by increasing production and that these measures took capital away from more useful, wealth-generating projects. However, unlike conservative liberals such as Salandra and Rossi who adopted analogous arguments,[58] he conceded that as long as Italian entrepreneurs derived their profits from state subsidies rather than productive investment, then the force of this reasoning was somewhat diminished. After all 'it is too much to hope to be able to rely on human ignorance, expecting to convince the workers of the uselessness, or worse of the damage, that would come from measures which are exactly similar to those used by the wealthier classes for their own ends.'[59] He rejected the applicability of the 'wages fund' theory to the Italian case, because in Italy wages were often below subsistence level and profits far from marginal. Whilst believing for his own part that the state should not meddle in the relations between capital and labour except to 'exercise the office of maintaining free competition', he affirmed that justice demanded that 'if it intervenes, it does so impartially, in everyone's favour, and not constantly for one side and to the detriment of the other.' As a result, he utterly deplored the use of troops to quell strikes and the imposition of low wages through the courts.[60]

In addition to the economic consequences of social legislation, he worried about its political and moral effects. He accused the Italian 'socialists of the chair', who promoted these measures, of seeking to incorporate new classes into the corrupting patronage network. Still, there is none of the cynicism towards humanitarian concerns which fills his later writings. He fully accepted similar laws as appropriate to a rich country such as Britain, regarding them as the outcome of a fair bargain between capital and labour whereby workers got a rightful share of the wealth they had helped to create. Similar regulations in Italy, in contrast, would be unearned paternalistic handouts imposed from above. He also gave qualified approval to mutual benefit schemes organized with government help but in the private sector. He even favoured a shift from indirect to direct taxation on the grounds of equity.[61] Needless to say, none of these socially progressive proposals had a hope of getting very far in Italy in any case. Pareto's reaction to them merely underlines the genuineness of his adherence to liberal values, especially as represented by British writers and a somewhat idealized version of British society.

Pareto's basic criterion for judging the worth of any policy was the utilitarian principle of the greatest happiness of the greatest number. He maintained that happiness would be more likely to be increased by raising salaries through maximizing production rather than redistributing the small and rather poor existing cake. Like the British radicals he admired, he believed the following three elements would best secure this goal. First, it was necessary by electoral reform to ensure the government represented the interests of the majority rather than a powerful minority. Second, governments should be subject to the rule of law, and laws in their turn ought to be equal for all and respectful of individual liberty of action and belief. Third, the economy must be freed from state control and regulated as far as possible by free competition.[62] A committed advocate of the entrepreneurial ideal, Pareto firmly opposed all unearned privilege – be it of the wealthy or the poor. He believed that only a free market in ideas, labour and capital was conducive to human material and moral progress and could make the people both more prosperous and more civilized.

As we noted above, the protectionist policies introduced after 1887 formed part of a more general political project which dominated Italian politics throughout the 1890s. Pareto's adherence to *laissez-faire* was similarly more than just an economic doctrine. Under the influence of Mill, Spencer, and the French liberals Yves Guyot and Gustav de Molinari, he made free trade but one aspect of a more comprehensive liberal theory. His involvement in the campaign against protectionism organised by the *Giornale degli economisti*, and his professional duties at Lausanne, where he succeeded Walras as Professor of Political Economy in 1893, now gave him the opportunity to elaborate this philosophy in a more systematic fashion.[63]

Pareto was alive to the political implications of the new tariffs from the first.[64] Writing in the *Journal des économistes* in October 1887, he baldly stated:

The customs tariff approved by the Italian Parliament has a dual purpose: on the one hand, to procure funds for the budget; on the other hand, to satisfy the interests which have sufficient representatives in the Chamber to wield power.[65]

Pareto could see no economic justification for the measures. On the contrary the tariff war with France seemed positively damaging. Protectionist policies reflected the essentially clientalistic nature of Italian politics. The 'triumph of the transformist system', they revealed how 'the perversion of the parliamentary system has sacrificed the interests of the people to those of a small number of persons strongly organized and resorting to all measures for extending their power over the country.'[66] Like many others, he bemoaned the decline of real parties after 1876 and the 'enormous extension of the functions of the state, which reduces almost to nullity the private initiative and economic independence of the citizens'. With exceptional clarity he pinpointed the connections between the two:

The absence of political parties favours the extension of the functions of government, because to obtain a majority the ministers are obliged to substitute motives of personal interest for motives of political interest or passions which do not exist. But the extension of governmental functions is, in its turn, a serious obstacle to the formation of parties.[67]

As he remarked, 'it is not easy to say whether the political disorganization of Italy is the cause or the result of the existing corruption.' In any case, it seemed impossible to break out of the circle. Looking as usual towards Britain, Pareto bemoaned the absence of movements like the Anti-Corn Law League or the campaign for parliamentary reform. Rather than seeking to change the state in a progressive direction for the advantage of all, the Italian bourgeoisie had abused their power to create a system of 'middle-class socialism' whereby landowners and industrialists used the resources of the state for their own exclusive interests. Drawing on Spencer's distinction between 'military' and 'industrial' societies, he had no difficulty in identifying protectionism with the revival of militarism in an attempt to give new life to traditional aristocratic and feudal values. The link between the subsidies for the iron and steel industries and the naval building programme and Italy's membership of the Triple Alliance and antagonism to France largely confirmed this thesis.[68] He regarded this development as inherently reactionary and unsuited to the requirements of a dynamic modern economy. It appeared to him that the future political struggle was thus 'between the protectionist system and the liberal system, the former essentially oligarchic, the latter democratic'.[69]

Pareto called socialists all those who wanted 'the intervention of the state to change the distribution of wealth'. 'Popular socialists' wished to favour the poor, 'bourgeois socialists' the wealthy. Pareto sympathised deeply with the former, accepting that the 'the luxury of the rich, their predominance, their privileges cause immense sufferings.'[70] Nevertheless, he was convinced that the only way to improve matters was to remove the influence of the state from the economy altogether, and to encourage the productive employment of capital in enterprises which would raise the standard of living of all. The error of the popular socialists was an understandable one, given the present political arrangements. However, 'the present condition of civil society is based not on private property and free competition, but on the intervention of the state.' 'Bourgeois socialism' redistributed wealth in an indirect manner by employing the following three mechanisms: 'customs duty protection, monopolies, public works and public debts; the prevalence of indirect over direct taxes; and war and the armed peace that precedes and follows it'. All three hurt the poor hardest. The first made industry less productive and imposed a tribute on the populace for the benefit of certain capitalists. The second was an anti-progressive measure which placed the burden of taxation on those least able to pay. The last 'are the most expensive luxuries that the ruling classes enjoy at the expense of the nation' and 'can do nothing but increase the sufferings of the majority'.[71] Whilst Pareto appreciated the popular socialists' desire to use the state to claw back the wealth which had been taken from them, and even believed this might be a salutory experience for the bourgeoisie, he argued that such an expedient could only have dire effects for the condition of the people. No matter how well meant, any planned redistribution of wealth removed capital from production and damaged national prosperity. Moreover, it risked giving excessive power to whoever controlled the state, and human nature being what it was this was bound to be abused.[72] Although he admired individual socialists for the independent stand they took against the government, often risking imprisonment, and strongly defended their right to free speech, he maintained that socialism was a 'metaphysical' or 'religious' theory, rather than a 'scientific' one. Pareto regarded his own task to consist in instructing the labouring classes and those members of the middle classes sympathetic to their plight in the lessons of political economy and the advantages of liberalism.[73]

In Pareto's opinion liberal systems were characterized by 'the repudiation of the use of coercive power, and the restitution of social welfare by the free use and free development of the intellectual faculties and attitudes of man'. Two arguments of an entirely Millian kind lay behind Pareto's defence of liberty. First, in the present state of ignorance in the fields of social science, freedom represented the lesser evil. In theory, a totally planned economy might prove more efficient and distribute wealth better than an unplanned one. However, he maintained we simply lacked the necessary information to make it work. The second, and most important, argument in favour of liberty was of an ethical kind, though:

The benefit that freedom can bring us is above all to educate men to be able to operate vigorously. The physiological law according to which any organ that is not used for many generations atrophies, extends also to the intellectual faculties, and the systems in which every manner of individual action is regulated can only produce men with no other ability than that of obeying, never that of commanding or directing others; and yet one needs such people, because the State of the socialists is an abstract term, and in reality there must be men of flesh and bone who can fulfil the offices, which become all the graver, and of greater importance, the more things the State seeks to provide. A society organised according to one of the most extreme socialist systems therefore would be unable to produce the men necessary to direct it; and as all the men provided by the liberal order it had replaced were used up, would ineluctably fall into decay.[74]

Pareto gave his most extensive discussion of his liberal philosophy in the *Cours d'économie politique* of 1896.[75] Here he took on the task of laying the foundations for a science of society grounded on the 'sure basis' of the logico-empirical method of the natural sciences. He aimed to expound the 'uniformities' underlying human behaviour, 'stripping man of a large number of accretions, ignoring the passions, whether good or bad, and reducing him eventually to a sort of molecule, susceptible solely to the influence of the forces of ophelimity [self-satisfaction]'.[76] He had graduated with a thesis on 'The Fundamental Principles of Equilibrium in Solid Bodies', and the mechanical model of the world as a system of mutually interacting particles which move from one state of equilibrium to another now provided him with his basic conception of the economy.[77] Following Spencer, he argued that society evolved through the progressive development of needs and desires as individuals sought ever more varied and higher forms of self-satisfaction. Societies consequently ceased to be simple homogeneous units and diversified into a heterogeneous organic community.[78] Different stages of social evolution gave rise to different forms of social equilibrium. However, experience demonstrated that in the most progressive stage maximum ophelimity was achieved by a system of free competition which rewarded merit and established a natural equilibrium between different individuals pursuing their divergent but ultimately compatible projects.[79] While Pareto disliked unearned privileges, he positively favoured a differentiated society which mirrored the inherent inequalities of ability and divergent tastes and needs of individuals.

Pareto disputed the socialist' contention that capitalism was inherently exploitative. The ownership of land and personal capital was not itself the cause of the 'spoilation' of the poor. He agreed with Marx that 'class struggle...is the great and dominant fact of history', but he argued that it took two forms. The first, beneficial, form was equivalent to economic competition. When this competition was free it produced maximum ophelimity, 'since free competition, far from destroying, produces wealth, it indirectly contributes to raising the minimum income level and to reducing inequalities of income.' The second, harmful, form, in contrast, 'is that whereby each class endeavours to get control of the government so as to make it an instrument for spoilation'. Class war in the healthy sense was simply an aspect of the Darwinian struggle for the survival of the fittest. It was an ineradicable consequence of natural differences between human beings and essential to social progress. The Marxist dream of an egalitarian communist society could only be achieved at the cost of stasis and an unnatural and hence enforced uniformity. However, class war in the unhealthy sense justifiably attacked by Marx, arose not from differences in ability but as a result of differential access to the organs of power. In this latter instance, the governing class abused its position as the upholder of order and security to serve its own narrow ends. Since this vice was common to all forms of government, the only solution was to reduce drastically the capacity of the state, no matter what its political character, to interfere with individual and economic freedom. In other words, it was necessary to have a minimal state bounded by regular laws which ensured its impartiality. Concluding, Pareto contended that socialists erred in believing it was the simple possession of private wealth which led people to despoil others. Rather, it depended on whether the political system favoured its use to win concessions from the public authorities instead of economic investment. 'Far from talking of the "oppression of capital"', he concluded, 'one must recognize that it is precisely when it is not transformed into capital' that wealth can be used 'in a way that harms society'. Britain and Italy once more served as his examples of the two types of polity, the one liberal and the other protectionist.[80]

As with his British counterparts, Pareto regarded capitalism not just as an economic system, but as a means of human progress. In true Enlightenment fashion, he viewed ignorance as the chief cause of human misery and placed great faith in our capacity to employ reason to improve our situation. Giving people the freedom to make mistakes led them to respond to experience and to substitute 'facts' for illusory 'metaphysical' ideals. Thus, free competition not only made the people materially better off, it made them more civilized as well. The key element in social evolution was 'human capital' – our potential to act as a force for change. The capitalist economic system therefore presupposed the emancipation of humankind's creative energies within a liberal system securing freedom of action and of thought. All forms of tutelage were both economically and morally wrong.[81]

During the 1890s Pareto tried hard to put these ideas into practice. He reminded both friends and foes of the present Italian system that it would be a mistake to pretend that it stood for individual freedom.[82] In the face of the vicious crackdown of popular protest, Pareto urged all those who called themselves liberals to have 'the courage…to stand firm in condemning any offense against freedom and justice, without caring who committed it, nor ever bending to flattery or threats'. To prevent social revolution, 'liberals must always abstain from the chicanery and tricks of politicians…and hold fast to a doctrine which is whole, upright, just and honest; beating a path where they can not be followed by those who have acquired their power by lies and deceit.'[83] Perversely, they did just the opposite, interfering with economic freedom themselves whilst denying workers freedom of contract and collective bargaining. By so doing they encouraged the very unrest they sought to combat. Pareto was attacked in the Italian press and even had one of his meetings broken up by the police for speaking out against the government. His friend Pantaleoni was forced to resign from his teaching post at the Scuola Superiore di Commercio di Bari because he had criticised the customs duty on wine in a scholarly journal, an event for which Pareto felt partly responsible since he had drawn attention to the piece in an article in the *Revue des deux mondes*.[84] The free traders found themselves making common cause with the socialists against government oppression and the bad effects of protectionism. It was the socialist deputy Napoleone Colajanni, for example, who revealed the bank scandals of 1893–4. Pareto firmly condemned the repression of the Sicilian *fasci* and the authoritarian measures of 1898. His house in Switzerland became a refuge for Italian and French radicals, Pareto passionately siding with the Dreyfusards in France and making friends with the syndicalist theorist Georges Sorel during this period. His sympathy for the socialists at this time should not be misunderstood, however. Although he defended their right to speak and organise, and admired the probity and honesty of a number of individual socialists, he remained as convinced as ever of the erroneous and pernicious nature of the doctrine. He feared that if people found that the only persons speaking out for justice were the socialists, then they would naturally turn to them for help. The social concerns of socialism, which were laudable, had to be distinguished from the economic theory, which he believed to be fundamentally mistaken. Indeed, because under socialism the 'spoilators' would outnumber the wealth creators, he maintained its effects would be even worse than protectionism. To prevent this disaster from occurring the bourgeoisie had 'to do better' than their rivals. They must imitate the middle-class radicalism of Cobden and Bright, bringing the working classes with them in their wake. As he noted, 'wherever in Europe the bourgeoisie are more honest, right and just, socialism flourishes less.'[85] The 'sentiment of freedom', however, seemed singularly absent from the Italian liberal bourgeoisie. 'In defiance of common sense and the dictionary' liberal now appeared to denote only those who encouraged 'every type of action against liberty'.[86] Far from being a class of entrepreneurs, the bourgeoisie were 'those who live in ease and enjoy protectionist duties, procure government offices for their sons, make money by burdening others, and when they get the chance, rip-off the banks'.[87] By 1899 he was writing how:

Not only in Italy, but in all Europe, one observes the strange phenomenon
of the socialists, who, in the battle for liberty, take the place deserted by
the liberals...Let us put theory to one side, in practice...the socialists more
or less alone put up an effective resistance to the oppression of
governments and fight against...militarism.[88]

It seems hard to believe that only two years later the same person would
be mounting a massive attack in his book on *Les systèmes socialistes* and
fulminating against the weakness of the bourgeoisie.

The 1890s represented the high point of Pareto's adherence to what I
have termed ethical liberalism. Yet only months into the new century a
change began to occur and he was warning of the 'dangers of socialism'
and elaborating his theory of ideology.[89] As his sociology took shape he
gradually lost his faith in the sincerity of humanitarian sentiments.
Spencer's evolutionism came to be rejected as 'metaphysical', expressing
the wishful thinking of a naive humanist rather than the cool reasoning
of an experimental scientist. Pareto wondered how he ever could have
valued such 'puerile' thinking.[90] Most important, his support for democracy was replaced by the conviction that far from ensuring that the best
people were chosen to govern, democratic methods compounded the
opportunities for the use of the state as an instrument of 'spoilation' on
behalf of the ruling class.[91] His major contribution to economic theory,
the *Manuale di economia politica* of 1906, sharply distinguished the logical
maximization of self-satisfaction assumed of economic agents and the
illogical rationalizations which guide the vast majority of human
actions.[92] Although the conception of the economy as an equilibrated
system still governed his thinking, he significantly dropped the notion
of an invisible hand mechanism indirectly leading individuals seeking
to optimise their own fulfilment to maximize the greatest happiness of
the greatest number. The dynamics of the economic system were too
complicated for anyone to be able to specify a certain state as the most
optimal for the economy to reach. Changes, such as technological
innovations, were unpredictable, and one person's benefit might well
damage others, making them less well-off. The free market based on
perfect competition was an economic ideal, achievable only when
isolated from other social phenomena. It was doubtful that people
would be likely to adopt it in practice. Pareto had become increasingly
convinced that 'economists have made the mistake of ascribing too
much importance to reason as the determining motive of human action.'[93]
Since the economy formed part of a larger society, economic functions,
like price and supply, could not be studied in isolation from other social
processes. In Pareto's opinion the 'science' capable of understanding the
interaction of the full range of social phenomena was no longer
economics but sociology.[94]

The alteration in Pareto's ideas was in some ways less dramatic than it
might seem at first. For example, he had severely criticised socialist
economics from the beginning. The new element in his attack on *Les*

systèmes socialistes of 1902 concerned his assertion that the socialist leaders, whose personal integrity he had defended before, would become in their turn the despoilers of the country. The thesis of the 'circulation of elites', whereby one group of corrupt politicians was simply replaced by a second more effective group, came to prevail over his earlier optimism concerning the eventual triumph of reason. Humanist ideas now appeared to him as a mere façade masking selfish interests, although he conceded that such views might be held in good faith. The seduction of large sections of the bourgeoisie by reformist sentiments simply testified to the terminal weakness of this class before the rising 'aristocracy of brigands' represented by the Socialist Party. As his favourite Genoese saying put it, 'whoever becomes a lamb will find a wolf to eat him.'[95] Pareto was careful to insist that unlike the conservative elitists who took up his theory he was not taking sides on the issue, merely making an observation. Giuseppe Prezzolini captured the differences between them when he concluded a famous interview for the nationalist review *Il Regno* with the observation that 'you [Pareto] see in the theory of aristocracies a scientific theory: I see it instead as a scientific justification of my present political needs.'[96]

His pretensions to 'scientific' aloofness notwithstanding, Pareto's sympathies had clearly drifted towards the anti-democratic and anti-socialist camp. What had produced this change?[97] Pareto had initially looked on Giolitti's intention to restore the rights of workers in the interests of balance with some favour.[98] Unfortunately, as we saw in the previous section, Giolitti's policy did not result in any real alterations in the political system, merely an adaptation of the politics of *trasformismo* to the new circumstances of mass politics. Pareto had been adamant that it would not suffice to change the personnel of government, the nature of the Italian state needed to be entirely rethought. As presently constituted, Italian politics were inherently corrupting.[99] The absence of any genuine institutional reform served to undermine his faith in democracy *tout court*. The years 1900–2, when *Les systèmes socialistes* was composed, witnessed an unprecedented wave of strikes – 1,034 in 1901 and 801 in 1902. Whilst Pareto recognised that they represented in part an understandable backlash after years of repression and exploitation, he believed Giolitti had begun to lean too far in the direction of the labour movement. He contended that the right not to strike deserved equal recognition to the right to strike, that the right of employers to lay off workers or employ others at lower rates was as important as the right of employees to free collective bargaining. Unlike Mill, he did not regard 'black legs' as 'free riders' who potentially harmed their colleagues by undermining the position of workers as a whole to improve their pay and conditions. As a result, he saw Giolitti's concessions to union power and wooing of the PSI (*Partito Socialista Italiano*) as ominous signs that 'bourgeois' socialism was giving way to the 'popular' kind. Clearly a new elite or aristocracy of power-brokers and 'spoilators' was forming, even more adept at manipulating the institutions of government than the bourgeoisie had been. Moreover, their influence was all the more pervasive, since socialism acted like a new religion and diverted the people's attention from their true interests with the hope of a mystical and totally illusory future paradise.[100] It now appeared to him that the liberals' stance in support of the socialists' rights to equality before the law had 'paved the way for the era of democratic oppresion which is now dawning'. The 'old special juris-dictions had been suppressed' only for 'the same thing in a new form to be instituted: a system of arbitration which always favours the workers'. 'Equal taxation to help the poor' had become 'progressive taxation at the expense of the rich', and the freedom to strike perverted into freedom for the strikers 'to beat up workers who want to continue working, and to burn down factories with impunity'.[101] Disappointment at the dashing of his hopes for a change in people's motivations and the victory of the liberal system turned into bitter recriminations against the socialists who he now believed posed the greatest threat to economic order. As he put it in an article of 1904:

> Before, the restrictive legislation was all to the advantage of the bour-geoisie, and against the people; whoever fought it, therefore, could honestly believe he was working to create a just regime, which would not favour either side with privileges. I do not see how you can demonstrate such a conception to be erroneous a priori, and it seems to me that only subsequent events have the power to give such a demonstration, as they have done. They have shown that we have not stopped even for a moment at a mid-point, where there are no privileges; instead the bourgeois privileges have been abolished only to make way for the popular pri-vileges, so that he who fought all privilege, in reality and contrary to his intention has succeeded only in substituting one kind for another.[102]

Pareto now took the bourgeoisie to task for going soft on the workers, remarking that 'the great error of the present age is believing that men can be governed by pure reasoning, without resort to force.'[103] As a commentary on the practices of Italian governments since unification, this can only be regarded as an extraordinary statement. In truth, it represented an autocritique of his own earlier views. Regrettably, the Italian bourgeoisie were only too ready to listen to his exhortations for them to resort to violence to defend their interests against threats from below.

The *Trattato di sociologia generale*, Pareto's major contribution to soci-ology, originated from these disappointments. It was significantly a work of *political* sociology of a singularly narrow kind. Pareto gave scant regard to the role played by social or economic structures in deter-mining human behaviour – indeed he implicitly denied they had any by drawing his examples willy-nilly from the past, and the ancient past at that, in the interests of 'scientific' detachment, paying no attention to their historical context. Although he claimed that the move to sociology arose from the inadequacies of economics, the image of human beings as self-interested utility maximisers still dominated his thinking. He simply shifted his attention from rational individuals acting in the market place to irrational classes operating through politics. Moreover, economy and society remained separated, despite his statements to the contrary. Crucial in this respect was his explanation of state intervention as the product of purely political forces, not as a result of the dynamics of capitalism itself. Indeed, his sociology might more properly be termed a study of political psychology, for social processes rarely enter into it. Far from remedying the defects of his unsociological economics, he had transferred its assumptions to his new subject. As in his economics, Pareto searched for 'scientific' laws of human acts on the model of the natural sciences. In both the aim was to discover regularities in economic and social life respectively, a process leading to a largely behavioural account of human action on the basis of supposedly 'uniform' character traits. In fact, as we shall see, he took the political practices of contemporary Italy as the norm and erected them into universal laws of human behaviour. This had the effect of blinding him to the possible alternative forms of political organization. The only other model he could contemplate was his ideal economic system – a sanitised apolitical free market society – which was taken as a given and so remained immune from a critical assessment of its practical viability. The result was that he ended up legitimising the very attitudes he sought to condemn and supporting the final transformation of liberal Italy, the fascist seizure of power.

Pareto's aim in the *Trattato* was to give an exhaustive analysis of 'non-logical' human behaviour. He distinguished three types of human action. Purely instinctual behaviour in which no reasoning intervenes; actions 'logically linked to an end, not only in respect to the person performing them, but also for those with more extensive knowledge'; and, most numerous, activities which have the appearance of being logical in the aforementioned sense and are often believed to be so by the agents, but in fact they are not.[104] The second, logical, class of acts was characteristic of economic activity whereby individuals sought to maximise their material interests in as direct a fashion as possible and in ways which were susceptible to correction by logico-empirical reasoning. Whilst the tastes which gave rise to our interests had no assignable rational origin, their pursuit followed reasoned methods. The majority of our acts, however, had only the semblance of reason. This did not mean they were illogical, only that they could not be empirically verified or refuted. Thus 'for Greek mariners, sacrifices to Poseidon and rowing with oars were equally logical means of navigation', but according to Pareto only the second was. The first belonged to the many 'verbal manifestations...which are mere manifestations of instincts, inclinations and so forth'. A chief purpose of the *Trattato* was to 'strip realities of these emotional veils'.[105]

Pareto contended that behind the whole gamut of non-logical acts lay certain constant psychic dispositions, which he termed 'sentiments'. Since only experimental psychology could verify the existence of these sentiments for sure, however, this could only be an hypothesis. In practice, all the sociologist had to work with were the various uniformities to be found at the root of particular types of non-logical theorising, in Pareto's terminology the 'residues' which were left when a false theory had been stripped of its verbal ornamentation. Pareto only assumed that they corresponded to certain mental or physical states. Moreover, not all sentiments were residues – interests and instincts, for example, only became so when they gave rise to spurious justifications or, to employ the Paretian term, 'derivations'.[106] Pareto's book attempted to classify and reduce to a manageable number of categories the various residues and derivations manifested by non-logical arguments, thereby unveiling the illusions dressing up most political ideologies.

Pareto claimed to have discovered some fifty-two residues, which he broke down into six classes. In spite of this diversity, he explained most political conduct in terms of the first two classes of residue. Class I he called the 'instinct of combinations'. The Italian word, *combinazione*, connotes a range of meanings suggesting shrewdness and wit, as well as the usual English sense of the word. According to Pareto, it functioned as both an intellectual and an imaginative attribute, employed equally by the scientist using the logico-empirical method, the poet in his creative fantasy, and the schemer playing on the sentiments of others.[107] Class II was a conservative tendency, the 'persistence of aggregates', which held on to conventional ways of seeing the world and resisted the establishment of new combinations.

In accordance with his equilibrium model of society, Pareto contended that political and economic change reflected alterations in the preponderance of particular sentiments within human beings. These fluctuations took on a cyclical pattern and formed one of the laws, or 'uniformities', of all societies. Pareto associated this cycle with the rise and fall of elites and parallel phases of boom and slump in the economy. Elite rule, another 'natural' law, arose from the inequalities and differences between human beings. No matter what form the government took, be it autocracy or democracy, 'always it is an oligarchy that governs.'[108] The composition of the ruling group was determined by the prevailing balance of Class I and Class II residues within the populace.[109] Government, he maintained, required both qualities: the invention, cunning and persuasiveness of 'foxes', in whom the combining sentiment predominated; and the strength of purpose and willingness to use force of the 'lions', moved more by the 'persistence of aggregates'.[110] History showed a constant circulation between these two types of ruling class. 'Foxes' held power by manipulating the political machine to their advantage and winning the support of the populace by playing on their sentiments with false promises or 'derivations'. But ultimately they would have to appease the opposition with economic and political concessions which undermined their dominance. They would then be replaced by the 'lions', who dropped consensus politics for coercion. However, an absence of imagination would lead their rule to become stultified and bureaucratic, and they in their turn would fall to the 'foxes' who cleverly exploited them for their own ends.[111] The political cycle was closely related to similar changes in the economy. Economic booms were associated with the accession of 'speculators' rich in Class I residues, since such people had an aptitude for money-making. Prosperity in its turn led traditional values to be called into question and helped the rise of 'foxes' within government. However, the ascendency of the speculator class ultimately proved self-defeating. Spoilation and over-consumption based on credit caused the government of foxes to go into debt and the economy to contract due to a scarcity of capital and a consequent lack of productive investment. The need for restraint and saving became apparent, and a *rentier* economic class full of Class II residues came to the fore together with a more conservative government of lions. Eventually, however, the economy would begin to stagnate, the restrictions would become oppressive, and the accumulated savings of this period would allow a business-led recovery to occur and the cycle to resume from the beginning again. No elite could hope to stay in power forever, therefore. It could either change gradually through replacement from below, or be ousted by a revolution. As only a system of open competition ensured that the most suitable individuals always ruled, periodic violent upheavals were to be expected.[112]

After the First World War, Pareto applied his ideas to the Italian situation in a number of pieces later collected together and published under the title *La trasformazione della democrazia* in 1921. In this book, he described Italy as a pluto-democracy on account of the dominance of the speculators and workers. Although the interests of these two classes did not coincide entirely, the fox-like reformist policies of the former had cleverly operated on the residues of the latter to produce a temporary union between them in using the state as a means for exploiting the other social classes.[113] Commenting on the wave of strikes that inundated Italy during the *biennio rosso* of 1919–20, Pareto foresaw that this relationship was coming to an end. The war had exhausted the resources of the plutocratic bourgeoisie, marking the climax of the protectionist-military block. As a result, they had reached the limits of their ability to make concessions to the working class, yet had lost the capacity for forceful action to withstand their demands. The future, he predicted, lay with the socialists in whom the sentiment of lions was stronger.[114] Pareto now refined the argument of the *Trattato* with a further theory linking the form of government to the balance of residues within the populace and hence to the type of rule employed by the elite. Drawing on his Newtonian model of society, he maintained that the cycle of sentiments was to be linked with the operation of 'centripetal' and 'centrifugal' social forces which influenced the nature of political sovereignty within the community. When the 'lions' were in power, the state tended to be highly centralized and traditional hierarchical patterns of authority predominated. The concessions made by 'foxes', in contrast, weakened central power and created a number of rival loci of authority. At first these would be united in their opposition to the government, but eventually anarchy would break out as they began to compete with each other for supremacy. This unrest would bring the return of a widespread desire for the re-establishment of law and order. Pareto opined that contemporary Italy had entered the anarchic phase of the cycle, a condition he likened to the assault on monarchical sovereignty by the feudal barons at the end of the Middle Ages. He associated the new feudalism with the trade unions.[115] Fascism marked the start of a new cycle, with a resurgence of lion-like sentiments and the centifugal forces linked with calls for the restoration of the authority of the state.

Few commentators have been convinced by Pareto's classification of residues and derivations or his law of the cyclical oscillation of sentiments within societies. He professed to have tested his system by an appeal to the 'facts of history'. He argued that he could provide empirical evidence of the presence of the two main classes of residues and then show an event to be produced by them – a claim he illustrated with the equation:

$$q \text{ (event)} = \frac{A \text{ (Class I)}}{B \text{ (Class II)}}$$

However, he then admitted that such a procedure was next to impossible, and that we must infer the presence of A and B from variations of q. Thus, he first described historical events in terms of his theory of residues, for example, Bismarck's victory over the French in 1870 as the result of his combination of cunning and force. He then explained and purportedly verified his thesis by explaining Bismarck's conduct by the existence of the appropriate balance of Class I and Class II residues! By this method Pareto could make any event fit his scheme.[116] The attempt to construct a science of society based on certain constant phenomena was vitiated from the start by the relation between thought and action. Changes in how we define ourselves produce changes in how we act. Since the conceptual scheme governing human behaviour has not been the same throughout human history, no sociological theory can fail to take philosophical and ideological mutations into account and accurately describe past acts. Instead of providing a factual account of, say, the politics of ancient Greece, one of his favourite examples, Pareto redescribed events in a fashion which misconstrued the motives of the principal actors so that they conformed to his schema. Indeed, he went further than this, to impose an image of politics in which anyone who did not seek to serve his or her narrowly defined egotistical interests was either a fool or a charlatan. Little surprise then, that Pareto should have fallen into the role of advocate of the Machiavellian use of force and consent to remain in power. Moreover, as all values were little more than subjective illusions, politics became the art of the practical rather than the desirable. The only way to judge a regime was by its success.

Pareto's theory turned the methods of Italian liberals into the only possible arts of government.[117] By reducing politics to the circulation of elites, Pareto effectively closed the door on other options, such as democracy or socialism. Different types of political organisation, such as constitutional arrangements protecting individual rights, were simply ruses generally adopted by foxish elites to pull the wool over the eyes of the people. At best, they could only weaken the existing ruling class and provide the means for the rise of another, who would abuse the concessions they had earlier fought for as soon as they got into power.[118] Statecraft, according to his theory, consisted solely in the manipulation of sentiments. Rational agreement on common goals was impossible, for values merely reflected subjective preferences. Whilst an engineer could sell a machine by appealing to the logico-empirical reasoning of potential customers, politicians had to gain consent to their policies by wooing the sentiments of their electorate by influencing residues via the appropriate derivations.[119] To call an agreement achieved by trickery and guile consent seems somewhat bizarre. Yet, once the Enlightenment faith in reason characteristic of ethical liberalism, as in Lockean contract theory for example, has been dropped, then there are few other options left for reaching collectively binding compacts. Moreover, when manipulation fails, force becomes as good a means of persuasion as any other.

Pareto's one genuine alternative was the procedural mechanism of the free market. However, this also produces difficulties for the genuine liberal. For Pareto, the advantage of the market arose from its tendency to achieve optimal solutions – that is to respond to the highest ranked preference of the whole community. The difficulties of achieving Paretian optimality in the presence of externalities are well known. However, as Sen has demonstrated, in certain configurations of individual preferences involving two or more alternatives it can also conflict with the very basic liberal principle respecting the right of individual choice in matters of a purely personal nature.[120] As he concludes, the moral to be drawn is that 'the ultimate guarantee for individual liberty may rest not on rules for social choice but on developing individual values that respect each other's personal choices.' Yet this solution was denied to Pareto by virtue of his cynical view of all ethical principles.

Pareto's advocacy of a free market economy involved him in a paradox which further compromised liberal principles. For all people to adopt the free market and accept the redistribution of rights necessary for the system to work optimally, there must be a prior commitment on their part to the type of society it entails. However, this requirement conflicts with the advantage claimed for free markets over centralised allocation – that they function by leaving the actor as the ultimate judge of his or her own preferences and objectives. In fact, the necessary measures would have to be imposed, or a single flash of altruism be assumed, if those currently benefiting from the injustices of society were to give up their privileges.[121] This difficulty provides one explanation for Pareto's later endorsement of fascism. Authoritarian politics seemed to be the only way to free the market from the political spoilation characteristic of a democracy. Had he lived long enough to see Mussolini's economic policy, he would undoubtedly have withdrawn his support.

In fairness to Pareto, one should point out that he never accepted fascist ideology. Whereas Pantaleoni became an ardent nationalist and anti-Semite, Pareto found his friend's enthusiasm somewhat disturbing. He had not dropped his democratic and Dreyfusard opinions in order to adopt others of the opposite tendency.[122] His adherence stemmed from the belief that 'the victory of fascism confirms splendidly the predictions of my *Sociology* and many of my articles. I can therefore rejoice both personally and as a scientist.'[123] Pareto welcomed fascism as marking the revival of the *rentier* class, the 'petit-bourgeoisie' and landowners who had lost most from the despoiling of the pluto-democratic state. As fascist violence spread through the countryside, he praised the movement for providing a salutary backlash to the years of 'red tyranny'.[124] Although initially worried that Mussolini would be Giolitti's pawn, he regarded the March on Rome as a brilliant tactical move. It revealed that the new leader possessed the fox-like cunning to woo the conservative forces to his side in equal measure to his ability to employ leonine strength. He applauded Mussolini's anti-democratic stance, for only in this manner 'could a radical change in Italian politics take place'. Jettisoning his earlier caution, he now hailed Mussolini as 'a statesman of the first rank', who would be a historical figure 'worthy of ancient Rome'. He was his Machiavellian Prince – 'the man the *Sociology* can invoke', who would bring about 'the resurgence of Italy'.[125] Little wonder that Mussolini should repay the compliment by claiming to have acquired his strategy during the brief period he attended Pareto's lectures in Lausanne.

Unfortunately, Pareto had deprived himself of any grounds for believing that Mussolini would act in the liberal direction he desired. Efficacy was the only standard by which he could judge a particular regime. Without defining an objective standard of human happiness, an aim at variance with his liberal belief that all such valuations were subjective, a successful government was merely that which had successfully persuaded or coerced people into believing their rule was better than another. The veracity of this claim was immaterial and in any case impossible to evaluate.[126] Thus, although Pareto might have warned Pantaleoni early on that 'the danger of using force is of slipping into abusing it',[127] this can only be taken as a prudential judgement, not a moral one.

Pareto's ideas can in many respects be compared with the views and policies put forward by New Right thinkers and politicians. They too start off as ethical liberals, praising the entrepreneurial spirit, talking of releasing private enterprise from state interference, etc. Yet, like Pareto, they have been forced to acknowledge that many groups fail to use this new found freedom that productively. People may seek to maximise profits, but not necessarily in ways which benefit the economy and the populace generally. The state is obliged to take an increasingly interventionist role in order to force economic self-interest into socially useful channels and to prevent the formation of cartels, monopolies and the like. Shorn of its ethical dimension, sheer economic liberalism becomes a far less attractive doctrine concerned with the pursuit of material power for its own sake. In this situation, freedom can no longer be expanded in an unproblematic way, simply by loosening the constraints on individual action, without endangering the stability of the social system.

There is a certain circularity in the reasoning behind Pareto's sociology. Disillusionment at the frustration of his liberal ideals led to a cynical view of politics as the preserve of various elites composed of foxes and lions. His sociology then elaborated upon this jaundiced interpretation. Finally, the application of these categories to the study of contemporary politics actually confirmed his thesis, though in a manner he would have repudiated. As a result, he failed to see what, in the previous section, we saw to be the chief defect of Italian liberalism, namely the absence of institutional reform. Nor did he detect explicitly its origins in the social and economic basis of Italy's liberal classes, although this is implicit in his early writings. The very dogmatism with which he held to liberal ideals blinded him to the way economic development itself generated certain types of state interference. The narrowness of his conception of liberty, as simply the absence of intentionally imposed physical restraint, meant that he could not see how certain forms of state activity might expand rather than curtail certain individual freedoms. In particular, he did not countenance the democratic state as a means whereby individuals might gain power over their lives. Nor, for similar reasons, did he acknowledge that market relations can be coercive, since these constraints were treated as 'natural'. He hugely overstated the socialist danger, as their easy defeat demonstrated, and underestimated the resilience of the liberal bourgeoisie and the importance of their connivance in Mussolini's rise and eventual success. In sum, once his liberalism was deprived of its ethical basis he found himself left with nothing but the forces of naked self-interest and with no compelling arguments for why they should ever be transcended. Not surprisingly, Croce, who had to endure twenty-odd years of opposition to fascism, was driven to drop economic liberalism and attempted to reconstruct its ethical foundations.

AN ELEGIAC LIBERAL: BENEDETTO CROCE AND LIBERALISM AS HISTORY

From 1903, when he began to publish his journal *La critica*, until his death in 1952, Croce dominated Italian culture. Although only a fraction of his copious writings was devoted to politics, he saw his scholarship as a civic duty, 'political in the widest sense'.[128] Croce regarded his Philosophy of Spirit as a comprehensive exposition of all the dimensions of our existence. He developed it with the aim of constructing a secular religion capable of providing direction and justification for human activity in the present. Croce attributed the decline of Italian politics into the bureaucratic management of interests to the loss of the ideals of the Risorgimento – a phenomenon he associated with the positivist and materialist doctrines which prevailed at that time.[129] He saw himself as renewing the nineteenth-century project of building a national liberal consciousness.

Because of the wider implications of his philosophy, it could not be isolated from the impact of the dramatic social and political changes of his day. Not only was Croce concerned to retain his cultural supremacy, his understanding of philosophy's role, as an attempt to comprehend and orientate humankind's concrete historical experience, committed him to coming to terms with contemporary events. As a result, Croce's views underwent a number of important transformations during his long career. It is possible to distinguish three rough periods in the development of Croce's philosophy, which are intimately related to his broader political concerns. During the first period, from 1900 to 1906, Croce was the *enfant terrible* of Italian philosophy, in revolt against positivism and praising humanity's infinite creative powers. This phase was succeeded by the containment of his earlier ideas within a system – the conservative historicism of Senator Croce from 1907 to 1924 can be seen as an attempt to quell the expectations he had aroused with his first major philosophical work, the *Aesthetic* of 1902, and his anti-establishment polemics. The final period, from 1925 to 1952, is the most crucial. For in opposing fascism, he came to elaborate a distinctively liberal philosophy and explicitly related his whole cultural project to the revival of the liberal order.

The antinomies of modern Italy that we noted in the first section, between the 'legal' and the 'real' nation, state and civil society, force and consensus, were incorporated into the very structure of Croce's Philosophy of Spirit, in which he sharply distinguished the economic from the ethical aspects of human activity. Running through his whole philosophical enterprise was the desire to bring into harmony the material, passional 'economic' side of human existence with the ideal, cultural and 'ethical' side in a manner which did not deny the autonomy of either, and to heal thereby the cleavages destroying the unity of Italian society. However, this attempted synthesis ultimately failed. Croce alternated between regarding politics as essentially amoral, concerned solely with questions of immediate utility, and the view that political action was orientated by certain ethical ideals. The reason for this ambivalence arose partly from a residual problem within his philosophical system and partly from his attempt to keep abreast of the fluctuations in the Italian political climate.

The precise meaning of spirit (*spirito*) for Croce is hard to grasp. Although the term originated with German idealism, he criticised the Hegelian conception of *Geist* for being an abstract metaphysical principle. Croce, in contrast, treated spirit as coextensive with the entire range of human accomplishments – from art to politics. However, it remains doubtful that he managed to rid it of the teleological properties he identified with Hegel's theory. He divided the activity of spirit into its theoretical and practical dimensions. The former was further subdivided into intuition and logic, the latter into economic and ethical willing, the various parts being so related that the second and third implied the first and second respectively, but not vice versa. These four subdivisions corresponded to the four aspects of spirit – the Beautiful, the True, the Useful and the Good. Croce did not believe that these concepts consisted of eternal ideals by which all human actions and beliefs could be judged, a position he believed inherently at odds with human freedom. On the contrary, they were 'pure concepts' which derived their content from the very activity of human beings. We were moved by the intuition of the moment and, if the stimulus was genuine, elaborated in the process a thought which expressed both Beauty and, by virtue of being an appropriate expression of the demands of spirit at a certain time, Truth as well. Similarly, by performing actions with regard to their apparent utility in given circumstances, people also furthered the unfolding of spirit and contributed both to the Useful and, indirectly, to the Good.

Croce's argument derived from the German neo-Kantians, particularly Windelband and Rickert. Like them, he denied that there were any fixed a priori categories for interpreting the world, as Kant had argued. The content of the forms of consciousness varied according to the needs of individuals in particular periods and places. However, Croce did not wish to avoid what he regarded as the perils of 'transcendence' in order to fall into the equally perilous clutches of relativism. Croce maintained that all human thought and action could be regarded as the manifestation of a single entity, namely spirit, and its development in history. Yet in so arguing he risked committing the very error he accused Hegel

of making, that of seeing all human history as part of a preconceived
metaphysical design. Croce never satisfactorily overcame this dilemma.
The ambivalence of his position can be seen from his varying
interpretations of the Hegelian motto that 'What is rational, is real, and
what is real, is rational',[130] which became the keystone of his mature
historicist doctrine. The German term rendered above as 'real' is *wirklich*
and derives from the German verb to act, *wirken*. By playing on the
double sense of *wirklich*, either as a given reality or as what has been
made actual by action, it is possible to argue either that history *per se* is
rational, or that it becomes rational through its actualisation. Croce
vacillated between the two interpretations. He consistently misquoted
Hegel by reversing the order of this sentence so that the real became
identified with the rational.[131] Although this was often done with the
intention of attacking the German philosopher, Croce himself frequently
adopted the somewhat conservative position of arguing that we must all
trust in the inherent rationality of the historical process. For example,
his riposte to his collaborator Giovanni Gentile's highly subjective form
of idealism, which significantly was called actualism, consisted largely
in the resolution of philosophy into history. However, when Croce
found himself in the position of having to attack the present, as he did
during the fascist era, he tended to adopt the more activist stance.

These vacillations were related to Croce's various shifts, noted above,
between the view that politics belonged primarily to the realm of
the Useful, judgements of good and evil being largely resolved by the
course of history, and the idea that human practical activity was
ethico-political in nature, involving the attempt to realise certain moral
ideals. Although these changes in emphasis can be linked to the internal
dynamics of Croce's philosophy, the main impetus came from outside.
For the ambiguity of his theory on this issue became a matter of some
political concern once Gentile and others began to employ his philosophy to interpret or justify events such as the First World War or the
rise of fascism. Needless to say, his own ideological preferences played
an important part in orientating his response. In general, when he
approved of what was happening he adopted the more passive 'economic' stance, and when he was critical of the dominant political trend he
leaned towards the more active 'ethico-political' view.

Broadly speaking, Croce identified with the liberalism of the Historical Right. The nephew of Silvio Spaventa, in whose house he briefly
lived following his parents' tragic death in an earthquake in 1883, Croce
shared his uncle's belief in the centrality of the rule of law, a sound
administration and the role of men of culture, together with many of his
misgivings concerning democracy. Introduced to Marxism by Antonio
Labriola, a frequent visitor to the Spaventa household, it was in this
period that Croce first formulated his distinction between the economic
and the ethical. He praised Marx for being a political realist in the
Machiavellian tradition, who had recognized that politicians must

concern themselves with the reality of social and political struggle and leave questions of morality alone as irrelevant. Ends and means were two entirely separate questions.[132] However, the distinction worked both ways. Ethical questions, according to Croce, were not to be confused with economic or political ones – a point which led him to attack all utilitarian and hedonistic moral doctrines as a category mistake, a subject he debated with Pareto.[133] Marxism could be similarly cordoned off as a practical rather than a philosophical doctrine. Joining forces with Georges Sorel, he maintained that without moral direction Marxism 'cannot give succour to socialism nor to any other practical endeavour'.[134] To Labriola's dismay, Croce did not follow him into the socialist movement but returned to his scholarly studies. Yet, as Croce observed in reply to his former mentor's taunts, his scholarship was far from apolitical.[135] Croce left his role lay in heading the cultural revival of Italy, bringing back to life the heroic spirit he fondly imagined had characterised the period of the Risorgimento.

The idealist school, to which Croce attached himself, had believed that political unity was impossible without a national cultural identity. As a result, they had striven to create a distinctively Italian intellectual tradition. The chief products of this project had been Francesco De Sanctis's *History of Italian Literature* and Bertrando Spaventa's studies of Italian philosophy. Yet De Sanctis expressed the disappointment of a whole generation when, in closing his magisterial work, he observed how 'at the very moment Italy was united, the intellectual and moral world out of which it was born dissolved.'[136] In setting forth the aims of his new review, *La critica*, Croce gave himself the task of reviving that tradition, appropriately continuing De Sanctis's history with a series of essays on Italian literature written since unification. Aided by Gentile, who had the job of completing Spaventa's studies with a survey of contemporary Italian philosophy, he sought 'to work for the formation of a modern Italian consciousness...which reproduces in new guise that of the Italian Risorgimento'.[137] Croce and Gentile became feared cultural censors, ridiculing the positivist and Catholic philosophies of the age. In their opinion, both doctrines shared the lamentable contemporary tendency of attempting 'to put the world in short pants' by presenting society and moral values as ready made. In their place, they advocated a 'realist idealism', which rejected the notion of the world as either a positively or theologically conceived given, for a view of reality as it was thought, acted upon and created by humanity.[138]

Their campaign fuelled the various attacks on the degeneration of Italian political life, a decline habitually associated with democracy and the flabbiness of the bourgeoisie.[139] As we saw, these criticisms were made by diverse elements of both left and right. Croce's success originated from the manner in which he managed to become associated with them all. Praise for Sorel, whose books he had translated by his own publisher, linked him with the revolutionary syndicalists.[140]

Enthusiasm for the poetry of the youthful Gabriele D'Annunzio brought him the adherence of pseudo-Nietzschean elitists such as Giovanni Papini and Giuseppe Prezzolini.[141] Support for Alfredo Oriani, a relatively unknown writer who turned Italy's abortive colonial ventures into the continuation of Italy's national mission, brought him into touch with the new imperialists.[142] Underlying his affinity with all of these movements was a shared contempt for the beliefs and practices of liberal and social democrats. According to Croce, their ideas exemplified the gross simplifications of what he termed the 'masonic mentality'. Croce associated this form of thought with the 'abstract' rationalism of the Enlightenment. Egalitarian doctrines were particular objects of his scorn, all being identified by a *reductio ad absurdum* with the most extreme forms of social levelling. Natural rights theories were similarly damned for attempting to judge the variety of human capacities and social forms by certain dull uniform criteria. Even tolerance was attacked for failing to take into account the context of particular acts. To condemn the Spanish Inquisition or the persecution of the Jews, for example, was to ignore the significant part they had played in their time in the formation of the modern world. In any case, toleration was ludicrously even-handed, since it was the duty of all critical and principled people to be intolerant of false or inferior points of view. Democracy represented the embodiment of this absurd mentality, for it had the supposed equality of all individuals as its rationale.[143]

In spite of these sentiments, Croce was not entirely happy to find himself in the same company as the reactionary modernists and posturing aesthetes who formed the most vocal members of the growing nationalist movement. Papini's 'mystical pragmatism' and D'Annunzio's bizarre mixture of patriotism, Nietzsche and sado-masochistic sex began to grate. A southern landowner, Croce remained a conservative liberal. Sonnino, who made him a senator in 1906, rather than the nationalist ex-republican Crispi, represented his political camp. From 1907, under the influence of Gentile, he began to emphasise the historicist aspect of his philosophy. He attacked the new literature as 'empty rhetoric' and accused the more extreme voluntarist philosphers of irrationalism, criticisms he was to repeat against futurism.[144] Quoting from his recent translation of Hegel's *Encyclopedia*, he argued that Italy's moral reawakening depended on 'the recognition of the objective necessity and rationality of the world as it exists and is made'.[145] Rather than seeking to create imaginary new worlds, he exhorted his contempories 'to continue to work on the old one, which is always new: to continue with growing self-consciousness and confidence that struggle, which is always spontaneously undertaken and develops out of things themselves'.[146]

Croce portrayed the 'D'Annunzian decadentism' of 'the young' as part of a general yearning for a new religion capable of fulfilling 'the need for orientation within reality and life'.[147] It represented a natural reaction to the mediocrity of Giolittian Italy. Socialism, which Croce regarded as the only secular alternative to his own philosophy, he solemnly proclaimed dead since taking a reformist turn, its ability to galvanize people into action had been fatally dissipated by involvement in the tedium of day-to-day politics and the adoption of the limp commonplaces of the 'massonic mentality'.[148] Given this spiritual void, it was not surprising that extreme opinions should predominate. Panaceas of all kinds were offered by nationalists and others to revital-ise the country. However, a political programme was necessarily a con-tingent matter. Since history was open-ended, we could only respond to problems in a piecemeal fashion. Comprehensive solutions were bogus, reflecting the restricted perspective of particular interests. The shrill tone of contemporary political debate derived from a situation in which various groups tried to force others to accept their partial views. The result had been a general collapse of social unity, signified by the fact that 'the great words that express this unity: King, Country, City, Nation, Church, Humanity have become cold and rhetorical.' Discipline and the ability to act together had collapsed – who, he wondered, could imagine today's artistic poseurs collaborating on building a public monument. Croce believed that the answer lay with a common faith capable of giving people the feeling that they counted for something. If everyone thought that their particular task involved work-ing for something worthwhile, then social harmony would be restored. Croce's historicism aimed to inculcate such opinions by showing how individuals had the obligation to carry out the duties allotted to them by history, secure in the knowledge that they were thereby aiding the development of spirit.[149]

Not surprisingly, Croce rejected the habitual call for the return of real parties in order to renew Italian political life. Parties would only strengthen ideological divisions. Like the programmes they represented, they served a transient purpose. The only permanent party consisted of those persons of culture who alone stood for the national interest.[150] Their duty consisted in mobilizing the allegiance of the people to the nation by getting them to identify with its distinctive moral and political mission. Patriotism, however, should be understood in an 'ethical manner and not in a naturalistic, ethnic, brutal, libidinous, capricious manner, as in the various nationalisms'.[151] Love of country (*patria*) stemmed from a feeling for its traditions and values and was above all the product of a sense of history. The difficulty with this thesis rests in deciding the particular historical project which one's nation is supposed to represent and lighting on the task one has in furthering it. In Croce's writings, an appeal to the patriotic sentiment all too often translated into a reactionary demand for a hierarchical social order in which each person knew their station and kept to it. Like the 'unpolitical' Thomas Mann, whose work he greatly admired, he contrasted politics with 'competence, order and decency' and thought 'parliament and party business [would] sour the whole life of the nation'.[152] Entering the electoral lists for the first and only time, he acted as President of the *Fascio dell'ordine*, a group got together to contest the 'block' of progressive parties in the Neapolitian municipal elections of July 1914. With the 'red week' of the previous month to the fore, Croce spelt out their ideals in the manifesto: they 'preferred order to disorder, serious study to rash chatter, work to disorganized agitations'.[153] Croce never overcame the inherent conservatism of his position, indeed he did not even seek to do so until he came into opposition with the not dissimilar ideas of the fascist regime.

The context and nature of the alteration in Croce's opinions charted above deserves to be spelt out. At the start of the Giolittian era, when reformism seemed to be working and it was fashionable to attack the mediocrity of the regime, Croce had supported the intellectual and moral rejection of the existing system. However, as Giolitti's political management foundered on the economic crisis of 1907–8 and social tensions and hostility increased, Croce backtracked to become the advocate of a return to order and stability. In terms of Croce's philosophical categories, the effect of these refinements of his position was to shift politics from the ethical sphere, as the elaboration of rival ideals, back into the economic realm of the Useful. Croce now argued that everyone must restrict themselves to resolving the problems which arose in the course of their everyday experience, trusting to the 'cunning of reason', that Hegelian version of the Smithean 'invisible hand', to harmonise their projects. The trouble with this argument was that it presupposed the compatibility of individual interests. British and French liberals may have frequently indulged a similar fantasy, but in Italy the reality of conflict could not be shelved so easily. As we saw, Croce had formulated his 'economic' theory of politics during his reading of Marx in the 1890s. Returning to this thesis, Croce now assimilated the Marxian notion of class struggle to an idealist version of the doctrine of natural selection.[154] The new synthesis could only come out of the dialectical clash of opposites. Individuals must therefore engage in the 'perpetual struggle' by which 'Reality makes itself'.[155] In so arguing, he ended up espousing a Machiavellian realism every bit as instrumentalist as Pareto's. For once the evaluation of different ideals had been ruled out, the only measure of who represented the true course of history was success.

Croce's interpretations of the First World War and the rise of fascism amply demonstrated the dangers of his 'economic' theory of politics. Unlike the nationalists, who called for a 'bath of blood' to rejuvenate the Italian people, Croce opposed entry into the war. He had the sense to see it would place a considerable strain upon Italian society. No humanitarian sentiments influenced Croce's position, he remained as opposed to the 'massonic mentality' as ever and felt uneasy at Italy's desertion of the Triple Alliance to join the democratic forces of France and Italy. He gave short shrift to all attempts at moral condemnation of the war, and defended the German armies against accusations of misconduct. Such judgements were out of place. The war should be regarded as 'a fight to which the German people, well aware that life is the right and duty of the strongest, have invited the other peoples, because events will prove who is best disposed or best prepared to give the imprint to the new historical epoch'.[156] The consequence was '…that one must practise *Realpolitik* so well as to succeed at it better than the Germans'.[157] States were economic rather than ethical entities, a mere locus of power through which the individual took part in the 'struggle for existence'. The citizen 'cannot arrogate to himself to change the divine laws of the world' by seeking to judge the rights or wrongs of the conflict, 'but must only defend the cause of the people of which he forms a part, and maintain to the utmost the post to which his particular conditions have assigned him'. Croce's belief that history offered the only valid moral judgement by showing which acts had been appropriate to the real and rational development of spirit came perilously close to suggesting might was right.

This peril became all too real in the course of Croce's analysis of fascism. Croce served in Giolitti's cabinet as Minister of Education from 1920 to 1921, he therefore had first-hand experience of the liberals' inability to control the post-war crisis. In common with most of his colleagues, Croce looked to fascism to remedy their failure to institutionalize political conflict by taking on the socialists in the country.[158] Unlike them, he could offer a theoretical justification for his position. Asked to pronounce on the future of liberalism on the first anniversary of the fascist seizure of power, he declared that his own liberalism was a mere personal preference. He was a liberal in much the same way that he was a Neapolitan, by birth rather than philosophical commitment. In any case, philosophers should not dabble in political questions, which were simply a matter of force and social utility. There could be no philosophical defence of the liberal state, because the form a state should take was not a theoretical issue but a practical one and varied according to the circumstances of the times. Thus, there was no contradiction between his liberal faith and his support for fascism:

> If the liberals have not had the force or the virtue to save Italy from the anarchy in which it was enmeshed, they must lament their condition, recite the *mea culpa*, and meanwhile accept and recognise good from whatever part it comes. This is their duty.[159]

Croce was still supporting Mussolini in the elections of April 1924,[160] when the electoral system was rigged in his favour. Even after the murder of Matteotti, when a good many liberals thought better of their earlier enthusiasm, he declared that a vote of confidence for the fascists was both 'prudent and patriotic'.[161]

Croce only entered the opposition later that year, when fascism went beyond the merely 'economic' role he had assigned to it of ensuring 'the restoration of a more severe liberal regime, in the context of a strong State',[162] and dissolved the liberal parliament altogether in the name of a new kind of fascist ethical state. To make matters worse, fascist intellectuals justified Mussolini's revolution in terms they claimed to have borrowed from Croce's own philosophy. Gentile, who had become the official philosopher of fascism, regarded Croce's continued adherence to liberalism as a sentimental affectation, for 'the entire philosophical education and the constant and most profound inspiration of Croce's thought make him a hardline fascist without a black shirt.'[163] He took up Croce's 'economic-political' thesis in a radical manner in order to argue explicitly that success offered its own moral justification. As he put it in a famous passage:

> Every force is moral force because it always addresses the will, and whatever method of argument is used – from sermon to cudgel – its efficacy cannot be other than that of entreating the inner man and persuading him to consent.[164]

The fascist state could therefore claim to have won the moral consent of the Italian people by gaining their submission through the force of its will.

From a theoretical point of view, Croce had no difficulty rejecting such sophistry as a fair representation of his thought. He had consistently distinguished between theory and action, ethics and politics and denied that the state could claim to be anything other than an economic as opposed to an ethical entity. Practically, however, this distinction was harder to maintain and Croce often seemed to blur it himself in the course of his own political judgements. Little wonder that Croce now felt that the Machiavellian emphasis on force had been somewhat overstressed.[165] Shifting his argument once again, he began to develop his 'ethico-political' theory of history and for the first time began to evolve a philosophical defence of liberalism.

Croce began by ridiculing the fascist doctrine of the 'ethical state' as a '"governmental" conception of morality'. 'Moral life', he observed, 'embraces the men of government and their adversaries, the conservatives and the revolutionaries, and the latter perhaps more than the others, because they open the paths to the future and procure the advancement of humanity.'[166] Liberalism, no longer a political creed or mere personal preference but a philosophical doctrine, built upon this insight by recognising:

> the necessity of giving, as far as possible, free play to the spontaneous and inventive forces of individuals and social groups, because only from these forces can one expect mental, moral and economic progress, and only in their free play does one trace out the road which history must follow.[167]

However, Croce saw no reason to elaborate on the form of state best able to ensure this sort of openness. Such questions remained 'abstract', and he retained his antipathy to the standard foundations of liberal democratic politics in the unhistorical doctrines of natural rights, equality and justice. The state remained a utilitarian entity, different forms having greater or lesser utility according to the needs of the times. The state was an organ of force, only the cultural associations found in civil society could mobilize the consent of the populace.

Rather than identify liberalism with a particular political system, Croce contended that it was a 'metapolitical' doctrine, coextensive with his historicist conception of reality as the progressive development of spirit.[168] In his earlier formulation of this thesis, in the *Teoria e storia della storiografia* (1912–15), Croce had identified the individual with spirit, so that history was seen as 'the work of that truly real individual, which is spirit eternally individualizing itself'. Thus the individual was but the particular act whereby spirit realized itself. In Hegelian manner, he regarded all 'real', successful actions as necessarily 'rational' developments of the Idea. In 'ethico-political' history, in contrast, he gave primacy to the ideals individuals set themselves as makers of history. This revision posed a problem, since it appeared to deny his original contention that the real entities in history were not human beings but their acts, seen as the product of an unknowable demiurge. He found a solution in the Hegelian belief that both points of view were valid ways of describing a single process, 'the Idea' and 'human will' being 'the warp and weft in the fabric of world history' whereby 'the Idea as it expresses itself through the medium of human will or human freedom gives rise to the entire ethical life of nations.'[169] Like Hegel, Croce maintained that human self-consciousness developed dialectically through the clash of ideals, whereby inferior forms of thought broke down under their own internal contradictions and gave rise to superior forms. He identified liberalism with this process on the grounds that liberty was both its goal and the means by which it advanced.[170] The freedom which came with complete self-knowledge could be achieved only by allowing for diversity and the free competition of ideals.

Croce made the liberal ideal, interpreted as the capacity for self-directed action by posing ideals for oneself, rather than being subject to determination by biological or material forces, the motivating force of history. Again following Hegel, he linked freedom, self-consciousness and the creation of new political forms. The elaboration of ever more inclusive ways of thinking widened the possibilities of human action and gave rise to new types of social organization. All history was the history of liberty, even if humankind had only become conscious of this fact during the Renaissance and Reformation and had not made it the unifying principle of society until the flowering of Romanticism in the nineteenth century – the liberal era.[171] The whole of history could be interpreted as a never-ending struggle to realise human freedom through the transformation of the world and the creation of the institutions and artifacts of human society, so that 'those aspects of social life still not permeated by liberty, represent...the material of future problems.'[172]

'The creators of these institutions are the political geniuses and the aristocrats or political classes which give them life and in turn are created and supported by them.'[173] Substituting Gaetano Mosca's 'political class' for Hegel's 'world historical individuals', Croce argued that the active members of any society came from the 'middling rank'.[174] This group could not be identified with the bourgeoisie, since they formed an ethical rather than an economic class. Neither 'rulers' nor 'ruled', they mediated between the two, linking the 'legal' state with the 'real' nation within a single ideological framework. Change occurred not through the circulation of interest groups, as Mosca (like his fellow elitist Pareto) claimed, but as a result of the elaboration of ideals. The intellectuals were therefore the most important component of this class, since their activity formed the customs and manners of the polity. As for the masses:

> One cannot expect that the truths, discovered by thinkers and made the common patrimony of culture, will easily penetrate them, but one must do one's utmost by educating them, to put them in a position, on the one hand, to increase the ruling class with ever fresh forces and new co-operators and elements and, on the other hand, to bring them gradually into harmony with it; and, when and where that does not occur, to treat them with the political shrewdness the occasions demand, so that they do not destroy the social order, that is to say civilisation.[175]

Although Croce never developed his argument more fully, it is possible to infer from it a limited defence of liberal democracy. Like Mill and his compatriot Mosca, he accepted democracy so long as it could be adjusted to ensure that only the best minds ruled. Subject to these restrictions, it provided a useful mechanism for educating the general populace and selecting the most able amongst them. In his history of liberal Italy, Croce even went so far as to interpret Giolitti's employment of *trasformismo* in this light.[176] However, when the masses threatened to use democracy as a tool for 'demagogy' or the 'tyranny of the majority', then undemocratic measures were justified to keep them in their place. As the resort of Italian liberals to fascism had shown, such aristocratic notions were hopelessly anachronistic in an era of mass democracy and deep social division. Croce glossed over the limitations of Giolitti's policies in his account of the period, not mentioning his election rigging and the guaranteed majority provided by his use of patronage to keep the southern deputies in his pocket. As we saw, these practices had the effect of delegitimising the parliamentary arena and encouraged the extra-parliamentary forms of protest Croce attacked. By ignoring this issue, Croce had hidden from view the central problem of Italian liberalism: namely, the inability and unwillingness of the political elite to institutionalize social conflict. Croce's conservative prejudices apart, he opposed on philosophical grounds any attempt to define the nature of the liberal state. Although his theory implied a form of elitist pluralism, the clash of competing aristocracies took place over the whole of history. He saw no need to provide a framework for it to occur at any one moment of time, even fascism would eventually fall under its own internal contradictions.

Croce illustrated his theory concerning the role of the 'political class' in a number of historical writings. The actions of liberal intellectuals during the Risorgimento served him particularly well.[177] For example, they formed the heroes of the concluding chapter of his *History of the Kingdom of Naples*, in which Croce was concerned to show that the south was not destined to backwardness by its social and economic conditions, but had been offered a political alternative by its intellectual and moral leaders.[178] However, Croce was not advocating a species of voluntarism and he remained firmly opposed to all 'utopian' attempts to build an ideal society. The 'ethical' remained conceptually distinct from the 'economic', but practically inseparable from it. The only valid ideals were those grounded in the 'real'. According to Croce, historical knowledge served as a preparation for moral action by yielding an awareness of the dispositions of spirit within us and the world, of the 'ideal' within the 'real'. However, it was 'indeterminate', the responsibility for new action lay with the individual alone. As he summed it up in a famous passage:

> We are products of the past and we live immersed within the past which presses upon us from all sides. How then can we move to a new life, how can we create our new action, without putting ourselves above the past if we are within it and it is us? There is only one way out, that of thought, which does not break the relationship with the past but ideally soars above it and converts it into knowledge.[179]

This argument did not neccesarily commit him to a form of reformism, as Gramsci supposed. Revolutionary action might be appropriate at a particular time and place. Nor, as Croce made clear in a famous debate with the liberal economist Luigi Einaudi, did his 'metapolitical' conception of liberalism place any special importance on the normal liberal political and social institutions of democracy and the free market. In itself, the liberal economic system, no less than the communist, was a utopian ideal which could never be realised in its entirety:

> The principle of liberalism [he wrote] is ethical and absolute, because it coincides with the moral principle itself, the most adequate formulation of which consists in the ever greater elevation of life, and hence in the liberty without which neither life nor activity is conceivable. To both free-market economists and communists liberalism says: I will accept or reject your

single and particular proposals according to whether, in the given conditions of time and place, they promote or depress human creativity and
liberty. In this way these self-same proposals, differently reasoned, are
converted into liberal measures.[180]

For similar reasons, Croce could still maintain that fascism had initially
responded to the need for law and order. Its mistake was to deny that
alternative methods could ever have any validity in the future. This
error bedevilled all ideologies, which conflated contingent economic
measures with the ethical demands of the human spirit. The genuine
liberal response resided in the recognition that human progress called
for different political programmes in different circumstances. Yet surely
we need to know what constitutes human progress in order to choose
those policies most conducive to its realization? Croce provided no
answer to this question, indeed, he maintained that it was unanswer-
able. Croce's very liberalism undermined the pretension to declare upon
the purpose of human history. To do so involved a denial of human
creativity by subordinating individuals to the preconceived plan of
some politician, philosopher or theologian. However, he was not
prepared to go so far as to deny that history had any meaning. Rather,
we must act as if it did have one, prompted by our inner 'vocation' and
trust in the inscrutable rationality of things. This conclusion, though,
landed him back identifying the historically rational with the successful – for on what grounds could he argue otherwise?

Croce's 'metapolitical' conception of liberalism meant that he could
only offer a limited defence of liberal practices. In fact, his studies
revealed the union of liberal beliefs and politics to have been little more
than a temporary historical conjunction of the period 1870–1915. And
once he admitted that his 'religion of liberty' was itself an historical
product, why should it not pass away in time? His *History of Europe in
the Nineteenth Century*, in particular, showed his liberal philosophy to
have been little more than a civilisational creed, which could have little
authority outside the particular society of which it was the expression.
As he admitted in the epilogue to this work:

> Others, with different minds, different concepts, a different quality of
> culture and a different temperament will choose other paths, and if they
> do so in a pure spirit, obeying an interior command, they too will be
> preparing the future well.[181]

Without pronouncing on the course of history, he could offer no
grounds for returning to the ways of the past. Indeed, Croce had great
difficulty in advocating any concrete policy.

Croce's dilemma was brought to the fore in his contribution to the
debates between liberals in the aftermath of the Second World War.
Influenced by the ideas of the 'liberal socialist' thinker Carlo Rosselli,
who had been killed by the fascists in 1937, members of the non-

communist anti-fascist organization the 'Party of Action' attempted to link the liberal concern with liberty with the socialist ideal of justice. Rosselli had agreed with Croce that 'the concrete content of liberalism changes with time; what is fundamental is the spirit, the immortal function, the dynamic and progressive element inherent within it.' However, he accused Croce of isolating his theory from the real forces of history, thereby rendering it totally vacuous. For 'a liberalism which rests entrusted to the virgin and sovereign mind of some philosopher and historian...a liberalism which does not graft itself onto a concrete mass movement, which does not seek to conquer the forces which express – perhaps unconsciously – a liberal function in society, is a pure abstraction.'[182] Like the 'revolutionary liberal' Piero Gobetti, Rosselli contended that 'the most energetic force of the modern world, the workers' movement, is the only one on which one can work for the conquest of a new civilization.'[183] Writing during the 1920s, he had no difficulty in attributing the crisis of Italian liberalism to its failure to incorporate this class. Guido de Ruggiero, another radical liberal of the period, summed up the position well when he argued that the 'crisis of authority' afflicting Italian political life could be 'resolved only by the gradual absorption into the state of those forces which now express themselves outside it... Give to the masses the clear, concrete sensation that the state is not aloof from and opposed to them, and they will obey the state, because they will feel themselves to be obeying their own law.'[184] Rosselli, like De Ruggiero, maintained that a theory of social justice offered the basis for incorporating the working class into Italian democratic institutions, for 'pure spiritual and political liberty is senseless when it is not accompanied and upheld by a relative autonomy and individual economic liberty.' Fearful of a return to the strife of the 1920s, Guido Calogero and the other leaders of the *Azionisti* took up this programme in the 1940s with the hope of building a new liberal democratic political party.[185]

Croce's dissent from the line taken by Calogero and his colleagues illustrated both his personal conservatism and the practical ineffectiveness of his 'metapolitical' liberalism. Croce argued that whilst liberty was an ethical ideal, justice was an economic concept. It was therefore wrong to place them on a par, since the conception of justice appropriate to the realisation of liberty varied according to the historical situation.[186] It would be out of place for the liberals to commit themselves to any particular policy. They should form a 'pre-party' drawn from the 'middling rank' of intellectuals, committed to upholding the 'religion of liberty' and mediating between the other parties.[187] The patriotism of the Risorgimento liberals, by which he meant a call for social unity, was all the programme they needed.[188] Needless to say, this strategy was doomed. Having alienated the reformists from the newly formed Italian Liberal Party (PLI), Croce found himself as the figure-head of an organization which served little purpose other than to rehabilitate numerous ex-fascists. The party was too conservative even for Croce's tastes, and he resigned the Presidency in 1947 after its disastrous showing at the polls. Croce had argued that fascism could be regarded as a mere 'parenthesis' in Italian history.[189] He soon discovered there was no question of the earlier liberal order being restored. The liberals' split deprived them of what chances they had of making any impact on Italian politics, which became dominated more than ever before by the rival religions of communism and Catholicism. The judgement of history had found Crocean liberalism seriously wanting.

Croce's reluctance to endorse any specific political or economic programme cannot be attributed to his personal conservatism alone, although this undoubtedly played a part. At a philosophical level, his absolute historicism deprived him of any basis for supporting one policy rather than another. By stripping the Hegelian dialectic of its ontology, he could no longer posit a foreordained goal of history which would prevent his identity of philosophy and history falling into relativism. All he could offer was a faith that the process was rational. Yet Croce was all too aware of the danger of doing otherwise, and his argument poses a serious problem for modern liberals. Hegel had regarded the fully rational state as providing the final conciliation of all opposing views.[190] The attempt by fascist philosophers, notably Gentile, to realize this ideal had shown just how coercive it could be. However, the failure of the Hegelian project reflects on all analogous attempts to pursue a stable consensus based on reason in which conflicting individual interests and purposes are harmonized. As we have seen, this had frequently been the aim of 'ethical' liberals such as Mill, Green and Durkheim, for whom conflicting ends were always a tractable issue, to be turned into fruitful competition. Croce followed the Hegelian critique of liberal theories of rights and justice whereby such reconciliations were to be achieved. Hegel had shown how none of these positions was self-sustaining, requiring faith in some transcendent principle, such as God or human nature, to support their claims to truth and universality. The liberal defence of pluralism paradoxically requires a grounding in a certain conception of the common good capable of obtaining the rational agreement of all concerned.[191] This poses liberalism with a dilemma. For its attraction as a doctrine arises precisely when the possibility of such a rational appeal to objective standards capable of overriding considerations of personal interest has broken down, and reciprocity has given way to conflict and oppression. As Croce retorted to De Ruggiero, who finally rejected Crocean historicism in favour of a 'return to reason' and the values of the Enlightenment in order to ground liberal commitments,[192] every ideal he chose would turn out in its turn to be partial, hiding the will to power of a particular group behind a metaphysical blanket. The age of transcendental security was over and could only issue in tyranny.[193] Hence Croce's insistence that liberalism was a 'metapolitical' conception, implicit in the dialectic of history itself.

However, whereas Hegel had believed that reason would ultimately work through all these internal contradictions to arrive at 'absolute knowing', Croce maintained that the process of internal critique must be never-ending. The liberal drama unfolded over the whole of history, with no final reconciliation in sight. The ideal remained in permanent contrast to the real, the economic with the ethical. At the practical level, we were confronted with the Paretian world of warring individuals and groups, with only a faith in the rationality of history itself to sustain us. In the end Croce's historicist 'religion of liberty' proved insufficient even for him. Once the social world no longer embodied the values of liberalism, an appeal to the inner life of the community could not provide a basis for a social existence orientated by liberal values. Force offered the only means to prevent the Hobbesian 'war of each against all'. Faced with this prospect, Croce died fearing a resurgence of a new barbarism.

Although Croce's philosophy developed out of the intellectual and political climate of turn-of-the-century Italy, his attempt to unite economic and ethical liberalism anticipated current arguments between liberal political philosophers, examined in chapter 5. These discussions have been characterised by a debate between utilitarian and Kantian 'neutralist' liberals on the one side and their 'communitarian' critics on the other. The former seek to mediate between the perceived conflicts of contemporary societies by appealing to impersonal and impartial rules which any rational person would assent to, independently of his or her interests. The latter argue that such accounts take insufficient notice of the particular attachments which define our sense of identity and make us moral agents in the first place. They maintain that unless the rules put forward by the neutralist liberals form part of the *Sittlichkeit* of ethical life of our community, they will have little grip on our lives. Indeed, the very abstractness of neutralist liberalism threatens to destroy the social ties which define and anchor our capacity for moral action. Like Croce, they contrast a patriotic morality of particularistic attachments and solidarities with the abstract liberal moralities of rational self-interest and of impartial, impersonal principles such as rights and justice. They argue citizens are inducted into morality through an understanding of the history and traditions of the nation of which they are a part. Like Croce, the communitarians adopt a neo-Hegelian historicism shorn of its metaphysical foundations to underpin their thesis. Like Croce's theory, theirs assumes but cannot create a given historical world. Not surprisingly, they face the selfsame dilemmas confronting the Italian philosopher. On the one hand, communitarianism frequently slips into a decidedly conservative and illiberal defence of existing morality. On the other hand, they can criticise, but are powerless to counteract, the collapse of community and the resulting plurality of values and interests within contemporary industrial societies. Unfortunately the neutralist liberal's response to this situation proves equally unconvincing. If Croce's inability to integrate utilitarian and Kantian ethics, force and consent, into a national morality foreshadows the difficulties of contemporary communitarians, his alternating and inconclusive appeals to abstract versions of these two sets of principles reveals the weakness of neutralist liberalism. For neither is likely to prove appealing unless embedded within certain shared practices which make a concern with collective security and an allegiance to just institutions meaningful for individuals. Neutralist liberalism, no less than its communitarian alternative, requires for its coherence an historically liberal political culture which has ceased to exist. Croce's dilemma has become very much our own. The project of 'making liberals', like that of 'making Italians', seems fraught with almost insuperable difficulties in a disenchanted world afflicted by the clash of competing 'economic' interests.

In this chapter, I have traced the breakdown of the ethical liberal tradition. The section on Pareto revealed the practical difficulty of transferring a set of assumptions and practices deriving largely from the British experience onto the very different terrain of Italian politics. Moral values, including those of self-styled liberals, were shown up as mere window-dressing for individual interests. Croce sought to avoid the emotivism of modern moral argument by finding an ethical basis for liberalism in history. However, with the decline of the historical world of liberalism this solution proved completely vacuous. It degenerated into a somewhat empty optimistic hope that out of the messy struggles of the present some good would emerge. The challenge facing liberalism, taken up by Weber in Germany, was to confront the reality of pluralism and the clashes it produces without either falling into a cynical realism or resorting to a contentious moralism to overcome these conflicts.

4

Germany: Liberalism Disenchanted

Much recent work on Max Weber's (1864–1920) political sociology has revolved around the question of whether or not his ideas merely reflect the peculiarities of German liberalism during the Wilhelmine period. His strong espousal of nationalism, in particular, has reinforced the view that his opinions simply mirrored the traditional willingness of German liberals to subordinate domestic social and political reforms to national power interests. With varying degrees of sophistication, Weber has come to be characterized as a typical exemplar of the failings of the German bourgeoisie. Supposedly disabused of their ethical ideals for social progress and individual freedom by their failure to unite the nation without the support of Bismarck's policies of blood and iron, the German middle classes are accused of sacrificing the political goals of liberalism to the pursuit of economic expansion. J. P. Mayer's belief that 'Weber was thoroughly...at home in the realm of German "Realpolitik"' and was the teacher of 'a new Machiavellism of the steel age' represents an extreme version of this view.[1] Wolfgang Mommsen offers a subtler interpretation.[2] He clears Weber of the charge of Bismarckianism,[3] but he regards Weber's nationalist sentiments as filling the vacuum left by his rejection of any ethical basis for liberal values in the rights of individuals. He argues Weber saw democracy and individual freedom as only a means for the promotion of Germany's economic and political ends.[4]

It is one of the strengths of Weber's thought that he elaborated his ideas through reflection on concrete contemporary problems. The German dimension of his political writings is undeniable, therefore. However, it was his belief that the German situation exemplified certain features of modern Western societies generally. Although his understanding of the nature of liberalism elaborated upon a number of characteristic concerns of the German liberal tradition, his ideas were not intended to apply to Germany alone. His theory formed part of a broader analysis of the fate of liberal values in a world characterised by economic competition between industrial states.[5] The aim of this chapter is to bring out the development of this broader thesis within his occasional writings. Such a reading of Weber's articles both requires and produces a more complex understanding of German liberalism than earlier interpreters have often used. This endeavour occupies the first two sections, which discuss the nature of Wilhelmine society and Weber's analysis of it respectively. The next two sections draw out the wider implications of Weber's views by examining in turn his interpretation of modern industrial society and his consequent reformulation of liberal democracy in the light of the contemporary social and moral challenges to it which he had identified. Far from being an exponent of the flawed liberalism of the Germans, I shall suggest that his thought offers a profound critique of the plausibility of liberal values within the modern world and provides a starting point for a much needed rethinking of liberal politics today.

THE GERMAN QUESTION

The Nazi era still casts its shadow over modern German historiography. As a result, post-war discussions of nineteenth- and early twentieth-century German history have tended to centre on the question: 'Why is it that so few in Germany embraced the principle of liberal democracy?'[6] Two related answers have been offered, connected to the character of German society and the German mind respectively. Those who take the first route emphasize the contrast between Imperial Germany's economic dynamism and its social and political backwardness.[7] They argue that the speed and relative tardiness of Germany's unification and industrialization had profound consequences for its political development. They contrast the German experience with the British. In Britain the slower pace of economic transformation brought about a gradual bourgeois revolution within both society and the state, so that the displacement of feudal economic structures went hand in hand with the development of liberal democratic political institutions and social values. Germany, in contrast, circumvented the entrepreneurial stage of capitalism and hence failed to produce the characteristic liberal social infrastructure based on a decentralized market economy involving competition between privately owned medium-sized firms. Instead, the German economy was characterised by large-scale units in the hands of a small group of powerful industrialists closely supported by the state. Comparing the statistics of joint-stock and limited-liability companies in 1910, for example, Ralf Dahrendorf notes that in Germany there were 5,000 such companies with a capital of approximately 16 billion marks, whereas in Britain they numbered about 50,000 with a total capital of 44 billion marks.[8] The German banks similarly merged into giant financial empires at an early stage. The rapid growth of large-scale industrial enterprises was further aided by the prominent role played by the state in fostering German industrialization. This involvement consisted not simply in loans and a favourable trade and foreign policy. The state also owned a large number of industrial concerns, from the railways and canals to some forty coal mines and twelve blast furnaces. Government also interfered in the economic process through the provision of sickness, accident, old-age and invalid insurance. Finally, the state further distorted the nature of German capitalism by actively facilitating the formation of the monopolies and cartels of the big industrialists.

These measures of state intervention are in contrast to the superficially analogous welfare and nationalisation schemes undertaken in Britain at a later date. For the German state remained dominated by the pre-industrial elites, notably the Prussian Junkers. Rather than challenging the landed estate owners, German commercial and industrial capital compromised with them. According to this line of interpretation, the revolution of 1848–9 marked the height of liberal success. Its collapse through the isolation of the German bourgeoisie from the rest of the nation prefigured their subsequent weakness. As the century went on, the very social and economic changes with which they identified most strongly both undermined their hold on the 'middling' strata by causing this group to drift to the right, and produced a growing threat of opposition from an increasingly self-conscious working class on the left. Deprived of a popular base for their reforms, the liberals were thrown into the hands of a state dominated by the old agrarian elites. Unification came about not through a popular movement spearheaded by the bourgeoisie but through the agency of Bismarck's diplomatic and military triumphs. Threatened by forces from below and captivated by Bismarck's success, the German liberals are said to have capitulated to the Prussian state – a decision marked by the formation of the National Liberal Party in 1867. The result was an unholy alliance between the Junker class and the bourgeoisie, in which the economic goals of the latter were traded for the continuing political predominance of the former. The subsequent tragic course of German history, from the entry into the First World War to the rise of Hitler, is attributed to the discrepancy between Germany's industrial economy on the one hand and the feudal and anti-democratic nature of state and society on the other resulting from German liberalism's fateful compromise. Nationalism replaced liberalism as the dominant ideology of the German middle classes, German aggrandisement sealing the 'marriage of iron and rye' uniting heavy industry and the Junker agriculturalists. Thus, a unique combination of social, economic and political factors meant that 'instead of developing it, industrialization in Germany swallowed the liberal principle.'[9]

The statist and nationalist turn of the German bourgeoisie is said to have derived additional support from the peculiarities of the German tradition of liberal thought, the second most widely canvassed answer to the German question.[10] This current of thought, it has been argued, was typified by the simultaneous advocacy of political conservatism and moral and spiritual freedom. This combination is itself attributed to the practical weakness of the liberal bourgeoisie and their prominence within the state bureaucracies of nineteenth-century Germany. Although the roots of the German idea of freedom get traced back to Luther, these intellectual historians believe that 'more than any other single man Immanuel Kant is the representative figure of German liberalism. In him its peculiar problems and its general mode of solution are made manifest.'[11] The various antinomies that characterise Kantian philosophy – the simultaneous separation of ethics and politics, and the basing of politics on an ethical foundation; the advocacy of republicanism and the doctrine of universal consent, and the rejection of democracy or the right to resistance against an unjust monarch; the emphasis on the liberty and equality of all individuals, and the insistence on the necessity of a superior authority and a measure of inequality for social progress – are all taken as instances of the dilemma facing German liberals.[12] For if Kant's defence of liberty, equality and security of property as fundamental rights mirrored 'the economic beliefs of the middle class', his thought also reflected the 'tendency prevailing amongst the [German] middle class to approach political problems in moral and philosophical terms instead of in terms of political power. This tendency revealed the political weakness of the middle classes and their lack of political consciousness.'[13] The resulting association of liberty with an authoritarian state reached its apotheosis in Thomas Mann's defence of the 'unpolitical German' at the end of the First World War.[14] Mann's belief that only the monarchical order 'offers freedom in the intellectual as well as the economic sphere', and his desire for the 'competence, order and decency' provided by a bureaucratic state upholding the rule of law, rather than the loathsome 'politics' of parties and parliament, are said to testify to the German liberals' supineness before authority and their retreat into the private world of family, business and literature. A direct connection is thereby asserted between 'the Germans' failure to achieve, under their own power, a liberal democracy in the western sense' and 'a peculiar German attitude to liberty'.[15]

Both of the above interpretations of German history contain a kernal of truth. What can be disputed, however, is the contention that Germany's path to modernity represented a deviation from the 'normal' Anglo-French route, rather than a variation on a common Western pattern of development. For this school of thought, the peculiarities of Germany's social, political and intellectual development is explained primarily by the persistence of supposedly pre-industrial or semi-feudal relations into an industrial era. Curiously, this thesis is often associated with Weber, particularly those writings examined in the next section.[16]

However, for Weber the weakness of German liberalism resulted as much from the internal dynamics of capitalist development within Wilhelmine Germany, as it did from the contingent survival of outmoded ideological traditions. One peculiarity that Germany's relatively late appearance as an industrial nation state did produce amongst German liberals was a concern with the problem of the very possibility of a liberal politics. In other words, they did not take the social world of liberalism for granted. Many of the supposed contradictions of German liberal thought and action derive from this fact – Kant's a priori definition and defence of liberal principles, and his practical willingness to compromise with tyranny, for example. Yet, that liberalism requires a certain environment which fosters individuality and experiment, whilst being politically impotent where these conditions are absent, is surely a paradox of the doctrine itself rather than of its German variant alone.[17] Weber shared this typical German concern with the preconditions of liberalism, but his disturbingly negative conclusions concerning their presence today must not be taken as instances of his illiberalism. They reflect his realism and pose a challenge all modern liberals must meet.

In order to understand Weber's position, we need to re-examine the relationship between liberalism, capitalism and the state in Imperial Germany. The coincidence of the processes of modernization and unification is often held responsible for the allegedly exceptional nature of Wilhelmine society, the one being carried out by the bourgeoisie, the other by the semi-feudal Junkers. However, the two cannot be separated so easily, for German liberalism was intimately connected within the creation of a national state in the context of the emergence of modern industrial society. As Professor Gellner has argued, in a distinctly Weberian analysis of the nationalist phenomenon,[18] the functioning of a complex and technologically advanced industrial system requires a more homogeneous society than exists in a pre-industrial agrarian economy. Agricultural societies tend to have a low degree of social mobility. They employ local labour, produce for local markets and place a premium on local knowledge of the region. The industrial workforce, in contrast, must be mobile and possess the generic training which enables them to acquire the skills necessary to shift from one job to another. They must also be able to communicate in a standard idiom employing impersonal and context-free terms. Universal literacy and numeracy are particularly important. Taken together, these elements create the need for an all-embracing education system tied to one culture. To this cultural dimension of industrialism can be added the social and economic requirements for a unified transport network, a single currency and system of weights and measures, and regular laws facilitating the ability of formally equal individuals to contract and exchange goods and services with each other in the market. All of these aspects of an industrial order radically transform the relationship between society, culture and the state. Above all they create a need for a degree of cultural and social homogeneity organized under the protection of a single political unit – a condition which nationalism reflects.

The nationalist aspirations of German liberals in the nineteenth century were entirely congruent with this characterisation of nationalism. They saw themselves as the agents of progressive social change, who would bring about a transformation of politics and society through the reconciliation of *Staat* and *Volk*. As the representatives of the most dynamic component of the *Volk*, the *Mittelstand*, they regarded their success to be inscribed in the course of history. The spread of enlightened opinion and economic change would assure their success. They viewed the political unification of Germany as the culmination of a process of social, economic and cultural development of which they were the principal agents and beneficiaries.[19]

As we have seen, the post-war historiography of the period has tended to regard the actual record of German liberalism in achieving its goals as a study in failure. However, a new generation of historians have modified this picture of liberal capitulation in three main respects.[20] First, they have questioned the contention that the persistence of pre-industrial elites in Germany was exceptional. As we saw in chapter 1, antagonism towards 'feudal' ideas and privileges and a fear that wealthy industrialists might fall into the aristocratic habits of the landowners formed constant themes amongst British liberals. Richard Cobden, appositely quoted by David Blackbourn, went so far as to complain that 'feudalism is every day more and more in the ascendent in [British] political and social life…Manufacturers and merchants as a rule seem only to desire riches that they may be enabled to prostrate themselves at the feet of feudalism.'[21] Indeed, a number of historians have regarded the feudalisation of the bourgeoisie as a peculiar feature of British political culture – the result of that nation's failure to experience the beneficial social effects of the French Revolution.[22] In fact, the phenomenon can be found throughout Europe.[23] As Weber commented, 'The *fidei-commissum* of the parvenu is one of the characteristic products of capitalism in an old country with aristocratic traditions and a military monarchy. In the German East, the same thing takes place now which has been going on in England for centuries'.[24] It was natural for new elites to legitimise themselves by aping the manners and symbols of those they sought to replace. Moreover, as Alfred Krupp's scorn for titles and decorations reveals, the capitalist barons were capable of creating a paternalism, snobbery and pomp all of their own. The revisionists argue that a whole series of social institutions provide evidence of a 'silent' bourgeois revolution, which reveal that the middle classes had no need for overt political gains in order to exert their power and influence within German society.

This observation links up to the second aspect of the revisionists' case – their stress on the gains made by the liberals. The 1860s and 1870s witnessed the achievement of many aspects of the liberal programme.

Most importantly, a series of reforms gradually worked towards the establishment of the *Rechtsstaat* advocated by Kantian liberalism[25] – That is, of a legal framework guaranteeing equal civil freedoms for all, most notably in those areas of property ownership, advancement to offices and the expression of opinions so essential for liberal capitalist economic and social relations. Thus, regulations of a particularist, mercantalist and semi-feudal type were abolished and a single internal market created on *laissez-faire* principles. Legal guarantees of personal and civil rights were also passed, establishing equality before the law, removing restrictions on freedom of movement and setting aside class and religious barriers to entry into government service. Important political liberties were also secured, such as press freedom to report parliamentary debates and legal immunity for deputies. Even the powers of the Reichstag were less limited than many historians have made out. It retained powers over federal taxes and in spite of the crucial compromise over military spending, Bismarck failed to get his 'iron budget' securing military expenditure from parliamentary scrutiny altogether. In the unification era at least, the liberals could with some justification regard the new state, to which so many of them belonged as officials, as a co-operator rather than a hindrance in promoting the transformation of German society in the direction they desired. The *Kulturkampf*, for example, far from representing the straightforward acquiescence of German liberalism to the illiberal practices of Bismarck, as many critics have maintained, can best be seen as an instance of the liberal employment of the state to bring a socially and economically 'backward' culture into line with the requirements of a 'progressive' industrial social order. The need to resort to aggressive state action of this kind was indeed a sign of the dearth of liberal support within the country at large, but it involved no compromise of liberal principles and objectives. Rather it reflected the social logic of the unification process, which paradoxically entailed the creation of the very cultural coalescence that in theory it had presupposed. Whatever else the new state involved, it helped bring about the legal and social structures required by a liberal capitalist economy.

This brings us to the third main revision of the older picture of German liberalism: the modification of the thesis that nationalist policies served thereafter to unite agrarian and industrial interests and provided them with a source of popular support which, they hoped, obviated the need for domestic reform. Many historians now believe that this view of Wilhelmine politics is too neat. After the fall of Bismarck, the interests of liberals committed to an industrial society and the conservative grouping around the Junkers and agriculturalists began to diverge. Although both espoused a variety of nationalism, their views of how national power should be pursued and conceived differed radically. The left-liberal industrial group, of which Weber was a leading member, saw the development of an expanionist national economic policy in the progressive terms characteristic of the earlier liberal tradition – namely, as part and parcel of the promotion of a new economic culture capable of absorbing the working class through social and political reform. This aim was quite different from the approach of the conservatives, who looked to aggressive nationalist policies as a means of staving off such reforms entirely. German liberals cannot be regarded as giving up the values of liberalism for those of nationalism. Rather, they regarded liberal values as intimately tied to the creation of a German national culture. If the state offered the necessary protection and promotion of the national ethos, state power for its own sake would ultimately prove sterile and incapable of retaining popular support. Herein lay the difference between liberal nationalism and that of the conservatives. The former sought to promote a national culture intimately tied up with the requirements of a modern industrial society. The latter attempted to substitute for that culture with pure *Realpolitik*. Unfortunately for the liberals, however, it became increasingly rational for the big industrialists such as Krupp or MAN and other members of the *Centralverband Deutscher Industrieller* (CVDI) to adopt paternalistic and authoritarian measures. As the high degree of labour mobility and competition of small-scale capitalism gave way to the more organized and monopolistic large-scale companies typical of advanced capitalism, anti-union and anti-democratic strategies became increasingly feasible and attractive and rendered liberal social and domestic reform redundant. Indirect and direct means of controlling their employees, from company paternalism to the blacklist, made it relatively easy for the larger employers to regulate capital–labour relations at the level of the individual firm and negated the need for more compromising political measures at a national level. The post-war orthodoxy assumed that the natural inclination of the industrialists should have been some accommodation with working-class demands for social and political equality on the Anglo-French model. But for the huge German combines, this was not the case – they had more attractive and less costly alternatives open to them. Although certain industrial interests were damaged by the CVDI policies, those requiring the dismantlement of the protective tariffs in order to gain access to cheaper raw materials for example, the authoritarian tendencies of the big employers coincided with their commercial interests rather than contradicted them. Not surprisingly, the liberal imperialists failed to construct a reformist coalition capable of challenging such powerful economic interests. By 1912 increased concentration and mergers amongst the main industries had combined with the German Social Democratic Party's (SPD) electoral achievement of becoming the largest party in the Reichstag to weaken fatally the anti-monopolist camp.

Although Weber has been associated with the post-war orthodoxy, his diagnosis of the ills of Wilhelmine Germany coincide more with the revisionist version of events. The main difference stems from the perspective from which he wrote, which produces a different evaluative slant to the generally Marxist orientation of the revisionist historians. For Weber was a committed liberal, whose criticism of German society arose from his despair at the gradual erosion of the social environment he perceived to be essential to the maintenance of the liberal ethos. If Germany illustrated this trend particularly vividly, he feared that the tendency towards novel and potentially illiberal forms of capitalism was universal. The dangers to liberalism came not so much from feudal continuities as from the new feudalism generated by capitalism itself.

MAX WEBER AND GERMAN POLITICS: NATIONALISM, IMPERIALISM AND THE LIBERAL STATE

Weber was linked by birth as well as temperament to the German National Liberal tradition. His father sat as a National Liberal in the Prussian House of Deputies and (for a shorter period) in the Reichstag. In the 1880s he even belonged to the party's central committee. His father's political colleague, the historian Hermann Baumgarten, exercised a particularly strong influence on Weber. Baumgarten's 'self-criticism' of liberalism in 1866, with its attack on the political ineptitude of the liberal bourgeoisie compared to Bismarck and the Prussian Junkers, is usually read as one of the prime documents of the liberal capitulation. Yet Baumgarten looked on the absence of the qualities necessary for political leadership amongst the bourgeoisie as a matter of regret rather than as an asset. He later came to attack the Bismarck cult of erstwhile liberals such as Treitschke, and to regard the great statesman's legacy in negative terms. Weber shared these concerns, and the need to develop political skills within the bourgeoisie formed one of the constant themes of his writing.[26] After 1887 Weber broke decisively with the National Liberal orientation of his father. From then on, he sharply distinguished between those nationalist policies which had an educative role in fostering a dynamic liberal culture and a nationalism based on mere Machtpolitik which served to keep the bourgeoisie and workers in a subordinate role.

Weber's writings on nationalism divide roughly into two phases, reflecting different periods of his intellectual development and changing circumstances in Germany's domestic and foreign affairs. The first phase relates primarily to the period 1892–7, during which Weber advocated a policy of liberal imperialism. The second phase, starting around 1905, follows on from the dashing of his hopes for the formation of a new party of bourgeois freedom on the basis of his imperialist proposals. A reappraisal of the economic, social and political consequences of national expansion, coupled with an appreciation of the need for national diversity and competition for the maintenance of liberal values, produced a more sophisticated theory. As a result, Weber came to be much more critical of Germany's official aims during the First World War than the traditional picture of him as a Machiavellian advocate of power politics would lead one to expect. Both phases are discussed in turn below. It will be shown that despite the changing emphasis of Weber's theorization of nationalism between the 1890s and the First World War, a fundamental continuity ran through his writings. This unity followed from what Mommsen has termed his universal-historical standpoint.[27] Weber regarded Western civilization to be undergoing a general process of rationalization and bureacratization which was placing liberal values at risk. Individuality could only be preserved within a pluralist economic and political structure which counteracted those tendencies of the industrial world which moved us towards the dull uniformity of a totally bureaucratized society. Both within and between states this required the maintenance of competition between different groups and individuals for their various ideal and material interests. Rivalry between nation states formed the counterpart to the struggle between classes, entrepreneurs and political parties in the domestic sphere. The contest between world powers, he believed, not only prevented their internal stultification, it hindered the possibility of any one of them becoming hegemonic over the rest. Thus, a plurality of competing states ensured liberal pluralism was preserved within states.

As Wilhelm Hennis has stressed, Weber's thought grew out of the political economy of the German historical school.[28] This movement originated as a reaction to what thinkers such as Adam Muller regarded as the abstract individualism and cosmopolitan approach of Smithean economics. They argued that economic phenomena had to be viewed as an integral part of the ethical and historical development of a nation. By the end of the century writers such as Friedrich List, Wilhelm Roscher and Karl Knies, whose lectures Weber attended, had established this doctrine within the universities. Their approach had a natural attraction for the generation of economists who grew to intellectual maturity under the influence of the liberal ideals for German unification and who were concerned by the threat to social unity posed by the political and social tensions arising from the dynamism of the German economy. They believed that liberalism's traditional *laissez-faire* attitude offered an inadequate response to the class divisions emerging within German society and called for a more positive approach to social and economic policy, a desire which led to the foundation of the influential *Verein für Sozialpolitik*. The 'young historical school', as they came to be called, was a fairly diverse group all the same. Weber, like Lujo Brentano and the majority of the second generation of post-unification social theorists, tended to retain much of the classical liberal distaste for excessive state intervention. As a result, he criticized the more bureaucratic and conservative theories of those older members of the school known as the *Kathedersozialisten*, or 'academic socialists', such as Gustav Schmoller and Adolf Wagner. Weber also distanced himself from the romantic and historicist elements of the school, which regarded the *Volkgeist* as a metaphysical entity providing the actual source of a people's distinct characteristics.[29] However, he was profoundly influenced by its insistence that economics had to be studied in association with the legal, political and cultural history of a nation. His aim was to ensure that the power of the German state rested on a national ethos appropriate to a modernising economy rather than one more suitable for an agrarian and backward-looking society.

This distinction between two kinds of nationalism was at the heart of his famous inaugural lecture at Freiburg in 1895 on 'The National State and Economic Policy'. His address took the form of a political programme rather than a scholarly discourse. Unashamedly declaring his bourgeois liberal allegiances, he sought to map out the possibilities open to his class within contemporary Germany.[30] Weber's discussion started off with an analysis of the rural labour question in eastern Prussia. He had been involved in an examination of this issue on behalf of the *Verein für Socialpolitik* and the *Evangelisch-sozialer Kongress* since the early 1890s.[31] This investigation had centred on the influx of migrant Polish workers into the East Elbian provinces and the exodus of German farm labourers to the West. Briefly, Weber argued that international competition had threatened the economic viability of the Junker estates. In order to survive, the landowners had been forced to adopt new techniques and crops and employ more entrepreneurial methods. As a result, the rural economy had shifted from a patriarchal to a capitalist type of organization. The agricultural worker had undergone a corresponding change in status, from being a contractually bound worker who lived on the estate, to the role of a 'potato-eating' proletarian who entered into service without a contract for varying lengths of time. The old patriarchal relationship between lord and vassal had led the superseded categories of labourers to identify their interests with those of the estate. Many of them lived in tied cottages and shared in the product of the harvest. The casual labourers, in contrast, worked for wages and so became the economic opponents of their employers. Class struggle thereby entered the countryside. Competition also existed amongst the workers themselves, favouring those whose expectations and living standards were lower. In consequence, the more enterprising German labourers were emigrating to the West and being replaced by Polish immigrants who could be hired on a seasonal basis.

Weber regarded aspects of this process as positive. Untied from their traditional bonds to the landlord, German workers had come to value their freedom. However, the inability of smallholdings to compete with the large estates had cut off any avenue for them to gain the economic independence and self-respect they desired as free men. Only Polish peasants satisfied with a subsistence existence found them a going concern. Economic pressures had produced an important cultural transformation in the region, therefore. With their newly acquired 'self-assertiveness' the German agricultural labourers found themselves psychologically more than materially incapable of adjusting to the purely proletarian existence that now confronted them. As a result, the new conditions had favoured the *'lower expectation of living standards*, in part physical, in part mental, which the Slav race either possesses as a gift from nature or has acquired through breeding in the course of its past history'.[32]

Weber drew a number of conclusions from his findings. First, they revealed that political economy did not provide a set of objective criteria by which all economic programmes might be judged. As a science of explanation and analysis economics had a certain neutrality, but as soon as one sought to employ its reasonings for specific purposes it ceased to be value-free. The problems of the production and distribution of commodities were not technical issues alone. Different solutions had implications for the *'quality of the human beings'* affected by them. The belief, promulgated by classical political economy, that economic growth could be seen as an end in itself, increasing human happiness by creating more wealth, ignored the ineradicability of the 'economic struggle for existence'. Weber's argument developed one of the central insights of the German historical school. Traditional liberal economics had maintained that *laissez-faire* would dissolve inter-state conflict by tying different countries together through the market by bonds of mutual advantage. The very title of Smith's famous work, the *Wealth of Nations*, had emphasised the internationalism of this doctrine. The *Nationalökonomie* of the historical school, in contrast, argued that *laissez-faire* had merely shifted the competition between different groups onto a new terrain, and that the tensions which arose from it were no less political than more traditional forms of rivalry. Far from creating domestic and foreign peace, *laissez-faire* manifested itself in class struggle within states and trade wars between them, both of which had profound effects on the social life of a nation, which a government ignored at its peril.[33] Weber noted that economic development intensified rather than eradicated this conflict, with finite resources meaning one group's gain was another's loss. As the East German situation illustrated, the outcome of a purely economic competition might well be to favour inferior types of cultural life. Economic policies, therefore, always had political consequences which no state could disregard. Letting the market decide and government intervention were both forms of regulation arising from political decisions. The merits of different economic strategies had to be weighed in terms of the human values those in power wished to uphold. In Weber's view, 'The economic policy of a German state, and the standard of value adopted by a German economic theorist, can therefore be nothing other than a German policy and a German standard.' For Weber this conclusion meant that economics must be placed at the service of 'the lasting power-political interests of the nation'.[34]

The second, and related, topic addressed by Weber concerned the implications of his study for the position of the Junkers. The manors of the East had been the source not just of the economic but also of the political power of the Junkers. The substitution of capitalist relations for patriarchal ones had undermined their influence over their workers and weakened their position in the wider economy, with agriculture forced into a subordinate economic role to the urban manufacturing centres. For such an economically declining class to remain politically dominant was 'dangerous, and in the long term incompatible with the interests of the nation'. The 'economic nationalist's' sole criterion for judging the leadership qualities of the various classes, Weber opined, was 'their *political maturity*, i.e. their understanding of the lasting economic interests of the nation's *power* and their ability to place these interests above all other considerations if the situation demands'. Whatever their past merits, the Junkers no longer had the capacity to lead in this way. Caught 'in the throes of an economic death-struggle', they would inevitably abuse whatever political power they possessed in a vain attempt to secure their faltering social position. The situation in the East typified this danger. For the Junkers' need for cheap labour had led them to oppose the national interest for a secure frontier and the upholding of German culture by employing Polish immigrants rather than the indigenous workers. Their desire for protective grain tariffs reflected a similar sacrifice of national goals to those of their class. Sadly, the Junkers remained the politically most important group within German society, their dominance of central state institutions giving them 'many paths to influence and power, many ways to the ear of the monarch, which are not available to the ordinary citizen'.[35] Weber traced most of the failings of Germany's foreign and economic policies to their continued sway.

Unfortunately, the bourgeoisie, to whom economic predominance had passed, remained politically immature. They acted as if all their goals had been achieved with the unification of Germany, rather than regarding national unity as the starting point for the promotion of German greatness. This 'unhistorical' mood stemmed from their 'unpolitical past'. Unable to unite the country themselves, they had seen Bismarck's success as proof of their political incompetence and had been content to live in his shadow. Bismarck's 'Caesar-like' qualities had accustomed them to having a strong leader in charge. They lacked any political education in consequence, yearning instead for a 'new Caesar' to fill the breach left by the great statesman and to mediate between the monarch and the masses for them.[36]

German workers manifested a similar disjunction between their increasing economic importance and their lack of political ability. They suffered in particular from the absence of a 'labour aristocracy' which could act as the 'repository of its political sense'. Their *petit-bourgeois* leaders had no conception of Germany's national greatness, and the class as a whole lacked the political training obtained by their British

counterparts through a prolonged organised fight for their own interests. Weber was particularly worried that the development of modern
industrial techniques was deskilling the majority of workers and
producing a mindless mass who would follow the populist dictates of
revolutionary or authoritarian demagogues – a matter which became the
subject of other surveys by the *Verein*.[37] Thus 'an immense labour of
political education' had to be undertaken of both the bourgeoisie and the
workers if they were to undertake their role as guardians of the
'*power*-interests of the nation'.[38]

Weber's affirmation of the national interest as the overriding aim of
German political and economic policy has earned him the undeserved
reputation of advocating mere *Machtpolitik*.[39] However, Weber had
nothing but disdain for that 'type of "satisfied" German for whom it is
was impossible not to support whatever was "presently successful"
with a breast inflated by *Realpolitik*'.[40] In his opinion, the 'power policy'
of contemporary Germany 'was not worthy of the name'.[41] As he noted,
German diplomacy was 'almost exclusively in the hands of noblemen'
and mirrored 'their political sympathies and antipathies'.[42] He associated its shortcomings with the baleful effects of Junker domination,
and his own view of national power politics cannot be understood
apart from his critique of their hegemony of German life. The chief
source of the Junkers' influence was their monopoly of positions in the
army and the bureaucracy. Even when members of other classes were
admitted to these bodies, the prestige attached to the norms and status
of the Junkers meant that they tended to be socialized into the aristocratic mode of behaviour. University fraternities, which had been
extended to the new technical and commercial colleges, and the civilian
officer reserve, all bore the Junker imprint and remained the acknowledged ladders for social and professional advancement. Weber
became an outspoken critic both of the system of *fideicommissum*, which
guaranteed an aristocratic title to the owners of certain estates and a
place in the administration to their sons, and of the Prussian three-class
voting system, which gave the landowners a determining position in the
Prussian House of Deputies out of all proportion to their numbers or
economic importance. He was particularly worried by the tendency of
successful manufacturers and merchants to buy into the aristocracy by
acquiring eastern estates and wished to close off this channel of social
mobility. This feudalization of the German bourgeoisie had been aided
by the conservativism of Lutheranism and the traditionalism of the
German educational system, both of which fostered a unique propensity
for hierarchy amongst the German middle classes. The result had been
an unholy alliance between industrial capitalism and the patriarchal
social values of the landowning classes. Although the bourgeoisie remained largely excluded from political office by the Junkers, their
acquiescence in this arrangement depended in part on the support of
the state for their economic goals – notably protective tariffs on

manufactured goods and a defence of the rights of employers to hire and fire at will. However, Weber believed these measures also testified to the extent the German industrialists had absorbed the Junker ethos. He feared that the bourgeoisie's transformation into a 'second-class aristocracy' was sapping their ability to engage in entrepreneurial activity and would lead to the stagnation of the German economy.

The coalition with the Junkers had also resulted in the adoption of a reactionary social policy and system of industrial relations which divided the bourgeoisie from the working classes. The obstruction of the political progress of this latter group had been one of the most pernicious consequences of the bourgeoisie's fateful choice. Weber believed that Bismarck had deliberately manoeuvred the bourgeoisie into the conservative camp by introducing universal suffrage before they had had a chance to organise themselves politically. Their fear that they would be incapable of withstanding the working classes in a democratic system had naturally grown with time and had strengthened their attachment to the authoritarian practices of the contemporary German state. The isolating of the working classes and their exclusion from the political sphere had in turn only served to radicalize and distance the proletariat from the capitalist system, throwing them into the arms of the Social Democrats. This development increased the worries of the bourgeoisie and moved them ever further in a conservative direction.

Weber sought to break this vicious circle, which only benefited the revolutionaries within the SPD and the Junkers. He advocated a reorientation of German politics centred on a new alliance between bourgeoisie and proletariat. A liberal imperialist policy of economic expansion provided the keystone of his political strategy. His proposals were inspired by the policies of Joseph Chamberlain and what he took to be the British experience.[43] He maintained that the British working class had been won to the state through involvement in its commercial success as a world power. He argued that modern economic developments had produced class divisions which were splitting German *society apart*. The *'social unification* of the nation' depended upon the German bourgeoisie having the political will to create a national culture capable of transcending class interests.[44] They had to break with the Junkers and absorb the working class into a liberal political system founded upon an expanding industrial economy.

The post-war school of German historians regard 'social imperialist' policies as having played a key role in the *Sammlungspolitik*, or 'politics of union', uniting heavy industry and agriculture in an anti-socialist and anti-liberal alliance.[45] According to this formulation, the industrialists obtained a programme of naval expansion providing them with lucrative contracts and a policy of *Weltpolitik* designed to acquire new markets. In exchange, they supported high grain tariffs and the continued social and political dominance of the landed aristocracy. The naval programme supposedly had the additional benefit of offering a political rallying point for the traditional middle classes and the masses which would obviate the need for domestic reform. Increased nationalist sentiments and the higher living standards which would result from foreign conquests were intended to draw the population to the existing regime and compensate them for their lack of power. As the revisionists have pointed out, Weber's writings suggest a flaw in this view of these events. As he commented of Turpitz's Navy Bill: 'Not a policy of so-called *"Sammlung"* with its anti-capitalist slogans, but only a decisive pursuit of the consequences of our powerful bourgeois-industrial development can lend sense for the bourgeois class to the demand for sea-power. For the protection of ground-rents we need no fleet.'[46] Far from serving a reactionary purpose, the Navy Bills were taken up by liberal imperialists seeking to sever the links between the industrialists and the Junker class. For this grouping, the economic, social and political privileges of the agrarian class were simply incompatible with Germany's becoming a world economic power. In the words of one of their number: 'World policy and social policy are the two poles in which one and the same power manifests itself. The national drive abroad must be accompanied by social progress at home.'[47]

Unlike the conservative social imperialists, Weber did not advocate reforms in order to buy off the workers with welfare measures. He criticized even the more progressive proposals for social reform through the state regulation of industry advocated by *Kathedersozialisten* such as Wagner and Schmoller. He regarded all welfare schemes granted from above as paternalistic devices designed to maintain the workers' subordination and dependency, a view confirmed for him by Bismarck's social insurance reforms. He raised similar objections to the proposals of Friedrich Naumann, whose shift from a Christian to a nationalist variety of socialism is generally attributed to Weber's Freiburg address.[48] As he provocatively declared to Naumann's *Evangeler-soziale Kongress* in 1894:

> We do not pursue a social policy in order to create human contentment…
> We wish and can only wish something else: that which is worthy in man,
> self-responsibility, aspiration for humanity's spiritual and moral legacy,
> that is what we wish to preserve and support.[49]

Weber wanted to encourage the workers to organize welfare arrangements for themselves in ways which would facilitate their independence and equality. Following Brentano, he saw trade unions on the British model as the best vehicle for this.[50] Unions would also place the workers in a position to win concessions from corporate capital through their own efforts. Weber insisted that bourgeois fears of the 'red spectre' were unfounded. Not only did he have a low opinion of the Social Democrat leaders, who he reckoned were too concerned to preserve the bureaucratic party organization which gave them their power and livelihood to risk it in revolutionary actions. He believed that once the working class could participate in the capitalist system on equal terms they would readily identify their interests with the continuing prosperity of the nation rather than with the creation of a spurious socialist utopia. A powerful trade union movement offered the mechanism for giving them the political education they sorely lacked, encouraging them to co-operate with bourgeois democracy rather than to seek its overthrow. The voluntary character of unions was of vital importance to him. He rejected Brentano's neo-Corporatist project for the creation of a number of mandatory labour organizations on the grounds that such bodies could not foster the sense of responsibility and comradeship which he regarded as the most significant elements of free union membership. Finally, an ability to engage in effective collective bargaining would provide a spur to the industrialists to increase profits through greater productivity and entrepreneurship instead of via the monopoly practices they currently employed.[51]

Further evidence for the liberal nature of Weber's imperialism is provided by his opposition to the autarchic and purely 'domestic', 'rentier' capitalism advocated by some of the other national economists, such as Karl Oldenburg. He believed this proposal would merely promote 'class struggle *from above*', for such a system generated profits not by 'the opening up of new markets but rather in the suppression of the workforce'. As a result, this policy 'sees its deadly enemy to be the rise of the of the working class and free institutions in the land'. However, since 'the economic struggle for existence' was inescapable, this programme could not be sustained. Weber argued that if the nation was not united by turning this struggle outwards through competition with other states, then it would inevitably be torn apart internally. In this case, only repression would hold the country together, and then not for very long. To avoid this scenario, the bourgeoisie had to liberate itself from the Junker embrace and 'return to the self-conscious cultivation of its own ideals, in the interests of a prosperous social development and the development of the country's political freedom'.[52]

Underlying Weber's reasoning was the theory of Ricardian political economy. According to this theory, there were finite limits to the productive surplus that could be extracted from a given supply of natural resources. At a certain level of productivity, industrial expansion required territorial expansion. Weber believed this stage had been reached. Only a 'naive optimism', he asserted, could fail to see that trade could no longer be extended through peaceful economic competition. The international economy had now reached a point 'where *only power* can decide the share each enjoys in the economic conquest of the earth and the extent of economic opportunity available to its population, especially to its working class'.[53] In Malthusian manner, he attributed the rising levels of unemployment to over-population. Hence, he affirmed that 'the expansion of Germany's power is the only thing that can ensure for [our people] a permanent livelihood at home and the possibility of progressive improvement.'[54] Moreover, a stagnating and ultimately subsistence economy would have an authoritarian character. Entrepreneurial initiative would be replaced by the bureaucratic administration of goods to satisfy basic needs.

For Weber the liberalizing of German domestic politics and a nationalist foreign policy were two sides of the same coin. Mommsen has argued that Weber only advocated the first to the extent that it served the second. Our analysis suggests that in Weber's mind they were simply inextricably interconnected. Germany could either remain a static, feudal and agrarian state or it could join the modern industrial world. The latter was incompatible with the authoritarian structure of Germany's present political institutions. The social forces industrialism unleashed could be domesticated only if they were allowed a political and economic voice. This in turn would create pressure for the expansion of German capitalism. The result, he maintained, would be a reinvigoration of German national culture around the work ethic and the entrepreneurial ideal. If anything, Weber's priorities were the opposite of those ascribed to him by Mommsen, with his advocacy of imperialism merely forming the inevitable consequence of his desire for a liberal political system and a dynamic economy.

Weber suffered a mental breakdown in 1897, which forced him to retire temporarily from active academic and political life. His next important publication was significantly the first part of his essay on Roscher and Knies criticizing the methodological foundations of the historical school. By this time the political climate had changed for the worse. Naumann's National Social Association, an attempt to create a new political movement uniting bourgeoisie and workers around the national-imperial ideal which had been largely influenced by Weber's ideas, had failed. Instead, the German political system became more reactionary with the passing of new laws, such as the infamous 'Prison Bill', restricting union activity and further alienating the proletariat from the bourgeoisie. Turpitz's naval building programme, far from offering a vehicle for liberal imperialism, had served only to antagonise Britain. Once naval spending began to conflict with agarian interests, in the form of calls for increased direct taxes to fund it, it was sacrificed in any case. With Germany more isolated diplomatically than ever before, Weber's concern for Germany's world-power role became increasingly linked to political rather than economic factors.

This shift in his thinking was facilitated by the fact that after 1911 he became both more optimistic about the prospects for continued econonomic growth and more shrewd in his analysis of imperialism. He now recognized that territorial expansion was often carried out simply to enhance the domestic prestige and power of the ruling class. Moreover, it was more likely to be associated with monopoly capitalism than with a capitalist system based on private enterprise and economic competition. The second form of capitalism tended to be orientated to peaceful exchange. Only the first was in a position to exploit the enhanced profits which accrued from the exploitation of captured territories. This 'booty-capitalism' was very different from the entrepreneurial variety Weber had initially associated with imperialist ventures in the 1890s. It arose from the very linking of capitalist interests to an authoritarian state which he had sought to prevent. Protectionist measures, monopolist loans and above all public subsidies to heavy industry through arms contracts all falsely enhanced the profitableness of imperialism compared to the gains to be made through peaceful competition with other firms in a free international market. Although superficially the whole population gained from colonial adventures, they withdrew capital from other uses and only really benefited certain sections of big business. Unfortunately, the proletariat and the *petitbourgeoisie* were easily swayed by emotional influences such as patriotism to ignore their genuine interests in peace. If a victorious war enhanced the cultural prestige of a nation, he conceded that it did not necessarily further the 'development of culture'. It might just as easily provide a spurious esteem for a debased and impoverished regime such as contemporary Germany's. Thus, Weber came to reverse his earlier position. He now linked imperialism with the *'rentier* capitalism' he had feared rather than the liberal industrial economy he continued to champion. Not that he was particularly optimistic about the abatement of imperialist ventures – on the contary, he believed that the universal tendency of capitalism towards increased cartelization meant that they were likely to become more frequent. He also doubted that socialist systems would be any different. Indeed, since he considered that the opportunites for monopolistic practices became more numerous as the public sector expanded, socialist economies could only enhance the material incentives fuelling imperialism.[55]

Weber's rethinking of the political and economic causes and consequences of imperialism drew on the experience of Germany's foreign policy on the eve of the First World War.[56] Weber attributed Germany's general mishandling of foreign affairs to the unaccountable and reactionary nature of its political system. Politicians and bureaucrats had indulged in dangerous sabre rattling that had gradually isolated Germany from the rest of Europe. By hiding behind the disastrous public pronouncements of the Kaiser, such as the Kruger telegramme, the real framers of policy had never been made responsible for their actions before the public. As a result, the national interest had been sacrificed to the limited concerns and ineptitude of the ruling elite, who were anxious for military successes to boost their flagging prestige at home. Only a genuine parliamentary party system could produce the right calibre of leadership and secure a foreign policy capable of responding to the needs of the nation as a whole. Thus, once again, liberal politics and nationalism were intimately connected in Weber's argument. Weber repeated his criticisms even during the war. For example, one of the

German war aims was the creation of a central European trade zone dominated by Germany which would render the country autarchic. Weber bravely spoke out against the annexionist plans put about by the German high command. The proposed annexation of Belgium in particular was 'unbelievable madness'. A war 'whose main result was that *Germany's boot stood on everyone's toes in Europe'* would prove a pyrrhic victory, perpetuating Germany's diplomatic isolation and the hostility of her European neighbours.[57]

Weber regarded Germany's chief war task to consist in the containment of Russian imperialism in the East. When investigating the Russian Revolution of 1905, Weber had been impressed by the works of the Ukranian federalist Dragomanov.[58] He had insisted on the need for the Russian state to concede a large degree of cultural autonomy to individual nations, such as Poland and Lithuania, within the Russian bloc. However, he had also contended that the realities of international power politics were such that relatively small nations could only survive with the protection of a powerful state. He therefore opposed the separatism of extreme nationalists. Weber's view of Germany's role in Eastern Europe elaborated upon Dragomanov's position.[59] Incorporation of Slavic peoples into the Reich would only antagonise fifteen million people and turn them into Germany's mortal enemies. Rather, Germany's historic responsibility as a great power lay in securing their independence from Russian aggrandisement:

> The small nations live around us in the shadow of our power. What would become of the independence of the Scandanavians, the Dutch, the people of Tessin, if Russia, France, England, Italy, did not have to respect our armies? Only the balance of the great powers against one another guarantees the freedom of the small states.[60]

The cultural interest of Germany did not reside solely in upholding German nationality. As a world power, she had a duty to prevent the division of the world between 'Russian bureaucracy' and the 'conventions of Anglo-Saxon society' by ensuring the autonomy of a number of nationalities.[61] Nothing illustrates the alteration in Weber's stance better than his changed attitude towards the Poles. His earliest writings had scarcely acknowledged that they were sufficiently civilized to possess a national culture. By 1908, however, he had become their champion, criticising the anti-Polish language clause of the Association Bill which required the use of German at political meetings. In 1917 a further shift in his views had led him to argue for the establishment of a Polish national state, albeit under the military protection of Germany.[62]

Weber's more analytical treatment of the state-nation relationship in *Economy and Society* reflected these changes in his position. Weber remained committed to the view that the concept of nationality was closely related to state power.[63] National identities resulted from the process of state formation rather than the spontaneous development of ethnic self-definition. Although he recognized nationality was undoubt-edly strengthened by the possession of a common language, ethnic make-up and religion, he did not regard these as either necessary or sufficient features for the existence of national feeling. He observed, for example, that 'German-speaking Alsatians considered themselves...as part of the French "nation"', and that the Swiss and North American nations both included a number of different ethnic, linguistic and religious groups.[64] Race theory, or 'zoological nationalism' as he dis-missively termed it, he regarded as the most dubious explanation of all. Consequently, he maintained that 'if the concept of "nation" can in any way be defined unambiguously, it certainly cannot be stated in terms of empirical qualities common to those who count as members of the nation.' The concept belonged to 'the sphere of values'. If the term had any meaning, then it meant 'above all, that *it is proper* to expect from certain sorts of groups a specific sentiment of solidarity in the face of other groups'.[65] Nationality, according to this definition, consisted of a shared set of beliefs and practices constituting the public culture of a political community. It provided the grounding for our attachment to the state and the mutual obligations uniting members of a particular polity together.

Weber's point was that the defining characteristic of a state, namely its *'monopoly of the legitimate use of physical force* within a given territory',[66] only obtained acceptance from its citizens when they felt bound together for a common purpose. He doubted if economic ties of mutual self-interest would prove sufficient. The contractual bonds of a political society, or *gesellschaft*, were unlikely to arise or have much durability unless they were founded upon the *Gemeinschaftlich* ties arising from nationalism.[67] This became evident particularly in wartime. The First World War, he remarked, had increased the prestige of the state: '"The State, not the Nation" runs the cry.' Yet, as he noted, Austrian officers were seriously hampered by the lack of a common vocabulary with their men and the defeat of the Russian army, 'the largest in the world', testified to the limits of the state to 'compel the *free allegiance of the indi-vidual'*. Only the sense of fellowship generated by a shared national identity commanded the voluntary consent of soldiers to risk their lives for the state in battle.[68]

The state was a means for the realization of other values. The increase of a state's power was only of worth to its members 'as long as it does not seek to transcend this merely auxiliary status'.[69] Contrary to the views of those commentators who regard him as a typical German *Realpolitiker*,[70] Weber believed that 'the mere "power politician", glori-fied amongst us by a passionate cult, may get strong effects, but actually his work leads nowhere and is meaningless.'[71] If the state was vital for the protection and promotion of national culture, he doubted whether even a victorious power could substitute raw military might for the identification between state and citizens resulting from a common

national background.[72] Of course, he recognized that national boundaries do not always coincide with state borders.[73] However, nationalist
movements were largely distinguishable from ethnic groups by being
tied to a desire for some degree of political autonomy. Thus, it was their
political ambitions which turned the Hungarians, Czechs, Greeks and,
some 150 years previously, the Germans into nations.[74] In the case of
both existing and emergent states, nationality offered a basis for citizenship, providing the sense of solidarity on which to build the reciprocal
rights and duties necessary to any political society. It supplied people
with a reason for their membership and concern for the citizens of one
state rather than another.[75] As modern commentators have shown,
nationality of this kind is often manufactured through the invention of
myths of descent and historical traditions.[76] Weber fully appreciated this
fact. For at the heart of his interest in nationality lay an understanding of
the interrelationship between the economic and political structures of a
community and the cultural values and national character of its
members. The two elements had a reciprocal influence upon each other,
with the type of power exercised by the state depending on the nature
of the nation and vice versa, so that 'the structure of a state must be
related exclusively to the actual world- and cultural-political tasks of the
nation.'[77] In the aftermath of the war, Weber's priority was to avoid the
mistakes of the past by ensuring that Germany had a liberal constitution
capable of providing the responsible leadership Germany had so conspicuously lacked under the Kaiser's regime. This goal in turn required
a nationalism which would foster liberal pluralism, not one opposed
to it.

It is hard not to be impressed by the contemporary relevance of
Weber's arguments. Many of the questions he addressed have once
again become pressing issues. The power role of a united Germany as a
buffer between East and West, the demands for national autonomy in
the Baltic, and the question of Germany's eastern border with Poland, to
name only the most obvious ones, have all returned to the top of the
European agenda. As in Weber's theorisation of these problems, the
manner of their resolution involves a choice between liberal and authoritarian options – although which is which is not always obvious.
Weber's own thinking on these subjects offers a predictably ambiguous
legacy. It might be argued that the consequences of his approach were
best reflected in the Cold War rather than in the present situation. Far
from promoting individual liberty and the autonomy of smaller states,
the competition between the superpowers after the Second World War
led to the progressive division of the world into two armed camps. Both
sides sought to squash any attempts at independence within their
respective spheres of influence and frequently used the military arms
race to justify restrictive internal security measures which infringed
important civil liberties. However, this view misrepresents Weber's
position. Part of Weber's case for Germany's world-power role was

to prevent just such a division of the world. The openness of the international system depended on the existence of a number of strong nation states, none of which could dominate the others alone. He hoped this situation would force states to negotiate and compromise with each other. He certainly believed that Germany's future political influence would reside in her ability to strike alliances rather than in displays of military power.

Weber doubted the teleological belief in human moral progress which underlies the Kantian conception of perpetual peace on the basis of universal principles of morality. Human fallibility and an appreciation of the plurality of often incompatible and incommensurable values made human conflict a permanent possibility for Weber. In such circumstances, the subordination of social and political concepts to the level of nation states or even more localized loyalties is ineliminable. Since the tensions between these divergent if equally valuable attachments and ways of life cannot be mediated within the context of a comprehensive ethical theory, the solution must be a political one. The distribution of power rather than abstract theories of justice or rights determines the ability of individuals and groups to pursue their ideals and interests in a disenchanted moral universe.[78] We shall take up this argument in the final section. We must turn now to the origins of that disenchantment.

LIBERALISM AND MODERNITY: CAPITALISM, RATIONALITY, BUREAUCRACY AND SOCIALISM

Wolfang Mommsen has described Weber as a 'liberal in despair' about the likely survival of liberalism within the bureaucratic and rationalized large-scale organizations of the modern world.[79] For it appeared that the very human qualities of individual freedom, entrepreneurship and working in a vocation which he believed had contributed to the rise of capitalism, were being undermined by the subsequent evolution of the capitalist system. Weber traced this dilemma to the double-edged nature of the process of rationalization which he believed characterized the modern social order.[80] Whilst he regarded the ability rationally to frame and pursue a plan of life as the quintessence of liberalism, he looked on the spread of bureaucratic rational techniques of social organization and the consequent regimentation of everyday life with considerable trepidation. The central difficulty of modern times lay in attempting to keep alive the beneficial individual attributes he linked to the first aspect of rationalization in the increasingly hostile environment spawned by its second aspect.

His articles on the Russian Revolution of 1905–6 take us to the heart of this problem.[81] Written soon after his work on *The Protestant Ethic and the Spirit of Capitalism*, these pieces reflected on 'the outlook for bourgeois democracy in Russia' in the absence of the special circumstances which had given rise to it in the West. Weber insisted on the historical specificity of the association between liberal values and capitalism:

> The historical development of modern 'freedom' presupposed a unique and unrepeatable constellation of factors, of which the following are the most important: first overseas expansion...secondly, the characteristic economic and social structure of the 'early capitalist' period in Western Europe; thirdly, the conquest of life through science...finally, certain ideal conceptions which grew out of the concrete historical uniqueness of a particular religious viewpoint, and which, working together with numerous unique political circumstances and the material preconditions mentioned above, combined to fashion the 'ethical' and 'cultural' character of modern man. The question, whether any process of material development, in particular that of present day advanced capitalism, could of itself maintain these unique historical circumstances in being or even create them anew, has only to be asked for the answer to be obvious.[82]

Weber thought that each of the four factors he listed as contributing to the origins of modern freedom were now under threat. The role he attributed to the first, 'overseas expansion', stemmed from the fact that Weber, like Mill and Ricardo before him, believed that natural resources placed a limit on industrial growth which would be felt as soon as the imperialist territorial gains of the Western powers came to an end. The 'exhaustion of the remaining "free" land and "free" markets' would produce a 'slowing-down of technological and economic "progress" and the victory of loan interest over commercial profit'.[83] The result had been the erosion of the social and economic structures of 'early' capitalism, the second factor he had drawn attention to. The small firms run by owner managers, such as Spencer had idealized for example, had been replaced by the huge cartels characteristic of monopoly capitalism. These concerns were orientated towards 'rent' rather than 'profit', with entrepreneurs giving way to professional managers who worked their way up through the corporate structure. This process had been facilitated by the further progress of the third factor, 'the conquest of life by science'. If the human mastery of nature had been liberating at first, the completion of the 'rational organization of outward life' had destroyed 'countless "values"'. He maintained that 'its universal consequence, under the present conditions of "commercial" life, has been to make our outward life-style uniform by means of the "standardisation" of production.' Science, as such, 'no longer creates today the "universal personality"' Weber associated with the liberal agent.[84] The new factories regimented workers along hierarchical lines, reducing them to a mass and sapping their capacity for self-help with paternalistic welfare measures which rendered them 'docile'. In all spheres of life, the drive for efficiency had produced the extension of bureaucratic methods and the consequent driving out of individual initiative: 'American "benevolent feudalism", the German so-called "welfare institutions", the Russian factory system. Everywhere, the *casing of a new serfdom* is ready.'[85]

Not only were the material conditions unpropitious for the rise of liberal democracy, Russia lacked the vital fourth factor. This comprised the intellectual traditions, most particularly ascetic forms of Protestantism such as Calvinism, which Weber reckoned had provided the essence of liberalism as a culture. He disputed the thesis of contemporary Marxists that the development of individualism and democracy could be left to 'the "lawlike" operation of material interests'. They owed their appearance to the fact that ascetic Protestantism had taken advantage of the other three factors in a special manner. Their coming together had been a chance event. 'There was not a shadow of plausibility', he affirmed, 'in the view that the economic development of society, as such, must nurture the growth either of inwardly "free" personalities or of "altruistic" ideals.' On the contrary, 'we "individualists" and supporters of "democratic" institutions are swimming "against the stream" of material developments.' For:

> If we had *only* to take account of 'material' conditions and the collective interests 'created' directly or indirectly by them, then the opinion of every reasonable man would be that all the *economic* weather signs point in the direction of increasing 'unfreedom'. It is utterly ridiculous to suppose that it is an 'inevitable' feature of our economic development under present-day advanced capitalism, as it has now been imported into Russia and as it exists in America, that it should have an elective affinity with 'democracy' or indeed with 'freedom' (in *any* sense of that word), when the only question to be asked is: how are all these things, in general and in the long term, *possible* where it prevails?[86]

Weber saw that 'high' capitalism, as he called it, differed greatly from the early capitalism to be found in Britain in the 1840s. Modern production methods and the organization of capital in large and often state-controlled cartels had driven out the competitive spirit so essential to liberal freedom. In consequence, the Russian liberal democrats could not expect that the introduction of capitalist methods would necessarily result in the growth of liberal institutions, for 'all the forms of development are excluded which in the West put the strong *economic* interests of the possessing classes in the service of the movement for bourgeois liberty.'[87] The upshot was far more likely to be a form of 'socialism', which according to Weber's definition sought to replace the dynamic process of market competition with a system of bureaucratic 'order', and the entrepreneur with state officials whose energies were confined to securing a position within the bureaucratic hierarchy.[88] Moreover, there was a danger that established capitalist societies might become corrupted themselves. This risk was all too apparent in Germany, where the bourgeoisie was politically weak and immature. Here, as the previous section showed, the threat was that industrialists would cease to be entrepreneurial and seek the quiet life of a *rentier* existence offered by state capitalism. Weber's fear was that this development formed but a single and particularly pronounced instance of a universal phenomenon.

Weber regarded the disturbing contemporary evolution of capitalism as a perversion of the original 'spirit' of early capitalist accumulation. In contrast to the mere desire for gain found in almost all cultures, capitalism had been characterised by the rationally calculated pursuit of profit through the exploitation of opportunities for exchange within a regular market. As such, capitalist economic action was quite different from acquisition by force, the use of political influence or irrational speculation. Weber maintained that although the necessary material conditions for the development of capitalism had existed elsewhere, only in the West had they coincided with the ability and disposition of individuals to employ instrumental reasoning in the peaceful pursuit of economic goals.[89] He now believed that, in an almost dialectical manner, this most distinctive feature of Occidental culture – the rationalization of economic behaviour as a calling or vocation (*Beruf*) – appeared to be turning against itself. Weber set out to chart this process in his famous essay, 'The Protestant Ethic'.

Weber argued that the Western bourgeoisie differed from other groups engaged in material accumulation in regarding this activity as of both religious and moral significance. Against utilitarian conceptions of economic behaviour, he affirmed that the capitalist was characterized by a unique combination of a devotion to earning wealth through the rationalisation of economic activity, and the avoidance of the use of this income for personal enjoyment. Thus rational means were linked to a seemingly irrational end.[90] Weber attributed this distinctive 'spirit' of Western capitalism to the ethic of the ascetic Protestant sects. He argued that an 'elective affinity' existed between the Calvinist doctrine of predestination and the capitalist's commitment to work, save and invest as a goal in itself. For this doctrine had the paradoxical effect of inducing individuals to demonstrate that they were graced in the next world by engaging in ascetic activity in this one. Cut off from the assurance of salvation through the sacraments, Calvinists were driven to a relentless striving to show they formed part of the divine order. They achieved this through methodically organizing their lives as if they comprised part of a meaningful plan. In Weber's opinion, it was the resulting notion that efficient performance showed a vocation or calling that gave rise to the peculiar rationalizing behaviour of the modern capitalist: a thesis he illustrated by comparing the moral attitudes of the English Puritan, Richard Baxter, with the capitalist creed expressed in the writings of Benjamin Franklin.

Weber's pathbreaking work in the field of comparative religion was intended to provide this thesis with counterfactual support.[91] He contended that other religions either separated the moral life from the material, or inhibited secular activity with religious proscriptions designed to ease the individual's passage into heaven. The possibility for atonement of sin offered by the Catholic confessional, for example, produced a more erratic approach to life than was characteristic of the Calvinist, since moral lapses could be corrected by priestly intervention. Weber blamed the submissive character of the German bourgeoisie on the preponderance of Lutheran Protestantism, since 'for Luther the concept of the calling remained traditionalistic. His calling is something which man has to accept as a divine ordinance, to which he must adapt himself.'[92] The ascetic Protestant sects, in contrast, ordained the conquest of the world rather than accommodation to it. They alone amongst the great world religions, by denying the usual consolations of religion and forcing the believer to prove him-or herself via success in the here and now, caused capitalist activity to take a central place in social life.

Both contemporary and subsequent historical scholarship has called into question the veracity of Weber's thesis. How, for example, did he explain the rise of capitalism in Catholic countries? Such criticisms rest partly on a misunderstanding stemming from an overly literal reading of Weber's argument. He is best understood as attempting to formulate an 'ideal type' of the early capitalist character, or *Personlichkeit*, which subtly combined normative and descriptive elements of the liberal personality Weber admired. As he made clear to contemporary critics, rather than offering a causal account of the origins of capitalism, his primary concern was to delineate the characteristics of bourgeois individualism, of which the profit motive was a major if not the only aspect. Seen in this light, Weber's picture of the liberal ideal was not so inaccurate, as our discussion of the concept of character in Smiles, Mill and Green in chapter 1 reveals.

Weber did not aim to substitute an intellectualist account of the origins of capitalism for a materialist one.[93] He appreciated that the spread of economic rationality, most particularly the use of book-keeping methods for the rational calculation of profits and losses in terms of money, could not be attributed to the Protestant ethic alone. He identified a variety of material factors, not dissimilar to those enumerated by Marx, that had provided the necessary preconditions for the rise of capitalism. These included: the separation of business from the household; the existence of a large supply of legally 'free' workers, both formally able and materially obliged to sell their labour power; a certain level of technological attainment; the removal of restrictions upon economic exchange in the market, such as the status monopolies on consumption and production of the Indian caste system; and the growth of the modern bureaucratic state, with the regular laws and administrative procedures essential for the co-ordination of a complex economic system.[94] Thus, Weber claimed only that Protestantism had facilitated the exploitation of these circumstances in a distinctively capitalist manner, not that it had caused them. It had merely determined the willingness of individuals to employ a specific type of practical rational conduct. The result had been the relentless extension not only of money-making but also of the ends–means rationality characteristic of capitalist accumulation throughout all aspects of modern Western societies. For the desire to obtain increased profits led to the rationalization of production in the direction of ever greater output and efficiency. Hence, the modern capitalist economy was distinguished from other economic systems by being:

> rationalised on the basis of rigorous calculation, directed with foresight and caution toward the economic success which is sought in sharp contrast to the hand-to-mouth existence of the peasant, and to the privileged traditionalism of the guild craftsman and of the adventurers' capitalism, orientated towards the exploitation of political opportunites and irrational speculation.[95]

Weber's attitude towards contemporary Western civilization was ambivalent to say the least. For whilst he certainly shared the values of the bourgeois classes, he feared the consequences of this remorseless rationalization of human existence which had accompanied their ascendency. Weber made a distinction between two types of rationality: *Wertrationalität*, or value-orientated rationality, and *Zweckrationalität*, or instrumental rationality. The first was geared to the attainment of substantive goals, the second referred to the adoption of formal procedures. Within the modern world, these two forms of practical reasoning had been split assunder. Weber traced two profound consequences to their division. First, he contended that the application of rational scientific criteria to all areas of human knowledge had produced the 'disenchantment of the world' – the realization that no single objective meaning could be ascribed to the nature of things. Whilst it was possible to ascertain by scientific criteria the best means to a given end, they could provide no guide to the choice of ends themselves.[96] As he put it in a famous passage:

> The fate of an epoch which has eaten of the tree of knowledge is that it must know that we cannot learn the *meaning* of the world from the results of its analysis, be it ever so perfect; it must rather be in a position to create this *meaning* itself. It must recognise that general views of life and the universe can never be the products of increasing empirical knowledge, and that the highest ideals, which move us most forcefully, are always formed only in the struggle with other ideals which are just as sacred to others as ours are to us.[97]

Empirical reasoning helped to clarify the consequences of adopting a given value position and to improve one's ability to attain one's chosen goals. However, it could not prove or disprove the ultimate validity of holding a particular position. As a result, no world view could hope to claim universal rational agreement. The 'ultimately possible attitudes toward life are irreconcilable, and hence their struggle can never be brought to a final conclusion.' In a pluralist universe, we alone had the ability to answer the questions 'What shall we do, and how shall we arrange our lives?' and had to decide 'Which of the warring gods should we serve?'[98] The Protestant ethic provided Weber with inspiration as to how we should act in this situation. The 'inner loneliness' of the Calvinist believer, who must meet a destiny decreed for him or her from eternity, matched well the fate of the modern individual living in a secular 'disenchanted' world. For the one God's purposes were inscrutable, for the other He had departed altogether. Neither could attain salvation through good works, they could only provide a sign of their commitment and have faith in the ultimate worth and meaning of their lives.[99] Like the Calvinist believer, we must act as if we had been called, seeking to achieve our self-chosen goals in a responsible manner through the rigorous rationalization of our conduct in accordance with a realistic appreciation of our social circumstances. This stoic figure epitomised Weber's liberalism. Contrary to many of his colleagues in German universities, Weber did not yearn for a return to a largely mythical Hellenic *Sittlichkeit*.[100] Nor did he attempt, like Durkheim or Green, to make liberalism the basis of a new ethical community. In a 'disenchanted world', meaning derived from the personal relations individuals established between their subjective values and their actions. Purpose in life was a matter of individual commitment rather than socialization to certain communal ideals. Although in a certain sense this placed an onerous burden upon us, the ability to give sense to the world through one's own actions was liberating as well. Indeed, Weber associated all that was most worthwhile in human existence, our individuality and creativity in particular, to this capacity for responsible free action.

If at the intellectual level the extension of calculative attitudes and scientific procedures and the consequent subversion of comprehensive belief systems had helped the rise of modern liberal individualism, their practical effects had not always been so happy. Weber was far more uncertain about the benefits of this second consequence of the rationalization of the modern world. For the formal rationalization of social life had increasingly become an end in itself, eroding those very qualities whereby 'the soul chooses the meaning of its own existence' which Weber most valued. What had been a choice for the Calvinist was now an 'iron cage' of bureaucratic rules and regulations:

> The Puritan wanted to work in a calling, we are forced to do so. For when ascetism was carried out of the monastic cells into everyday life, and began to dominate worldly morality, it did its part in building the tremendous cosmos of the modern economic order. This order is now bound to the technical and economic conditions of the machine production which today determine the lives of all the individuals who are born into this

mechanism, not only those directly concerned with economic acquisition, with irresistible force. Perhaps it will so determine them until the last ton of fossilised coal is burnt. In Baxter's view the care for external goods should only lie on the shoulders of the 'saint like a light cloak which can be thrown aside at any moment'. But fate decreed that the cloak should become an iron cage.[101]

The extension of the division of labour had increased the professionalization and specialization of work. The rationalization of individual behaviour no longer rested on a religious but on a mechanical foundation. Weber was deeply disturbed by the consequences for the personality of individuals living in the cage of modernity. Whereas the small-scale, privately owned enterprises of early capitalism had encouraged the capitalist spirit Weber associated with the Protestant ethic, contemporary corporate capitalism fostered a society of egoistic, rational, utility maximisers. The bureaucrats and self-centred materialists produced by modern social conditions were 'specialists without spirit, sensualists without heart'.

Weber did not by any means regard the formal rationality of bureaucratic administration entirely negatively.[102] Bureaucratic methods offered 'the most rational known means of exercising authority over human beings,...superior to any other form in precision, in stability, in the stringency of its discipline, and in its reliability' and as such were 'completely indispensable'.[103] Their development reflected the quantitative and qualitative growth of administrative tasks within modern societies. Political and economic organizations were not only bigger, their affairs had become more complicated and technical as well. Inter-state rivalry and the resulting need for secure public finances to equip and maintain a standing army had provided the initial impetus for the rise of bureaucratic management. Today the chief demand for efficient administration came from the capitalist market economy. Weber distinguished the modern 'legal-rational' type of bureaucracy from the 'irrational' patriarchal and patrimonial forms of authority found in traditional societies. The latter were governed by custom and the personal whim of the ruler and staffed by unpaid notables, personal retainers, elected officials, etc. Weber believed they lacked the expertise, consistency and purposiveness to co-ordinate successfully a complex, technically sophisticated, large-scale modern economy involving extensive functional differentiation. They operated in too haphazard a manner. 'Legal-rational' bureaucracies, in contrast, offered the stability and order industrial social systems required. By legality, Weber had in mind a set of universal and impersonal rules which prevented arbitrary decision-making.[104] Rationality in this instance meant instrumental means–end reasoning. Combining the two within a set of clearly formulated procedures enacted by professional administrators enabled specialised knowledge to be directed towards the achievement of specific goals in a coherent and efficient manner. This framework greatly facilitated the distinctively capitalist rationalization of human action on the basis of calculations of profit and loss. Thus, 'precision, speed, unambiguity, knowledge of files, continuity, discretion, unity, strict subordination, reduction of friction and of material and costs' were all 'raised to the optimum point in the strictly bureaucratic administration'. From these points of view, Weber held 'the fully developed bureaucratic apparatus compares with other organizations exactly as does the machine with the non-mechanical modes of production.'[105]

Weber has been criticized for overestimating the merits of bureaucratic methods. We shall see below that he was far from unaware of their negative side. He granted that bureaucracy can create 'definite impediments for the discharge of business in a manner best adapted to the individuality of each case'.[106] Its inflexibility often rendered it inefficient and cumbersome in particular instances which diverged from the norm. For this reason, he acknowledged the need for capable individuals to direct and programme the bureaucratic machine – an issue we shall discuss later. However, in general it was impossible to treat all decisions as *sui generis*. The immense problems of co-ordination in the contemporary world made routine administrative work 'inescapable'.

Weber's doubts about the increased diffusion of bureaucracy arose primarily from his worries concerning the cultural effects of a completely bureaucratized society. Germany, which had 'shown great virtuosity in the development of the rational...bureaucratic organization over the whole field of human associations, from the factory to the army and the state', revealed these dangers particularly vividly.[107] The role of bureaucracy within the German state had formed a major topic of discussion within the *Verein für Sozialpolitik* and the debate offers crucial insights into why Weber's thinking took the direction it did.[108] The 'conservative' wing of the association, represented by Adolph Wagner and the historian of Prussian administration Gustav Schmoller, viewed the state bureaucracy as an independent force above class and party. Their faith in the moral probity and intellectual superiority of German officialdom led them to see the state regulation of industry as the best solution to the 'social problem'. They regarded democracy as inevitably leading to the politicization and subversion of a hitherto neutral and efficient body. Weber, in common with his brother Alfred, Lujo Brentano and other members of the 'liberal' wing, dissented from this view. The debate came to a head at the 1909 meeting of the *Verein*, when Alfred Weber made an impassioned speech against Wagner's idealization of the German bureaucrat's virtues in contrast with the supposed corruption of private capitalism in the USA. Like Max Weber, Alfred granted the undoubted technical efficiency of bureaucracy. However, he questioned both its political independence and the moral and intellectual advantages its more enthusiastic supporters claimed it had bestowed on German life. On the contrary, he observed that as a result of its pernicious pervasiveness 'our entire society is being rendered narrow-minded and philistine.' It threatened 'to stifle any independent stirrings' by turning everyone into a 'loyal and pensionable' time server. As for being above class interests, this was a 'fundamental error', since 'it finds its social basis in those power groups which control the organization of society.'[109]

Max Weber essentially agreed with his brother's diagnosis, which indeed he had inspired.[110] He remained convinced that the progress of bureaucracy was as 'irresistible' as the mechanization of industry, and its technical superiority as 'unshaken' as that 'of the machine over the handworker'. In this respect, there was little difference between the state or a private organization, since both were driven by the same social and economic forces towards ever greater bureaucratization. However, the gains in technical efficiency were more than off-set by the psychological consequences of the introduction of formal methods of rational calculation (*Rechenhaftigkeit*) throughout society. The need for an established command structure and decision-making procedure turned each individual into a 'little cog in the machine' whose 'one preoccupation is whether he can become a bigger cog'. Bureaucrats typically sought status and security. Just as workers had had their control of the means of production expropriated from them, so office clerks and administrators had been separated from ownership of the means of administration. Sinecures, nepotism and the like had all been abolished. Appointment on the basis of competitive examinations, tenure, payment by salary, fixed career lines and a rigid hierarchical structure were all designed to ensure the characteristics of independence, impersonality, procedural rectitude and devotion to duty which were the hallmarks of the ideal modern official. If such features had their positive side for the smooth running of the bureaucratic machine, they produced a limited type of person. For Weber, bureaucrats were 'men who need "order" and nothing but order' and who were 'so totally adjusted to it that they become nervous and cowardly if this order falters, and helpless if they are torn away from it'. He could imagine nothing more 'horrible' than that 'the world could one day be filled with nothing but those little cogs, little men clinging to little jobs and striving towards bigger ones' 'passion for bureaucracy' of his colleagues drove him 'to despair':

> that the world should know nothing but these men of order – this is the development in which we are caught up, and the central question is not how we may still further promote and accelerate it, but what we can oppose to this machinery, in order to keep a portion of humanity free from this parcelling out of the soul, from this total dominance of the bureaucratic ideal of life.[111]

Weber regarded the routinization of labour in office and factory as one of the most soul-destroying features of modern life, although typically the resulting sapping of individual initiative preoccupied him more than its alienating effects. In keeping with his elitist perspective, he was particularly perturbed that it would prevent the emergence of the enterprising captains of industry and far-sighted political leaders on whom he believed a society's dynamism depended. For the attributes of the good administrator, notably procedural correctness, tended to stifle the capacity for original thought and innovative action needed to give a company or a state a sense of direction or to respond to exceptional circumstances. These drawbacks constituted positive virtues so long as bureaucracies had appropriate guidance from individuals possessing these qualities. Damage only occurred when bureaucrats sought to deny their subordinate function and actually run the economy and the state. It was Wagner and Schmoller's advocacy of this very move which had particularly concerned Weber. For it lent legitimacy to what he already perceived to be a disturbing trend within bureaucratic systems in any case.

Weber's analysis in *Economy and Society* elaborated upon this peril by pinpointing the sources of status and power open to bureaucrats. He conceded that bureaucracy had had some beneficial social effects, replacing privileges based on birth with a meritocracy based on learning. To this extent, it was promoted by the democratic desire to remove distinctions of rank from society. But this general levelling tendency was itself counteracted by the fact that bureaucrats increasingly formed a status group of their own deriving from their monopoly of specialized knowledge. A new hierarchy of education and expertise was replacing those of property, economic function and inherited standing found in traditional societies. University qualifications and professional certificates were taking over from 'proof of ancestry' as titles to offices. The need for specialists who had received an approved training rendered bureaucracies largely self-selecting, since only fellow professionals could legitimately claim to vet potential employees. 'To this extent', he wrote, 'bureaucracy, both in business offices and in public service, promotes the rise of a specific status group, just as did the quite different office holders of the past.' The enhanced social prestige of officials encouraged the spread of bureaucratic values throughout society as a whole, since all talented individuals aspired to join their ranks. Their independence was also undermined by virtue of the fact that they came to form a special group with an interest in preserving their privileged position – usually by restricting access to education. Such measures frequently threw them into the arms of the older propertied elites, who possessed the wealth if not the talent for prolonged periods of learning. Weber cited the dominance of duelling fraternities in the universities as evidence of the unhealthy combination of feudal and educational elites in Germany, and noted how public schools, London clubs and Oxbridge performed the same service in Britain.[112]

Their monopoly of knowledge gave bureaucracies power as well. Weber distinguished two types of bureaucratic knowledge. The first kind consisted of 'technical know-how in the widest sense of the word, acquired through specialized training'. This expertise gave the bureaucrats an obvious advantage over a lay audience. The second, and far more insidious sort of knowledge, originated from the *'official information*, which is only available through administrative channels' which the bureaucracy strove to maintain secret.[113] This power hindered considerably the ability even of other specialists to control the bureaucratic machine, since 'only he who can get access to these facts independently of the officials' good will can effectively supervise the administration.' Only capitalist entrepreneurs, he believed, were generally superior to bureaucrats in knowledge and techniques – and even they solely within their own sphere of interest. Democratic accountability was particularly hard to ensure. In Germany, for example, the Prussian bureaucracy had consistently supported Junker dominance against all attempts at electoral reform through their hold on census data. The statistical bureau, in particular, so mastered the 'science' of voting arithmetic as to ensure that 'not too many of the centre party and left liberals, and for God's sake no social democrats, should find their way into the Prussian Parliament'.[114] Yet Weber did not believe the bureaucrats could be dislodged from their superior positions. The proposal of radical democrats that official appointments be rotated amongst all citizens or be subject to periodic recall by them he regarded as completely impractical.[115] The need for expertise and consistency rendered a professional bureaucracy irreplaceable. In both the USA and revolutionary Russia, elected officials were gradually giving way to a permanent trained staff.

All modern government, therefore, was in a general sense run by bureaucrats, who oversaw the everyday execution of policies. Weber's fear was that they might exploit the power inherent to this situation and attempt actually to rule. He regarded the prospect of 'bureaucratic rule' (*Beamtenherrschaft*) with dismay. Technical knowledge and procedures were necessary but not sufficient mechanisms for governing complex societies. Improvisation, vision and good judgement were also essential to prevent them from malfunctioning in a variety of ways and becoming hidebound by red tape. Weber's early studies of the Ancient World had accounted for the decline of Rome and Egypt by the stultifying effects of bureaucracy as it 'destroyed every economic as well as political initiative of its subjects' and inhibited their capacity to adapt to changing circumstances. Contemporary Germany offered, he believed, an even more pressing example of the dangers of bureaucratic rule. He blamed both Germany's disastrous foreign policy and the poor conduct of the war it had precipitated on bureaucrats usurping the role of politicians, for example. Administrators lacked the training in making quick and flexible decisions so necessary for successful diplomacy and in wartime.[116] To escape the bureaucratic sclerosis and servility that had afflicted the great civilizations of antiquity constituted the most urgent problem confronting the present age. Indeed, the technical perfection of modern bureaucracies made the danger even greater than it had been in the past.

Weber's fear of a totally bureaucratized world lay behind his criticism of socialism and his preference for capitalism. Weber disputed the Marxist version of the imminent collapse of capitalism. The logic of the falling rate of profit and the prospect of recurrent crises of production had been disproved by events. Capitalist enterprises had evinced a remarkable capacity for technical innovation, diversification and self-regulation through the organization of cartels and the like. Far from dropping, production had dramatically risen and living standards had steadily improved since the early nineteenth century. As a result of these developments, the social preconditions for revolution had also been undermined. Following Eduard Bernstein, he saw the increase in white-collar workers as falsifying Marx's contention that capitalist society would become polarised between the bourgeoisie and an ever larger and impoverished proletarian mass. In Weber's opinion, Marx had overlooked the genuine flaw in capitalism, namely its tendency to become ever more bureaucratic as a result of the formal rationalization of production and exchange. This trend reached its culmination in socialism rather than being abolished by it.[117]

Marx regarded the separation of the worker from ownership of the means of production as distinctive of a capitalist system based on private property. Under socialism all property would be held in common, thereby giving workers control over their own labour. Weber rejected this hypothesis. He argued that the separation of the worker from the tools of his or her trade arose for purely technical reasons linked to the extension of the division of labour, the nature of modern machinery, the growth of an international market requiring new communications networks, etc. Factories, mines, furnaces and railways, for example, could 'never be the property of an individual or of several individuals in the sense in which the materials of a mediaeval craft were the property of one guild-master or of a local trade association or guild'.[118] For this reason, Weber dismissed as unrealistic syndicalist and soviet-style schemes for a workers' democracy based on factory councils which aimed to replace management and the state by enabling society to regulate itself.[119]

Marx's argument confused ownership with control. For the elimination of private property still left the problem of how the economy was to be co-ordinated. We have already noted that Weber thought that only a professional bureaucracy could manage an industrialised society. However, this fact meant that the problem of domination could not be transcended. Weber generalized the Marxist notion concerning the separation of the worker beyond the field of production to bureaucratic organizations. Wage workers, administrative and technical employees, civil servants, university professors, and soldiers were all 'separated' from the material means of production, administration, academic research, and destruction respectively, which were owned by either private entrepreneurs or the state. In either case, all employees were in the power of the managers, administrators or officers in charge of the bureaucratic apparatus. The inevitable centralization of bureaucracies, combined with their necessarily hierarchical structure, resulted in the lower echelons becoming subordinated to those higher up. Moreover, the rule-governed nature of bureaucratic decision-making bound bureaucrat and client alike, acting as an impersonal force restricting their freedom of action. In consequence, the 'alienation' of workers and officials was an unavoidable aspect of living in the modern world.[120]

Of course, many socialists accepted that socialism would require a state bureaucracy to run the economy, especially in the short run. Weber also took issue with them, denying that a planned economy could either eliminate the capitalist 'anarchy of production' and secure genuine human needs or bring an end to exploitation. A capitalist market economy, for all its faults, proved both more efficient and freer than socialist planning. Weber thought that a socialist economy would operate with labour credits and payment in kind rather than money.[121] This arrangement assumed the existence of an objective standard for the just allocation of burdens and benefits and the distribution of resources within society, an assumption contradicted by Weber's value pluralism. He also believed that the profit motive would be required to provide the people with adequate incentives to improve their performance, although he accepted that amongst individuals strongly committed to socialist ideals this might not be so. Nevertheless, it remained the case that only a market system responding through the price mechanism to the forces of supply and demand could direct production and set a fair rate of exchange between incommensurable goods and services in a calculable manner. Moreover, it had been this ability that accounted for the formal rationalization and high productivity of Western capitalism. The competition for profit between economic rivals had formed an important precondition of this development. A planned economy had no comparable means for adjudicating between the comparative importance of satisfying different wants. This problem could only be resolved 'by adherence to tradition or by an arbitrary dictatorial regulation which, on whatever basis, lays down the pattern of consumption *and* enforces obedience'.[122] The same difficulty arose when attempting to measure the relative contribution made by different factors of production. Only calculations of profitability on the basis of money allowed the provision for mass demand by mass production characteristic of a developed economy.

This last point brings us to Weber's primary objection to a planned economy – namely, that 'increasing public ownership in the economic sphere today unavoidably means increasing bureaucratization.'[123] The advocates of a state-run economy had overlooked the fact that it would enhance the power and status of officials. The oppression resulting from differential access to private property would be replaced by that stemming from differential access to the organs of bureaucratic control. For Weber, the 'free struggle for economic existence' promoted not only efficiency but individuality and freedom as well. Individuality arose from the competition of entrepreneurs in the market place. The economic 'struggle of man against man' encouraged, in Darwinian fashion, the emergence of a superior and more dynamic personality than the bureaucratic lover of order. 'The *Communist Manifesto*', he wrote, 'emphasised the *economically...revolutionary* character of the work of the capitalist entrepreneurs with good reason. No trade union, much less a state-socialist official, can perform this role for us in their place.'[124] Bureaucrats lacked the will and the training to take risks or exercise personal judgement. Yet only such qualities produced innovation or could cope with unexpected crises. A planned economy would, Weber maintained, soon stagnate and collapse because 'the abolition of private capitalism would simply mean that also the *top management* of the nationalized or socialized enterprises would become bureaucratic.'[125]

This situation would also reduce freedom. For the existence of private industry resulted in the presence of a counter-bureaucracy to that of the state, offering an alternative source of knowledge and power. State and industry could check the power of the other as a result. If private capitalism were eliminated:

> State bureaucracy would rule alone...The private and public bureaucracies, which now work next to, and potentially against, each other and hence check one another to a degree, would be merged into a single hierarchy.[126]

As the employment conditions of the state-owned mines in Prussia revealed, the worker was much less free in such circumstances 'since there is no appeal to an agency which as a matter of principle would be interested in limiting the employer's power, such as there is in the case of a private enterprise'.[127] As the sole employer, the state would have an interest in keeping wages down and workers submissive and there would be no balancing force to make it act otherwise. In a capitalist system, in contrast, there existed a constant tension between trade unions, different employers and the state, which gave workers a degree of bargaining power. The future proferred by state socialists paralleled that of the right-wingers in the *Verein*, therefore, in holding out the horrendous prospect of a society in which a technically superior administration constituted the only body ordering our affairs. Such a 'shell of bondage' would render us 'as powerless as the fellahs of ancient Egypt', whose unhappy fate it had been to live in the first bureaucratic autocracy.

Although Weber idealized capitalist relations to a certain extent, Marcuse was wrong to accuse him of confusing its 'formal rationality' with its 'rationality' as such.[128] Weber fully appreciated that from a substantive point of view capitalism often appeared irrational. He accepted, for example, that it responded to the effective demand of the wealthy rather than the needs of the poor. Above all, he realized that in encouraging the ever greater formal rationalization of production, capitalism was undermining itself by building up the 'iron cage' of a bureaucratic world. Weber was well aware of the contrast between 'early' and 'high' capitalism in this respect. He pointed out, for example, how the entrepreneur had slowly become an appointed manager at the top of a bureaucratic machine, and how competition between small businesses operating in a free market had been replaced by monopolies and cartels. He presented little if any advice as to how this process might be halted or reversed, other than inter-state rivalry. In the future, the main block on bureaucracy would come from the political rather than the economic sphere.

RETHINKING LIBERAL DEMOCRACY

Weber perceived that the same developments which had undermined liberal values within capitalist economies had transformed the liberal nature of democratic politics. As a result, the theory and practice of liberal democracy needed to be rethought. Two factors in particular lay behind this rethinking: (a) the social constraints placed on democratic procedures by the development of both a mass electorate and a complex economy requiring bureaucratic regulation; and (b), the undermining of any objective foundation for liberal individualism in natural law due to the 'disenchantment' of the world. Although for the purposes of exposition it is convenient to treat each element separately, Weber's analysis linked these two problems and his democratic theory consequently involved a combined response.

The philosophical purpose of his model of democracy has not always been noticed by his commentators. Unlike earlier liberal thinkers, who started off from considerations concerning the best possible society, Weber was led to argue from an empirical account of existing phenomena to an assessment of the feasibility of adopting particular political options. A number of interpreters have assumed that Weber consequently aimed at a 'value-free', 'empirical' theory of democracy, modelled on the current practices of modern politics. They have criticised him accordingly for confusing 'is' and 'ought', in order to provide contemporary political systems falsely claiming to be democratic with a spurious legitimacy.[129] However, Weber was quite open about his own normative priorities, writing in the essay on 'The Meaning of Value Freedom' of 1917 that:

> every order of social relations (however constituted) is, if one wishes to *evaluate* it, ultimately to be examined in terms of the human type

(*menschlichen Typus*) to which it, by way of external or internal (motivational) selection, provides the optimal chances of becoming the dominant type. Otherwise empirical research is neither really exhaustive, nor is there the necessary real foundation for such an evaluation, be it consciously subjective, or an evaluation claiming objective validity.[130]

Weber's concern with the relationship between environment and individual character reflected his sociological understanding of liberalism. Liberal values, in his opinion, derived less from the inherent rights or attributes of human beings, so much as from a specific cultural and social environment – namely, the Protestant ethic and the nature of early capitalism. These historical circumstances had given rise to a certain kind of individual, one capable of autonomous, self-directed action. But in a mass society dominated by large-scale organizations, he considered the type of free individual action characteristic of classical liberalism could now be found only in a few persons at the top – the industrial managers and political leaders. By virtue of their subordinate positions in some bureaucratic hierarchy, most other people had been deprived of this aptitude. His entire scheme was designed, therefore, to procure a certain quality of individual leadership rather than to diffuse power and the ability to act freely throughout society as a whole. Thus, Weber's theory mixed normative and empirical elements. On the one hand, he remained committed to the liberal conception of the creative and responsible individual. On the other hand, he believed such agency could only be preserved for the few. This section will begin by examining Weber's analysis of the empirical constraints on democracy, before turning to a study of his original defence of liberal values in terms of the ethic of responsibility. I shall argue that whilst his conclusions regarding the first were elitist, his understanding of the second was not. Rather, his thesis poses a challenge for the reconstruction of democracy in a realistic way so as to render liberalism a practical possibility for all.

Defeat in 1918 and the abdication of the Kaiser provided the opportunity for the framing of a liberal democratic constitution in Germany. Most of Weber's writings on democracy arose out of this situation and often had an occasional air to them. The main line of his argument was nevertheless clear, and its central elements had been established rather earlier.[131] Weber aimed at adapting existing political institutions in order to secure the democratic selection of leaders in a way appropriate to large-scale mass industrial societies. Weber's design contained two chief components, both heavily influenced by his interpretation of British politics: a defence of the role of parties in organizing a mass electorate, and an account of parliamentary institutions. The two aspects reinforced each other in providing a pluralistic political system which would serve as a training ground in the skills of political leadership.

Weber's understanding of modern democratic politics drew heavily on Ostrogorski's classic account of the British and North American party systems.[132] However, he reached quite different conclusions about the character of this process from his source. Ostrogorski believed the new organized parties and their charismatic leaders were destructive of democracy. Like many earlier liberals, he idealized the virtues of men of independent views and means, who devoted themselves to public service out of a desire to contribute to the common good rather than for the purposes of self-aggrandisement. He favoured a return to the informal coalitions of likeminded men of good will, who had a personal relationship of trust with their constituents. Weber, in contrast, whilst regretting the passing of these largely mythical political paragons, acknowledged that the days of notable politics had gone. Local worthies with the private wealth and spare time to live 'for' rather than 'off' politics no longer existed. Those with the money were either too self-interested or too absorbed in making more to provide suitable candidates, economic competition having obliged even the landed gentry to adopt entrepreneurial methods. Even if such public-spirited individuals had survived the pressures of capitalism, they would no longer be capable of doing the job. The division of labour had entered the political sphere like every other, so that government now needed the expertise of trained specialists rather than well-intentioned amateurs. Above all, they needed the capacity to attract a mass following. Weber saw that the process of social democratisation had fatally undermined the deferential structures on which the *Honoratioren* system depended. The same factors had rendered anything less than universal suffrage unacceptable and impractical within modern states. Equal voting rights simply followed on from the formal equality of status of all which underpinned the capitalist and bureaucratic systems. All of the intricate proposals put forward to limit the franchise on the basis of educational, property or some other qualification, ignored the levelling tendencies inherent to modern economies.[133]

This extension of voting rights to the masses was an irreversible development that had changed dramatically the nature of liberal politics. Party machines had now become necessary for the mobilisation of the vote. Parties, on Weber's definition, were voluntary associations devoted 'to securing power within an organization for its leaders in order to attain ideal or material advantages for its members'.[134] Whilst such groups were not products of a mass electorate, universal suffrage had altered their character. The far greater number of voters and the enhanced competition brought about by the broadening of interests demanding representation, made bureaucratic methods indispensable for their efficient functioning. As a result, the party boss and professional election agents gradually displaced the relatively disorganized and technically less rational arrangements of local dignitaries.[135] Their 'petty patronage' could not rival the funds raised by the new type of 'political capitalist entrepreneur' who ran the modern parties. Unlike the *Honoratiores*, they did not necessarily have a good education and enjoyed a low social status, 'since the "professional" is despised in "respectable society"'. The only skills they required were the ability to manage and finance the party's propaganda and administration. These shadowy figures secured the party finances from the contributions of members and even shadier 'great financial Maecenases', concerned to get a particular individual elected. Seekers after power for its own sake, they did not jeopardise their careers by entering the electoral lists personally. Their position rested on getting the party into office, and they supported whatever candidates or policies were necessary to achieve it: for the 'boss has no firm political "principles"...and asks merely: what will capture votes?'[136]

The growth of parties had also reduced the importance of the individual MP, killing the traditional liberal conception of the independent representative. Except in a few rare cases, candidates did not possess a sufficient local following to get themselves elected. They required the canvassing facilities and finance of the party. Hence, 'all attempts to subordinate the representative to the will of the voters have in the long run only one effect: they reinforce the ascendency of the party organization over him, since it is the party organization alone that can mobilise the people.'[137] With the exception of a handful of Cabinet Ministers and the odd eccentric, most MPs were creatures of the party apparatus, serving as 'nothing better than well-disciplined lobby fodder'.[138]

The key figures were increasingly the political leaders at the head of the party machine. For a party's success depended on their personal charisma, since the masses identified a party largely with the personality of its leader. Weber regarded the masses as incapable of initiating political action for themselves. They merely responded to the lead given by others, providing them with supporters. As Gladstone's campaigning had demonstrated,[139] 'even under the most democratic form of state', 'it is not the politically passive "mass" that produces the leader from its midst, but the political leader who recruits his following and wins the mass through "demagogy".'[140]

Liberals seeking to restrict or exclude the involvement of the masses in politics have traditionally justified this policy out of a fear of the tyranny of the majority and the demagoguery of electoral politics. Weber shared many of the prejudices against the masses which motivated these fears.[141] However, he insisted that in a mass society characterised by job mobility, general literacy and a popular press, the political influence of the populace at large was inevitable. Far from avoiding the problem, restricting the franchise exacerbated it. Weber offered the Kaiser's manipulation of public opinion with speeches and telegrams and the U-boat agitation whipped up by Turpitz during the war as eloquent examples of the dangers of undemocratic politicians exploiting mass feelings to gain support for their policies. Nobody aware of recent German politics, he wrote, 'could claim that "dema-goguery" is a characteristic of a constitutionally democratic polity...In Germany we have *demagoguery* and the pressure of the rabble *without democracy*, or rather *because of the absence* of an orderly democracy.'[142] If Weber felt some sympathy for the liberal antipathy towards popular democracy, he regarded it as preferable to the 'irrational', emotive and uncontrolled political interventions of the mass which would erupt without it. For universal suffrage led not to direct democracy or mob rule, but to the organization of the masses into political parties under the control of a charismatic leader.[143]

Like the contemporary elite theorists Pareto, Mosca and Michels,[144] Weber held that democracy reinforced rather than challenged the 'law of the small number', decreeing that 'political action is always deter-mined by...the superior political maneuverability of small leading groups.'[145] Because a ruling minority 'can quickly reach an understand-ing amongst its members', Weber contended that 'it is thus able at any time to initiate that rationally organized action necessary to preserve its position of power.' Mass democracy merely enhanced their authority. For the larger the number of people involved, the harder it was for them to co-ordinate their opposition to the will of their rulers. Consequently, the liberals need have no fear of a tyrannous majority. For an organized minority 'can easily squelch any action of the masses threatening its power'.[146] Modern political parties reflected this elitist logic. Controlled by party leaders and their staffs, the common voter was kept 'com-pletely inactive'. The masses were 'mere objects whose votes are solicited at election time'. Even 'the participation of the rank and file is limited to assistance and voting during elections, which take place at relatively long intervals, and to the discussion of resolutions, the outcome of which is always controlled by the leaders.'[147]

Democratization did not lead to the rule of the people, therefore, it simply brought about a change in the methods whereby elites recruited their popular support.[148] The other elite theorists looked on this fact with a degree of cynicism, ultimately rejecting democracy altogether as an intrinsically corrupt practice whereby a small group hoodwinked the rest of the population for private gain.[149] Weber assessed these developments rather differently, for he considered the party system to have produced a new type of elite of a largely praiseworthy nature. He dismissed fears that the party system encouraged a dangerous mixture of bureaucratic time-servers and power-crazed rabble rousers. Both the corruption and rigidity endemic to all bureaucracies and the excesses of the extremist were curbed by 'the competitive struggle to win the favour of the voter'. Weber maintained that the pluralist nature of modern society – a function of its class, religious and other divisions – meant that most polities would contain several parties vying with each other for the people's vote.[150] Indeed, he asserted that 'parties can exist by definition only within an organization, whether political or other, and only when there is a struggle for its control.' 'All associations which are prescribed and controlled by the polity', such as the Nazi Party after 1933 or the former Soviet Communist Party, failed to meet his criterion of being groups dependent on the voluntary adherence of their members for their existence.[151] The essence of democracy, on Weber's reconceptualization, derived from the need for different parties to strive against each other to attract voters in order to achieve power.

The benefits of this electoral market were supposedly similar to those traditionally associated with the economic market.[152] The resulting competition kept the party organizations efficient and ensured that good candidates emerged, in much the same way that the need to attract consumers and workers from rival companies encouraged entrepreneurship and efficiency in business. Above all, it provided the parties with an incentive to pick leaders capable of gaining an electoral victory.[153] In order to preserve their own position, the party bosses nominated any person of proven 'vote-getting' ability, regardless of their opinions. These pressures also made certain that the politicians remained open to the concerns of the electorate, making them receptive to new ideas. For, 'the professional politician...who must live "off" the party, least of all wants to see his intellectual equipment of ideas and slogans outmoded.'[154] Although Weber rejected the conception of democracy as the expression of the 'will of the people', his own view was not unresponsive to popular demands. Once again, the market analogy provided Weber with his model. Even though it was absurd 'to speak of the will of the shoe buyer who has to decide what skills the shoemaker should employ', consumer pressure still worked because 'the shoe buyer knows, to be sure, *where* the shoe *pinches*.'[155] Similarly, if the masses lacked the expertise to rule themselves, they could nevertheless evaluate the effect of policies on their lives and throw out those politicians who failed to provide them with what they wanted. This was not the chief advantage of the voting market for Weber, however. The main virtue of the electoral fight consisted in the way it tempered the politician, giving him or her the breadth of vision and decisiveness so conspicuously lacking in the bureaucrat. It ensured that the rulers who emerged were capable of coping with the conflicts endemic to politics in a responsible and committed manner. In contrast to Ostrogorski, Weber looked favourably on the Caesarist qualities selected by the modern 'electoral battlefield'. The plebiscitarian nature of contemporary democracy, he claimed, ensured that only those with a genuine calling for politics rose to the top. 'Since the essence of politics is struggle', then 'for the tasks of national leadership only such men are prepared who have been selected in the course of the political struggle...It simply happens to be a fact that such preparation is, on the average, accomplished better by the much-maligned "craft of demagoguery" than by the clerk's office.'[156]

Weber recognized that 'political demagoguery can lead to striking abuses.'[157] The presence of a working parliament formed a necessary additional component of Weber's conception of democratic politics in order to guard against this danger. Weber made an important distinction between 'negative' and 'positive' politics. So long as parliament could control the government solely by approving or refusing financial and other legislation, or by putting forward the petitions of citizens, then its role was restricted to 'negative' politics. 'Positive' politics involved the ability to initiate legislation and to participate actively 'in the *direction* of political affairs' and the running of the administration. It had been Bismarck's legacy to restrict the German Reichstag to a largely negative function, by preventing parliamentary leaders from having a positive share in government.[158] Weber singled out for especial criticism Article 9 of the Reich constitution of 1871, which excluded anyone from being simultaneously a member of the Bundesrat and of the Reichstag. This rule meant that party leaders in the national parliament could only enter the government at the cost of losing their political base – something that they were not keen to do for obvious reasons. Because of this reluctance, the top officials rarely had a parliamentary mandate or much political experience. In any case, the powerlessness of parliament meant that the calibre of politician tended to be fairly low, and the training provided by a parliamentary career worse than useless.[159] Purely negative politics encouraged an unhealthy antagonism between parliament and government. Parliamentary members regarded the administration 'as a hostile power', full of 'careerists and henchmen who subject the people to their annoying and largely superfluous activities'. The bureaucrats, in their turn, suffered from a lack of adequate supervision. They looked on parliament as 'a mere drag chain, an assembly of impotent fault-finders and know-it-alls', to 'be given only the indispensable minimum of information'.[160] As a result, politics had become increasingly extreme and ideological in nature. Denied access both to power and to the full facts – the necessary prerequisites for a responsible and informed debate of the issues – German politicians were condemned to 'amateurish ignorance'.[161] They compensated by indulging in extravagant posturing. The only constructive outlet for their energies lay in 'representing the local economic interests of influential voters' and 'the patronage of minor subordinate positions'. Those parties excluded from even these petty offices, like the Social Democrats, 'compensate themselves by running the municipal administrations and the public health insurance funds, and pursue in parliament...policies hostile to the government or alienated from the state'.[162] In sum, 'ignorant demagogy or routinized impotence – or both – prevail in a parliament which can only criticise without getting access to the facts and whose leaders are never put into a situation in which they must prove their mettle.'[163]

Thus, negative politics encouraged the 'negative selection' of politicians. Those with true leadership qualities were deterred from

following a political career, and went into business instead.[164] In consequence, German politics was dominated by bureaucratic placemen occupying the major positions, who sought office without the responsibilities
of power, on the one hand; and a parliament packed with nonentities and
windbags, content with minor roles and a purely oppositional stance,
respectively, on the other. The resulting absence of real leaders became
painfully obvious whenever a crisis occurred which gave the Reichstag
one of its rare opportunites to act positively. The fall of Bethmann-
Hollweg from the Chancellorship in 1917 following the failure of the
U-boat campaign, for example, occasioned 'complete anarchy' amongst
the parties and the bureaucrats alike. They found themselves confronted
'with a completely novel task to which neither their organization nor
their personnel could measure up – the formation of a government.'[165]

Whereas Germany provided Weber with his example of the faults of
'negative' politics, he regarded Britain as exemplifying the virtues of
'positive' politics. If a weak parliamentary system led to 'negative' politics, a strong parliament, from which the government was directly
recruited and to which it was answerable, produced 'positive' politics.
This arrangement not only encouraged the selection of able leaders by
giving them the chance to exercise power, it also guaranteed their
accountability by forcing them to justify their actions, and, when they
failed, allowed them to be dismissed with a minimum of fuss.[166] Weber
particularly admired the role of committees in the British parliament.
These gave the politician a valuable training in 'steady strenuous work'
as opposed to the talent for making 'ostentatious and decorative
speeches before parliament' developed by the German model.
Politicians needed to have detailed practical knowledge of the mechanisms of government, so that their words and deeds would be tempered
by 'sober experience'. 'Only such intensive training, through which the
politician must pass in the committees of a *working* parliament,' he
wrote, 'turns such an assembly into a recruiting ground not for mere
demagogues but for positively participating politicians.' Committees
forced politicians to consider the detailed implications of implementing
their policies and hence accustomed them to weighing the consequences
of their decisions, the true mark of a responsible politician. Finally, only
the professional deputy with a comprehension of the intricate affairs of
state could adequately check the civil service. Once again committees
offered the best way of informing politicians of the role of the
administration and of submitting it to public scrutiny. Weber went so
far as to maintain that 'only such co-operation between civil servants
and politicians can guarantee the continuous supervision of the administration and, with it, political education of leaders and led.'[167]

Parliament supplemented his theory of party competition in elections
in important ways, therefore, by serving as an important safeguard
against a number of the dangers of the Caesarism encouraged by a
mass democracy. First, parliamentary institutions ensured a peaceful

succession, 'since the rise, neutralization and elimination of a caesarist leader occur most easily without the danger of domestic catastrophe when the effective co-domination of powerful representative bodies preserves the political continuity and the constitutional guarantees of the civil order'.[168] Second, parliament offered a forum for debating public policy. This trained leaders in the technique and details of government, and forced them to persuade others of the practicality of their schemes. The high standard of oratory demanded, made it 'a suitable practical proving ground of the politicians wooing the confidence of the masses'. Debate also enabled the conciliation and modification of opposing positions by negotiation. Third, parliamentary committees were the best means of supervising the bureaucracy, obliging MPs to master the mechanics of administration as well as the civil servants themselves. Fourth and last, parliament helped 'the preservation of civil liberties' via its ability to dismiss leaders and the mutual checks it placed on politicians and bureaucrats alike.[169]

Weber desired to convince the German bourgeoisie that their antipathy to modern parliamentary democracy was misplaced. Unfortunately, German liberals had reacted badly to the erosion of their former authority. Industrialisation, the growth of urban centres and the development of new forms of interest group politics had undermined their support and revealed the inadequacies of their lack of organization. Increasingly marginalized from national politics, where universal suffrage operated, they became defenders of the often highly discriminatory electoral systems of many of the town councils and federal states.[170] The most glaringly unfair of these was the Prussian three-class voting system. During the war, Weber engaged in a fierce attack on this arrangement, for the war had brought out the anomaly it involved particularly clearly. Characteristically, Weber grounded his argument in historical sociology. In the past, access to citizenship had been limited to those able to provide their own military equipment. But today no one owned their own arms. In a modern bureaucratic army, soldiers were functionaries of the state and conscription had made all men equally eligible to enter the field of death. That the business men and financiers who stayed at home should have political rights denied to the majority of soldiers risking their lives for their policies was doubly dangerous. It encouraged the irresponsibility of both sides: the first as a result of their excessive power, the second as a result of their powerlessness. Unchecked, the former would undoubtedly sacrifice the public interest to their own, as indeed he believed they had done by milking the war to secure themselves maximum profits. Unrepresented, the latter would cease to identify with the nation and the collective spirit needed to rebuild German society would be lacking. Revolutionary schemes offering insubstantial utopias would prove much more attractive.[171]

Far from protecting them from the masses, the authoritarian structures of the German state had encouraged the 'democracy of the streets'. Rather than fearing the rise of the Social Democrats, by 1912 the largest party in the Reichstag, their progress was to be welcomed. As Michels's 1911 study had shown, the SPD had succumbed to the 'iron law of oligarchy' affecting all parties, its democratic socialist aspirations notwithstanding.[172] Such organizations, Weber noted, 'constitute a very important counterbalance against the direct and irrational mob rule typical of purely plebiscitary peoples'. The dangers of revolutionary disturbances were always 'strongest in countries with either a powerless or a politically discredited parliament, that means, above all, in countries without *rationally organized parties*'.[173] A working parliamentary system would transform the SPD into a responsible party and obtain the consent of the proletariat to the liberal social and political system.[174] The liberals' energies must now be directed towards the formation of a left-of-centre party capable of building a progressive coalition of the industrial classes, and Weber became involved in the founding of a new German Democratic Party for this purpose.[175]

Above all, Weber attacked the quality of leadership provided by the autocratic system. Instead of being strong and efficient, as its apologists had claimed, German governments had proved weak and indecisive. Weber blamed this state of affairs on the usurpation of the leading positions by bureaucratic officials as a result of Bismarck's elimination of all political talent. Whilst it was good for an official to work dutifully according to the rules and to act as instructed, regardless of who was in power, this ability to obey orders was totally unsuited to the task of governing a country. Whereas the official's role was to remain above parties and the struggle for power, 'this struggle for personal power, and the resulting personal responsibility, is the lifeblood of the politician.'[176] As we have seen, Weber regarded the chief benefit of democracy to inhere in its promotion of a gladiatorial contest for election from which a true leader would perforce emerge.

Weber outlined the attributes he hoped would occur in a political leader chosen in a parliamentary democracy in his classic essay on 'Politics as a Vocation'.[177] He considered that 'three pre-eminant qualities are decisive for the politician: passion, a feeling of responsibility, and a sense of proportion.'[178] The combination was crucial. Passion was the engine of serious political motivation; without it, politics degenerated into sheer opportunism. But the passion Weber commended was not the romantic passion of the person who has lost a grip on reality, but rather that of a person devoted to a cause (whatever it may be). It was this cause, resting ultimately on faith in a belief, which gave passion its depth and pathos. Finally, a degree of distance and detachment was required if the cause was to be pursued with responsibility.

The problem then 'is simply how can warm passion and a cool sense of proportion be forged together in one and the same soul?'[179] This quandary was closely related to the vexed question of the relationship between politics and ethics. The issue was an intensely difficult one for

Weber because violence and politics were intimately linked in his schema. Since no overarching moral framework existed within which all viewpoints could be reconciled, Weber thought human societies were permanently characterized by the struggle for power between rival groups, classes and individuals seeking to promote their various interests. Herein lay the essence of politics. Unlike Marx, Weber believed these conflicts could not be ascribed totally to an unjust economic system, although he did not deny the presence of class struggles throughout history either. Divergent ethical ideals provided a far more potent and ultimately ineradicable source of political disputes. The ethical complexity of the world rendered all policies contentious. Someone's interests and ideals would always suffer relative to those of someone else. Given that complete rational agreement amongst citizens could not be counted on in principle, coercion formed an inherent aspect of every state. Without the ability to oblige its citizens to obey it, a state would soon decline into anarchy. Thus, the wielding of power was an intrinsic part of all political activity, and politicians were faced frequently with having either to use force or to compromise when implementing their programmes.[180]

In confronting this problem, Weber made an important distinction between the 'ethic of ultimate ends' and the 'ethic of responsibility'. For the conviction politician who totally subscribed to the first ethos, the ends always justified the means. 'If an action of good intent leads to bad results, then, in the actor's eyes, not he but the world, or the stupidity of other men, or God's will who made them thus, is responsible for the evil.' The central flaw of this attitude arose from its denial of the 'ethical irrationality of the world'. It was not correct that no evil could follow from good actions or vice versa, nor was it the case that something could not be true without being beautiful, holy and good as well. This 'irreconcilable conflict' between different value spheres rendered politics an inevitably messy and dangerous business. The follower of the 'ethic of responsibility' recognized this fact. Hence, the responsible politician 'takes account of the average deficiencies of people;...he does not even have the right to presuppose their goodness and perfection. He does not feel in a position to burden others with the results of his own actions so far as he was able to foresee them; he will say: these results are ascribed to my action.' Politicians of this kind acknowledged the paradoxes of human experience, lived with the tensions they generated, and accepted culpability for actions that went awry. They saw that politics was a tangle of righteous intentions; that the quest for power involved a struggle with 'diabolical forces lurking in all violence'. Most important, they appreciated the need to weigh the consequences of any action they undertook, and understood that difficult choices between equally worthy but incompatible goals would often be necessary. They therefore adopted a crucially different attitude from the conviction politicians, who would brook no compromise, who could not accept that a good tree was capable of bearing evil fruit, who blamed others for the fate of their own plans, and who generally lacked the inner poise to endure with dignity the existence of 'an irrational world of undeserved suffering, unpunished injustice, and hopeless stupidity'.[181]

The contrast between the responsible and the conviction politician should not be overstated, however. Although Weber condemned the fanatical revolutionary who believed the righteous end justified any means, he admired, for instance, the genuine pacifist prepared to turn the other cheek and pay the price for his or her convictions – even if he thought their attitude showed them to be 'political infants'. He did not maintain either that 'an ethic of ultimate ends is identical with irresponsibility, or that an ethic of responsibility is identical with unprincipled opportunism.'[182] A politician totally lacking in convictions would be an abomination. If power was the unavoidable means, and striving for power one of the driving forces of all politics, he believed 'there is no more powerful distortion of political force than the parvenu-like braggart with power, and the vain self-reflection in the feeling of power, and in general every worship of power *per se*.'[183] It was the cynicism of those conviction politicians who tell us There Is No Alternative, without ever having to suffer personally, or fully consider the consequences of their policies, that he attacked. The genuinely responsible politician, though willing to compromise, retained 'a bed-rock integrity to insist finally, "Here I stand: I can do no other."' In this respect, he concluded, 'an ethic of ultimate ends and an ethic of responsibility are not absolute contrasts but rather supplements, which only in unison constitute a genuine man – a man who *can* have the "calling for politics."'[184]

Thus, Weber sought to promote a very specific form of charismatic leadership, one not without certain attractions. Those scholars who claim he failed to allow 'any distinction between the "genuine charisma of responsible democratic leaders, as for instance, Gladstone or Roosevelt, and the pernicious charisma of personalities like Kurt Eisner or Adolf Hitler"'[185] are clearly mistaken. Such criticism does not distinguish between Weber's intention in designing his version of democracy, namely the production of a certain kind of leader, and very proper worries about the effectiveness of his proposed schema in securing this end. On this latter score, even Weber began to have serious doubts.

Most of the articles discussed so far were written in the final years of the First World War. However, by 1919 his confidence in Parliament and the party system had waned. He now insisted that only a strong President elected directly by the people, and hence with a power base outside Parliament, could provide the leadership and focus for national unity Germany so badly needed.[186] Since this proposal plausibly influenced the framing of the Weimer constitution, on which Weber was consulted, we must examine briefly the reasons behind this measure before turning to a final assessment of his theory.[187] In the eyes of many commentators it brought out a number of the inherent shortcomings of Weber's conception of liberal democracy as a whole, revealing its pronouncedly anti-democratic and dictatorial nature.[188]

Three main reasons lay behind Weber's proposal. First, he regarded a popularly elected national leader as a means for overcoming regional and economic particularism. He became convinced that the Bundesrat, the German Federal Council, would continue to be important, producing a corresponding weakening of the Reichstag. The survival of subnational allegiances also meant that political parties would remain essentially regionally based and provincial in outlook. The introduction of proportional representation would further fragment the German political system, turning parties into vehicles for narrowly based interest groups. A Reichstag elected after this fashion would be 'a parliament of philistines – incapable of being in any sense a place where political leaders are selected'.[189] Whereas during the Wilhelmine era democracy had been endangered by the absence of parliamentary checks on the executive, he now feared that it was imperilled by there being too many. Second, he maintained that at a time when major economic restructuring was necessary, a figurehead with the authority to impose often unpopular policies was vital. 'Only a President who has millions of votes behind him' would be capable of doing this. The other political leaders would be too closely identified with the sectional interests of their particular parties to have the vision or the freedom of action to undertake a genuinely national programme of economic and social reform.[190] Third, he believed a plebiscitarian presidency offered the best mechanism for ensuring responsible, strong, personal leadership. The coalition government endemic to a Reichstag dominated by several parties would be unstable and produce no dominant figure. Any President elected by parliamentary representives, on the model of the French Third Republic, would be subservient to the particular groups which voted him or her in and was 'politically a dead man when these constellations shift'. A popularly elected President, in contrast, possessing a delaying veto and the power to dissolve parliament and call referenda, 'is the guarantor of true democracy, which means not feeble surrender to cliques but subjection to leaders chosen by the people themselves'.[191]

Although Weber stressed the Caesarist and dictatorial qualities of the Reich President, he insisted that he was not a despot. Weber held that direct election meant that he would pay for his mistakes, unlike the Kaiser and his entourage. Constitutional guarantees were also necessary to ensure that 'whenever the President of the Reich attempts to tamper with the laws or to govern autocratically, he sees the "noose and gallows" before his eyes.' Significantly, Weber had no part in the notorious Article 48, which allowed the President to rule by decree. Although he counselled giving the President certain emergency powers, such as a suspensory veto, he cautioned that intervention in the machinery of the Reich must be limited to the 'case of temporarily insoluble crises...and in other circumstances only by calling a referendum'.[192] However, Weber was somewhat too sanguine over the likelihood of Parliament exercising these controls. Its divisiveness made concerted action difficult, and the President's monopoly of patronage and ability to ignore Parliament by going straight to the people, would have further constrained the assembly's capacity to check his power.

No doubt Weber's own failure to secure a place on the German Democratic Party list due to the opposition of party worthies contributed to the sudden souring of his opinion of parliamentary politics. However, the unprecedented social unrest of 1918–19 probably played the greatest role in convincing him of the need for decisive leadership to unite the nation.[193] Instead of proving creative, the clash of different interest groups now seemed more likely to lead to stalemate and unsatisfactory compromises at best, and at worst open conflict and violent revolution. With the country divided and the parties dominated by narrow cliques, he believed parliament would become a mere centre for horse trading. This atmosphere could only produce a 'leaderless democracy, in other words the rule of professional politicians without a calling, without the inner charismatic qualities which make a leader'.[194] The sole way to obtain independent leadership capable of coping with the demands of competing sectional interests and the 'irrational' pressures of the mass was by transcending the parliamentary and party mechanisms, and allowing individuals of the right calibre to appeal directly to the people themselves. However, in weakening parliament and the parties in this way, Weber had undermined their ability to curb the demagoguery of the leader. The balance between the elitist and liberal elements of his earlier theory suffered as a consequence. The only block on the President's power lay with the people themselves, who could demand a referendum calling for his or her dismissal. Yet it is hard to see this as much of a safeguard, when one remembers that Weber considered the mass incapable of originating political action for themselves.

Weber's revision of his theory in an increasingly elitist direction not only contradicts a number of elements of his earlier position, it also casts doubt on some of the empirical presuppositions underpinning his thesis. First, Weber's competitive elite model of democracy assumed that the plurality of values posited by his epistemology would be reflected in a plurality of political positions. However, the political market he described was far more likely to be 'oligopolistic' than genuinely free, with the elite groups sharing certain common interests distinct from those of the voters which caused them to collude to hold certain items off the political agenda.[195] Second, his model relied on there being an essential tolerance of differences of opinion and a general acceptance of the constitutional rules of the game. The political culture of Weimar Germany, as Weber quickly realised, exhibited neither of these features. Opinions were polarised across a number of dimensions and many groups regarded the post-war constitutional settlement with open hostility. Since Weimar both lacked the 'traditional' legitimacy of older political systems, and failed to gain widespread consent for its procedures, Weber believed that only a charismatic figure could bring about some degree of national unity. In the process, the democratic elements of Weber's argument gave way to the demagogic. Third, an awareness of a plurality of different moral codes need not generate respect for the views of others in the political leader any more than it does in the populace at large. Weber sought to inculcate responsibility by getting politicians to attend to the effects of imposing their ideas upon the population. However, since we judge the acceptability or unacceptability of consequences according to our own particular scale of values, Weber's reasoning was in danger of becoming circular, and of offering no brake on the fanaticism of the conviction politician. Finally, Weber's assessment of the electorate was in many respects self-contradictory.[196] On the one hand he regarded them as incapable of judging political matters for themselves; but, on the other, he thought them quite capable of discriminating between different styles of leadership and of providing a check against the rise of a tyrant. Yet, if anything, a system designed to keep the masses passive will tend to increase the feelings of disaffection which puts them into the hands of political charlatans offering miracle cures. His poor opinion of the demos was likely to prove self-confirming.

Weber has been accused not only of providing an ideological legitimation of Hitler's style of leadership, but also of helping put in place the constitutional mechanisms that enabled him to seize power in the first place.[197] The second charge is easily dismissed. Although many of Weber's suggestions concerning the President were enshrined in the Weimar constitution, they appear to have owed more to the influence of similar proposals by others than to Weber. Interestingly enough, the motivation of these thinkers was quite different to Weber's, springing more from a liberal concern with the 'balance of powers'. Not surprisingly, the explicitly Caesarist elements of Weber's design were rejected.[198] In any case, as Baehr points out, the role of the President in Hitler's rise has been overdone.[199] The paralysis of parliament, which Weber correctly foresaw, was far more decisive, whilst Article 76, which allowed the constitution to be altered by a bill with the support of two-thirds of the Reichstag, provided the main legal instrument for the setting up of the Third Reich.

The first charge, that Weber provided a spurious legitimation for Hitler's demagoguery, has greater plausibility. Weber's own commitment to the traditional liberal freedoms is undeniable, so that he would undoubtedly have opposed Hitler's regime had he lived to see it. However, he doubted that there could be any philosophical basis for these freedoms in natural law or human rights. They could only be expressed in the actions of exceptional individuals capable of over-coming the enervating and stultifying pressures of modern bureaucratic societies. His critics argue that this conclusion led him to emphasise strong leadership at the expense of parliamentary or legal guarantees protecting the liberties of ordinary folk. The elitist and decisionistic element within Weber's liberalism fitted uneasily even with his version of democracy, arguably sharing a close affinity to Carl Schmitt's subsequent overt defence of the Nazi dictatorship.[200] These criticisms pose a serious challenge to Weber's political theory. However, they also reveal problems for liberalism generally, for whatever the shortcomings of Weber's own rethinking of liberal politics, the dilemmas he identified with traditional defences of liberalism remain genuine ones which cannot be ignored.

Weber's rejection of the classical liberal concept of the 'constitutional state' or *Rechtsstaat* has been regarded by many critics as the fatal flaw of his model of democracy. Weber contended that the theological foundations on which doctrines of natural rights ultimately rested had gradually lost their appeal, revealing the contestable ontological assumptions lying behind most rights claims. Far from representing universal attributes of human beings as such, rights functioned to legit-imise the position of diverse groups and classes. For example, Weber noted how 'both the formal rationalistic natural law of freedom and the substantive natural law of the exclusive legitimacy of the product of labour have definite class implications.' The first suited bourgeois capi-talism best, the latter a proletarian society. Moreover, the implications of each system were ambiguous. The latter, for example, could be cashed out to mean either the 'right to work', or the 'right to a minimum stand-ard of living', or a combination of the two, as the 'right to the full prod-uct of one's labour'. This plethora of competing and contradictory 'intrinsic' and 'inalienable' human rights considerably reduced the concept's usefulness and offered few distinct directions for a political or social programme.[201]

Since neither human rights nor any other set of putatively objective values, such as justice, could be applied to decide the legitimacy of the state, Weber was forced to provide an alternative account of legitimate authority to underpin his version of democracy. In his view, domination became legitimate simply through being voluntarily complied with by those subject to its authority, without the need for force or argument.[202] Weber identified three ways of obtaining such compliance, none of which necessarily involved any substantive considerations concerning the validity of the ends being pursued by those in power. The authority claims of the state could be based on:

1 rational grounds – resting on a belief in the legality of enacted rules and the right of those elevated to authority under such such rules to issue commands (legal authority),

2 traditional grounds – resting on an established belief in the sanctity of immemorial traditions and the legitimacy of those exercising authority under them (traditional authority); or finally,

3 charismatic grounds – resting on devotion to the exceptional sanctity, heroism or exemplary character of an individual person, and of the normative patterns or order revealed or ordained by him (charismatic authority).[203]

Most political systems combined these three 'pure' types in some form or other. However, the process of rationalization was causing traditional sources of legitimation to lose their hold upon people. Weber contended that value-orientated justifications of authority, such as arguments from natural law, were an example of the traditional type. Belief in the legitimacy conferred by certain set procedures, in contrast, had grown alongside the advance of bureaucratic methods. Although such formal rules and regulations provided political organizations with stability and order, they also suffocated the sort of individual creative action on which the dynamism of a society depended. Fortunately, charismatic leadership still constituted an alternative to bureaucratic red tape. Weber associated charisma with the sway of figures such as Christ and Napoleon. Such personalities had the capacity of gaining popular assent to innovative ideas and policies. Like Nietzsche's *Übermenschen*, they set new values for themselves and their followers in an heroic attempt to raise humankind to a higher level.[204] Weber realised that truly great political leaders, who endowed their state's activities and those of its citizens with purpose and meaning, would only appear very rarely. However, even lesser figures could overcome the bureaucratic stranglehold and inject some flexibility into the running of the government.[205] Nevertheless, this form of domination had its drawbacks as well. Leaders could be wilful and their decisions erratic. Their rule risked becoming autocratic and corrupt, features which could make their peaceful removal difficult when they failed. Indeed, without traditional mechanisms for choosing a successor, such as the hereditary principle in the case of monarchies, the transition from one leader to the next was always fraught with problems.[206] Weber's concept of 'Leadership Democracy' was intended to combine the virtues of legal and charismatic authority whilst overcoming their respective shortcomings. Democracy offered a procedure for the selection and rejection of charismatic leaders, with a state administration ensuring efficient enactment of their decrees and providing an element of continuity and stability. Charismatic leaders in their turn gave the direction and dynamism otherwise lacking in bureaucratic systems.[207]

As always with Weber, it is hard to disentangle the descriptive from the evaluative aspects of his argument. Is his typology supposed to exhaust all the theoretical possibilities for obtaining legitimate authority, or does it simply categorise all forms that have actually existed? Mommsen argues that Weber's theory 'does not allow a distinction between what would nowadays be called government by consent on the one hand and tyrannical dictatorships which force people into submission by means of manipulation or oppression on the other'.[208] This is not entirely true, for Weber made a clear distinction between the various reasons, such as fear and hope, that might make people obey and the legitimation of this obedience. According to Weber's schema, consent must be voluntary for authority to be legitimate.[209] However, Mommsen is correct to note that one category seems conspicuous by its absence – the free consent of rational agents, surely a more standard characterisation of the democratic ideal. On a practical level, Weber appears to have regarded ordinary citizens as incapable of free self-determination. Their consent could only be won by demagogic means, and in Weber's opinion their reasons for consenting would almost certainly be irrational and emotive in nature. It is a moot point whether apathetic acquiescence or compliance resulting from false consciousness can constitute true agreement on the part of agents. As Mommsen rightly remarks, such formal criteria for consent can be met no matter how deluded those who give it are, and may be obtained for policies which from a substantive point of view are positively anti-democratic. Yet, as I shall argue below, Weber's philosophical defence of liberalism allowed a quite different understanding of democracy deriving from his recognition of the consequences of value pluralism.

Critics of Weber confuse his philosophical defence of liberalism with his practical assessment of the best political means for realizing liberal values.[210] The confusion is understandable given Weber's propensity to turn 'apparent historical necessities into positive theoretical virtues'.[211] In this respect, his method was better than his practice, for the norms underlying Weber's thesis can and should be separated in an almost archetypally Weberian manner from both his own personal commitments and his empirical evaluation of the best means of realizing them.

In spite of his rejection of any objective basis for human rights, Weber felt that 'it is a gross self-deception to believe that without the achievements of the age of the Rights of Man any one of us, including the most conservative, can go on living his life.'[212] Fortunately, Weber believed a philosophical grounding for liberalism could be found in the very arguments that had undermined its former basis in natural law. The discovery that there were no rationally objective moral and political values, but that they were matters of personal choice and commitment instead, provided a new foundation for liberalism in the related concepts of individualism and pluralism. The liberal commitment to an open society derived its rationale, in Weber's view, from the individual's need to affirm the meaning of his or her existence by choosing from amongst numerous competing and often irreconcilable values. This quasi-Nietzschean defence of liberal institutions disturbs most commentators, who regard it as intrinsically elitist.[213] They argue that Weber's emphasis on individualism ignored the universalism of traditional rights theories and confused the exercise of rights by a few superior beings with the securing of equal rights for all, which is the true goal of liberalism. Returning to the familiar comparison with Britain, they contrast Weber's restatement of liberalism unfavourably with the redefinition offered contemporaneously by the new liberals. They characterise this latter group as attempting to enlarge the freedoms open to all through state intervention aimed at extending rights to include equal access to the social and cultural prerequisites for action.[214] However, our examination of the new liberals in chapter 1 revealed a Weberian analysis of this episode to be nearer the mark, for such interpretations miss the paternalistic and avowedly class nature of these reforms, which excluded certain categories of individual behaviour as 'unfit' as well as endorsing and facilitating approved forms of self-realization. Indeed, unless one believes that a certain type of existence can be objectively defined as the best life possible for humankind, then, as Weber appreciated, any theory of rights will end up reflecting but one out of a range of plausible forms of human flourishing and delegitimise others.

Individualism and pluralism were intimately connected in Weber's version of liberalism. Weber contended that no ethical code existed capable of integrating the diverse dimensions – erotic, economic, familial, aesthetic, etc. – of human life into one scheme of values.[215] These different spheres of our existence operated with principles and logics of their own, which were not always mutually compatible. In a secular era, we could not escape this dilemma by placing our trust in the ultimate rationality and meaningfulness of a world that defied our own limited understanding, nor could we responsibly ignore the presence of competing values in our lives. Weber denied that this position was relativistic in the crude sense. He rejected totally the vulgar relativist's belief that the presence of conflicting value systems prevents us from making judgements which allow us to choose between them. On the contrary, Weber insisted we had a duty to make such choices, for meaning and coherence only came from the conscious decisions individuals made for themselves. Weber acknowledged that in 'the shallowness of our routinized daily existence' people tended to muddle through and avoid facing up to this responsibility by ignoring the incoherences within their lives. However:

> The fruit of the tree of knowledge, which is distasteful to the complacent but which is, nonetheless, inescapable, consists in the insight that every single important activity and ultimately life as a whole, if it is not to be permitted to run on as an event in nature but is instead to be consciously guided, is a series of ultimate decisions through which the soul – as in Plato – chooses its own fate, i.e., the meaning of its activity and existence.[216]

The range of moral positions was too extensive for them all to be fully compatible with each other all of the time. Most of our decisions would involve some loss by excluding certain alternatives of equal value. Conflict between different subjective commitments of comparable worth formed part of the human condition. The only responsible attitude was to face up to this situation and to acknowledge the painful consequences which resulted when hard choices had to be made. Thus, Weber's individualistic ethic was a corollary of his contention that we lived in a disenchanted and pluralistic world. His liberalism followed on from a recognition of the importance for different groups of people of a diversity of sometimes incompatible values. A liberal attitude resulted from seeking to mediate between the conflicts which arose from this circumstance in as responsible a way as possible – one which took the claims of others seriously.

Weber did not believe either individualism or pluralism were inherent aspects of the human condition. The novelty of his sociological understanding of liberalism came from his perception that both elements were but the products of the peculiar set of historical circumstances which had formed Western culture. As we saw, Weber feared that this special context was threatened now by the very forces which had brought it into being. Bureaucratic patterns of behaviour were depriving us of the capacity to act in an independent manner by forcing people to operate in accordance with formal rules and regulations. The instrumental rationality of bureaucratic procedures appeared to obviate the need for making substantive decisions. However, such methods were directionless in themselves, providing no criteria as to why one goal should be adopted rather than another.

Weber's solution was to create a set of institutions which would give rise to politicians with the ability to offer such guidance. He attempted to embody his value pluralist and individualist ethic within a pluralist political system which promoted responsible individuals into positions of power.[217] The elitism of his model reflected his belief that the charisma of a few aristocratic souls had ever been the 'specifically creative revolutionary force of history'[218] Yet nothing in Weber's philosophical position necessarily committed him to elitism. Mark Warren has suggested that his individualist ethic can be largely assimilated to the eminently universalisable Kantian conception of self-determination, whereby we constitute ourselves as free persons through rational value choices. Unlike Kant, however, instead of regarding certain values as *objectively* valid for human self-realization, Weber's position involved merely 'that we regard as objectively valuable those innermost elements of the "personality", those highest and most ultimate value-judgements which determine our conduct and give meaning and significance to our life'.[219] Such a commitment need not involve any transcendental grounding, emerging instead as an implicit aspect of all social interaction with others.[220] From this perspective, a democratic acknowledgement of each person's entitlement to equal concern and respect flowed not from certain inherent rights of human beings as such, so much as the recognition of the validity for different human beings of a plurality of values. What individuals lost in the way of transcendental reassurance was more than compensated for by their enhanced moral freedom and personal responsibility. Acting justly no longer consisted in behaving according to a set moral code handed down by others. The responsibility fell on our shoulders to act as we believed right. This duty entailed a willingness to justify our actions to others and to accept the consequences of our chosen path. In other words, we all had an obligation to behave in the manner of Weber's ideal politician, outlined above. The political task was to ensure an institutional framework existed which encouraged and allowed people to take on this burden.

A normative basis for a genuinely liberal, democratic and pluralist politics can be found in Weber's writings, therefore. It remains to be asked whether this ethic could be realized in practice. We have already found Weber's own proposals wanting. Whatever their merits as a characterization of contemporary democratic practice in the West, our political leaders fall woefully short of achieving his ideal. What, then, of the model he rejected? Is more democracy not only desirable, but plausible as well?

Weber did not dismiss more participatory forms of democracy out of hand. But he claimed the size of modern societies, the absence of face-to-face relations, the growing complexity and technicality of administrative tasks, and the need for a permanent bureaucracy staffed by experts, all worked against the classical democratic ideal.[221] For direct democracy to be feasible, the following conditions had to be met:

1 the organization must be local or otherwise limited in the number of members;
2 the social positions of the members must not greatly differ from each other;
3 the administrative functions must be relatively simple and stable;
4 ... there must be a certain minimum development of training in objectively determining ways and means.[222]

According to Weber, none of these factors obtained in the large-scale and socially and economically differentiated societies of the developed world. Advocates of direct democracy ignored the effects of the increasing complexity of modern societies on the ability of the mass of people to make reasoned political judgements. People did not have the time or expertise to devote themselves to politics, as this model demanded. Cut off from the possibility of any personal experience or knowledge of public affairs and the processes effecting them, the average citizen acted on the basis of irrational prejudices resulting from numerous kinds of misinformation, much of it deliberately disseminated by those in power. Similar factors made it unrealistic to expect the demos to express a common will, a concept denied in principle by Weber's value pluralism in any case. Yet without such agreement, the mandating of delegates and administrative officers would only result in irresolvable conflicts between competing interests. One of the assets of the representative system lay in the possibility for parliamentary members to arrange trade-offs and compromises between each other which would have been impossible for their constituents to agree upon for themselves. They also managed to work alongside a professional bureaucracy, which provided the expertise and continuity vital for the running of a modern economy.

Weber's account of the obstacles to wider political involvement is salutary and in many respects valid. But he had a habit of turning a problem into an impasse, and his attitude to increased democracy was unduly pessimistic. Weber never considered the ways in which the ability of people to participate might be improved by removing some of the obstacles they currently have to overcome, such as the huge concentrations of economic and social power. He also exaggerated the degree to which public opinion is manipulable. Those in charge of the media and in positions of prestige and influence form a rather less coherent group than elite theorists have often thought, making the manufacture from above of a coherent viewpoint unlikely. The various perspectives derived from school, family, friends, work, newspapers and television, etc., interact with each other in numerous ways to produce diverse and often critical opinions amongst a far from unthinking mass.[223] Weber greatly overestimated the distance of politics from people's everyday lives. We continually have to confront political issues such as the price of food, the provision of welfare services, employment opportunities, the availability of housing, etc. Whilst it would be difficult to involve people directly at a macro level in making decisions about foreign or monetary policy, it is still possible to give people greater control over the implementation of such policies at a micro level in their local communities and in the workplace, etc.

The distribution of power in this manner would have three further benefits. First, it offers a means of alleviating Weber's great fear of bureaucratic domination. Weber rather overstated this danger, for the very social complexity which he believed rendered bureaucratic methods necessary has evolved to a stage which makes the effective co-ordination of any society by a centralised administration deeply problematic, as the planners of the former Communist bloc in Eastern Europe discovered. Consequently, political direction which operates from the centre alone will be similarly inefficient. In this respect, greater democracy constitutes a valid response to the enhanced pluralism and differentiation of society. Since different people are experts in different spheres, decentralization would not only reduce the monopoly of power of any one group, but prove more efficient as well. Of course, some overall co-ordination of the system would still be necessary, and representatives operating through parties and parliaments in tandem with a central administration still offers a plausible means of achieving this. However, to turn to the second benefit of enhanced democratization, the continued sway of the state is not incompatible with the empowerment of civil society. Intermediate institutions need not just serve as a more efficient mechanism for enacting policies made from on high, they could also act as a means for channelling the demands of people up to their representatives. The competitive elite and the participatory models of democracy are not necessarily mutually exclusive, they can be combined in ways which employ their respective virtues to overcome the other's weaknesses.[224] Finally, the existence of a diverse civil society containing a variety of voluntary self-governing associations – political parties, religious sects, economic and cultural organizations, etc. – can off-set the reifying effects of bureaucracy and capitalism. On the one hand, they help preserve the individual's capacity for exercising judgement and commitment, for they play a major role in maintaining the vocational values and spiritual ideals through which individuals assert their personal identity and moral responsibility. On the other hand, they add to the countervailing social forces opposing the state and business bureaucracies.[225]

Weber's philosophical and sociological arguments concerning the basis of liberalism can be employed to rethink liberal democracy even more thoroughly than he thought possible. He rejected ethical liberalism as but one more example of 'that soft-headed attitude, so agreeable from the human point of view, but nevertheless so unutterably narrowing in its effects, which thinks it possible to replace political with "ethical" ideals, and to innocently identify these with optimistic expectations of felicity'.[226] In place of a doctrine of rights or justice, he reconceived liberalism in realist terms as a set of procedures and institutions, which via the redistribution of power became capable of giving expression to a plurality of competing values in society, and of securing an accommodation between them. This reconceptualization of the liberal project provides the foundations for a pluralistic political liberalism based on the democratization of the ethic of responsibility and suited to the needs of a disenchanted and bureaucratic world suffocated by corporate power. We shall return to this argument in the conclusion. Before doing so, it remains for us to examine the attempts of those contemporary liberals who, unlike Weber, still try to offer a neutral moral framework capable of restraining the class and value conflicts of a post-Marxist and post-Nietzschean world.[227]

5

Contemporary Liberal Philosophy: Liberalism Neutralized

The rise of fascist and communist regimes in the 1920s and 1930s appeared to confirm Weber's gloomy predictions concerning the demise of liberal values in the modern world. Yet, if for many contemporaries the rival authoritarianisms of left and right made liberalism seem outmoded or inadequate, for others its values attained a new urgency. The period after the Second World War saw a renewed defence of liberal ideas and methods and of the political and economic institutions and practices held to embody them – notably the social and constitutional systems of Britain and the USA. Although the Cold War rendered much of this writing avowedly anti-socialist and dogmatic in tone, liberal thinking continued to range across a fairly wide ideological spectrum – from New Right neo-conservative libertarians to New Left sympathisers with the new social movements of the West and the dissident groups in the East. Avowedly liberal parties may have declined in most countries, but liberal concepts have threatened to become the only legitimate form of political discourse.

A notable feature of the most recent liberal theorising of all ideological persuasions has been its mixture of philosophical sophistication and social and political naivety. With the partial exception of the British tradition, to which these philosophers largely align themselves, this weakness had not been a general characteristic of earlier liberal thinking. As this book has attempted to show, earlier thinkers were all too aware of the degree to which liberal ideas were parasitic upon a particular social and political context which rendered them morally and sociologically plausible. It would appear that the more the actual practices of Western states diverged from the liberal ideal, the more abstract liberal theorising became. Thus, the putatively empirical defences of liberal democracy typical of political scientists of the 1950s and 1960s[1] gradually gave way to the philosophical defences of the next three decades. Whereas the former sought to define liberalism in terms of an idealised view of the prevailing Western social and political systems, the chief purpose of the latter is to provide definitions of liberalism that are prior to, and hence supposedly untainted by, any political or social considerations. They aim to prescribe the proper boundaries of politics and economics, rather than to describe or extrapolate from those that exist.

Many reasons can be given for this revival of liberal political philosophy, not least the end of the post-war boom and the neo-Keynesian consensus which provided both its rationale and its ideological legitimation.[2] These theories have responded to this situation by offering justifications for various visions of the liberal social order which aspire to be of universal validity. Moreover, their proponents appear to have succeeded to an extraordinary extent in getting this claim accepted. Although most of these thinkers are either British or North American by birth or adoption, their books have been widely translated and are regularly referred to as authorities in general political debate throughout the West and increasingly in former Eastern bloc countries as well. Nevertheless, one of the chief perils of abstract argument resides in a lack of engagement with the social and political problems confronting the implementation of the theory you seek to propose.[3] I shall argue that this lacuna proves fatal to contemporary liberal political philosophy, preventing it from facing up to the erosion of the ethical liberal assumptions on which its arguments either tacitly or explicitly rely.

Contemporary philosophical defences of liberalism have adopted two main, and divergent, methodological positions. First, both chronologically and in numbers of adherents, there are those writers who argue from individualist premises and define liberalism as a doctrine which is neutral between different conceptions of the good. They acknowledge we live in a 'disenchanted' world, lacking any overall moral consensus. They maintain that in such circumstances the only acceptable doctrine is one which treats the various values and projects of different people in an even-handed manner. Second, and more recently, a group of theorists have criticized this stance as incoherent and have sought to define liberalism as avowedly communitarian in nature: that is, as linked to a definite type of society and presupposing a shared understanding of its values.[4] In other words, they have urged a return to the ethical liberal tradition explored in this book. Although neutralist liberals have accused their communitarian critics of conservatism,[5] I shall argue that both schools rely upon similar assumptions for their respective positions, so that communitarian liberalism is indeed in many respects the more coherent of the two. However, I conclude that, given certain features of modern societies, if liberalism does require such moral and social foundations, it may well be time to abandon it in this form. In the conclusion, however, I shall outline a democratic view of liberalism which attempts to skirt around some of these difficulties.

NEUTRALIST LIBERALISM: NOZICK, HAYEK, DWORKIN, RAWLS

A number of theorists have made neutrality the defining political characteristic of liberalism. This feature merits emphasis, for they do not value neutrality *per se*. In their opinion, its virtue consists in showing equal concern and respect to individuals, groups and communities and their conceptions of the good in a way suited to societies characterized by a plurality of competing values. The doctrine has a healthy Kantian ancestry, insisting that we must find 'principles of right [*Recht*]' distinct from any particular moral purpose if we are to treat individuals as ends in themselves rather than as means to the attainment of some pre-conceived goal of our own.[6] In consequence, neutralist liberals are avowedly anti-perfectionist and anti-utilitarian on the grounds that the moral ends assumed by the former and the aggregative methods adopted by the latter fail to show sufficient respect to different individual lives. Nevertheless, as we shall see below, neutralist liberals frequently fall into the trap of adopting such procedures themselves. I shall contend that these lapses stem from the impossibility of separating the right from the good in the manner they propose.

In spite of agreement on this basic methodological point, neutralist theorists differ considerably over which principles best promote equality and respect. Ideologically, neutralist liberals range from neo-conservative libertarians like F. A. Hayek and R. Nozick, through more centrist liberals such as B. A. Ackerman, to social democrats like R. Dworkin and J. Rawls.[7] This diversity reflects an essential indeterminacy in the notion of neutrality which renders it somewhat vacuous for practical purposes, for it inevitably takes on the characteristics of the theory of the good held by its interpreter.

Following Joseph Raz, we may identify three types of neutrality.[8] The first type, neutrality in the narrowest sense, merely requires that the state take no action which aims to help individuals pursue a given conception of the good. The second type, neutrality in the comprehensive sense, in contrast, requires that the state ensure that all individuals are able equally to pursue and achieve any conception of the good that they choose. Finally, a third, mid-way position, moderate neutrality, requires that the state not do anything that will make it more likely that an individual will pursue one conception of the good rather than another unless it compensates those disadvantaged by policies which do discriminate in this way. Libertarian theorists have generally favoured the first sort of neutrality, socialists the second, and centre liberals and social democrats the third. The first seems the easiest to achieve but, as the following discussion shows, this simplicity proves deceptive. The second appears the most obviously neutral, yet it is impractical. In a world possessed of limited resources, no government can guarantee that all its citizens' desires will be satisfied. The achievement of equal satisfaction for all, therefore, involves everyone being restrained to some degree. However, it also raises problematical decisions concerning the intensity of different people's wants, the differential costs between those with expensive and cheap tastes, etc. Even if it were possible to arrange trade-offs between all these various groups in a neutral manner, a highly complex matter involving intractable technical and logical problems, those with the lowest expectations will end up subsidising the most greedy and ambitious – a rather curious policy to say the least! The final version of neutrality is the most complex, but, as we shall see, tends to merge into one or other of the previous two.

For the libertarians, the market alone treats people as equals because a person's success is a measure of his or her productive use of common resources. The norms governing market transactions provide the simplest form of neutrality by neither helping nor hindering any of the competing parties, beyond the minimal requirement of preventing them from intentionally causing each other direct physical harm. Libertarian thinkers maintain that this is the only attitude either compatible with equality of respect or truly neutral. Any attempt to introduce a 'patterned' distribution of resources, which evens up the life chances of unequally talented individuals in some way, fails to treat them as ends in themselves. They do not defend the market on the grounds that it rewards the meritorious or deserving, therefore, because one could only decide on what counts as merit or desert by making the sorts of value judgements they seek to rule out. Rather, markets distribute goods in an 'unpatterned' way on the basis of entitlement and luck. Needless to say, these thinkers regard distribution on the basis of need as the most contentious and illiberal form of social justice. I shall examine two examples of this narrow version of neutrality – those of Robert Nozick and Friedrich Hayek.[9]

Nozick has argued that we must view the varied capacities and degrees of inherited wealth of different individuals as the blind gifts of fortune, and accept any state of affairs that results from them legitimately exercising their entitlements as just, provided that there is not a legacy of previous violations of entitlements to compensate for.[10] The redistribution of resources infringes what Nozick asserts is our basic right to self-ownership, from which all property rights protecting the rights of individuals to pursue their projects without the interference of others ultimately derive. In spite of its apparent simplicity, Nozick's theory is not immune from the criticisms of indeterminacy and arbitrariness levelled at more complex neutralist theories of justice. In following Locke and postulating a single basic right to which all other entitlements can be traced, Nozick seeks to avoid the chief difficulty confronting natural rights theorists – namely, how to adjudicate between conflicting yet equally fundamental rights. For a philosopher aspiring to provide a theory that is neutral between rival conceptions of the good, the problems of having to make 'on-balance' judgements between incompatible liberties poses seemingly insuperable problems. How, for example, can one decide the relative merits of freedom of speech and freedom of privacy in a manner that does not explicitly or implicitly involve value judgements?[11] Even a system composed entirely of negative or passive rights, which only require forbearance rather than positive measures by governments or individuals for their enforcement, is liable to give rise to such conflicts. As inhabitants of flats or apartments know all too well, for example, rights to privacy and property rights can frequently clash in a variety of ways.

Nozick's attempt to get around this difficulty by grafting all rights onto a single primordial right does not work. Leaving aside the fact that, unlike Locke who offers a theological framework for his theory, he provides no argument for why we have the basic right of self-ownership in the first place, the relationship between self-ownership and other rights remains obscure. He appears simply to assert that a right of initial acquisition is derivable from it, although he rightly notes that Locke's labour-mixing theory is fraught with problems. The obscurity of this connection suggests that Nozick's thesis requires the existence of two basic rights rather than one. Moreover, the notion of 'first possession', on which Nozick's entitlement thesis rests, still needs further specification to avoid extension to an excessively wide number of goods. For example, would aesthetic pleasures deriving from being the first to see a beautiful vista prohibit a subsequent landowner from developing the spot? Both claims can be defended equally well in neo-Lockean Nozickean terms. It also raises the question of why those earlier in time should be favoured over those who come later. Neither sort of issue can be addressed without embarking upon the slippery slope of advocating a particular 'pattern' of distribution – something his thesis had sought to avoid.[12] Nozick half admits that he can think of no theory of acquisition capable of resolving conflicts between the divergent property rights to which it might give rise.[13] However, he simply skirts around the problem in his usual cavalier fashion, going so far as to refer in a footnote to the very redistributionist principles he purports to dismiss.[14] This admission is fatal to his theory but inescapable, for even Nozick cannot avoid the abrogation of some property rights. For example, he claims that our inviolable right to the products of our skill, labour and luck in the market renders taxation an infringement of the integrity of the individual akin to physical coercion.[15] Yet, like most libertarians, he appreciates that a minimal state will be needed to enforce recognition of the contractual rights and duties basic to the free market economy. But if taxation is equivalent to coercion, how is this to be funded? He would appear to be hoist with his own petard.

A more subtle advocate of the market mechanism and libertarian values is F. A. Hayek. Hayek's theory is especially interesting for us, since he alone amongst contemporary liberal thinkers consciously tries to combine the social and philosophical theses which I have identified as typical of liberalism. The social thesis Hayek associates above all with Hume and other thinkers of the Scottish Enlightenment, such as Adam Smith. Hayek accuses all 'constructivist' endeavours rationally to control and plan society of the most dangerous hubris. He contends that social processes and individual goals are too diverse and complex to be so organised, and any attempt to do so will result in the illiberal imposition of a particular set of putatively rational ends on all those who do not endorse them. Liberalism, on this view, arises from an appreciation of the role of unplanned individual action in the development of society, a proposition developed by Hayek in his theory of the market as a spontaneous order or 'catallaxy', composed of free exchanges between independent individuals serving their mutual wants.[16] However, Hayek is not so sanguine that he believes that a liberal polity will automatically emerge from the evolutionary process so long as it is left alone. The co-ordination of spontaneous orders can break down, for example as a result of prisoners' dilemmas generating 'negative externalities'.[17] These failures cannot be rectified by market forces alone, since the structure of rights and entitlements supporting the market either rules out such transactions or makes them uneconomic. Without some intervention both to secure those public goods necessary to the functioning of the market itself, and to eliminate the public bads generated by its own unregulated operations, the spontaneous order gives way to disorder. Hayek appreciates some of these difficulties. Unlike Nozick, he accepts a limited role for the state to alleviate extreme cases of hardship and to provide essential public goods, although he is opposed to anything approaching a welfare state.[18] More important, he sees the need for a new constitutional settlement capable of upholding the rule of law and of defining and protecting those rights essential to the freedom of individuals.[19] This leads him to defend what I have called liberalism's philosophical thesis – the maximization of individual liberty. For this purpose, he turns principally to Kant and argues that human rationality and autonomy require that each individual has an equal right to freedom. Again following Kant, he insists that this is best secured by a legal framework consisting solely of universal rules of just conduct, protecting a recognisable private domain of individuals.[20]

Hayek claims that his theory is not the result of any theoretical construction, but that it merely reflects the desire of earlier liberals to extend and generalise the beneficial effects of the social and political order of eighteenth- and nineteenth-century Britain.[21] Thus, like the earlier liberals he admires, he believes the social and the philosophical aspects of his doctrine are mutually supporting, the one implying the other. However, as Chandren Kukathas has demonstrated in his study of Hayek's political thought, they are incompatible.[22] The first contends that the role of reason in social life must be severely circumscribed. The second offers a systematic defence of the liberal order on rational grounds. Thus, the second thesis contradicts the anti-constructivism of the first. Hayek fails to recognize this dilemma, yet he cannot escape it: for the claim of the first thesis to derive liberalism from the discovery of a spontaneous order in social affairs can only be sustained within the context of the moral theory contained in the second thesis. Only the latter is capable of identifying a specifically liberal set of individual entitlements and of justifying them as essential to the very nature of a social order as Hayek conceives it. In itself, the social thesis leads not to liberalism but a form of traditionalist conservatism that Hayek explicitly repudiates. As he points out, for the liberal 'the decisive objection to any conservatism which deserves to be called such...is that by its very nature it cannot offer an alternative to the direction in which we are moving...It has, for this reason, invariably been the fate of conservatism to be dragged along a path not of its own choosing.'[23] Since the social thesis cannot point in an explicitly liberal direction, it must be supplemented by a philosophical thesis which does.

To defend liberal principles, therefore, Hayek is forced to adopt the very rationalist reasoning he attacks. In the process, he impugns the narrow neutrality embodied in his social theory. Take the account of liberty which Hayek places at the centre of his social and political thought.[24] From the perspective of his social thesis, Hayek appears to adopt a 'negative' conception of liberty as simply 'the absence...of coercion by other men'. On this view, our freedom suffers no restriction even if our options are few and unattractive, so long as no person has intentionally and directly limited them. Freedom 'becomes positive only through what we make of it. It does not assure us of any particular opportunities, but leaves it to us to decide what use we shall make of the circumstances in which we shall find ourselves.' Accordingly, for Hayek 'the penniless vagabond who lives precariously by constant improvisation is...freer than the conscripted soldier with all his security and relative comfort.'[25] Now, Hayek argues that 'while the uses of liberty are many, liberty is one. Liberties only appear when liberty is lacking.'[26] As a result, he regards the trading off of certain liberties against others as incoherent. Since liberty is a unitary concept, it can only be increased or diminished. However, we have observed at a number of points in this book that this argument is only tenable on the basis of a strongly normative view of what counts as liberty – the hallmark of the positive conception of liberty. Otherwise, conflicts between different sets of compossible liberties will arise, which because of their incommensurability cannot be weighed up against each other. Not surprisingly, when we turn to Hayek's philosophical defence of liberty, we discover that he does indeed adopt the very sort of positive notion of freedom his social theory condemns. This aspect becomes apparent in his definition of coercion. He condemns coercion on the largely Kantian grounds that it 'eliminates an individual as a thinking and valuing person and makes him a bare tool in the achievement of the ends of another'. However, as he notes, coercion 'cannot be altogether avoided because the only way to prevent it is by the threat of coercion'.[27] Practically, the solution is to confer a monopoly of coercion on the state. But to avoid arbitrary rule, a line needs to be drawn between legitimate and illegitimate coercion. Hayek adopts Kant's solution to this question, and argues that laws are only legitimate so long as they are universalizable so as to apply equally to all. Indeed, again following Kant, he maintains that 'when we obey laws, in the sense of general abstract rules irrespective of their application to us, we are not subject to another's will and are therefore free.'[28] As John Gray remarks, Hayek's argument closely resembles the central tenet of positive conceptions of liberty – namely, that we are only free when we obey the general will, and hence that what Hayek calls 'true law' cannot limit freedom.[29] Thus, as with most ethical liberal theories, Hayek's liberalism turns out to assume a certain sort of rational moral agency, and not to be neutral as regards divergent conceptions of the good at all.

Hayek attempts to get around this problem in a number of ways, but these solutions only compound his difficulties. For example, he tries to avoid the charge of constructivism by stressing the formalism of the Kantian test of universalizability.[30] The trouble with this criterion is that it is so weak that with a little ingenuity numerous injunctions totally incompatible with individual liberty in either the positive or negative senses can be made to pass it.[31] Nor does it determine adequately the protected domains of individuals, within which they cannot be coerced and outside which they have no absolute entitlement to stray. Gray's suggestion,[32] that the universalizability thesis be rendered more specific by insisting that only rules which fulfil the demands of consistency, impartiality and moral neutrality pass the test, does not resolve this particular problem. Instead, it risks making the criteria so stringent that hardly any law would prove acceptable.

Hayek's other possible solution creates similar difficulties. This reading, again propounded by Gray, suggests that Hayek's theory be seen as a form of indirect utilitarianism, in which a social system incorporating certain kinds of individual rights and liberties is valued for its conduciveness to the maximization of human welfare.[33] Whilst it is true that Hayek refers at a number of points to the beneficial consequences of a liberal regime in terms of increased population, material prosperity and human progress,[34] he makes an implausible utilitarian. As Kukathas has stressed,[35] the strongly anti-rationalist stance of his social theory, with its antipathy to all constructivist ethics, rules out even the most sophisticated forms of utilitarianism. Hayek rejects totally the possibility of any sort of end-state comparative judgements concerning human happiness or preference satisfaction, vital for utilitarian doctrines of all kinds. From the standpoint of his social theory, the chief virtue of the liberal order is not that it promotes any given goal but that it simply enables human beings to adapt to an ever-changing environment, the moral quality of which remains an open question. Since preferences are moulded in the evolutionary process, 'progress in the sense of the cumulative growth of knowledge and power over nature is a term that says little about whether the new state will give us more satisfaction than the old.' Progress, according to Hayek, is simply 'movement for movement's sake' rather than an advance to some putative state of human fulfilment – a definition which would be radically at odds with his liberalism. Nor can knowledge of the general character of this process enable us deliberately to construct the conditions most amenable to its unfolding. For human reason itself is a product of evolution and hence 'can neither predict nor deliberately shape its own future'.[36] Once again, the attempt to provide a philosophical defence of the liberal social order is undercut by the social thesis which denies the validity of any such undertaking.

Hayek cannot resolve the central dilemma at the heart of his doctrine. The neutrality and openness which he insists constitute the great virtue of the liberal social system rule out all attempts rationally to justify the nature and scope of the individual entitlements which he asserts are vital to its functioning. Yet, without such a justification, he cannot show that the evolutionary process enjoins a specifically liberal order at all.

Writers at the social democratic end of the liberal spectrum tend to employ more explicitly constructivist kinds of reasoning. They reject the simpler forms of neutrality adopted by libertarians on the grounds of fairness. According to Ronald Dworkin and John Rawls, the scope of neutrality implies that not only must the political framework be neutral, but also that no laws or programmes should be passed which make it easier to pursue one conception of the good rather than another. Nozick and Hayek claim that the minimal state is neutral in the first sense, because its justification depends on reasons independent of any particular theory of the good. However, the neutrality of their proposal could still be impugned, since a failure to secure the conditions enabling all persons to have an equal possibility of pursuing and promoting their chosen ideal of the good effectively hinders them from so doing. For these reasons, both Rawls and Dworkin seek to secure a neutral distribution of resources which will offer every person equality of opportunity to follow a given way of life with an equal chance of success. Nevertheless, Dworkin in particular rejects the extension of this argument into an attempt to guarantee all members of society equality of fulfilment. He notes that personal satisfaction is highly subjective, so that to apply any universal measure, such as the degree of wealth achieved, would not respect the incommensurable values held by different individuals. Indeed, even individuals themselves hold divergent views of success in different spheres and stages of their lives. As we noted, to let everyone draw up their own assessment of their degree of fulfilment raises the problem of those choosing low levels of attainment or cheap pleasures subsidising the hopelessly overambitious or egocentric. Moreover, some people may not value success or fulfilment at all, preferring instead a life of continuous striving or the disinterested and selfless pursuit of certain goals, neither of which will necessarily maximize personal satisfaction. Aside from these practical difficulties, Dworkin regards the whole exercise of using individuals' conceptions of the good to determine their claims upon a society as misconceived. For people adopt a given way of life in the light of the available resources, so that to fix on the former in ignorance of the latter would be meaningless.[37] Finally, a further assumption concerning the scope of neutrality underlies Dworkin's and Rawls's caveats about welfarism. What, following Raz, we earlier called a theory of 'comprehensive neutrality' will see every aspect of an individual's well-being as the proper concern of the state, and hence regard a policy of equal satisfaction as the only way not to favour any conception of the good more than others.[38] As we saw, at the other extreme lies a 'narrow' theory of neutrality, such as Nozick's, which sees practically any interference as an infringement of personal autonomy. Rawls and Dworkin take a mid-position, arguably based more on its intuitive appeal than on logic, which regards individuals as responsible for the success of their own chosen goals to the extent that they are not prejudiced by features of the world or of themselves that are not of their own making. Despite the apparent reasonableness of this position, it proves hard to sustain.

In his essay on 'Liberalism', Dworkin succinctly sums up the essential neutralist case outlined above. According to Dworkin the 'constitutive morality' of liberalism consists of a theory of equality which 'supposes that political decisions must be, so far as is possible, independent of any particular conception of the good life, or of what gives value to life'. He continues:

> Since the citizens of a society differ in their conceptions, the government does not treat them as equals if it prefers one conception to another, either because the officials believe that one is intrinsically superior, or because one is held by the more numerous or more powerful group.[39]

Dworkin regards the familiar liberal institutions of the market economy and representative democracy as providing the most satisfactory institutional means for meeting this requirement, since both are procedural mechanisms for the neutral aggregation and exchange of individual preferences.[40] Nevertheless, they frequently fail to operate in the desired manner. Differences and inequalities of social and economic power mean that biases develop against certain groups, and redistributive measures and civil rights are needed to ensure that the system accurately reflects different citizens' preferences and treats them all with equal respect.[41] I shall examine both proposals in turn below.[42]

Dworkin agrees with traditional liberals that in an efficient market the cost to individuals of what they consume in the way of goods and leisure, and the value of what they add by their own efforts, is reflected in the net benefit of their contribution to the community as determined by the willingness of other individuals to pay for their services. He maintains that two aspects of the real world prevent the realization of this liberal idyll. First, people do not begin on equal terms; some have advantages of inherited wealth and better social circumstances, or have better luck than others. Second, people are not equal in their 'raw' skill, intelligence or other capacities and, through no deliberate choice of their own, the market may reward some better than others. In consequence, individuals who are willing to work just as hard as others more fortunately endowed can still end up with fewer resources. Thus Dworkin favours the market in so far as it rewards the 'genuine choices' individuals have made for life-styles which cost or benefit society in ways which reflect what other people want from their lives. However, he seeks to correct it to the extent that some people are disadvantaged not because they *will* not respond to market forces but because they *cannot* due to some misfortune, an inherent incapacity or social disadvantage.[43]

Dworkin's own proposal concentrates on producing an equal distribution of resources against which individuals choose their plan of life, but he believes they must rely on their own abilities and those of like-minded fellow citizens for their success. He bases his solution on a hypothetical auction in which participants bargain with an equal number of otherwise worthless counters (clam shells) for the resources of an imagined island.[44] Unlike Rawls's 'original position', discussed below, the participants are aware of the actual disposition of existing resources and hence can base their conceptions of the good upon that knowledge. He therefore gets around the criticism that he assumes people would choose a certain set of resources, such as Rawls's 'primary goods', which deliberately stack the odds in favour of essentially liberal patterns of life. The island example is meant to replicate an idealized market.

Before looking at the problems Dworkin raises himself, it is worth pondering upon those he does not. A major difficulty arises from the way the aggregation of different individual preferences may have the consequence of blocking the availability of resources for use by a minority. One response to this possibility might be that although unfortunate, it was unintended and hence quite fair. Dworkin seems to find it perfectly acceptable that we should be influenced by the market's channelling of individual demands when deciding whether to pursue a lucrative career or not. The important point seems to be that no one intends to impose a particular career on anyone else by desiring a certain commodity. I shall return to the assumptions concerning our ability to choose careers and the invisible hand mechanism at work in Dworkin's theory later. For the moment, I wish only to point out that in given circumstances his reasoning could lead to some individuals being deprived of materials essential to their particular kind of existence. In the essay on 'Liberalism' Dworkin uses an argument for the protection of the environment which suggests that he might restrict the auction to individually consumable goods, ruling out public goods such as air, beautiful views, etc. He argues that:

> the conquest of unspoilt terrain by the consumer economy is self-fuelling and irreversible, and…will make a way of life that has been desired and found satisfying in the past unavailable to future generations,…the process is not neutral amongst competing ideas of the good life, but in fact destructive of the very possibility of some of these.[45]

This argument provides an example of the indeterminacy characteristic of Dworkin's position. He claims that this decision arises not from the presumption that conservation is good for future generations or what they will want. Rather, it derives from the need to keep open the choice between lives linked to the natural environment and those premised upon industrialization. Are we then to suppose that all choices must be kept open? Should we, for example, retain a malarial swamp for the benefit of future aspirant victims? Moreover, how can we specify any mix of industrialisation and conservation without running the risk of arbitrariness? We would appear doomed to inactivity, consuming only abundant and renewable resources widely available to all. Yet even this decision requires justification. To take Dworkin's example, surely not building a factory or banning strip-mining could prejudice the likely life styles of future generations just as much as doing so would. The difficulty seems endemic to the attempt to identify public goods independently of any appeal to their intrinsic value for human life, or of what individuals prefer.

Presumably it is to avoid an appeal of the first kind that Dworkin skirts around the issue by treating his auction as a totally individualistic affair. He raises the problem of dividing out 'unique' resources, but suggests that distributions are acceptable so long as they are 'envy free', in the economist's sense, meaning that no one prefers anyone else's bundle to his or her own. If they did, the auction would have to be run again. However, his main reason for not tackling it stems from his faith in his proposed insurance scheme. He imagines everyone insuring themselves against both unsuitable talents and handicaps or special cravings for rare resources that impede a successful life, whilst still in a Rawlsian-style state of ignorance about their actual abilities. Thus, because individuals would have insurance against these two sorts of misfortune, they would have protection against the vagaries of market forces. Dworkin wishes to distinguish 'expensive' tastes from disadvantages which have not been actively desired or willed by people themselves.[46] An example of the latter might be a diabetic who would want protection against the price of insulin becoming prohibitive. But surely insuring against both is just as rational for individuals behind the veil of ignorance? After all, certain of my tastes may become expensive –

consider the case of the addicted smoker, whose habit has become increasingly costly. In addition, to compensate handicaps and cravings effectively renders other tastes and talents expensive, with the more favourably endowed having to work harder to maximise the utility of the low earners. It may prove more acceptable for them to level down rather than up. Finally, faced with the ever increasing possibilities created by medical science for very expensive treatment to save life, Dworkin's scheme risks writing certain categories of people a blank cheque which cuts off important discussions about the competing use of resources for equally worthwhile goals.[47]

These problems basically boil down to two: the inability of his theory to cope with the issue of public goods, and the difficulty of applying the equality of resources model over time. The relative value we place on our private goods will depend on both these factors. The appreciation we have for a motor car, for example, will depend on how many other people possess them, what the road system is like, what the consequences for the environment are likely to be – elements that have a collective and temporal dimension. Questions of distribution cannot be isolated from social processes and contexts, therefore, in the manner Dworkin attempts. For related reasons, Dworkin's distinction between 'natural' and willed inequalities, which lies at the heart of his whole theory, is similarly tendentious. He accepts that the needs of society at any given time will favour some people more than others, and that we can insure against our talents not being wanted. Merit is a product of social demand, rather than an intrinsic feature of our abilities or character.[48] But he attempts to retain the belief that those aptitudes and traits we do possess are 'natural' and are not themselves socially constituted. This distinction strikes me as forced, at the very least the relative weighting of nature and nurture seems hard to disentangle. Whether it collapses or not, it is very difficult to see how his proposal can escape shading into the principle of equal fulfilment which he rightly rejects.

A major obstacle confronting neutralist theorists stems from the dubious possibility of devising any notion of social justice without making qualitative judgements. Such theories always have to specify which resources should be shared and how, in ways which will favour some life styles and hinder others. Dworkin claims that having ensured through various devices a base-line of equality of resources (including personal abilities) the choices over which ones and how we use them becomes a personal matter. If I do not want to maximise my wealth, for example, I can opt for a life of self-denial rather than entering the City or Wall Street. However, as we saw with the environment example above, we cannot always be insulated from the consequences of other people's choices. Decisions to modernise the economy, etc., become grounded in certain conceptions of life which curtail others. Dworkin hopes to avoid the problem of choosing any given structural principle by arguing that even if the eventual distributions do reflect conceptions of the good, one can arrive at them by neutral methods. He bases the neutrality of the market upon its procedural virtues. In the market individuals remain ignorant of the likely effects of their preferences for specific commodities. When I choose a range of goods it becomes impossible for me to trace all the likely effects of these decisions on the economy as a whole. As we saw, Dworkin is not so callous as to accept all the non-neutral effects of its operations. Yet there is no reason for matters to stop there, for why should not people insure against the non-neutrality of the market itself? Given that certain types of social structure favour particular notions of the good, the right cannot be separated from the good: for what I regard as the right society largely depends upon the goals I feel are worth pursuing. Clearly the market favours entrepreneurial individuals who are willing to exploit their talents to their best advantage. Dworkin specifically endorses this type of agent through his emphasis on individual responsibility. However, why should someone who desires an alternative social set-up, who believes they would do rather better under feudalism or primitive communism for example, not demand compensation? In other words, once Dworkin acknowledges that non-neutral outcomes can have repugnant consequences, how can he devise methods to avoid only some of them without himself infringing neutrality? The only alternative would appear to be either to leave the content of equality completely empty, as in the 'narrow' conception of neutrality, or to broaden it to promote equal satisfaction.

Dworkin's advocacy of the market involves more than a commitment to the rather abstract position of 'treating people as equals'. It rests on his incorporating the whole value system of liberal capitalism into his theory. For there is nothing in Dworkin's argument, beyond his own cultural preferences, to suggest that market societies offer the only plausible and coherent form of equality of respect. Take the examples of feudalism and primitive communism adverted to above. Arguably both involve a certain conception of showing people 'equality of concern and respect' every bit as valid as the liberal's. Distinctions of birth count as 'natural' inequalities under feudalism, much as putatively 'natural' differences in ability are held to legitimate large differentials in wealth and power under capitalism. The king shows no lack of respect in regarding his vassal as a subordinate, for their difference in status counts as a relevant reason for unequal treatment in such a society. Primitive communism offers a much simpler version of an egalitarian society. Liberals usually reject it on the grounds that the common ownership of goods stultifies individual initiative – a view relying on the sort of contentious assumptions concerning human nature which a neutralist liberal ought to avoid.[49] However, such a society is likely to be committed to the principle of ensuring each person has resources to pursue his or her goals to an equal degree – a radical formulation of the notion of 'treating people as equals' which Dworkin approves. My point is that the quality of life, and hence what counts as a relevant reason for according people equality of respect, will be different under each of these systems. Feudal societies base it on status, communist societies on need, and market societies on desert.[50] The liberal notion of desert and of what constitutes equality of opportunity on the one hand, and Dworkin's belief in the intrinsic fairness of market societies on the other, are two sides of the same coin. Since there are no 'objective' moral reasons for believing liberal capitalism to be the best form of society, the attempt to show that there are will inevitably end in failure.

Analogous difficulties bedevil his account of rights and the operation of democracy. Democratic decisions by majority vote can similarly undermine the possibilities for minorities to pursue their conception of the good. The usual response of liberals is to place constraints on the outcomes of votes in the form of individual rights. Once again, neutralists find themselves in the tricky situation of devising rights without discriminating amongst goods in ways which favour or imply some notions of human fulfilment rather than others. The problems parallel those associated with the distribution of resources. Any metric for the protection or restriction of liberty, be it Mill's 'simple principle' or Rawls's 'first principle' advocating the 'most extensive liberty', will implicitly carry value judgements about the relative worth of different types of human action embedded within it. For instance, Mill's notion of harm is either too wide, encompassing such a variety of controversial and contradictory claims that it cannot determine action, or too narrow to remain morally neutral between the alternatives. In order to avoid this problem, Dworkin seeks to devise a neutral method for arriving at our rights which screens out judgements based upon conceptions of the good. Dworkin maintains that the objection to a simple utilitarian aggregation of preferences rests upon their inclusion of not only 'personal' preferences, which apply solely to ourselves, but also 'external' preferences, which dictate a certain way of life for others.[51] He claims such decisions could be rendered neutral by excluding the latter. He proposes that we require a set of rights, similar to the American Bill of Rights, which would overrule ('trump' in Dworkin's terminology) any decision which intended to prescribe a particular way of life and impose it on other people against their consent.[52] Thus, in Dworkin's account, I do not have any rights to a specified set of goods, such as the freedoms of speech and assembly, only the right not to be imposed upon by the 'external' preferences of others. Personal preferences, however, can have external effects. The desire for non-smokers not to inhale tobacco fumes requires that people do not smoke in their presence, for example. Indeed, most of our important preferences entail a particular ordering of affairs, without us necessarily wishing to impose forms of behaviour on others. Even individualistic preferences potentially produce the same result, for they involve a particular social set-up which renders alternative life styles based on collective arrangements or enforced orthodoxy unobtainable. Of course no liberal theory need be ashamed of rejecting Hitler or the Ayatollah Khomeini, but Dworkin's arguments from equality and neutrality are too weak to achieve even this in all circumstances. Fascists, say, might always argue that they merely wanted the chance to live in a particular way. If a sufficient number of people held similar views, they could say it was merely a 'personal' preference for fascism that led to the prohibition of non-fascist activities, not an 'external' preference to achieve that result.[53]

Dworkin might want to save his theory by drawing a third distinction, between 'personal' preferences with external effects, such as those given above, and self-regarding personal preferences which affect only the person who has the preference – like sleeping on your side. Even such trivial examples raise problems, of course – how many relationships break up because of a lack of complementarity as to which side you prefer, for instance? Suppose one *could* find a morally neutral definition of self-regarding preferences, though (a controversial issue, for all the reasons raised in relation to the Millian principle); it is still likely to be either too wide, making our rights too all-encompassing, or too narrow, protecting us against very little. On the 'narrow' interpretation, we can only have rights to protect purely self-regarding areas of our lives. On the 'wider' view, our rights can 'trump' any personal preferences with external effects. Choosing between them seems in itself quite arbitrary and points up the difficulty of neutrality noted above. Dworkin generally employs whichever suits his purpose at a given moment. Thus, in the environment example, cited above, he conceivably adopts a variant of the 'wide' view. However, as we saw, this version has debilitating consequences of the sort Dworkin generally wishes to avoid. He wants to employ a revised form of utilitarianism, based on personal preferences, in order to resolve such problems as the allocation of scant resources for competing ends in a 'neutral' manner. For instance, he has consistently argued that a decision of this kind could justify a policy of reverse discrimination favouring specified under-privileged racial groups. He maintains that a certain arbitrariness is unavoidable when choosing criteria for selecting people for jobs or university places. Once the pool of acceptable candidates, possessing the minimum level of ability necessary to perform the requisite tasks, grows beyond the number of available places, then the choice depends on other qualities deemed to be in the best interests of the community at large. So long as these reflect a 'rational calculation about the socially most beneficial use of limited resources' rather than 'prejudice or contempt', the unsuccessful applicants suffer no curtailment of their right to equality of respect.[54] Yet, even if Dworkin's arguments successfully rebut the charge of inverted racism, they can be applied in ways which offend liberal susceptibilities. By similar reasoning one could justify a policy of enforced friendship and love for social outcasts, for example. This latter suggestion causes offence because it conflicts with our notions of the integrity and dignity of the person –

inherently value-laden concepts, to which Dworkin purportedly makes no appeal.

When it comes to civil liberties the 'narrow' view can have similarly unfortunate results. Dworkin possibly employs some such distinction when he argues that a 'personal' preference not to be offended or upset is insufficient either to curtail the use of strong language in demonstrations or to ban displays of pornographic material in principle.[55] Since people can surely find behaviour or displays disagreeable or embarrassing without holding that they are wrong for any separate reason, his objection is presumably to their external effects going beyond the self-regarding sphere of the privacy of their own homes. Yet if he supports the anti-Vietnam protester's right to offend public morality by using obscene language like 'fuck the draft', why not extend similar rights to someone wishing to expose himself in public? The flasher may even have a better case than the demonstrator, since the second is presumably agitating for some social cause or external preference which could affect us all, whilst the first is just doing what comes naturally and could dismiss complaints as the product of excessive prudery. Dworkin rightly insists that he need not be neutral about forms of expression which attack the *raison d'être* of neutrality itself – such as Nazis promoting racial legislation which would curtail equality of respect – but this still leaves open a very wide field of potentially anti-social activity.

Although Dworkin's neutralism allows him to cope with straight external preferences, it debars any satisfactory discrimination amongst personal preferences in terms of their content. However, without making such choices he cannot erect rights as barriers against the effects of certain sorts of personal preferences, for to do this involves justifying why particular areas of an individual's life are especially important and valuable and ought to receive special protection, in other words ought not to be subject to utilitarian trade-offs. Such judgements violate neutrality, for they implicitly rely upon an idea of what is valuable for individuals. This dilemma is unavoidable. The questions of equality and social justice, which motivate Dworkin's liberalism, ultimately assume a shared commitment to certain essential forms of human fulfilment and the intrinsic worth of the capacity for self-development. The main weakness of his theory arises from the lack of any account of how we come to recognize these common goals. Indeed, his whole rights-based approach militates against such recognition. Respect for the environment, for example, cannot be generated in this way. Suppose I own a piece of land, I have a right to do with it what I please. I can build on it, mine it, let it go wild, etc. I may have instrumental reasons to do all these things in a responsible way, because of the money I'll make from selling a beautiful rather than an ugly building, for example. But the interests of others cannot produce a duty on my part to respect them without absurdly extending the claims of individuals to restrict someone's action on the grounds of a potential conflict of interest – the difficulty of the 'wide' reading of self-regarding personal preferences discussed earlier. Ultimately the rights of others can only be appreciated in the context of certain shared notions of what makes for a valuable and worthwhile life. These values cannot be arrived at by separating out our personal from our external preferences, since we habitually evaluate what we regard as a good for ourselves against a background understanding of how it relates to the range of goods available in society as a whole. Moreover, we frequently acknowledge the intrinsic importance of goods and activities we have no interest in or ability to pursue ourselves, simply on the grounds of their value for human fulfilment. We can be tone deaf and still recognise the importance of music.

Dworkin ignores such questions largely by assuming we all share roughly the same scale of values as he does: that we rank anti-draft demonstrations above old ladies' feelings, but have little regard for the rights of flashers. In fact, he explicitly admits to a theory of human worth when he explains why we should value 'equality of respect' in the first place. The whole notion of rights, he states, 'supposes that there are ways of treating a man that are inconsistent with regarding him as a full member of the human community, and holds such treatment is profoundly unjust'.[56] He asserts that governments must show concern for their citizens as 'beings who are capable of forming and acting on intelligent conceptions of how their lives should be lived'.[57] In other words, he appeals to the liberal model of the self-developing rational chooser of ends, characteristic of the rationalist tradition of Kant and Mill. It is this conception of human agency which does the real work in his theory, allowing him to rank the rights of the individualist above those of the conformist, the pursuer of intellectual argument and debate above the prudish and the prurient. Indeed, when it comes to the tricky problem of settling 'hard cases', Dworkin imagines a judge of Herculean powers explicitly drawing on such values in order to uphold the moral fabric of liberal society. Thus, Dworkin's argument subtly moves from being individualist and neutralist to adopting an ethical and communitarian viewpoint.

Rawls's theory has undergone a similar change of perspective for similar reasons. In his book *A Theory of Justice*, Rawls attempts to find 'an Archimedean point for judging the basic structure of society'.[58] To attain this perspective, he adopts the device of a hypothetical 'original position' to arrive at two principles of justice, which he believes rational individuals would choose freely if they were ignorant of their present abilities and social position, as fair for society as a whole. According to Rawls, these principles are:

First principle
Each person is to have an equal right to the most extensive total system of equal basic liberties compatible with a similar system of liberty for all.

Second principle
Social and economic inequalities are to be arranged so that they are both:
    (a) to the greatest benefit of the least advantaged,
    (b) attached to offices and positions open to all under conditions of fair equality of opportunity.[59]

Participants in the original position also agree on a 'lexical order' for the application of the principles, according to which the first takes precedence over the second and 2(b) has priority over 2(a). Rawls maintains the choosers in the original position possess only a 'thin theory of the good', consisting of a number of 'primary goods' which he assumes it is rational for all persons, regardless of their views, to want to maximize. They do not have particular interests, but only a generalized interest in being able to secure whatever particular interests they may acquire. Similarly, they have no knowledge or known preference for any specific kind of society, merely general information about social processes. As a result, Rawls claims that the derivation of these principles is purely procedural and hence neutral between different conceptions of the good.

Rawls's project has attracted a torrent of criticism.[60] Numerous commentators have remarked that the principles themselves are inadequate and certainly not neutral. The first attempts to be so by proposing the construction of a maximal system of equal rights for all. We have already criticised this classical liberal project in the introduction and elsewhere for its failure to recognise that judgements about liberty are necessarily qualitative rather than quantitative in nature. The individualist bias of the second principle ignores the importance to people of collective goods, such as peace, a clean environment etc., which cannot be distributed in the form of individualisable resources. Yet, the maximin criteria (2a) also curiously avoids any reference to individual desert, need or entitlement in the apportionment of burdens and benefits, thereby undercutting the notions of personal responsibility, effort or contribution central to the liberal conception of autonomy Rawls largely defends.[61] Moreover, it does not capture the importance of people's relative standing for their evaluation of their sense of equal worth and respect. Finally, Marxist and feminist critics have attacked the division between state and civil society, private and public, implied by Rawls's lexical ordering and separation of his two principles. They argue that he underestimates the extent to which the equal freedoms of the first require a more substantial social and economic empowerment than he appears to concede with the second.

These weaknesses are related to a general difficulty in Rawls's derivation of his two principles: namely, his tacit reliance on the naive moral and social assumptions characteristic of the ethical liberal tradition. Many commentators have pointed out the impossibility of abstracting individuals from any historical and social contexts, or of finding criteria of rationality and justification in morals which are not relative to particular ethical perspectives. For some critics, Rawls only arrives at his liberal-democratic consensus by endowing the members of the original position with the characteristics typical of idealised liberal citizens. Others have regarded that had he taken his 'thin theory of the good' and the principles of pure instrumental rationality seriously, they would not have supported the particular index of primary goods which he requires for his proposed theory of justice.[62] Either these cyphers are too thin to be able to conceive of any conception of justice, or, if they can, then it is because Rawls has endowed them with certain culturally specific attitudes and modes of reasoning. Like the other neutralist theorists, Rawls seems caught between the Scylla of arbitrariness and the Charybdis of indeterminacy.

Communitarian writers, some of whom are discussed in the next section, have developed these sorts of criticism in order to call into question the whole Rawlsian project. They point out that we only acquire the capacity for judgement through living in real societies embodying those conceptions of the good which give our lives their particular purpose, meaning and character. They contend that Rawls's appeal to abstract principles jeopardises our attachment to the social practices and values which make us moral agents in the first place. Not only does he employ models of rational choice which make highly unrealistic assumptions about the availability of information, the coherence of people's different needs and aspirations, and their capacity for calculation, it is doubtful whether many people, outside certain special situations such as shopping or stockbroking, could or should aspire to them in any case. To do so would be to destroy the genuine moral bonds of community and to replace them with the inherently unstable ties of reciprocal self-interest. Taking this criticism further, social theorists remark that within pluralistic and differentiated societies the categories of universalistic ethics invoked by Rawls break down. Individuals and groups formulate and justify their demands in a particularistic and constrained manner. They point out that Rawls can only achieve his consensus by ignoring the divergent historical identities and social and economic inequalities that in the real world mould and limit moral and political decisions. From this perspective, his theory is simply irrelevant. I shall return to this latter argument in the final section of this chapter.

In a series of articles, Rawls has sought to defend himself from his critics, modifying his argument in ways which grant a number of their points and fill out the background assumptions of his theory. He now admits to explicitly defending a liberal theory of justice, premised upon a basic acceptance of the institutions of Western democracies and based upon a 'model-conception of a moral person' which he assumes belongs to that tradition.[63] Nevertheless, he insists that his critics misunderstood his intention to offer a political as opposed to a metaphysical conception of justice.[64] In other words, he does not deny that human beings come to the political arena with conceptions of the good formed through their various experiences of community life. However, he maintains that they are able to abstract from their divergent conceptions to arrive at an 'overlapping consensus' on the basic structure of a democratic society. This consensus consists of certain moral norms that all members of democracy must abide by for the procedures to have any meaning for them at all. Rawls believes that the democratic ideal rests on the 'fundamental intuitive idea' of society as a fair system of co-operation between free and equal moral persons. According to Rawls, democratic citizens possess two distinctive moral powers, namely a sense of justice and 'the capacity to form, to revise and rationally to pursue a conception of the good', and 'two corresponding highest order interests in realising and exercising these powers'.[66] He concludes that a democratic constitution consists not just of a fair set of procedures for the settling of disputes, such as majority rule, it must also ensure an equitable division of those primary social goods necessary for participation in the democratic process. Since the ability to realise and exercise our two moral powers constitute, in Rawls's opinion, the preconditions for democratic citizenship, they cannot themselves be subject to democratic bargaining. Rather, they need constitutional protection within a bill of rights or a set of fundamental laws guaranteeing each person's highest order interests.

Rawls claims that his theory of justice merely specifies the basic requirements of a legitimate democratic political system. Against the communitarians, he maintains that this liberal consensus need not itself be based on a 'comprehensive' theory of the good, such as Mill's theory of individuality for example. He correctly remarks that today public agreement on the sort of moral doctrine typical of the ethical liberal tradition could be achieved 'only by the oppressive use of state power'.[66] Indeed, our very acceptance of a democratic political system originates from what he calls the 'fact of pluralism'. – That is, the empirical existence of competing moral codes and faiths, rather than a meta-ethical commitment to the plurality of values, scepticism about the good, or the intrinsic worth of individual choice. 'The aim of justice as fairness', he insists, 'is practical...it presents itself not as a conception of justice that is true, but one that can serve as a basis of informed and willing political agreement' and thereby 'help ensure stability from one generation to the next'.[67] Yet, the 'overlapping consensus' is more than a mere *modus vivendi* brought about by a contingent coalition of individual and group interests. Although it may start out as such, the stability of society requires that it comes to define the political sphere rather than being itself subject to continued political bargaining. Nor can every consensus be regarded as legitimate. To be so, it must be both internally coherent and capable of acceptance 'as true, or as reasonable, [for all] from the standpoint of their own comprehensive view, whatever it may be'.[68] Moreover, he persists in believing that a suitably modified version of his two principles will serve this purpose better than any other conception of justice.

Thus, Rawls's 'overlapping consensus' may not be based on a comprehensive morality, but it does supposedly represent a minimal moral position which he maintains can form a stable common denominator regulating public interaction between people holding a wide range of different philosophical and religious views. He seeks to abstain from grounding his theory of justice in controversial views of either the nature of truth or morality, whilst nevertheless contending that it should be embraced by all rational, moral agents within a pluralist democracy. How coherent is this argument? Doesn't Rawls want to have his cake and eat it? His disclaimer notwithstanding, surely the contention that the value of his theory rests on its ability to command the reflective allegiance of free and equal democratic citizens amounts to the claim that meeting such conditions attests to its validity and truth? Otherwise, he must rest his case on the purely empirical assertion that only such an agreement on principles which people, rightly or wrongly, simply happen to believe are just can produce lasting social stability. If this is Rawls's position, then his theory amounts to no more than an account of the preconditions of uncoerced social peace and unity. It could hardly be called a theory of justice, and offers no normative account of why people ought to abide by these principles rather than any others.[69] As such, it would be an extremely poor argument. It is even debatable whether the thesis that social stability depends on principled agreement is correct. Within contemporary complex societies, the achievement of a willed consensus such as Rawls appeals to seems as illogical and unattainable as the 'general will' or the 'common good'. The social homogeneity assumed by such concepts has been progressively undermined by the process of differentiation associated with industrialization. Within the large-scale and complex societies of today, far less reasoned emotions, such as a natural affection for the traditions and ways of doing things of the land of one's birth and upbringing, play a far greater role in holding societies together than rationally sanctioned principles.

Rawls cannot (and in my view does not) take the line attributed to him by Richard Rorty of offering his theory as no more than an account of liberal democratic society, for that historical and social inheritance is under attack.[70] To make his theory at all persuasive, therefore, Rawls cannot avoid grounding it in a more comprehensive conception of the good. Not surprisingly, closer examination of his argument reveals that he draws on the resources of the ethical liberal tradition to do just this. A major innovation of Rawls's recent writings lies in his development of his theory of moral personality. Rawls claims that his view of moral personality represents the self-understanding of members of a democratic society rather than a metaphysical ideal. This contention is highly suspect. Most modern democratic theorists, for instance, take a far more pessimistic view of the moral capacities of their fellow citizens.

They maintain that passion and interest play a greater role than a sense of justice in the average voter, a phenomenon reflected in the factional nature of contemporary politics. For these political analysts, Rawls's view of moral personality seems too ambitious. Other groups within contemporary societies will find it simply unacceptable. Those who believe our morality stems from the unquestioned authority of some religious text or person, for example, will regard Rawls's advocacy of a power 'to form, to revise, and to rationally pursue a conception of the good' as deeply subversive of their own moral system. Nor does everyone agree that all moral action can be accommodated with a higher interest 'to apply and to act from...the principles of justice', as Rawls contends. Thus, some feminists have argued that emphasis on abstract principles of justice devalues the virtues of love and concern for particular others which provide the centre of many women's moral lives. They maintain the priority of justice is at odds with the partiality of the ethic of care they endorse.[71] Rawls acknowledges that certain conceptions of the good will be unlikely to endure or gain adherents under institutions of equal freedom and toleration. In his earlier formulations of his theory, this loss did not bother him. He argued that the precarious viability of such conceptions threw doubts on their worthiness as well.[72] He now regards 'that optimistic view' to be mistaken, regarding them merely as unfortunate victims of the fact that no social world can escape excluding certain fundamental values.[73] From the point of view of the losers, however, it makes little difference whether they are seen as inferior or simply unlucky. Either way, their attachment to a liberal society which has no place for them will be seriously weakened.

Rawls minimises the impact of these problems for his theory by assuming that members of a pluralistic society will naturally seek to reduce conflict and find forms of just social co-operation. However, he reaches this happy conclusion largely because his account of moral personality makes freedom and justice essential aspects of human well-being. Within Rawls's theory, the right does not precede, it forms part of the human good. We have returned to the world of ethical liberalism and its most distinctive inhabitant, the autonomous individual. As Galston has remarked, an implicit and highly contentious 'democratic perfectionism' underlies his theory, whereby we realise ourselves through developing the capacity to choose.[74] Without such an assumption, his theory of justice seems unlikely to gain the universal adherence he seeks for it. Yet it remains hard to believe that many people within the pluralist societies which he addresses can or do accept the requirements of moral agency he stipulates.

Rawls seeks to defend himself from these sorts of criticisms by insisting that his theory of justice only refers to the public as opposed to the private aspect of our lives. Individuals may privately think only women should perform certain domestic duties or that homosexuality is evil, they must only refrain from trying to impose these beliefs on others. Similarly, Rawls's theory does not stop people joining religious groups requiring strict conformity from their members, it merely rules out the setting up of a theocratic state. The trouble with this distinction between public and private spheres, however, is that it requires all but the liberal to be endowed with an implausibly schizophrenic personality. Because liberalism regards a whole range of beliefs as mere personal opinions, liberals have no difficulty in tolerating a variety of views on most questions. True believers, in contrast, admit no such scepticism and would be inconsistent to do so. They could only embrace Rawls's public morality by sacrificing many of their core commitments. In any case, as feminists have pointed out, even liberals should be worried about this distinction if it merely serves to legitimate domestic and intra-community oppression. To ignore this possibility opens up liberalism to the charge that the public freedoms and equality it advocates will only be available to some and implicitly require the oppression of others for their exercise.[75]

One would have thought that bargaining and clashes between a plurality of opposed beliefs formed the stuff of politics. However, Rawls's concern with stability leads him to exclude politics proper completely. What Rawls calls political liberalism deliberately 'removes from the political agenda the most divisive issues, pervasive uncertainty and serious contention about which must undermine the bases of social cooperation'.[76] Yet within contemporary societies, much of what Rawls sees as basic to a democratic overlapping consensus is currently regarded as a legitimate matter of public discussion. Debates about abortion, censorship, education or welfare provision, for example, reveal that no agreement about the conception of moral personality that Rawls's theory trades on currently exists. A truly political liberalism must find room to accommodate debates about such important issues. To ban political argument about these matters, as Rawls effectively proposes, would necessitate the imposition of a comprehensive liberal morality – a position he had sought to avoid.

The chief difficulty with the principle of neutrality is that only liberals find it convincing. No non-liberal could countenance placing all positions on an equal footing in the manner its proponents desire. Neutrality turns out to be dependent on a more constitutive liberal moral belief such as autonomy and the existence of a reasonably homogenous moral community. It would appear, then, that the gap separating neutralist and communitarian liberals is now exceedingly narrow. It remains to be seen how satisfactory that conception of liberalism is.

COMMUNITARIAN LIBERALISM: WALZER, RAZ

Not all communitarian critics of neutralist liberalism are liberals. As a result, lumping them all together has made it easy for neutralists to treat the doctrine as inherently conservative.[77] Certainly the emphasis placed on settled traditions and established identities often leads some writers to oppose, or doubt the wisdom of, a variety of typical liberal causes. This divergence has been particularly evident in the support some communitarians have offered to defenders of the 'moral majority', who seek to ban 'offensive' activities in the name of preserving their community's 'way of life and the values that sustain it'.[78] Our concern here, however, is with those communitarians who explicitly endorse liberal values. Two different strands of thought exist amongst this group: the relativist and the rationalist.

To take the relativists first, I have in mind arguments along the lines of Michael Walzer's book *Spheres of Justice*. Walzer shares the neutralists' antipathy to perfectionist and utilitarian reasoning, but not their methodological individualism. He believes that if we truly endorse endorse the liberal values of equality and pluralism, then we must accept the different standards communities adopt when evaluating the justice of their social arrangements. Goods are not conceived abstractly as something we may or may not want as a result of our personal preference for this or that object or life style:

> Rather, goods with their meanings – because of their meanings – are the crucial medium of social relations; they come into people's minds before they come into their hands; distributions are patterned in accordance with shared conceptions of what the goods are and what they are for.[79]

According to Walzer, we must respect not only the various conceptions of the good life held by different communities, but also the divergent natures of the goods people choose to pursue. Each good operates within its own sphere and must be distributed according to its own inner logic. Walzer wishes to avoid the familiar arguments against relativism: namely, that it leaves too much to the contingencies of cultural self-understanding by reducing judgements on the arrangements of different societies to a matter of subjective taste or a criticism of the coherence of the chosen rules. He provides two criteria for assessing the justice both of the range of goods available in a given society and of the chosen patterns of distribution. First, he maintains that the set-up must have the uncoerced allegiance of all the members of that society. As long as everyone affected endorses the caste system, to use Walzer's example, we cannot legitimately condemn it. However, once members come to challenge the system of beliefs on which it is based, then it ceases to be just. Walzer suggests that we can certainly invite a given people to subject its shared norms to an immanent critique of their genesis and optimistically believes that any genuinely unjust arrangement, one which served the interests of a narrow clique for example, would be rejected spontaneously by such a procedure.[80] Second, he argues that each good generates a set of relevant reasons for its distribution inherent to its meaning for the community as a whole. Thus, to use his examples again, access to medical care depends upon the ill-health of would-be recipients, not their wealth or standing in the community. [81] Similarly, and against Dworkin, places in higher education belong to those who merit them by virtue of their intellectual abilities and should not be allocated for reasons of social utility to less suitable candidates.[82]

Despite certain differences over policy and approach, Walzer's political position is akin to Dworkin's, namely, that of a left-of-centre liberal. We should not be surprised, therefore, when a similar set of assumptions turn out to be doing the real work in his theory once his declared arguments begin to run into trouble. The distinctiveness of Walzer's thesis derives from his two revisions of the standard relativist approach, yet neither is unproblematic.[83] The first aims to allow us to criticise from within the social beliefs which determine both the available goods and their pattern of distribution. By this means Walzer hopes to tackle the problem of false consciousness without referring to putatively universalistic criteria, such as some set of basic human needs. The difficulty here is that our appreciation of what goods are in our interest arises in Walzer's view from shared meanings. Once this consensus breaks down one is faced with the problem of adjudicating between different conceptions of where our interests lie based upon incommensurable interpretations of our needs. This requirement poses the question of how to evaluate the adequacy of divergent conceptions of our real interests, and in particular of how to escape the viciousness of the hermeneutic circle – the fact that different interpretations only make sense within a total interpretative framework which is in turn made up of particular interpretations. In the end, gaining a critical distance from our beliefs risks turning into the application of non-socially relative considerations of the sort Walzer wants to avoid. When he raises this issue, he gets out of it simply by assuming that people would make the sort of decision we would expect of a liberal individual; that given a conflict between the system of castes and the requirements of a modern bureaucracy based on equality of opportunity and merit, the latter will win out. Indeed, Walzer goes so far as to argue that liberalism should prevail, for this is a corollary of his second revision of relativism whereby all goods are said to have an appropriate distributive principle. For example, he admits that different groups within the black community in the USA can muster good communitarian arguments both for and against the policy of bussing.[84] Radical black leaders often voice the opinion that it destroys the black consciousness of children by teaching them to adopt the white values of American capitalism and hence distances them from their own ethnic origins. It is viewed as a policy of enforced social control. Concerned black liberals, in contrast, retort that to remain in the ghetto is just as much a form of social conditioning, offering fewer avenues for escape. The appeal to education as a good in itself is not directly open to Walzer in this instance, because he sees it being interpreted differently in different social circumstances. However, he simply asserts that the black community should opt for the greater opportunities offered by the liberal to compete on equal terms with their fellow white citizens on the grounds that the world outside the ghetto is the more inclusive community. A counter-example will underline the presumption of Walzer's view. Jewish schools in the ghettos of turn-of-the-century Eastern Europe were faced with a similar dilemma to the one discussed by Walzer. No one can doubt the learning and scholarship of the Rabbinical tradition, but their religious teaching was often in opposition to the secular values of the nations of which they were citizens. The enforced secular education of Jewish children was in their eyes no 'equality of opportunity' but a dilution of the traditional beliefs holding together a very special kind of community.

Walzer's relativism seems motivated by similar intuitions to the neutralists' concerning the need to accord different concepts of the good equality of respect. However, he encounters analogous difficulties to theirs when forced to rule on 'boundary disputes' between competing conceptions, since setting rules governing the distribution of goods necessarily involves making qualitative judgements. Different types of education conflict with each other and preferring one to the other will depend upon what you believe to be most valuable in life – democratic participation or group cohesion. A good liberal, Walzer prefers the former, but not everyone would and it is difficult to see how his model of 'internal critique' will resolve these disputes. Such problems not only undermine the usefulness of Walzer's thesis concerning the 'social meanings' of goods, but equally his attempt to isolate them in different spheres. Goods compete with each other and count for more or less according to how we rank them in our lives. Walzer ignores the fact that distributions in one sphere will have knock-on effects in others, and that entitlements to one good will generate obligations which may impair our enjoyment, or that of others, of another. It is instructive to note that Walzer has likened his interpretative model to the reasoning adopted by Dworkin's Herculean judge for the resolution of 'hard' cases.[85] Both represent attempts to discover a meta-language expressive of the inner rationale of conflicting spheres and moral claims which are attuned to the basic interests of the community. In both cases this exercise degenerates into the imposition of a somewhat parochial set of East Coast progressive liberal beliefs.

Walzer's theory is based on two powerful intuitions: (a) that when we think about justice we are influenced by a background sense of the worth of a particular pattern for the life of our community, and (b) that we need to respect a variety of goods as valuable for different sorts of reasons and not allow the pursuit of some goods by people endowed with one set of capacities and tastes to restrict unduly the possibilities for individuals possessed of divergent needs and abilities successfully to follow paths of their own. These are important concerns which no viable form of liberalism can ignore, and I shall return to them in the conclusion. Yet we have found Walzer's argument unequal to the task of defending these beliefs for much the same reasons we associated with neutralist liberalism: namely, the apparent impossibility of not drawing upon a particular conception of the range of worthwhile forms of human development, conduct and interaction within the community and of specifying the rights and distributions which favour it, and hence inevitably hinder others.

The second school of communitarian liberals deliberately grasp this nettle and attempt to describe 'the full theory of the good latent within liberal practice'.[86] For these thinkers the central form of human flourishing within a liberal society is individual autonomy. They argue that the individualist strand within neutralist liberalism produces a confusion between a commitment to the capacity for autonomy and the belief that this capacity can be achieved autonomously. They point out that the conditions necessary for an autonomous life cannot be created simply by protecting the individual against the incursions of others. Eschewing the individualist, rights-based approach of neutralist liberals, they observe that liberalism represents a certain quality of life for a whole community. The only way to resolve the problem of specifying rights and adjudicating between them when they conflict is to regard them as 'fundamental components in the way of life of a community' committed to certain forms of human flourishing for all.[87] Rights cannot just refer to the protection of 'individuated political aims' against the claims of the 'aggregative collective good',[88] they must attend to 'the quality of inter-action among persons' as well.[89] The neutralists' mistake, to quote Raz, 'is to think that one can identify, say, the rights of others, while being completely ignorant of what values make a life meaningful and satisfying and what personal goals one has in life [or, conversely]...to think that one can understand the values which can give meaning to life and have goals and ideals while remaining ignorant of one's duties to others'.[90] The source of both our goals and obligations stems from the common good, those values and goods important for an autonomous life, which indeed provide the precondition for it.

Although these thinkers share Walzer's contention that the primary bond of society is a 'shared understanding both of the good for man and the good of that community',[91] they do not leave the definition and understanding of those goods to the vagaries of historical contingency. In Aristotelian manner, they seek to arrive at them through a process of practical reasoning deemed to be distinctive of the human species. On critical evaluation, our desires are held to imply a form of life which would provide the full expression of the potentialities specific to human beings. Within Aristotle's philosophy, we arrive by this means at the standard of what the good man wants, since he seeks to manifest in his person and actions all these distinctively human characteristics. The theorists under discussion admit that the circle cannot be completed in quite so pat a fashion, and acknowledge that our desires and interests do not all necessarily point to some single all-inclusive way of life. They concede that they are assuming a certain sort of moral agent, one who values autonomy, and that even autonomous choices admit of a plurality of reasonable goals. Unlike Aristotle, they do not expect citizens of a liberal polity to fulfil in their own person all the virtues of human nature in order to lead a complete and full life, merely that they be open to these possibilities and do not prevent others from enjoying them. However, even this revised doctrine would appear to assume a moral order in the universe in order to avoid a conflict between rational endeavours, so that these different goods are at the very least assumed to be compatible. Some such assumption clearly emerges from Raz's statement that his thesis rests on:

> the belief...that personal autonomy depends on the persistence of collect-ive goods, and therefore that the notion of an inherent general conflict between individual freedom and the needs of others is illusory. Though an individual's freedom, understood as personal autonomy, sometimes conflicts with the interests of others, it also depends on those interests and can be obtained only through the collective goods which do not benefit anyone unless they benefit everyone. This fact, rather than any definition, undermines the individualist emphasis on rights.[92]

John Finnis makes a similar claim when he states as an 'absolute right' the following 'requirement of practical reasonableness...that it is always unreasonable to choose directly against any basic value, whether in oneself or in one's fellow human beings. [For] the basic values are not mere abstractions; they are aspects of the real well-being of flesh-and-blood individuals.'[93] Now it may be the case that one can only respond to the moral sceptic, such as Thrasymachus, by invoking some form of ethical naturalism sufficient at least to generate something akin to Hart's 'minimum content of natural law'.[94] However, whilst some such notion might enable you to condemn Nazism, for example, it will not be particularly determinate beyond such extremes. The difficulty of going further does not depend simply on the diversity of distinguishing marks of humankind, not all of them particularly savoury, which makes it unlikely that practical reason will be able to resolve all conflicts between them in the desired manner. Rather, as Stuart Hampshire has stressed, it is because:

> the distinguishing capacity for thought, which for Aristotle opened the way to a rational choice between kinds of life and kinds of human ex-cellence, at the same time complicates and multiplies choice, and, more important, puts a limit on its rationality. As a direct consequence of the capacity to recognise and to name differences, a whole range of complete lives is represented as normal for human beings; and the capacity to conceive these multitude alternatives is recognised as a natural power

common to the whole species, alongside the power to calculate and to argue logically. Therefore the capacity to envisage conflicts between norms for a complete life, conflicts of ends and values, is natural to human beings.[95]

Hampshire goes on to argue that we evince this faculty in the creation and development of moral languages which reinforce differences between groups of human beings. To a large extent liberalism can only be understood in such historical terms, so that an Aristotelian defence of either a minimal (Rawls, Dworkin) or developed (Finnis, Galston, Raz) nature is bound to fail. Our capacity for reflection upon our moral aims and ideals, whereby we evolve the variety of ethical codes which prevail within human societies, renders the aspiration to achieve a fundamental agreement or convergence of moralities not only flawed but harmful. Hence, as Hampshire observes, 'the modern liberals' conception of justice is not generalizable as a virtue that could be embedded in other admired ways of life without conflict with their other sustaining virtues and ideals.'[96] Indeed, the dilemma facing liberals today may well be that the historical community sustaining liberalism has been irretrievably torn apart in ways which make attempts to revive it moralistic and eventually intolerant. This circumstance no doubt accounts for the contemporary image of the wishy-washy liberal whose appreciation of all sides of an argument and the diversity of values underlying them condemns him or her to being a perpetual, and largely impotent, observer of the conflicts of others – a far cry from their all too confident nineteenth-century predecessors. When liberalism asserts itself today, it risks becoming strangely illiberal.

This criticism may seem unfair. Raz, in particular, does explicitly defend a similar thesis concerning the incommensurability of values and maintains that autonomy presupposes what he calls 'competitive pluralism' of the kind described above. He accepts that genuine moral dilemmas arise as a result, involving tragic choices when 'whatever a person does he would irreparably damage one of the projects or relationships which he pursued or which shape his life.'[97] Moreover, he insists that the morally good person tolerates the presence of such conflicts within society as a whole as essential to autonomy. Nevertheless, I believe certain key assumptions in his theory reveal that, practically, such toleration would be much more limited in scope than Raz allows. Raz argues that moral goals, securing 'worthwhile' options basic to our well-being, are generally compatible in ways in which mainly self-interested projects are not. This distinction between 'self-interest' and 'personal well-being' begs a number of questions. The first relates primarily to our biological requirements, and arouses pleasure which, according to Raz's definition, is both insatiable and non-diminishing. The second is orientated towards goals or pursuits of independent value, and produces happiness, which Raz regards as a satiable and diminishing emotion. Whilst personal well-being usually entails the satisfaction of our biological needs and a capacity for pleasure, these are not necessary components. We can sacrifice them to pursue a worth-while goal, ranging from the trivial instance of giving up a favourite television programme in order to continue studying to the more significant case of being prepared to die for a cause. Although success forms an element in our happiness, he believes that after a certain level it is the mere pursuit of the activity which is important and further pleasures, whilst welcome, will not truly add to our sense of fulfilment.[98] As the picture of what autonomy requires begins to fill out, the pluralism Raz claims it entails looks somewhat narrower than we might have supposed. This familiar image of the autonomous agent who overcomes the baser impulses and strives after achievement in various improving higher endeavours is frequently presented by its proponents as a liberated figure. Yet for those who have struggled to rid themselves of the middle-class culture and institutions which sustained it, it has a more oppressive feel. As Raz rightly points out, autonomy is not a totally personal creation but only flourishes within a community which provides the requisite social forms to sustain it. Our most important activities are structured by the forms they can take. The hobbies we pursue, the careers we follow, how we interrelate with others on various occasions, are moulded by the conventions governing them in different societies. The conditions of autonomy cannot be separated from its exercise, since the available options will condition the type of choice we make. Reinterpreting the Millian harm principle, he argues that harm properly embraces all commissions and omissions which diminish autonomy. This argument justifies not only the public provision of worth-while options, such as education, but also coercion against autonomy-inhibiting acts. Not surprisingly he concludes, 'for those who live in an autonomy-supporting environment there is no choice but to be autonomous: there is no other way to prosper in such a society.'[99] If the social forms only 'enshrine sound moral conceptions' then, as Raz says:

> it is easy for people generally...to choose for themselves goals which lead to a rough coincidence in their own lives of moral and personal concerns. In their careers, personal relations and other interests they will be engaged on activities which serve themselves and others at the same time. By being teachers, production workers, drivers, public servants, loyal friends and family people, loyal to their communities, nature loving and so on, they will be pursuing their own goals, enhancing their own well-being, and also serving their communities, and generally living in a morally worthy way.[100]

Easy, certainly, and a form of society not without its attractions, yet, as Susan Mendus has observed, it is curiously intolerant and illiberal as well.[101] The tolerance allowed within such a community is only between autonomous lives. Different moral values, whilst posing conflicts for the individual, appear to belong to 'part of a mosaic which in its entirety makes for a valuable social life',[102] so that each of the parts ultimately enhances the other. The real dilemmas have been put to one side, as concerning immoral or unworthy choices. As Mendus points out, the difficulty arises from trying to reconcile the requirements of the conditions for autonomy, which only flourishes in a certain type of social set-up, with the notion of the capacity of autonomy, seen as our ability to create our own moral world. Once our capacity for autonomy becomes itself a conditioned social product, then one can no longer appeal to it as an independent standard to prevent paternalistic inter-ferences with individual liberty. Raz recognizes no inherent worth in recognising those forms of life which do not value autonomy, although he admits it may be prudent to do so.[103] The potential dangers of this approach in a multicultural society such as modern Britain seem self-evident. The tutelary nature of this moralised liberal community may well reflect the ethos behind liberalism during its better days, when it represented a progressive creed for the transformation of both society and state (the *Kulturkampf* comes readily to mind), but today it appears both anachronistic and reactionary. This danger is not restricted to communitarian liberals, since we saw that their neutralist counterparts ultimately adopted similar assumptions to justify their position.

LIBERALISM AND MODERN SOCIETY

The various contemporary theories of liberalism examined above all turn out to be ethical theories. They are based on perfectionist reasoning construing the good life for human beings as consisting in an auton-omous existence. Far from being of universal application, they advocate an idealised form of a particular historical community – essentially the bourgeois utopia of the ethical liberal tradition. The weaknesses of this vision of social relations have already been commented on in earlier chapters, most particularly in the examination of Mill and Durkheim. To revive such theories now suggests a social and political naivety which is hard to credit.

Raz provides a succinct statement of why he believes the ideal of autonomy is 'particularly suited to the conditions of the industrial age and its aftermath with their fast changing technologies and free move-ment of labour'. These developments, he says, 'call for an ability to cope with changing technological, economic and social conditions, for an ability to adjust, to acquire new skills, to move from one subculture to another, to come to terms with new scientific and moral views'.[104] Some such background picture of modern society is held by most of the other theorists, and if accurate would greatly enhance the plausibility of their case. Large market societies, increased education, the pluralism of modern culture, are all assumed to have brought into being a liberal ethos. Whilst it is nevertheless worth reiterating the point made earlier, namely the restricted types of subculture and moral values that such a society allows, those liberal theorists who acknowledge this argument contend it is a price worth paying for a more individualistic society. In this section, however, I want to insist on the implausibility of this argument, and its total failure to tackle the pervasive influences of power and structure on people's lives within complex industrial societies.[105]

Societies are not the product of the reflective consensus of autonomous agents, but mirror the balance of power of the various groups within them and the conventions and customs of the economic and political practices in which their members are engaged. Neutralist liberals are especially guilty of failing to see how the institutions of the market and democracy do not operate according to neutral norms of universal rationality, but reflect the organizational capacities of different corporate and group interests. Distributions are not a function of how we fared in some 'natural' lottery, but of our bargaining power within a given structure of economic and political relations. The greater functional differentiation and the variety of organisational structures generated by modern economies, far from liberating individuals and enhancing their capacity for reflection and action, serve to inculcate appropriate personal motivations and goals, often with different logics of their own. The accommodations that result between, say, work, the family and our obligations to the state are not based on individual rational choices, but the relative coercive power and emotional attachment generated by these different spheres of our lives – a far messier business. To the extent that these theorists greatly exaggerate the independence and opportunities available to individuals to pursue their conceptions of the good, their work fails to address the circumstances of the vast majority of people. As a result, they risk legitimating the exclusion of those who do not meet their criteria by providing a spurious moral justification for the present political system. Witness the way many earlier liberals dismissed past protests of women, workers and ethnic minorities within Western democracies by dubbing them 'irrational'. Of course, Rawls, Dworkin et al. argue that their prescriptions would radically alter current social, political and economic arrangements. Such changes as they advocate are highly unlikely, however. First, we have seen their reforms would entail forcing a particular conception of human agency on people, which many might resent and actively oppose. Second, and most important, contemporary social conditions challenge the very possibility of the well-ordered, co-operative society based upon the sort of shared universal principles that they defend. Their methodological individualism and reliance upon parochial standards of rationality seem sociologically misconceived when the increasing complexity of modern societies is calling such assumptions into question by increasing the plurality and contingency of values and social affiliations and enhancing the power of organised structures to shape people's lives. By ignoring such factors, Rawls, Dworkin et al. have simply offered an elegiac theoretical justification of an idealized past social equilibrium which now seems in crisis.

The communitarian liberals can be praised for at least being aware of how autonomy presupposes certain societal conditions. Yet, as the neutralists partly recognize, a moralized liberalism seems both oddly unpluralistic and easily manipulable to provide a Smilsean ethic of self-help which suits capitalist relations by conveniently explaining their deficiencies with regard to those who are unsuccessful. Raz and Galston, like Dworkin and Rawls, deny the validity of such interpretations. Their advocacy of autonomy entails their own version of the bourgeois utopia in which everyone gets his or her just reward in the course of pursuing a worthy existence. Admirable though it is in many respects, there are both moral and practical doubts about the acceptability of such a social order. The moral doubt was raised above, and concerned the compatibility of autonomy with a society which effectively coerces the development of worthy talents at the expense of others people might want to develop. The practical doubt arises from the suggestion, found in the quotation from Raz at the end of the previous section, that (only slightly to amend a famous phrase) the autonomy of each is the condition for the autonomy of all. There may be some co-operative ventures of this nature, such as certain team games or collaborative academic work, but it is doubtful whether industrial production (*pace* Durkheim) has this characteristic. As the industrial process has become more integrated and functional differentiation has increased, the tendency has been for autonomy to decrease and for the individual to become ever more circumscribed within the confines of a narrow, and often degrading, task. Even more than the neutralist theories it opposes, communitarian liberalism seems at best irrelevant and at worst either a legitimising creed for powerful interests or a paternalistic scheme which would involve the wholesale imposition of a certain way of life upon a reluctant populace.

Although in their different ways both neutralists and communitarians accept 'the fact of pluralism', they remain remarkably sanguine about the possibility of achieving some agreement on shared moral principles. This belief derives from a failure to confront the social source of this pluralism, and the challenge it poses to the moral assumptions of ethical liberalism. Pluralism stems from the differentiation of modern societies. This process has resulted not only in people desiring diverse and often incommensurable goods, but has fostered their adoption of distinct and occasionally contradictory kinds of reasoning in the different contexts within which they operate. As a result, the identities and loyalties even of single individuals can become divided between their membership of various groups – their professional, neighbourhood, family, sexual, ethnic and religious ties can all clash at times. No ethical code, capable of integrating without remainder the diverse dimensions of human life into one scheme of values, exists in such circumstance. Needless to say, these tensions between the various spheres of our social existence are exacerbated when seeking to produce a rational consensus between groups and individuals. The division of labour and the fragmentation of our lives not only splits up our own sense of personal identity, it seriously weakens our ability to relate to others as members of a common moral, social and political world. The size of modern societies and the concomitant absence of face-to-face relations; the growing complexity and technicality of many social and economic tasks and the resulting reliance on experts, including permanent professional bureaucracies; the intrusion of new technologies into all areas of life, especially the mass media; and the enhanced functional differentiation and specialization which accompany these innovations – all these forces have progressively weakened the individual's capacity for autonomous rational action and choice. The dependence on unknown, unpredictable and uncontrollable others involved in an integrated global economy; our containment within managerial hierarchies of various kinds; the proliferation of sources of information and persuasion resulting from the technological revolution within the media, etc., have rendered it increasingly hard for anyone to make reasoned judgements about the world, since we cannot reduce its complexity to manageable levels. Our moral intuitions, far from offering guidance as Rawls et al. assume, will often be inadequate in the world's baffling diversity and flux, so that to insist on them reflects the attitude of a narrow-minded and ignorant dogmatist rather than of a reasonable person. We may be capable of coherent moral and practical reasoning within specific local contexts of which we have direct experience, but on a whole range of wider issues we fall into an unavoidable deference to expertise and authority and become increasingly susceptible to psychological and non-rational forms of suasion. In this situation, the only moral and political consensus likely to emerge is one that has been manufactured by the propaganda, advertising and organized manipulation of those in power. The possibility for a revived liberal moral community, no matter how watered down it may be, has definitely ceased. If liberalism is to remain relevant within modern conditions, therefore, it must drop the ethical approach and recast liberal concerns within a perspective adequate to the complexity and pluralism of the contemporary world. As I shall suggest in the conclusion, the basis for such a project lies in Weber's political and realist rethinking of liberalism discussed in chapter 4.

Conclusion: From Liberal Democracy to Democratic Liberalism

This study has had two main purposes. The first has been to bring to light the social and moral assumptions of modern liberalism. This aim constituted the principal task of chapters 1 and 2, on Britain and France respectively. Whereas much contemporary analysis and elaboration of the liberal tradition treats this doctrine as a set of universal verities concerning the nature of human organization, I have insisted on its historically contingent character. Second, I have challenged the continuing viability of those assumptions with the erosion of the historical conditions which gave rise to them. I have maintained that the further evolution of advanced capitalist economies has undermined the social environment that leant ethical liberalism its coherence. This criticism formed the main object of chapters 3 and 4, which traced the disillusionment with the ideals of ethical liberalism experienced by Italian and German thinkers. Far from reflecting and stabilizing the social relations of modern societies, as Durkheim believed, liberal morality has proved unable to cope with their growing differentiation and complexity. Chapter 5 developed this thesis by showing the inadequacy of those recent liberal theories which seek to adapt or extend the ethical liberal tradition to encompass the pluralism of the modern world. Such theories continue to rely on models of human rationality and moral agency that belong to the liberal ideology of early capitalism. Of dubious plausibility then, within today's complex social systems they can no longer be assumed as either possible or desirable. Outside the historical context which gave them practical force, liberal principles cease to be compelling. They cannot function as neutral presuppositions of universal validity. At best, they represent highly problematic goals to be achieved, and as such in competition with other, equally valuable, forms of human well-being. I shall now argue that the reworking of liberal thought, born out of the frustration experienced by the Italian and

German theorists we examined, provides the materials for constructing a realist conception of liberalism far more suited to the complex political and moral issues currently confronting us.[1]

Ethical and realist liberals offer two contrasting ways of conceiving the nature of social order. The former subscribe to a consensual model of society, the latter focus on conflict and the role of power in holding a community together. Ethical liberals maintain that social stability rests on a set of shared norms, beliefs and values which are intrinsic to modern industrial societies. They identify this morality with a set of basic rights and entitlements capable of ensuring the maximum equal liberty for all. Earlier writers in this tradition, such as Durkheim, believed social progress itself was producing a growing convergence on these general principles. More recent ethical liberal philosophers, such as Rawls, have modified this position and merely claimed that it offers the minimal morality required for any form of uncoerced social co-operation in the contemporary world. Realist liberals, like Weber, dispute the view of social relations underlying even the minimalist Rawlsian 'overlapping consensus', however. Influenced by Marx, Nietzsche and Machiavelli, they offer a very different picture of modernity. Drawing on Marx, they point to the sources of conflict between different classes and interests in modern economies, relating these to the clashes of values between groups and individuals. Observing the various collective and structural forces moulding and perverting the will of individuals, they question the ethical liberal assumption of an independent rational convergence of views. They regard such agreements as more often than not the product of socialization and various forms of covert and overt persuasion or coercion. Drawing on Nietzsche now to take this critique further, they identify all moralizing with the 'will to power' and the effort to stem the nihilism of a disenchanted world. Conflict does not just originate from differential access to scarce resources and the organs of authority – it is part of the existential condition of human beings possessed of free will and disabused of all metaphysical consolations. In the face of numerous equally plausible yet rationally irreconcilable attitudes to life, there can be no objective way of judging the legitimacy of different and competing claims to authority. The neutral Archimedian point desired by contemporary ethical liberal theorists is revealed as just one perspective amongst others. Drawing finally on Machiavelli, they examine the way the political system operates as a mechanism for the organization of coercion and consent by different ruling groups and individuals. Far from being an open forum for the expression of the popular will, they see mass democracy as an instrument of social control. From the perspective of realist liberalism, therefore, the ethical liberal tradition fails adequately to explore the connection between the distribution of power and the legitimation of values.

Ethical and realist liberalism give rise to two correspondingly different ways of conceiving the public sphere: liberal democracy and democratic liberalism. Whereas liberal democracy assumes (or seeks to create) a moral consensus which provides a framework for political deliberation, democratic liberalism gives central place to fair procedures that favour the expression and temporary conciliation of a plurality of ideals. Consequently, democratic liberalism responds to the complexity and particularist pluralism of modern life by regarding liberal constitutional principles and arrangements in terms of a *modus vivendi*. They arise out of the current circumstances of justice, rather than being the preconditions of all legitimate social coexistence. The heterogeneity of rules generated by highly differentiated societies has rendered the notion of any pre-political 'overlapping consensus' suspect. Instead, consensus is an outcome of the political system, which seeks to reduce the complexity and conflicts of society to manageable proportions. Seen in this realist light, pragmatic rather than absolutist considerations apply. The important goal is to ensure that the making of agreements is equitable, rather than that the outcomes are just in some absolute sense.

Democratic liberalism, therefore, disputes the liberal democratic aim to ground politics in a set of universal ethical principles. From a realist point of view, such an attempt merely reflects the desire of a particular group to legitimise its own position and restrict the actions of others. It forms a part of political debates and struggles rather than transcending them. Take, for example, the liberal democratic argument for a constitutionally entrenched bill of rights. This proposal seeks to answer the realist's objections concerning the feasibility of liberal agency in the modern world by building the prerequisites for autonomous action into the political system. Unlike a number of earlier liberal thinkers, contemporary liberal theorists do not base their account of democratic rights on either theological foundations or perfectionist reasoning stemming from some contestable view of human nature. They try to construct rather than deduce the largest set of rights capable of being held simultaneously by a society of roughly free and equal but widely divergent individuals. David Held's model of democratic autonomy, which tries to synthesise the whole gamut of liberal theorising on this issue, provides a fine example of the type of argument under discussion. He states the principle of autonomy as follows:

> Persons should enjoy equal rights (and, accordingly, equal obligations) in the framework which generates and limits the opportunities available to them; that is they should be free and equal in the determination of the conditions of their own lives, so long as they do not deploy this framework to negate the rights of others.[2]

Constructions of rights along these lines fit most easily with physicalist theories of action and accounts of liberty which conceive freedom in terms of authority over a specific domain. On this view, each person must be accorded the maximal sphere of action compatible with an equivalent space for others. Setting the boundaries of these individual territories, however, is impossibly difficult once we leave the realm of metaphor and seek actually to apply this theory to the real world. The problem with this approach, as we have seen, becomes clear when we consider the difficulty of making 'on-balance' judgements about freedom in the event of a clash of liberties.[3] What metric do we use to sort out the potential clashes between, say, freedom of association and the freedom not to be discriminated against, so as to increase freedom over all? Can either of these be judged greater or lesser than the other? In these sorts of cases, prioritising liberty in itself proves indeterminate, for judgements about the greatest liberty are necessarily qualitative rather than quantitative. They can only proceed on the basis of some view of the value of different human activities, which regards certain liberties as being more intrinsic to human flourishing and well-being than others. As a result, many different (and often conflicting) sets of equal liberties could be consistently assigned to all people, with each set emphasising some liberties at the expense of others. Thus, a negative interpretation of liberty yields a libertarian construction of rights against interference from others, whereas a positive conception of liberty gives rise to welfare rights requiring us to provide people with certain goods and services. These two views of liberty produce not only two divergent sets of rights, but two incompatible sets. For if, for example, I have an unrestricted *right* to private property and to trade in the market, others cannot have *rights* to welfare, and vice versa. Socialists often seek to combine the two by claiming that social rights extend the traditional civil and political rights by enabling citizens to exercise them. However, such arguments – like those of the new liberals and T. H. Marshall which inspire them – only make sense on the basis of some form of perfectionism. Reliance on such ethical naturalist assumptions undercuts the supposed pluralism of rights-based theories, though, and are in any case very hard to justify. For why should New Right theorists, who largely resist welfare rights on the grounds that they undermine individual and social morality, accept that these rights are more essential to human fulfilment than property rights? Moreover, the problems of identifying a basic set of compossible rights, common to all moralities, mirror those of constructing a maximal set. As the debate over abortion between those championing the right of the mother over her own body and those defending the right of the unborn foetus has shown, even the most basic of negative liberty rights can conflict at times. Indeed, the various parties have found it impossible even to agree on a common conception of what counts as life. Rights-based liberal moralities cannot provide the basic structure for all legitimate political systems, therefore, because rights only make sense as the co-ordinating principles of particular forms of life. Different communities fostering different kinds of human flourishing will give rise to different conceptions of rights. This communitarian aspect of rights comes to light most obviously when rights clash, as we have seen they inevitably do. Conflicts of rights can only be resolved, as the examples above illustrate, with reference to the common good or type of moral life valued by the community. This feature makes rights singularly ill-suited to providing the foundations of a political system in a disenchanted world such as our own, characterised by the fragmentation of our moral framework.

Once cut off from an agreed comprehensive conception of the good, assertions of basic human rights are liable to generate irreconcilable conflicts between rival ontological claims. Contemporary moral experience lacks the regularity the advocates of a framework of absolute basic rights require. Even the most essential of civil and political rights come into conflict with each other at times. For example, it is correctly believed to be essential in a liberal democracy that everyone has a right to the fair procedures which guarantee an unprejudiced trial. However, suppose it is discovered that some of these rights lead to guilty persons going free and committing crimes which infringe the equally important rights of innocent citizens? The British government's decision under Mrs Thatcher to modify the right to silence reflects just such a perceived conflict of rights. In such instances we are faced with tragic choices in which doing right involves committing wrong. No ethical theory can adequately resolve such questions. If policy decisions are to be possible, then argument about the merits of different proposals has to be pitched at a less absolute level. The constitutional entrenchment of a given set of rights attempts to make a given conception of social life unalterable. Yet discussion of what sort of world we would like to live in and the kinds of collective goods the state ought to provide form a vital part of the subject matter of politics, and cannot legitimately be excluded from the political agenda.[4] To do so has the effect of raising the temperature of political debate so that every challenge to the political system gets turned into a revolutionary demand. It places political disputes on a level where the opposing positions of the contesting parties cannot be redeemed discursively. This strategy could only succeed at the unacceptable price of a significant homogenisation and simplification of modern societies.

Attempts to construct neutral principles of rights or justice fail because they inevitably rest on ungrounded and contentious idealizations of particular conceptions of human agency. Within the liberal tradition these typically involve notions of autonomy and of self-sufficiency, such as one finds in Rawls's 'Kantian ideal of the person'.[5] However, we saw in chapter 5 that it is dubious whether many people can or should measure up to these ideals. To avoid a moralistic politics, politics must be kept separate from ethics. In the modern world, the distinctive function of the political system is to arrange compromises amongst a plurality of often conflicting views, rather than to achieve a rational consensus upon a non-existent common good.[6]

To attack ethical liberal attempts to provide a moralistic foundation for politics is not to suggest that we do not require any notion of law, rights or justice. Some Marxists and anarchists have dreamed of the withering away of the state altogether. They have regarded the liberal legal framework as the product of a class-divided society, to be replaced by a harmonious society in which 'the free development of each is the condition of the free development for all.'[7] Ironically, this utopia is in formal terms not that different from the ethical liberal ideal. However, this socialist idyll is only plausible on the basis of a number of highly unrealistic assumptions.[8] Whereas one could reasonably expect that under socialism people might be better disposed towards each other, and their social relations more solidaristic and fraternal, it is unreasonable to suppose that the ordinary human weaknesses resulting from imperfect knowledge, carelessness, and our essential infallibility will have been transcended by a new race of superbeings. Similarly, whilst socialists can argue that wealth will be distributed more equitably and that people will be less materialist in their desires, to believe that there will be such superabundance that no constraints of resources exist stretches the bounds of credibility too far. Yet, if we remove the assumptions that human beings could be transformed into omniscient creatures possessing a saintly rectitude, and that the world could be made so bountiful as to satisfy each of our wildest desires, then the picture of a society without laws, rights or the need for politics ceases to be plausible. Even if citizens agree on which ends are to be pursued, social processes within a society of any size and sophistication will be so complicated that people will be liable to err due to either insufficient information about their fellow citizens' needs, or a lack of expertise about how best to meet them. The road to hell is paved with good intentions, and even the most altruistic individuals may be misguided as to what other people require. For all but the smallest groups, therefore, some formal framework establishing the norms of conduct and the conditions for entering into agreements is unavoidable. However, if those Marxists who stigmatise all laws and rights as intrinsically bourgeois are mistaken, so are those of their critics who contend that the ethical liberal framework represents the only legitimate legal system capable of upholding individual freedom. As we have seen, it is fraught with contradictions and inadequacies.

A democratic liberalism overcomes the respective difficulties of both the ethical liberal and the Marxian view of justice by regarding the laws, rights, and distributive principles by which societies co-ordinate their affairs as mere rules of thumb. Far from reflecting universal ethical norms, they emerge from individual judgements in particular circumstances. As such, they have an *ad hoc* character which facilitates their revision when circumstances or needs alter. They serve to reduce the chaos and uncertainty of social life to manageable proportions, providing the regularity of expectations necessary for leading a reasonably stable life. From this perspective, the freedom of individuals and groups is not protected by written guarantees, however worthy, but by the existence of agencies which enable citizens to act in certain ways and which provide them with a means of defence against being hindered by others. Since the rights and liberties we enjoy depend on the structure of laws, the values and the priorities of the society we live in, we are only free when we have a role in determining the character of our communities. This activity requires democratic institutions through which we can deliberate on our particular and collective interests. The laws and regulations emanating from such bodies create positive rights which have none of the drawbacks I have associated with various versions of ethical liberal pre-political human rights. Instead of representing inherent ontological attributes, they reflect socially determined purposes which are capable of reformulation to meet changing situations and attitudes. Legislation can be used to mediate between competing claims, granting rights which reflect the divergent requirements of different areas of social life, rather than conforming to some idealised image of the human subject which imposes a particular pattern of human agency upon society. Moreover, these political institutions not only allow us to define our freedom, they enable us to defend it. After all, even under Stalin the USSR boasted a written constitution guaranteeing certain fundamental human rights. Their denial stemmed from the concentration of power within the party apparatus. The enjoyment of our rights and liberties depends to an important extent on a democratic institutional structure which distributes power amongst the citizen body. Without the possibility of widespread political participation, the state apparatus can fall into the hands of narrow cliques who seek to use it to further the particular interests of their class, group, religion, ideology or leader. The protection of minority groups, which forms a major part in the desire of rights theorists to limit the scope of democratic decisions, can best be served by having a variety of different loci of power and decision-making which restrict the possibilities for any one agency or group to dominate all others. Without a differentiation of political functions which recognizes the plurality of society by preserving the autonomy of different spheres and levels of social life, separating, for example, judicial and executive functions, and local from central government, constitutional rights will be worthless. Once disproportionate power falls into the restricted group or a single agency, individual freedom will soon be curtailed.

Thus, for liberalism to meet the challenge posed by the complexity and pluralism of modern societies, a complex plurality of political mechanisms must be devised which facilitates the influence and scrutiny of government policy by all relevant groups and individuals. This objective requires the distribution of decision-making power throughout society and the designation of distinct areas of competence so as to limit the scope of central authority. Such a system replaces substantive 'moralistic' constitutional constraints on majority rule and government action with 'realistic' procedural democratic checks and controls. Procedures allowing a plurality of views to be expressed, and which encourage their mediation, take the place of pre-political notions of rights and justice. The preservation of pluralism in this manner constitutes a liberal as much as a democratic commitment, for only a pluralist society provides a sufficient range of worthwhile options for the equal exercise of liberty through choice to make sense. A system of democratic institutions, which reflects the diversity of values and interests within society and enables accommodations to be arranged between them, provides the framework for a genuinely political liberalism, therefore, adequate to 'the fact of pluralism'.

This way of thinking harks back to the classical republican tradition of thought.[9] Unlike the civic humanist tradition, classical republicanism sees politics as a means rather than an end in itself. A form of Aristotelianism, civic humanism regards human beings as essentially political animals for whom political participation is a necessary aspect of the good life. Classical republicanism, in contrast, originates with Machiavelli and treats civic involvement as merely the condition for retaining our liberty. Since it involves no special commitment to a particular conception of the good, it is compatible with a pluralist democratic liberalism.[10] The virtues of political involvement are purely instrumental and prudential in character. The procedural norms of democratic liberalism, such as majority rule based on an equal vote, are simply functional components of the political system necessary for the peaceful resolution of social conflict. As such, their observance arises from a prudentially motivated political duty (in other words, if you do not uphold them, no one else will), rather than a moral right.[11]

Libertarians argue that the main locus of individual choice and freedom is the market rather than the political sphere. So long as the market is free, then the price mechanism will reflect in an objective way the value people place on certain commodities. As we saw, Pareto was led to this economic liberal solution after his disillusionment with ethical liberalism. However, the market fails to provide an adequate mechanism for the neutral or fair mediation of a plurality of all human values and desires. Leaving aside the difficulties with the perfect competition model of the market mentioned in the introduction,[12] there are three basic objections to the extension of market principles to cover the whole range of social and political issues. First, as Brian Barry has pointed out, this version of liberalism assumes that all preferences reflect essentially material private wants.[13] Such preferences are entirely amenable to the market mechanism. Having no intrinsic worth, they may be traded off against each other, the only object being to achieve the greatest aggregate satisfaction of wants over all. Market operations prove unsatisfactory, however, when people hold ideal-regarding preferences. When I regard an object as intrinsically valuable I shall not be satisfied with such trade-offs. Considering the relative merits of various educational policies, for example, is different from bargaining with various stall holders over the relative price of different items of food and clothing. In the second case, I can consider my wants and seek to maximise their satisfaction, sacrificing a banana here for an extra couple of apples there, etc. The first case is not like that. I shall have opinions about what a basic educational curriculum ought to include, say, and shall expect those of opposing views to argue their case with me. If I believe children require a certain kind of teaching, I shall not necessarily be satisfied just to be told that school productivity has been increased by doubling the number of pupils in each class and introducing rote learning. When evaluative as opposed to merely quantitative considerations apply, the market is no longer the appropriate decision-making medium. By providing a forum for public discussion, politics enables ideal-regarding preferences to be transformed and not just aggregated, allowing opposed interests to find acceptable compromises or even agreement on common values. Political participation can educate citizens into a perception of the dependency of their social relations and group and individual autonomy upon collective rules and arrangements. This process discourages the free-riding and other self-defeating forms of self-interest which bedevil markets.[14] The need for collective decisions provides the second main objection to a totally market-orientated liberalism. In the modern world, many of the goods which most concern us are not individualizable. The environment, peace, population control, information exchange – in sum, the most pressing policy issues of our time – all require concerted action for their solution. Indeed, the market is itself a collective good needing constant political regulation. Moreover, its very scope is a matter of political decision calling for constant discussion, for–my third and last point–markets do not avoid the problem of power within society. Markets are traditionally associated with a capitalist economic system. However, unregulated markets, based on private property rights in the means of production, distribution and exchange, result in discrepancies in wealth and hierarchical relationships which create grave inequalities of power and influence that restrict the range of democratic control. The consequent private domination of the financial and industrial corporations may be better than that of a monolithic bureaucratic socialist state, but it is far from realising the liberal ideas of freedom and equality that are often said to be synonymous with capitalism. Within a market system distorted by the concentration of capital and the power of organization, the average consumer's pull is severely limited. A socialist society composed of co-operatively owned and democratically self-managing enterprises arguably disperses economic power more effectively and equitably, and so proves more pluralist than capitalism. It is compatible with both democratic decision-making in the area of public goods and the conciliation of ideal-regarding preferences, and the use of market and price mechanisms for the co-ordination of material preferences and ordinary consumption.[15]

Liberalism remains important for anyone who takes the plurality and complexity of the modern world seriously. Traditional liberal arguments, such as the importance of autonomy and diversity for human progress or mere scepticism about the existence of any objective values, fail to do so, for they are all based on recognisably liberal moral conceptions which do not do justice to alternative ethical systems.[16] Attempts to devise supposedly neutral legal frameworks, protecting certain rights and liberties, privilege particular points of view at the expense of others of equal importance. As a result, they become a source of conflict rather than of stability. Contemporary societies lack the convenient moral symmetry such theories require. In an increasingly functionally and ethically differentiated world, clashes between competing aspects of our lives and our social system are inevitable. No overarching moral theory can resolve all the tensions within them. The compromises and rules required for peaceful coexistence can only emerge in an *ad hoc* manner. A democratic liberalism tries to perform this task by constructing a workable set of democratic institutions capable of providing the *modus vivendi* necessary to arrive at these agreements. It seeks to preserve individual and group freedom through the distribution of power. Unlike ethical liberalism, democratic liberalism does not aim at the construction of the just society *sub specie aeternitatis*. More modestly, it attempts to allow people in the here and now to articulate their needs and ideals and map out a basis for their present co-operation. A liberalism of this kind is not only necessary, it is the only way we can all be liberals now.

Notes

Introduction: from Ethical to Economic Liberalism

1 Francis Fukuyama, 'The World Against a Family', *Guardian*, 12 Sept. 1990, p. 19. See too *idem*, 'The End of History', *The National Interest*, Summer 1989, esp. pp. 3–5, 8–15, 18.

2 My analysis of this thesis is indebted to the work of O. O'Neill, 'The Most Extensive Liberty', *Proceedings of the Aristotelian Society*, 80 (1979/80), pp. 45–59; and J. Gray, *Liberalisms: Essays in Political Philosophy* (London, 1989), esp. ch. 9.

3 See J. Dunn, 'From Applied Theology to Social Analysis: The Break between John Locke and the Scottish Enlightenment', in I. Hont and M. Ignatieff (eds), *Wealth and Virtue: The Shaping of Political Economy in the Scottish Enlightenment* (Cambridge, 1983).

4 The insistence by critics of liberalism on both the left, e.g. A. Arblaster, *The Rise and Decline of Western Liberalism* (Oxford, 1984), and the right, e.g. L. Strauss, *Liberalism: Ancient and Modern* (New York, 1968), that possessive individualism is a basic aspect of the doctrine is therefore mistaken. This argument is made at greater length in chapter 1.

5 E.g. A. Smith, *An Inquiry into the Nature and Causes of the Wealth of Nations*, eds R. H. Campbell, A. S. Skinner and W. B. Todd (Oxford, 1976), IV, ix, 51, pp. 687–8.

6 This argument is clearly indebted to J. Habermas, *The Structural Transformation of the Public Sphere: An Inquiry into a Category of Bourgeois Society* (Cambridge, 1989).

7 J. T. Kloppenberg, *Uncertain Victory: Social Democracy and Progressivism in European and American Thought, 1870–1920* (Oxford, 1986) provides such a history, although Italy is not discussed. The author largely shares the views of the ethical liberal tradition, with the result that the book is often uncritical in its analysis and evaluation of the thinkers discussed. A very useful source of information none the less.

Chapter 1   Britain: Liberalism Defined

1 For this first section I have drawn on A. Briggs, *Victorian People* (London, 1954); *idem, The Age of Improvement 1783–1867* (London, 1959); J. R. Vincent, *The Formation of the British Liberal Party 1856–1868* (London, 1966); H. Perkin, *The Origins of Modern English Society 1780–1880* (London, 1969); R. Shannon, *The Crisis of Imperialism 1865–1915* (London, 1976); C. Harvie, *The Lights of Liberalism: University Liberals and the Challenge of Democracy* (London, 1976); S. Collini, *Liberalism and Sociology: L. T. Hobhouse and Political Argument in England 1880–1914* (Cambridge, 1979), esp. part I; I. Bradley, *The Optimists: Themes and Personalities in Victorian Liberalism* (London, 1980); M. Pugh, *The Making of Modern British Politics* (Oxford, 1982) and my 'Introduction' to Richard Bellamy (ed.), *Victorian Liberalism: Nineteenth Century Political Thought and Practice* (London, 1990).

2 This view was classically expressed by C. B. Macpherson, *The Political Theory of Possessive Individualism* (Oxford, 1962), and is often repeated by radical critics of liberalism, e.g. A. Arblaster, *The Rise and Decline of Western liberalism* (Oxford, 1984), and more curiously by present-day libertarians, e.g. J. Gray, *Liberalism* (Milton Keynes, 1986).

3 S. Collini, 'The Idea of "Character" in Victorian Political Thought', *Transactions of the Royal Historical Society*, 5th series, 35 (1985), pp. 29–50.

4 For two useful studies of Smiles, see Briggs, *Victorian People*, ch. 5, and K. Fielden, 'Samuel Smiles and Self-Help', *Victorian Studies*, 12 (1968–9), pp. 155–72.

5 D. Ricardo, *Principles of Political Economy and Taxation*, in *Works and Correspondence*, ed. P. Sraffa (Cambridge, 1962), I, pp. 151–2, 290, 108–9.

6 S. Smiles, *Self-Help, with Illustrations of Conduct and Perseverance* (London, 1925), p. 3.

7 *Westminster Review*, I (1824), pp. 68–9.

8 See Bradley, *The Optimists*, ch. 4. The quotation, from Gladstone, is on p. 99.

9 Smiles, *Self-Help*, p. 348.

10 Ibid., pp. 341–2.

11 Collini, 'Character', pp. 35–6.

12 S. Smiles, *Thrift* (London, 1875), p. 292.

13 Cobden to Bright, quoted in Bradley, *The Optimists*, p. 59.

14 Smiles quoted in Briggs, *Victorian People*, p. 141.

15 S. Smiles, *Duty* (London, 1880), pp. 267–70.

16 J. S. Mill, *Autobiography*, ed. J. Stillinger (Oxford, 1971), p. 103.

17 Smiles quoted in Briggs, *Victorian People*, pp. 142–3.

18 For the relationship between liberalism and the establishment of middle-class hegemony see Perkin, *Origins of Modern English Society*, chs VII to IX, and T. R. Tholfson, 'The Intellectual Origins of Mid-Victorian Stability', *Political Science Quarterly*, LXXXVI (1971), pp. 57–91.

19 Perkin, *Origins of Modern English Society*, pp. 226–7.

20 Gladstone, quoted in B. Hilton, 'Gladstone's Theological Politics', in M. Bentley and J. Stevenson (eds), *High and Low Politics in Modern Britain* (Oxford, 1983), p. 42.

21 Vincent, *Liberal Party*, p. xxix. See J. Burrow, *A Liberal Descent: Victorian*

Historians and the English Past (Cambridge, 1981) for a full discussion of this historical vision.

22 See the two articles by T. R. Tholfson, 'The Transition to Democracy in Victorian England', *International Review of Social History*, VI (1961), pp. 226–48, and 'The Intellectual Origins of Mid-Victorian Stability', *Political Quarterly*, LXXVI (1971), pp. 57–91.

23 E.g. E. Miall, *Reconciliation between the Middle and the Working Classes* (Birmingham, 1842), pp. 18–20.

24 Bradley, *The Optimists*, pp. 154–5.

25 Smiles, quoted in Briggs, *Victorian People*, pp. 129, 137, 139.

26 B. Webb, *My Apprenticeship* (Harmondsworth, 1971), p. 40, cited in D. Miller, *Social Justice* (Oxford, 1976), p. 290, whose discussion of market societies on pp. 286–300 provides the basis for this and the next paragraph.

27 Miller, *Social Justice*, p. 294.

28 See J. D. Y. Peel, *Herbert Spencer: The Evolution of a Sociologist* (London, 1971), esp. chs 2–4 and 8, and Miller, *Social Justice*, ch. 6.

29 H. Spencer, *Social Statics*, 1st edn (London, 1851), p. 77.

30 This problem is discussed by O. O'Neill, 'The Most Extensive Liberty', *Proceedings of the Aristotelian Society*, 80 (1979–80), pp. 45–59.

31 H. Spencer, *The Principles of Sociology* (3 vols, London, 1876–96), III, pp. 563–4, and Peel, *Spencer*, pp. 212–5.

32 H. Spencer, *The Principles of Sociology*, I, p. 563.

33 This view was typical of the older textbooks, e.g. R. C. K. Ensor, *England 1870–1914* (Oxford, 1936), pp. 162–3; H. J. Laski *The Decline of Liberalism* (London, 1940), pp. 11–12; A. Bullock and M. Shock (eds), *The Liberal Tradition* (Oxford, 1956), p. xliv, and still resurfaces in more recent ones, e.g. W. H. Greenleaf, *The British Political Tradition* (4 vols, London, 1983), II, pp. 124–41.

34 The following discussion draws heavily upon Collini, *Liberalism and Sociology*, part 1.

35 J. S. Mill, 'Bentham', in *Mill on Coleridge and Bentham*, ed. F. R. Leavis (Cambridge, 1980), p. 66, and *Autobiography*, ch. V.

36 Mill, *Utilitarianism*, in *Utilitarianism, On Liberty and Representative Government* (London, 1972), pp. 8–9.

37 See T. H. Green, 'Popular Philosophy in its Relation to Life', in *Works of T. H. Green*, ed. R. L. Nettleship (3 vols, London, 1888), III, pp. 92–125, and his *Prolegomena to Ethics* (1883), ed. A. C. Bradley (Oxford, 1924); para. 1.

38 Green, *Prolegomena*, para. 167.

39 Ibid., para. 166.

40 I have compared their views on liberty more fully in my 'J. S. Mill, T. H. Green and Isaiah Berlin on the Nature of Liberty and Liberalism', in H. Gross and R. Harrison (eds), *Cambridge Essays in Jurisprudence* (Oxford, 1992).

41 Berlin, 'Two Concepts of Liberty', in *Four Essays on Liberty* (Oxford, 1969), esp. p. 133n.

42 Ibid., pp. 131, 128.

43 Berlin, 'Introduction', *Four Essays*, pp. xxxvii–xl.

44 T. Baldwin, 'MacCallum and the Two Concepts of Freedom', *Ratio*, 26 (1984), p. 130. A similar point is made by W. E. Connolly, *The Terms of Political Discourse*, 2nd edn (Oxford, 1983), pp. 143–6.

45 E.g. G. C. MacCallum, 'Negative and Positive Freedom', *Philosophical Review*, 76 (1967), pp. 312–34; Connolly, *Terms of Political Discourse*, pp. 143–6; Baldwin, 'MacCallum and the Two Concepts', pp. 124–42; J. Gray, 'On Negative and Positive Liberty', *Political Studies*, 28 (1980), pp. 508–26.

46 T. H. Green, 'Lecture on "Liberal Legislation and Freedom of Contract"' (1881), reprinted in his *Lectures on the Principles of Political Obligation and other writings*, ed. P. Harris and J. Morrow (Cambridge, 1986), p. 202.

47 T. H. Green, 'On the Different Senses of "Freedom" as Applied to Will and the Moral Progress of Man' (1879), reprinted in *Principles*, para. 17.

48 J. C. Rees, *Mill and his Early Critics* (Leicester, 1956), pp. 48–9.

49 Mill, *On Liberty*, in *idem*, *Utilitarianism, On Liberty and Representative Government*, p. 72.

50 E.g. D. Miller, 'Constraints on Freedom', *Ethics*, 94 (1983), pp. 66–86, and the ensuing debate with F. Oppenheim, *Ethics*, 95 (1985), pp. 205–14.

51 Collini, *Liberalism and Sociology*, pp. 28–9, 46–9.

52 I. Berlin, 'From Fear and Hope Set Free', *Concepts and Categories* (London, 1978), pp. 173–98.

53 Baldwin, 'MacCallum and the Two Concepts', p. 140, quoting H. Sidgwick, *Lectures on Green, Spencer and Martineau* (London, 1902) p. 168 n. 58.

54 Smiles, *Self-Help*, p. 3.

55 Ibid., p. 31.

56 See Peel, *Spencer*, ch. 6, and J. Burrow, *Evolution and Society: A Study in Victorian Social Theory* (Cambridge, 1966).

57 Smiles, *Thrift*, p. 337. See Briggs, *Victorian People*, p. 134, and Fielden, 'Samuel Smiles', p. 172.

58 A. J. Taylor, *Laissez-faire and State Intervention in Nineteenth Century Britain* (London, 1972) surveys the relevant literature.

59 For a development of these points see Collini, 'Character', pp. 35–6, and the same author's *Liberalism and Sociology*, pp. 26–32. S. Mendus, 'Liberty and Autonomy', *Proceedings of the Aristotelian Society*, 87 (1986–7), pp. 107–20, makes the same point with regard to contemporary liberal theory.

60 S. Ball, 'The Moral Aspects of Socialism', *International Journal of Ethics*, VI (1896), p. 302, quoted in Collini, *Liberalism and Sociology*, p. 31.

61 Mill, *On Liberty*, p. 72.

62 Mill, *Autobiography*, p. 150.

63 Mill, *On Liberty*, p. 16.

64 J. S. Mill, *Principles of Political Economy*, in *Collected Works*, II (Toronto, 1965), p. 367.

65 J. S. Mill, *System of Logic*, in *Collected Works*, VIII (Toronto, 1974), pp. 904–5.

66 The following discussion of Mill is much indebted to that of Susan Mendus in her *Toleration and the Limits of Liberalism* (London, 1989), ch. 3.

67 Mill, *On Liberty*, p. 125.

68 Ibid., p. 125.

69 Mill, *Autobiography*, p. 93.

70 Mill, *On Liberty*, p. 117.

71 Ibid., p. 74.

72 J. Gray, *Mill on Liberty: A Defence* (London, 1983).

73 Mill, *On Liberty*, p. 121.

74 See J. Gibbins, 'Mill, Liberalism and Progress', in Bellamy (ed.), *Victorian Liberalism*, ch. 5.

75 Stefan Collini, 'Introduction', J. S. Mill, *Essays on Equality, Law and Education*, in *Collected Works*, XXI (Toronto, 1984), p. xiii.
76 Mill, *Utilitarianism*, pp. 9–10.
77 This distinction adapts a similar one in Mendus, 'Liberty and Autonomy' between the condition and the development of autonomy.
78 Mill, *On Liberty*, pp. 116–17.
79 Mill, *Logic*, pp. 836–43. For a fine analysis of this passage, see G. W. Smith, 'The Logic of J. S. Mill on Freedom', *Political Studies*, 28 (1980), pp. 239–52, and P. Smart, 'Mill and Human Nature', in I. Forbes and S. Smith (eds), *Politics and Human Nature* (London, 1983), ch. 3.
80 Mill, *On Liberty*, p. 73.
81 Mill, *Utilitarianism*, p. 9.
82 Mill, *On Liberty*, pp. 157–8. Cf. Mill, *Principles*, pp. 953–4.
83 J. S. Mill, 'Civilisation', in *Collected Works*, XVIII (Toronto, 1977), pp. 119–35, and *idem*, *On Liberty*, pp. 123–4, 130–1.
84 Mill, *On Liberty*, p. 120.
85 Mill, *Civilisation*, p. 135.
86 Mill, *Considerations on Representative Government*, in *idem*, *Utilitarianism, On Liberty and Representative Government*, p. 177.
87 Ibid., p. 197.
88 Ibid., pp. 178–9, 198, 202–8.
89 Ibid., pp. 250–1. These were the assumptions of James Mill's *Essay on Government* (1820).
90 'The principle of individual liberty is not involved in the doctrine of Free Trade,…neither is it in most of the questions which arise respecting the limits of doctrine' (Mill, *On Liberty*, p. 151).
91 Mill, *On Liberty*, pp. 145, 150.
92 Ibid., pp. 150–1.
93 Mill, *Principles*, pp. 954–56. Given current privatization schemes in Britain, it is worth mentioning that Mill shared the liberal prejudice against joint-stock companies as an effective form of consumer control of such concerns. He believed that the power of shareholders over their directors compared very unfavourably with 'the greater publicity and more active discussion and comment, to be expected in free countries with regard to affairs in which the general government takes part' (p. 954). To increase this accountability, Mill favoured devolving the management of such enterprises onto local authorities wherever possible.
94 Mill, *Principles*, pp. 968–70.
95 Mill, *On Liberty*, pp. 167–8.
96 Mill, *Principles*, p. 943.
97 Ibid., p. 943.
98 Ibid., p. 944.
99 Ibid., p. 970.
100 Mill, *On Liberty*, p. 169.
101 Mill, *Principles*, V, xi, 16, p. 970.
102 Mill, *Principles*, p. 956.
103 Cf. M. Hollis, 'The Social Liberty Game', in A. P. Griffiths (ed.), *Of Liberty*, (Cambridge, 1983).
104 Mill, *On Liberty*, pp. 146–7.
105 Ibid., p. 163.

106 Mill, *Principles*, p. 970.
107 O'Neill, 'The Most Extensive Liberty', p. 56.
108 Mill, *On Liberty*, p. 134.
109 Ibid., p. 121.
110 J. S. Mill, *Subjection of Women*, in *Essays on Equality, Law and Education*, pp. 306, 336.
111 B. Bosanquet, 'The Antithesis between Individualism and Socialism Philosophically Considered' (1980), in his *The Civilisation of Christendom and Other Studies* (London, 1893), pp. 356–7, and Sidgwick, *Elements of Politics*, p. 42, as cited by Collini, *Liberalism and Sociology*, p. 50.
112 My account draws on A. Ryan, *Property and Political Theory* (Oxford, 1984), ch. 6, and W. Wolfe, *From Radicalism to Socialism: Men and Ideas in the Formation of Fabian Socialist Doctrines, 1881–1889* (New Haven, 1975), pp. 52–65.
113 Mill, *Principles*, p. 199.
114 Ibid., p. 208.
115 Ibid., p. 225.
116 Ibid., pp. 226–30.
117 Ibid., p. 819.
118 The best account, on which I have drawn, is L. Zastoupil, 'Moral Government: J. S. Mill on Ireland', *Historical Journal*, XXVI (1983), pp. 707–17.
119 Mill, *Principles*, pp. 230–1.
120 Mill, *Morning Chronicle*, 2 November 1846.
121 Mill, *Principles*, pp. 212–13.
122 Mill, *Autobiography*, p. 139.
123 Ibid., pp. 106–7, 138–9.
124 Ibid., p. 138, and cf. *idem*, *Principles*, pp. 793–4.
125 Mill, *Principles*, p. 792.
126 Mill, *Logic*, p. 841.
127 M. Richter, 'T. H. Green and his Audience: Liberalism as a Surrogate Religion', *Review of Politics*, 18 (1956), pp. 444–72; Richter, *Politics of Conscience* (London, 1964).
128 H. H. Asquith, A. Acland, Edward Grey, H. Samuel, L. T. Hobhouse, J. A. Hobson, W. H. Beveridge, R. B. Morant and W. J. Braitwaite figure amongst the prominant liberals said to have been influenced by Green at Oxford. R. B. Haldane, although educated at Edinburgh, was the most self-conscious disciple amongst politicians. Other members of the idealist school with a Greenian turn of mind included H. Jones, D. G. Ritchie, B. Bosanquet, W. Wallace, E. Caird and the economist A. Toynbee. The *Prolegomena to Ethics* sold 17,000 copies in five editions from 1883 to 1949, when it first went out of print, whilst a separate edition of the *Lectures on the Principles of Political Obligation*, issued with a preface by B. Bosanquet in 1895, went through eleven editions from 1901 to 1950 (Richter, *Politics of Conscience*, p. 294n.).
129 Green, *Prolegomena*, para. 8.
130 Ibid., para. 33.
131 Ibid., para. 125.
132 T. H. Green, *Lectures on the Principles of Political Obligation* (1886), paras 5–7.
133 Green, *Prolegomena*, paras 186–9.
134 Ibid., para. 190.
135 Green, *Lectures*, para. 114.
136 Green, *Prolegomena*, para. 216.

137 Ibid., para. 184.
138 Green, *Lectures*, para. 25.
139 Green, *Prolegomena*, para. 332.
140 Ibid., para. 365; *idem, Lectures*, para. 121.
141 Green, *Prolegomena*, paras 183, 190; *Lectures*, paras 113, 114. J. Raz, *The Morality of Freedom* (Oxford, 1986), esp. ch. 8, offers an analogous view of freedom which I have found useful in elucidating Green's conception.
142 Green, *Lectures*, para. 114.
143 Compare Green's views, discussed below, with Mill's in *Representative Government*, ch. 16, and *Coleridge*, pp. 124–6 (repeated in the *Logic* with slight amendments, pp. 923–4).
144 For the influence of Mazzinian nationalism on Victorian liberals see Harvie, *Lights of Liberalism*, ch. 5, and Bradley, *The Optimists*, ch. 5.
145 For an interesting comparison between the views of Green and those of I. Kant, *Political Writings*, tr. H. Nisbet and ed. H. Reiss (Cambridge, 1977), p. 74, see H. Williams, *Kant's Political Philosophy* (Oxford, 1983), pp. 129–37.
146 Green, *Lectures*, para. 123.
147 Green, *Prolegomena*, para. 184.
148 Green, *Lectures*, para. 122.
149 Ibid., para. 171.
150 Green, *Prolegomena*, paras 232, 286.
151 'The danger of legislation, either in the interests of a privileged class, or for the promotion of particular religious opinions, we may fairly assume to be over. The popular jealousy of law, once justifiable enough, is therefore out of date. The citizens of England now make its law' (Green, 'Liberal Legislation', p. 212).
152 Green, *Lectures*, para. 17.
153 Green, 'Liberal Legislation', p. 196.
154 Green, *Lectures*, para. 17.
155 My understanding of this issue owes much to the excellent article by P. Nicholson, 'T. H. Green and State Action: Liquor Legislation', *History of Political Thought*, VI (1985), pp. 517–50.
156 Speech at Oxford, 1872, quoted in Nicholson, 'Green and State Action', pp. 539.
157 Green, *Lectures*, para. 18.
158 Nicholson, 'Green and State Action', pp. 525–7; Green, 'Liberal Legislation', p. 209; Nettleship, 'Memoir', in *Works of T. H. Green*, I, p. cxvi.
159 Green, 'Liberal Legislation', pp. 210–11.
160 Green, Letter to Harcourt, Jan. 1873, quoted in Nicholson, 'Green and State Action', p. 542.
161 Green, 'Liberal Legislation', p. 210. Compare Mill, *On Liberty*, pp. 145–6, 155–6.
162 Nettleship, 'Memoir', p. cxviii; Nicholson, 'Green and State Action', pp. 520–5.
163 Green, 'Liberal Legislation', pp. 203–4.
164 C. B. Macpherson, *Property: Mainstream and Critical Positions* (Toronto, 1978), pp. 303–4. The following discussion draws upon the fine analysis of J. Morrow, 'Property and Personal Development: an interpretation of T. H. Green's political philosophy', *Politics*, 18 (1983), pp. 84–92.
165 Green, *Lectures*, para. 213.

166 Ibid., para. 223; *idem, Prolegomena,* para. 191.
167 Green, *Lectures,* paras 220, 227.
168 Ibid., para. 217.
169 Ibid., para. 221.
170 Ibid., para. 217.
171 Ibid., para. 229.
172 Green, quoted in Nettleship, 'Memoir', p. cxii.
173 Green, *Lectures,* para. 229.
174 Green, 'Liberal Legislation', p. 205; *idem, Lectures,* para. 228.
175 Green, *Lectures,* para. 230.
176 Ibid., para. 226.
177 Green, quoted in Nettleship, 'Memoir', p. cxii.
178 Green, *Lectures,* para. 226.
179 Ibid., para. 227.
180 Ibid., para. 174.
181 Nettleship, 'Memoir', p. xxiv, and Green, *Lectures,* para. 173. Compare the views of Cobden and Bright as reported by Briggs, *Victorian People,* pp. 223, 224.
182 Green, *Lectures,* para. 223.
183 Ibid., para. 17.
184 Ibid., para. 223.
185 Mill, *Principles,* pp. 752–7; Spencer, *Social Statics,* p. 123.
186 Morrow, 'Property', p. 90, quotes the relevant passage from Green's marginal annotations of Plato's *Republic,* book V, 464–D to this effect.
187 Green, *Lectures,* para. 142; *idem, Prolegomena,* paras 206–7.
188 Green, *Lectures,* paras 142, 144.
189 See Green's speech to the Oxford Reform League, reported in the *Oxford Chronicle,* 30 March 1866, and cited in Harvie, *Lights of Liberalism,* p. 118.
190 Green, quoted in Nettleship, 'Memoir', p. cxviii.
191 A. Milne, 'The Idealist Criticism of Utilitarian Social Philosophy', *Archives Européenes de Sociologie,* VIII (1967), p. 322.
192 Green, *Lectures,* para. 129.
193 F. Hirsch, *Social Limits to Growth* (London, 1976). I have borrowed this example from R. Plant and A. Vincent, *Philosophy, Politics and Citizenship: The Life and Thought of the British Idealists* (Oxford, 1984), pp. 177–8, although my point is somewhat different from theirs. I spell out this divergence in R. Bellamy, 'A Green Revolution?: Idealism, Liberalism and the Welfare State', *The Bulletin of the Hegel Society of Great Britain,* X (1984), p. 38.
194 Green, *Prolegomena,* para. 245.
195 H. Sidgwick, 'Green's Ethics', *Mind,* 9 (1884), pp. 183–4.
196 For a general treatment of this issue, see B. Harrison, 'State Legislation and Moral Reform in Nineteenth Century England', in P. Hollis (ed.), *Pressure from Without in Early Victorian England* (London, 1974), pp. 289–322.
197 A. Toynbee, 'Are Radicals Socialists?' (1882), in *Lectures on the Industrial Revolution in England* (London, 1884), p. 219.
198 As Asa Briggs has warned, 'It is easy to caricature the outlook of the COS' (*Social Thought and Social Action: A Study of the Work of Seebohm Rowntree 1871–1954* (London, 1961), p. 21). For contrasting accounts of its policies see G. Stedman Jones, *Outcast London: A Study in the Relationship between Classes in Victorian Society* (Oxford, 1971), esp. ch. 15, and the less critical view of Vincent and Plant, *Philosophy, Politics and Citizenship,* ch. 6.

199 The following paragraph summarizes the argument of Perkin, *The Origins of Modern English Society 1780–1880*, ch. X, from which all the figures and illustrations have been taken.

200 See Mill, *Principles*, pp. 137–40, 954–5; H. Spencer, 'Railway Morals and Railway Policy' (1854), in *Essays Scientific, Political, Speculative* (3 vols, London, 1891), III, esp. pp. 88–96.

201 These points draw together the collective wisdom of earlier scholars in the field: especially H. V. Emy, *Liberals, Radicals and Social Politics, 1892–1914* (Cambridge, 1973); P. Clark, 'The Progressive Movement in England', *Transactions of the Royal Historical Society*, 5th series, 24 (1974), pp. 159–81; Collini, *Liberalism and Sociology; idem,* 'Political Theory and the "Science of Society" in Victorian England', *Historical Journal*, XXIII (1980), pp. 227–31; Vincent and Plant, *Philosophy, Politics and Citizenship*, pp. 443–8; and M. Freeden, 'New Liberalism and its Aftermath', in Bellamy (ed.), *Victorian Liberalism*, to whom I owe these distinctions.

202 H. Spencer, *The Man Versus the State* (1884), ed. D. MacRae (Harmondsworth, 1964), p. 83, and see p. 110.

203 A. Marshall, *Principles of Economics* 8th edn. (London, 1920), p. 528, and *idem,* 'Industrial Remuneration Conference' (1885), pp. 173–4, quoted in Stedman Jones, *Outcast London*, pp. 7, 8. On Marshall's moralistic economics see Winch and Collini's essay 'A Separate Science: Polity and Society in Marshall's Economics', in S. Collini, D. Winch and J. Burrow, *That Noble Science of Politics: A Study in Nineteenth Century Intellectual History* (Cambridge, 1983), pp. 309–37.

204 G. De Ruggiero, *The History of European Liberalism*, tr. R. G. Collingwood (London, 1927), p. 155. For a discussion of De Ruggiero's intellectual affinity to Hobhouse see R. Bellamy, 'Idealism and Liberalism in an Italian "New Liberal Theorist": Guido De Ruggiero's *History of European Liberalism*', *Historical Journal*, 30 (1987), pp. 191–200.

205 L. T. Hobhouse, *Democracy and Reaction* (1904, 2nd edn 1909), ed. P. Clarke (Brighton, 1972), p. 211; Collini, *Liberalism and Sociology*, ch. 3.

206 Hobhouse, *Democracy and Reaction*, p. 237.

207 M. Freeden, *The New Liberalism: An Ideology of Social Reform* (Oxford, 1978), pp. 16–19, 55–60, correctly argues that Green's ideas were not intended to justify later collectivist policies, and draws attention to the greater prevalence of arguments drawn from biological analogies over those explicitly resting on some form of idealism. However, he goes on to talk as if Hobson, Hobhouse and Ritchie literally 'derived their conclusions about the nature of society from biological and evolutionary data' (p. 19). As Collini remarks 'many of his quotations overwhelmingly suggest rather that they used these models to *legitimate* their proposals' ('Science of Society', p. 227). The title of D. G. Ritchie's study, *Darwin and Hegel* (London, 1893) illustrates how they saw no incompatibility between idealism and evolutionary doctrine, and I follow Collini, *Liberalism and Sociology*, pp. 125–8, 174, in regarding Hobhouse's 'organic' conception of society as fundamentally inspired by Green and, to a lesser extent, Mill.

208 See Collini, *Liberalism and Sociology*, ch. 8.

209 L. T. Hobhouse, *Development and Purpose: An Essay Towards a Philosophy of Evolution* (London, 1913), pp. xix, xxvi.

210 Hobhouse, *Development and Purpose*, pp. xxi, xxvii.

211 Ibid., p. 195.
212 Ibid., p. 198.
213 Ibid., p. 195.
214 Ibid., pp. xxii–iii.
215 E.g. D. G. Ritchie, *The Principles of State Interference* (London, 1891), pp. 14–22, who challenges Spencer's use of this analogy in just this fashion.
216 L. T. Hobhouse, *Liberalism* (1911) (Oxford, 1964), p. 91.
217 Mill, *On Liberty*, p. 69; Hobhouse, *Liberalism*, pp. 50–1, 74, 78.
218 Hobhouse, *Liberalism*, pp. 78–81.
219 Ibid., p. 69, my emphasis.
220 Ibid., p. 81.
221 Ibid., p. 76.
222 Ibid., pp. 80–1.
223 Ibid., pp. 98–9.
224 Ibid., p. 104.
225 Ibid., pp. 53–4, 91–2.
226 Ibid., 100–102.
227 Ibid., p. 103.
228 Ibid., p. 99.
229 Ibid., p. 104 n. 1.
230 Ibid., p. 83.
231 Ibid., p. 86.
232 Ibid., p. 106.
233 For a full discussion see J. Harris, *Unemployment and Politics: A Study in English Social Policy 1886–1914* (Oxford, 1971), esp. chs 5 and 7.
234 W. H. Beveridge, 'The Problem of the Unemployed', *Sociological Papers*, 3 (1906), p. 327. Compare the comments on this passage of Freeden, *New Liberalism*, pp. 184–5, who regards this statement as an 'inexplicable' lapse, with those of Stedman Jones, *Outcast London*, p. 335 and Harris, *Unemployment and Politics*, pp. 189–90, who do not.
235 See Freeden, *New Liberalism*, pp. 185–94.
236 Collini, *Liberalism and Sociology*, pp. 82–4; Hobhouse, *Democracy and Reaction*, pp. 119–24. On the 'national efficiency' current within the liberal movement see B. Semmel, *Imperialism and Social Reform: English Social-Imperial Thought 1895–1914* (London, 1960); G. R. Searle, *The Quest for National Efficiency: A Study in British Politics and Political Thought* (Oxford, 1971); and H. C. G. Matthew, *The Liberal Imperialists: The Ideas and Politics of a Post-Gladstonian Elite* (Oxford, 1973).
237 Hobhouse, *Liberalism*, pp. 89–90.
238 L. T. Hobhouse, *Social Evolution and Political Theory* (New York, 1911), p. 71.
239 Ibid., p. 179.
240 E.g. H. H. Asquith's statement in his 'Introduction' to H. Samuel, *Liberalism: An Attempt to State the Principles and Proposals of Contemporary Liberalism in England* (London, 1902), where he defines positive liberty as making 'the best use of faculty, opportunity, energy, life...everything, in short, that tends to national, communal and personal efficiency' (quoted in Freeden, *New Liberalism*, p. 183).
241 See P. Clarke, *Liberals and Social Democrats* (Cambridge, 1978), and M. Freeden, *Liberalism Divided): A Study in British Political Thought 1914–1939* (Oxford, 1986).

242 Hobson's view of Old Age Pensions, quoted in Freeden, *New Liberalism*, p. 241.
243 Mill, *Representative Government*, p. 227. See L. Siedentop, 'Two Liberal Traditions', in Ryan (ed.), *Idea of Freedom*, pp. 153–74, for the contrast with France.
244 Freeden, *Liberalism Divided*, pp. 285ff shows how power was progressive liberalism's 'blind spot'; S. Lukes, *Power: A Radical View* (London, 1974) indicates how it still is.
245 I owe this reflection to G. Hawthorn, *Enlightenment and Despair: A History of Sociology* (Cambridge, 1976), p. 112.

Chapter 2   France: Liberalism Socialized

1 E. Durkheim, *The Division of Labour in Society* (1893), tr. W. D. Halls (London, 1984), p. xxx.
2 A few examples from each camp drawn from the vast Durkheim secondary literature must suffice: L. Coser, 'Durkheim's Conservatism and its Implications for his Sociological Theory' in K. H. Wolff (ed.), *Emile Durkheim, 1858–1917* (Columbus, 1960), pp. 211–32 and R. Nisbet, 'Conservatism and Sociology', *American Journal of Sociology*, 58 (1952), pp. 165–75, are the main proponents of the 'Conservative'view; M. Richter, 'Durkheim's Politics and Political Theory', in Wolff (ed.), *Durkheim*, pp. 170–210, A Giddens, 'Durkheim's Political Sociology', *Sociological Review*, 19 (1971), pp. 477–519, B. Lacroix, *Durkheim et la politique* (Paris, 1981) and W. Logue, *From Philosophy to Sociology: The Evolution of French Liberalism, 1870–1914* (Illinois, 1983), ch. VII, see him as a liberal; finally S. Lukes, *Emile Durkheim: His Life and Work* (London, 1973), J-C. Filloux, 'Introduction', E. Durkheim, *La science social et l'action* (Paris, 1970), pp. 5–68 and F. Pearce, *The Radical Durkheim* (London, 1989) emphasise his affinities to socialism.
3 The view of the French school of Marxist historians, e.g. G. Lefebvre, *The Coming of the French Revolution* (New York, 1957).
4 E.g. W. Doyle, *Origins of the French Revolution* (Oxford, 1985), ch. 13.
5 This and the following paragraph draw on A. Jardin, *Histoire du liberalisme politique: de la crise de l'absolutisme à la constitution de 1875* (Paris, 1985), P. Rosanvallon, *Le moment Guizot* (Paris, 1985), Guido De Ruggiero, *Storia del liberalismo europeo* (Bari, 1925), pp. 154–204, and E. K. Bramstead and K. J. Melhuish (eds), *Western Liberalism: A History in Documents from Locke to Croce* (London, 1978), pp. 52–79.
6 See L. Siedentop, 'Two Liberal Traditions', in A. Ryan (ed.), *The Idea of Freedom* (Oxford, 1979).
7 F. Guizot, *Mémoires pour servir à l'histoire de mons temps* (Paris, 1872), VI, p. 346, cited in Bramstead and Melhuish, *Western Liberalism*, pp. 335–6.
8 Both Jardin, *Historie* and Rosanvallon, *Guizot* stress that French liberalism cannot be identified with *laissez-faire* economics. This view requires some qualification. Whilst it is true that French liberals, no less than the British, cannot be identified with a crude economic individualism, their liberal politics did assume the capitalist organisation of society. See C. Welch, *Liberty and Utility: French Ideologues and the Transformation of Liberalism* (New York, 1984) and B. Fontana, 'The Shaping of Modern Liberty: Commerce and

Civilization in the Writings of Benjamin Constant', *Annales Benjamin Constant*, 5 (1985), pp. 5–15.

9 A. de Tocqueville, *De la Democratie en Amérique* (Paris, 1981), II, pp. 125–7.

10 For the classic, and much misunderstood, expression of this view, see B. Constant, 'The Liberty of the Ancients compared with that of the Moderns', in *Political Writings*, ed. and tr. B. Fontana (Cambridge, 1988), esp. pp. 326–8. Both Jardin, *Histoire*, especially ch. XIII, and Rosanvallon, *Guizot* emphasise this specifically political dimension of French liberalism, as does S. Holmes, *Benjamin Constant and the Making of Modern Liberalism* (New Haven, 1985).

11 Guizot, *Mémoires*, VI, p. 349.

12 Cf. Lukes, *Durkheim*, pp. 195–9.

13 My account draws on S. Elwitt, *The Making of the Third Republic* (Baton Rouge, 1975); J. Mayeur, *Les débuts de la IIIe République* (Paris, 1973); R. D. Anderson, *France 1870–1914* (London, 1977) and R. Magraw, *France 1815–1914: The Bourgeois Century* (London, 1983).

14 Ferry, cited in Lukes, *Durkheim*, p. 355.

15 E. Durkheim, 'Individualism and the Intellectuals' (1898), tr. S. and J. Lukes, *Political Studies*, XVII (1969), p. 29.

16 S. Elwitt, *The Third Republic Defended: Bourgeois Reform in France*, 1880–1914 (Baton Rouge, 1986), pp. 4–5.

17 General Boulanger was appointed Minister of War because of his supposed Radical sympathies in an attempt to control the army. The move backfired when he used his growing popularity following the Schnaebele affair, a border incident involving Germany, to boost his own political fortunes. He was dismissed in 1888, but won a dramatic succession of electoral victories in 1889 on a platform of populist nationalism. Fearing a resurgence of Bonapartism, he was threatened with prosecution for treason and fled to Belgium, where he commited suicide on the grave of his mistress.

18 The controversy surrounding the Dreyfus affair reached its height in 1898–9, but went back to 1894 when it was discovered that military secrets were being passed to the German embassy. Dreyfus was convicted on the basis of his handwriting and sent to Devil's Island. In 1897 the new head of the secret service, Col. Picquart, discovered that the real traitor was another officer, Esterhazy. Prejudice against Dreyfus's Jewishness and low military rank, combined with an inability to admit having made a mistake, made the army reluctant to re-open the case. Picquart was transferred and Esterhazy acquitted in a rigged trial. In January 1898 a public debate broke out after Zola's famous open letter 'J'accuse'. The Dreyfusards stood for Republican values – hence the ambivalence of the socialists, with Jaurès supporting them and Guesde remaining aloof; the Anti-Dreyfusards, mainly centred on the Church and Army, argued that one should always support the central institutions of the country, regardless of whether they are right or wrong. Durkheim's contribution to this debate on the side of the Republicans will be examined further on in this chapter.

19 The best discussions of radicalism and solidarism can be found in M. Réberioux, *La république radicale?* (Paris, 1975), for a sound political chronology; and Elwitt, *the Third Republic Defended*, and T. Zeldin, *France 1848–1945: Politics and Anger*, paperback edn (Oxford, 1979), chs 8–9 for an examination of their social policy. The fullest analysis of their ideas remains the

following series of articles by J. E. S. Hayward, 'Solidarity: The Social History of an Idea in Nineteenth Century France', *International Review of Social History*, 4 (1959), pp. 261–84; 'The Official Social Philosophy of the French Third Republic: Léon Bourgeois and Solidarism', *Int. Rev. Soc. Hist.*, 6 (1961), pp. 20–48 and 'Educational Pressure Groups and the Indoctrination of the Radical Ideology of Solidarism, 1895–1914', *Int. Rev. Soc. Hist.*, 8 (1963), pp. 1–17. He relates Durkheim's project to theirs in his 'Solidarist Syndicalism: Durkheim and Duguit', *Sociological Review*, 8 (1960), pp. 17–36, 185–202.

20 Detailed accounts of Renouvier's ideas are given in R. H. Soltau, *French Political Thought in the 19th Century* (London, 1931), ch. X, and Logue, *From Philosophy to Sociology*, ch. III.
21 C. Renouvier, *Science de la morale* (1869), 2nd edn (Paris, 1908), I, p. 58.
22 Ibid., I, pp. 219–27.
23 Ibid., I, pp. 107–8, 264; II, p. 2, 18.
24 Ibid., I, pp. 134–42.
25 Ibid., II, pp. 30, 35, 126–7.
26 Elwitt, *The Third Republic Defended*, esp. ch. 1.
27 Biographical information comes from Hayward, 'Bourgeois', who also provides a sustained analysis of his ideas.
28 Clemençeau quoted in Hayward, 'Bourgeois', p. 24.
29 L. Bourgeois, *Solidarité*, 11th edn (Paris, 1926), pp. 7–10.
30 Ibid., pp. 12, 166–9.
31 Ibid., p. 37.
32 Ibid., p. 37.
33 Ibid., pp. 19–20, 85.
34 Ibid., pp. 162–7.
35 Ibid., p. 54.
36 Ibid., pp. 60–72, 190–200.
37 Bourgeois's ideas were enthusiastically received by new liberals in Britain, a positive notice in *The Progressive Review*, Dec, 1896, pp. 283–6 remarking on the similarities between his doctrine and theirs.
38 Bourgeois, *Solidarité*, pp. 200–7.
39 See the debate appended to the various talks given by Bourgeois to the Ecoles des Hautes Etudes Sociales 1901–3, and collected in later editions of *Solidarité* under the title 'L'idée de solidarité et ses consequences sociales', pp. 157–283.
40 Bourgeois, *Solidarité*, pp. 234, 238.
41 Ibid., p. 188.
42 Ibid., pp. 244–6.
43 Ibid., pp. 240–1.
44 A. Fouillée, *La propriété sociale et la democratie* (Paris, 1884), discussed by Bourgeois in *Solidarité*, p. 248.
45 Bourgeois, *Solidarité*, pp. 242–4, 248–50.
46 Paul Deschanel, quoted in Zeldin, *Politics and Anger*, p. 296.
47 E. de Boyve, *Histoire de la cooperation à Nimes* (Paris, 1889), pp. 6–12, 15–16, quoted in Elwitt, *The Third Republic Defended*, p. 192.
48 Quotations from the *Revue des Institutions de Prevoyance*, IV (1890), p. 153, cited in Elwitt, *The Third Republic Defended*, p. 188.
49 C. Gide, 'De la cooperation et des transformations qu'elle est appelée à

réaliser dans l'ordre économique', *Revue d'Economie Politique*, III (1889), pp. 476–88, quoted in Elwitt, *The Third Republic Defended*, pp. 194–5, whose analysis I reproduce.

50 Bourgeois, *Solidarité*, p. 188.
51 Ibid., p. 96.
52 A. Fouillée, *L'Enseignement au point de vue national* (Paris, 1891), pp. 255, 260, 289, cited in Elwitt, *The Third Republic Defended*, pp. 223–4.
53 F. Buisson, *Congrès* internationale de l'éducation sociale: *Proces-verbale sommaire* (Paris, 1902), pp. 114–15, quoted in Elwitt, *The Third Republic Defended*, p. 222.
54 Bourgeois, *Solidarité*, pp. 97–9.
55 Ferdinand Faure quoted in Zeldin, *Politics and Anger*, pp. 299–300.
56 Durkheim, Review of A. Fouillée, *La Propriété sociale et la democratie*, *Revue philosophique*, XIX (1885), pp. 446–53, translated in A. Giddens (ed.), *Durkheim on Politics and the State* (Cambridge, 1987), tr. W. D. Halls, pp. 86–96.
57 E. Durkheim, 'Cours de science sociale, leçon d'ouverture' (1888), in *La science sociale et l'action*, pp. 109–10.
58 Durkheim, *Division of Labour*, pp. xxv–xxvii.
59 On Espinas see Logue, *From Philosophy to Sociology*, p. 104.
60 Quotations from E. Durkheim, 'La science positive de la morale en Allemagne', *Revue philosophique*, 24 (1887), pp. 33–58, 113–42, 275–84, cited in A. Giddens, *Capitalism and Modern Social Theory* (Cambridge, 1971), pp. 67–71.
61 Durkheim, *Division of Labour*, pp. 24–9.
62 Ibid., p. 84.
63 Ibid., p. 172.
64 Ibid., pp. 200–5.
65 Ibid., pp. 179–99.
66 Ibid., pp. 218–19.
67 Ibid., pp. 220–1.
68 Ibid., p. 152.
69 Ibid., p. 302.
70 E. Durkheim, Review of F. Tonnies, *Gemeinschaft und Gesellschaft*, *Revue philosophique*, 27 (1889), pp. 416–22, translated in E. Durkheim, *Selected Writings*, ed. and tr. A. Giddens (Cambridge, 1972), pp. 146–7.
71 Durkheim, *Division of Labour*, p. 122 (revised translation R. Bellamy).
72 Ibid., p. 333.
73 Ibid., pp. 337–8, 302.
74 Ibid., p. 122.
75 Ibid., pp. 153–4.
76 Ibid., p. 304.
77 Ibid., p. 308.
78 Ibid., p. 310.
79 Ibid., p. 319.
80 Ibid., p. 312.
81 Ibid., p. 316.
82 Ibid., pp. 317–18.
83 Ibid., pp. 323–8.
84 Ibid., p. 321.
85 Quotation and figures come from Magraw, *France 1815–1914*, ch. 8.

86 Durkheim, *Division of Labour*, p. 313.
87 Durkheim, *Leçons*, p. 238.
88 Ibid., p. 237.
89 Ibid., pp. 68–9.
90 Ibid., pp. 50–1.
91 Ibid., pp. 241–2.
92 Ibid., p. 239.
93 Ibid., pp. 242–4.
94 E. Durkheim, *Suicide: A Study in Sociology* (1897), tr. J. A. Spaulding and G. Simpson (London, 1952), p. 37 (amended translation).
95 See D. Pick, *Faces of Degeneration: A European Disorder, c.1848–1918* (Cambridge, 1989).
96 See Lukes, *Durkheim*, ch. 9 for details of the contemporary debate.
97 Durkheim, *Suicide*, p. 37.
98 Ibid., p. 258.
99 Ibid., p. 258.
100 E. Durkheim, 'Le dualisme de la nature humaine et ses conditions sociales', *Scientia*, XV (1914), pp. 206–21, reprinted in Durkheim, *La science sociale et l'action*, p. 330.
101 Barclay Johnson, 'Durkheim's One Cause of Suicide', *American Sociological Review*, 30 (1965), pp. 875–86.
102 Durkheim, *Suicide*, p. 212.
103 Ibid., p. 288.
104 Ibid., pp. 246–50.
105 Ibid., pp. 252–3.
106 Ibid., p. 254.
107 Ibid., pp. 255, 257.
108 Ibid., p. 253 (amended translation).
109 E. Durkheim, *Socialism and Saint-Simon*, tr. C. Sattler, ed. A. W. Gouldner (1928) (London, 1959), pp. 1–28, 196–204.
110 E. Durkheim, Review of S. Merlino, *Formes et essence du socialisme* (Paris, 1897), *Revue philosophique*, XLVIII (1899), pp. 433–9, translated in Giddens (ed.), *Durkheim on Politics and the State*, p. 143.
111 Durkheim, *Socialism*, pp. 7–9.
112 E. Durkheim, Review of A. Labriola, *Essais sur la conception matérialiste de l'historie* (Paris, 1897), *Revue philosophique*, XLIV (1897), pp. 645–51, translated in Giddens (ed.), *Durkheim on Politics and the State*, p. 136.
113 Durkheim, *Socialism*, p. 204.
114 Ibid., pp. 241–2.
115 S. Lukes, *Marxism and Morality* (Oxford, 1986) provides the most convenient summary of the debate. It is perhaps no accident that the author is also a leading Durkheim scholar.
116 The argument of Pearce, *The Radical Durkheim*, esp. ch. 8, is particularly vitiated in this respect.
117 M. Barres, *Scènes et doctrines du nationalisme* (Paris, 1902) livre 2e, pp. 209–10, cited in Lukes, 'Introduction' to Durkheim, 'Individualism and the Intellectuals', p. 16.
118 Durkheim, 'Individualism and the Intellectuals', pp. 23, 25.
119 Ibid., pp. 25–6.
120 Ibid., pp. 20–1.

121 Ibid., p. 27.
122 Ibid., pp. 20–4.
123 Ibid., p. 29.
124 I. Kant, *The Metaphysics of Morals*, in *Werke* (Berlin, 1902), vol. 6, p. 423.
125 G. Tarde, 'Criminalité et santé sociale', *Revue philosophique* XXXIX (1895), pp. 148–62.
126 See S. Lukes, 'Alienation and Anomie', in P. Laslett and W. G. Runciman (eds), *Philosophy, Politics and Society*, Series III (Oxford, 1967).
127 E. Durkheim, *Sociology and Philosophy* (1924), tr. D. F. Pocock (London, 1953), p. 72. For similar statements, see E. Durkheim, *Moral Education* (1925) tr. E. K. Wilson and H. Schnurer (New York, 1961), pp. 40–6, 54.
128 Durkheim, *Division of Labour*, p. 333.
129 Giddens, 'Durkheim's Political Sociology', p. 492.
130 Durkheim, *Sociology and Philosophy*, pp. 60–1. These views were expressed in an article of 1906.
131 E. Durkheim, *The Rules of Sociological Method* (1895), tr. W. D. Halls, ed. S. Lukes (Oxford, 1982), pp. 94, 104.
132 E. Durkheim, *Pragmatisme et sociologie* (Paris, 1955), p. 174. This book consists of posthumously published lecture notes, from a course delivered at the Sorbonne 1913–14.
133 Durkheim, *Suicide*, p. 360.
134 Durkheim, *Sociology and Philosophy*, pp. 50–1.
135 Durkheim, 'The Contribution of Sociology to Psychology and Philosophy' (1909), in *Rules*, pp. 238–9.
136 Durkheim, *Sociology and Philosophy*, p. 52.
137 Durkheim, *Suicide*, p. 360.
138 E.g. J. Rawls, *A Theory of Justice* (Oxford, 1971).
139 E. Durkheim, 'Deux lois d'évolution penale', *Année Sociologique*, 4 (1901), pp. 65–95, translated in S. Lukes and A. Scull (eds), *Durkheim and the Law* (Oxford, 1983), ch. 4. The quotations come from pp. 106 and 104 respectively.
140 Durkheim, 'Deux lois', p. 129.
141 Durkheim, *Suicide*, pp. 379–80. *idem*, *Division of Labour*, p. liv.
142 Durkheim, *Division of Labour*, p. liv.
143 Ibid., p. liv. These remarks on the professional groups were added in a preface to the second edition of 1902. Durkheim had already indicated their importance in the conclusion to *Suicide* (1897), pp. 378–92, and had sketched out some of his ideas as early as 1885 in his first published writing, an analysis of the ideas of the *Kathedersozialisten*, Review of A. Schaeffle, *Bau und Leben des sozialen Korpers: Erster Band*, *Revue philosophique*, XIX (1885), pp. 84–101. The most comprehensive treatment of his revised political system came in the *Leçons* which derive from a course of lectures on 'Physique Générale du Droit et des Moeurs' delivered twice in Bordeaux between 1896 and 1900, and repeated at the Sorbonne in 1904 and 1912. The earliest published account of their new role within his revised theory of politics and the state was in his review of Merlino, *Formes et essence du socialisme*.
144 Durkheim, *Division of Labour*, p. 1 xiv; *idem*, *Suicide*, pp. 378–9, 389–90; *idem*, *Leçons*, pp. 135–6.
145 Durkheim, *Division of Labour*, pp. xxxv–vi, liii.
146 Durkheim, contribution to a discussion 'Sur l'état, les fonctionnaires et

le public: le fonctionnaire citoyen; syndicats de fonctionnaires', in *Libres entretiens*, 4th series, translated in *Durkheim on Politics and the State*, pp. 145–53.

147 Durkheim, *Suicide*, pp. 386–7.
148 Durkheim, *Division of Labour*, p. lvi.
149 Durkheim, *Suicide*, pp. 386–7.
150 Durkheim, *Suicide*, p. 380; *idem*, *Leçons*, p. 78.
151 Durkheim, *Suicide*, p. 384.
152 Durkheim, *Leçons*, p. 122.
153 For a useful contemporary discussion of democracy in terms of the erosion of these features, see N. Bobbio, *The Future of Democracy* (Cambridge, 1987), pp. 33–4, 86–91, whose terminology I have borrowed.
154 Durkheim, *Leçons*, pp. 124–5.
155 Although Durkheim identified Rousseau as the main exponent of 'direct democracy', it is doubtful that the citizen of Geneva held the views he attributed to him. Rousseau was no less a critic than Durkheim of the 'will of all', and his notion of the 'general will' equated well with the sociologist's ideal.
156 Durkheim, *Leçons*, pp. 124–5.
157 Ibid., p. 125.
158 Ibid., pp. 127–9, 138–9.
159 Ibid., p. 137.
160 Ibid., p. 105.
161 Ibid., p. 99.
162 Ibid., pp. 98, 99, 100–9.
163 Ibid., p. 98.
164 Ibid., p. 140.
165 Ibid., p. 78.
166 E.g. J. Rawls, *A Theory of Justice* (Oxford, 1971) and R. Dworkin, 'Liberalism' in S. Hampshire (ed.), *Public and Private Morality* (Cambridge, 1978).
167 Durkheim, *Moral Education*, p. 155.
168 Durkheim, *Leçons*, p. 109.
169 Durkheim, *L'Allemagne au-dessus de tout: la mentalité allemande et la guerre* (Paris, 1915), pp. 42, 44.
170 E.g. M. M. Mitchell, 'Emile Durkheim and the Philosophy of Nationalism', *Political Science Quarterly*, 46 (1931), pp. 87–106, who sees in his work 'the transition from the humanitarian ideas of Positivists of the middle of the nineteenth century to the jingoist nationalism of the twentieth'. This view derives from Mitchell's misinterpretation of Durkheim's view of the state as 'a psychic being more than the sum-total of its members'. Durkheim strongly denied this 'mystical' notion of the state in *Leçons*, p. 104 and *L'Allemagne*, pp. 27, 38.

Chapter 3   Italy: Liberalism Transformed

1 This point is particularly well made by A. Lyttleton, 'Landlords, Peasants and the Limits of Liberalism', in J. A. Davis (ed.), *Gramsci and Italy's Passive Revolution* (London, 1979), ch. 4. The subordinate role of the commercial or industrial bourgeoisie in the making of liberal Italy during the Risorgimento is the subject of K. R. Greenfield's classic study *Economics and Liberalism in the Risorgimento* (Baltimore, 1965).

2 See G. Baglioni, *L'ideologia della borghesia industriale nell'Italia liberale* (Turin, 1974), esp. ch. 2.
3 Lyttleton, 'Landlords, Peasants', pp. 107–8, 115.
4 See J. A. Davis, *Conflict and Control: Law and Order in Nineteenth Century Italy* (London, 1988), pp. 160–8, on which this and the next paragraph are based.
5 Cavour, quoted in Davis, *Conflict and Control*, p. 161.
6 For a discussion of how the suppression of the south determined the future course of Italian liberal politics see R. Vivarelli, *Il fallimento del liberalismo* (Bologna, 1981), ch. 1, and Davis, *Conflict and Control*, chs 6–12. I have also referred to R. Romanelli, *L'Italia liberale (1861–1900)* (Bologna, 1979), ch. 1.
7 The quotation, written in 1861 from a former intimate of Cavour to the liberal politician Marco Minghetti, is cited by Romanelli, *L'Italia liberale*, p. 31. Earlier he had remarked, 'This is a country that one can only hold with force or the terror of force.'
8 For a useful overview of the structure of the Liberal state after unification see M. Clark, *Modern Italy 1871–1982* (London, 1984), ch. 3.
9 For subtle versions of the argument that fascism 'revealed' the weaknesses of liberal Italy, which I largely follow, see Vivarelli, *Il fallimento del liberalismo*, esp. ch. 1, A. Lyttleton, *The Seizure of Power: Fascism in Italy 1919–29* (London, 1973), chs 1–2, and P. Corner, 'Liberalism, Pre-Fascism, Fascism', in D. Forgacs (ed.), *Rethinking Italian Fascism: Capitalism, Populism and Culture* (London, 1986), pp. 11–20. For a corrective against more extreme proponents of this view see A. Acquarone, *Alla ricerca dell'Italia liberale* (Naples, 1972), ch. 6.
10 E.g. D. Mack Smith, *Italy: A Modern History*, 2nd edn (Ann Arbor, 1969), p. 104; Romanelli, *L'Italia liberale*, pp. 22–7.
11 For a full account of the political ideals of the Neapolitan Hegelians, see S. Onufrio, 'Lo "Stato etico" e gli hegeliani di Napoli', *Nuovi Quaderni Meridionali*, VII (1969), pp. 76–90, 171–88, 271–87, 436–57, 466–80, VIII (1970), pp. 64–78, 196–214.
12 S. Spaventa, *Dal 1845 al 1861: Lettere, scritti, documenti*, ed. B. Croce, 2nd edn (Bari, 1923), pp. 148, 149.
13 S. Spaventa, 'Discorso parlamentare del 24 giugno 1876', in S. Spaventa, *Discorsi parlamentari* (Rome, 1913), p. 413.
14 Quoted in Romanelli, *L'Italia liberale*, p. 25. See too F. De Sanctis, 'La scuola liberale', in *La letteratura italiana nel secolo xix: scuola liberale – scuola democratica*, ed. F. Torraca (Naples, 1898), pp. 379–80. For an interesting comparison of the liberalism of S. Spaventa and F. De Sanctis see Onufrio, 'Lo "Stato etico" ', pp. 480–3.
15 See S. Spaventa's famous autocritique of 1879, 'La politica e l'amministrazione della Destra e l'opera della Sinistra', in *La giustizia nell'amministrazione* (Turin, 1949), ch. 1, where both these sentiments are expressed. Indeed, Spaventa (pp. 44–5) even reproaches the Right with having been too soft on the peasant revolts!
16 B. Spaventa, *Studi sull'etica de Hegel* (Naples, 1869), pp. 153–4.
17 See note 10.
18 This tendency to seek out the laws governing the social system was particularly true of Roberto Ardigo and his school, e.g. his *La morale dei positivisti* (1879).

19 C. Lombroso, *L'uomo delinquente* (Turin, 1878). For an analysis of Lombroso's ideas see Davis, *Conflict and Control*, pp. 326–38 and D. Pick, 'The Faces of Anarchy: Lombroso and the Politics of Criminal Science in Post-Unification Italy', *Historical Workshop*, 21 (1986), pp. 60–86.

20 Spaventa, *Discorsi parlamentari*, pp. 419–20. The lack of faith in the control operated by shareholders over directors was shared by Smith, Spencer, Mill and Sidgwick – that is, the main representatives of British classical political economy.

21 Acquarone, *Alla ricerca dell'Italia liberale*, p. 281.

22 These figures, which are for 1861, come from Clark, *Modern Italy*, pp. 35–6.

23 E.g. F. De Sanctis, 'L'uomo dei Guicciardini', in *Saggi critici*, III (Bari, 1969), pp. 1–25. The theme is surprisingly echoed in the political science literature of the 1950s, e.g. G. A. Almond and S. Verba, *The Civic Culture: Political Attitudes and Democracy in Five Nations* (Princeton, 1963), pp. 402–3.

24 Stefano Jacini, *Sulle condizioni della cosa pubblica in Italia dopo il '66* (Florence, 1870).

25 P. Turiello, *Governo e governati in Italia* (2 vols, Bologna, 1882).

26 P. Villari, *Le lettere meridionali ed altri scritti sulla questione sociale in Italia* (Florence, 1898), and L. Franchetti and S. Sonnino, *La Sicilia nel 1876* (2 vols, Florence, 1876).

27 For a good summary of recent research along these lines see Clark, *Modern Italy*, ch. 1.

28 See Davis, *Conflict and Control*, ch. 11.

29 R. Villari, *Mezzogiorno e democrazia* (Bari, 1978), p. 75. For Mill's arguments see ch. 1, pp. 33–4.

30 For the reality see F. Snowden, 'From Sharecropper to Proletarian: the Background to Fascism in Rural Tuscany', in Davis (ed.), *Gramsci and Italy's Passive Revolution*, ch. 5.

31 Villari, *Lettere meridionali*, quoted in Davis, *Conflict and Control*, p. 348. On this group see Villari, *Mezzogiorno e democrazia*, ch. 3, and A. Asor Rosa, *La cultura*, in *Storia d'Italia*, vol. 4 ii (Turin, 1975), pp. 893ff.

32 For a fascinating study of the reception of Mill in Italy, see Nadia Urbinati, 'John Stuart Mill e il liberalismo italiano nell'età del positivismo', Tesi presentata per il conseguimento del dottorato di ricerca in Scienze Politiche e Sociali presso l'Istituto Universitario Europeo, Florence, June 1989.

33 The classic text in this regard is of course B. Moore jun., *Social Origins of Dictatorship and Democracy* (Boston, 1967), esp. pp. 418–9, 422, 429–30, 451–2, whose thesis has been modified to fit the Italian case by Lyttleton, 'Landlords, Peasants'.

34 E.g. M. Minghetti, *I partiti politici e la ingerenza loro nella giustizia e nell' amministrazione* (Bologna, 1881) as quoted by V. Pareto, 'State Intervention in Italy', *The Speaker*, 14 May 1892, reproduced in *Ecrits épars*, ed. G. Busino (Geneva, 1974), pp. 50–1. Pareto ruefully remarks on Minghetti's simultaneous cogent criticism and practical support of Depretis's political management.

35 For the debate see A. Gerschenkron, *Economic Backwardness in Historical Perspective* (Cambridge, Mass., 1962) pp. 72–89, R. Romeo, *Risorgimento e capitalismo* (Bari, 1959), pp. 91–203 and A. Caracciolo, *La formazione dell' Italia industriale* (Bari, 1969).

36 Clark, *Modern Italy*, pp. 93–9.

37 Baglioni, *L'ideologia della borghesia*, ch. 4 provides a full account of Rossi, from which the quotations (at pp. 255–6) are taken. See too S. Lanaro, *Nazione e lavoro: saggio sulla cultura della borghesia in Italia 1870–1925 (Venice, 1979)*.

38 See Baglioni's tracing of the curious fortunes of the Smilsean ethos in Italy in *L'ideologia della borghesia*, ch. 5.

39 See A. Cardini, *Stato liberale e protezionismo in Italia (1880–1990)* (Bologna, 1981).

40 For details of the Crispi era and the ensuing crisis of the Liberal state see Mack Smith, *Italy*, sections 5–6, Romanelli, *L'Italia liberale*, ch. V; Clark, *Modern Italy*, ch. 5 and Davis, *Conflict and Control*, 'Epilogue'.

41 S. Sonnino, 'Torniamo allo statuto', *Nuova antologia*, 1–1–1897, in N. Valeri (ed.), *La lotta politica in Italia dall'unità al 1925: idee e documenti*, 2nd edn (Florence, 1958), p. 251–69.

42 See the fresh rebuttal of Sonnino's reactionary programme in favour of a democratic agenda in the following exchange: S. Sonnino, 'Quid agendum?', *Nuova antologia*, 16–9–1900, and G. Alessio, 'Risposta al "Quid agendum?" ', Ibid., in Valeri (ed.), *La lotta politica*, pp. 281–6.

43 G. Giolitti, 'Il nuovo indirizzo della politica liberale', speech to the Chamber of Deputies, 4–2–1901, in Valeri (ed.), *La lotta politica*, pp. 286–9.

44 See D. Roberts, *The Syndicalist Tradition and Italian Fascism* (Manchester, 1979) and E. Gentile, *Il mito dello stato nuovo dall'antigiolittismo al fascismo* (Rome/Bari, 1982).

45 See G. Salvemini, *Il ministro della malavita*, in *Opere*, IV, ed. E. Apih (Milan, 1962).

46 For details see M. Clark, *Gramsci and the Revolution that Failed* (Yale, 1977).

47 C. Maier, *Recasting Bourgeois Europe: Stabilisation in France, Germany and Italy in the Decade after World War One* (Princeton, 1975), pp. 317, 329. My own account of the final crisis of the liberal regime draws on chs 2 and 5 of this book, as well as Lyttleton, *The Seizure of Power* and Clark, *Modern Italy*, ch. 10.

48 See Maier, *Recasting Bourgeois Europe*, pp. 328, 338–9.

49 A speaker at the conference of the Italian Liberal Party at Bologna, 8–10 October 1922, quoted in Maier, *Recasting Bourgeois Europe*, p. 342.

50 E.g. F. Borkenau, *Pareto* (New York, 1930), H. Stuart Hughes, *Consciousness and Society: The Reorientation of European Social Thought* (Brighton, 1979), pp. 260–1.

51 J. A. Schumpeter, *Ten Great Economists from Marx to Keynes* (New York, 1951), pp. 116–17.

52 The following account draws on and modifies my chapter on Pareto in *Modern Italian Social Theory: Ideology and Politics from Pareto to the Present* (Cambridge, 1987), ch. 2. Like all other Pareto scholars I am indebted to the editorial work of G. Busino in making available the twenty volumes of Pareto's complete work (*Oeuvres complètes de Vilfredo Pareto* (20 vols, Geneva, 1964–75). The outlines of Busino's own interpretation can be gained from his review article, 'Vilfredo Pareto: sociologo della borguesia e dello sviluppo capitalistico?', *Rivista storica italiana*, LXXXIII (1971), pp. 385–438. I also owe a lot to the pioneering work of S. E. Finer's 'Introduction' to his selection of Pareto's *Sociological Writings*, tr. D. Mirfin (Oxford, 1966) and his article 'Pareto and Pluto-democracy', *American Political Science Review*, LXII (1968), pp. 440–50.

53 V. Pareto, 'Sulla rappresentanza proporzionale', *Atti della Reale Accademia dei Georgofili di Firenze*, series IV, vol. II (1872), pp. 138–56 and 'Suffragio Universale', *L'Italiano – Gazzetta del Popolo*, 12 Nov. 1872, pp. 3–4, in V. Pareto, *Ecrits politiques*, ed. G. Busino (2 vols, Geneva, 1974), I, *Lo sviluppo del capitalismo 1872–95*, pp. 33–46, 47–51.

54 Pareto, 'Suffragio universale', p. 49.

55 Ibid., p. 49.

56 V. Pareto, 'La legge sulla responsabilità civile dei padroni e imprenditori pei casi d' infortunio sul lavoro', *Rassegna di scienze sociale e politiche*, 15 July 1883, pp. 521–41, *Lo sviluppo*, pp. 158–80.

57 For a powerful statement of this view see for example Pareto's *Cronaca* of April 1893 in the *Giornale degli economisti*, in *Lo sviluppo*, pp. 618–19.

58 Romanelli, *L'Italia liberale*, p. 295.

59 V. Pareto, 'Se convenga fissare per legge un minimo al salario guadagnato e un massimo alla ricchezza speculata', *Atti della Reale Accademia Economico-agraria dei Georgofili di Firenze*, series IV, vol. IX (1886), pp. 103–30, in *Lo sviluppo*, p. 205.

60 Pareto, 'Se convenga fissare', pp. 192ff.

61 V. Pareto, ' Due disegni di leggi sociale', *Rassegna di scienze sociale e politiche*, 15 June 1883, pp. 353–64, in *Lo sviluppo*, pp. 144–57.

62 Pareto enunciated this programme many times, most particularly in the *Cours d'économie politique* (1896) examined below. For a shorter statement see his summary of his programme in the *Cronaca* of April 1894 in the *Giornale degli economisti*, pp. 407–12, in *Lo sviluppo*, esp. 767–8.

63 The following account of this period of Pareto's life and his involvement with the anti-protectionist campaign draws on A. Cardini, *Stato liberale e protezionismo in Italia (1890–1900)* (Bologna, 1981) and most especially Vivarelli, *Il fallimento del liberalismo*, ch. IV.

64 V. Pareto, 'Sulla recrudescenza della protezione doganale in Italia', *Atti della Reale Accademia Economico-agraria dei Georgofili di Firenze*, series IV, vol. X, 1887, pp. 27–52, and 'Ancora sulla recrudescenza dogonale', Ibid., pp. 303–7, 312–15, in *Lo sviluppo*, pp. 218–34, 235–40.

65 V. Pareto, 'La nuova tariffa doganale italiana', *Journal des économistes*, Oct. 1887, pp. 5–23, in *Lo sviluppo*, p. 241.

66 V. Pareto, ' Practical Questions in the Italian Government', *The Chautauquan*, Jan. 1892, pp. 448–51, in *Ecrits épars*, pp. 44, 48.

67 V. Pareto, 'The Parliamentary Regime in Italy', *Political Science Quarterly*, Dec. 1893, pp. 677–721, in *Ecrits épars*, p. 93.

68 E.g. V. Pareto, 'Letters from Italy I', *Liberty*, IV (1888), pp. 6–7, in *Ecrits épars*, p. 15, 'Dell'unione doganale od altri sistemi di rapporti commerciali fra le nazioni come mezzo inteso a migliorare le relazioni politiche ed a renderle pacifiche', *Relazione al Congresso di Rome per la pace* (Lapi, 1889), pp. 85–94, *Lo sviluppo*, p. 289, and 'Parliamentary Regime', p. 94.

69 V. Pareto, ' Il signor Yves Guyot e il suo libro *La scienza economica*', *L'économista*, 26 Aug. 1888, pp. 559–64, *Lo sviluppo*, p. 276.

70 V. Pareto, Letter to F. Papafava, 2 Dec. 1888, in G. Busino, *Vilfredo Pareto e l'industria del ferro nel Valdarno. Contributo alla storia dell'imprenditorialità italiana* (Milan, 1977), p. 824.

71 V. Pareto, 'Socialismo e libertà', *Il pensiero italiano*, Feb, 1891, pp. 227–37, in *Lo sviluppo*, pp. 378–9, 384.

72 See Pareto's 'Introduction' to K. Marx, *Le Capital, extraits faits par P. Lafargue* (Paris, 1893), pp. iii–lxxx, in V. Pareto, *Marxisme et économie pure* (Lausanne, 1966), p. 70.

73 Pareto, 'Socialismo e libertà', pp. 384–89.

74 Ibid., pp. 404–5.

75 See the excellent discussion in Vivarelli, *Il fallimento del liberalismo*, pp. 241–52, on which I have drawn.

76 V. Pareto, *Cours d'économie politique* (2 vols, Lausanne, 1896–7), II, 'Il resume', pp. 1–2.

77 Pareto, *Cours*, II, paras 580, 585–93.

78 Ibid., II, book 1.

79 Ibid., II, paras 735–6, 743.

80 Pareto, *Cours*, II, paras 1053–65. For specific applications of these ideas to contemporary Italy see the *Cronaca*, *Giornale degli economisti*, Feb. 1895, in *Lo sviluppo*, esp. pp. 848–9 and 'Finanza e partiti politici', *Rivista popolare di politica, lettere e scienze sociale*, 30 May 1897, pp. 424–6, in *Ecrits politiques*, vol. 2, *Reazione, libertà, fascismo*, pp. 188–92.

81 Pareto, *Cours*, II paras 606, 625, 661–5. For further evidence of Pareto's Enlightenment rationalism and evolutionism see the following letters to Pantaleoni of 7 Feb. and 27 July 1892, in *Lettere a Maffeo Pantaleoni* nos 55 and 96, I, pp. 177, 255.

82 Pareto, 'Socialismo e libertà', p. 384.

83 V. Pareto, 'Le sorti future della parte liberale', *L'idea liberale*, 28 Aug. and 4 Sept. 1892, in *Lo sviluppo*, pp. 549, 550.

84 For details see G. De Rosa's editorial note in V. Pareto, *Lettere a Maffeo Pantaleoni* (3 vols, Geneva, 1984), I, pp. 134–9, 143.

85 V. Pareto, 'Pro e contro socialismo', *Il secolo* 20–21 June 1896, in *Reazione, libertà*, fascismo, pp. 84–6. For similar sentiments see 'La parte economica e la parte sociale delle dottrine socialiste', *Critica sociale*, 1 Aug. 1895, pp. 230–1, in *Lo sviluppo*, pp. 890–4.

86 V. Pareto, 'Il sentimento della libertà', *Il secolo*, 2–3 and 4 April 1899, in *Reazione, libertà, fascismo*, p. 302.

87 V. Pareto, Letter to Maffeo Pantaleoni, 23 Dec. 1896, in *Lettere a Maffeo Pantaleone*, no. 246, III, p. 500.

88 V. Pareto, 'Liberali e socialisti', *Critica sociale*, 1 Sept. 1889, pp. 215–6, in *Reazione, libertà, fascismo*, pp. 322–3.

89 V. Pareto, 'Le péril socialiste', *Journal des économistes*, May 1900, in *Libre-échangisme, protectionisme et socialisme*, ed. G. Busino (Geneva, 1965), pp. 322–39, and 'Un applicazione di teorie sociologiche', *Rivista italiana di sociologia*, July 1900, in *Ecrits sociologiques mineurs*, ed. G. Busino (Geneva, 1980), pp. 178–238. This latter article contains all the main elements of Pareto's later sociology.

90 V. Pareto, Letter to Ernest Roguin, 6 Feb. 1907, in *Correspondance 1890–1923*, ed. G. Busino (2 vols, Geneva, 1975), no. 486, I, p. 587. Pareto later recalled his earlier attachment in two interesting letters to James Harvey Rogers dated 9 Feb. 1916 and 7 April 1916 in Ibid., nos. 965, 974, II, pp. 915, 921–2. For similar criticisms of Spencer in his scholarly works see, e.g. V. Pareto, *Manuel d'économie politique*, 2nd edn (Geneva, 1909), ch. 2, paras 29, 31, 50, 101.

91 E.g. Letter to Tullio Martello, 17 Feb. 1905, in *Correspondance*, no. 420, I, p. 538.

92 Pareto's continuing reputation as an economist largely rests on the mathematical appendix added to the 1909 (French) edition of the work.
93 V. Pareto, *Les systèmes socialistes* (2 vols, Paris, 1902), I, p. 125.
94 E.g. see the two chapters on sociological method and its relevance to economic which open the *Manuel* and the article 'L'économie et la sociologie au point de vue scientifique', *Rivista di scienza* (1907), pp. 293–312, in V. Pareto, *Ecrits sociologiques mineurs*, pp. 324–43.
95 V. Pareto, *Les systèmes socialistes*, I, pp. 15, 21–2, 24–5, 34–41, 58–62, 132–3, II, pp. 380–4, 419–9, 454–6.
96 V. Pareto and G. Prezzolini, 'L'aristocrazia dei briganti', in *Il Regno*, I (1903), in D. Frigessi (ed.), *La culture italiana attraverso le riviste* (2 vols Turin, 1960), II, pp. 455–60, 467–8.
97 For Pareto's own fascinating accounts of the reasons, see his letters to Antonio Antonucci of 7 Dec. 1907 and Emanuele Sella, 11 june 1913, in *Correspondance*, no. 513, I, pp. 613–16 and no. 828, II, pp. 831–3.
98 V. Pareto, 'Gli scioperi e il ministro Giolitti', *La vita internazionale*, 20 July 1901, in *Reazione, Libertà, fascismo*, pp. 356–64.
99 E.g. V. Pareto, 'Perche' l'economia politica non gode favore presso il popolo?', *Atti della Reale Accademia dei Georgofili di Firenze*, series, IV, vol. XII (1889), pp. 26–44, in *Lo sviluppo*, p. 321.
100 The development of Pareto's critical attitude towards the socialists and Giolitti's programme can be traced in the following articles: 'Il pericolo del socialismo', 'Gli scioperi e il ministro Giolitti', 'Giustizia' and 'Sempre giustizia', *La vita internazionale*, 20 Aug. 1900 and 5 Nov. 1900, pp. 489–90, 520–3, in *Reazione, libertà, fascismo*, pp. 332–6, 337–44 and 'Un poco di fisiologia sociale', *La vita internazionale*, 5 Sept. 1901, pp. 529–32, in Ibid., pp. 365–73, 'L'eclissi della liberta', *Giornale deqli economisti*, June 1903, pp. 568–70, in Ibid., pp. 387–90, 'Decadenza borgnese', 'Scioperanti in Francia' and 'Umanitari e rivoluzionari', in *Il Regno*, 4 May 1904, pp. 1–3, 31 July 1904, pp. 6–7, 30 Oct. 1904, pp. 1–2, in Ibid., pp. 420–4, 425–9, 433–6.
101 Pareto, *Manuale, para. 107*.
102 V. Pareto, 'Il crepuscolo della libertà', *Rivista d'Italia*, Feb. 1904, pp. 193–205, *Reazione, libertà, fascismo*, p. 408. For similar sentiments, privately expressed, see the Letter to Tullio Martello of 17 Feb. 1905, in *Correspondance*, no. 420, I, p. 538.
103 Pareto, *Manuale*, para. 107. He went on sententiously to declare that 'force is the foundation of all social organisation' and 'to note that the antipathy of the contemporary bourgeoisie to force results is giving a free hand to violence.'
104 V. Pareto, *Trattato di sociologia generale*, ed. N. Bobbio, 2nd Italian edn (Milan, 1964), paras 149, 151.
105 Pareto, *Trattato*, Index summary of theorems: 1b.
106 Pareto, *Trattato*, paras 842–6, 866–70, 875, 881, 885–6, 1690 and note. Pareto's distinction between residue and sentiment is particularly important to bear in mind, since he tends to use the former to denote the latter. Failure to comprehend the distinction properly can lead to disastrous misinterpretations. E.g. C. Powers, *Vilfredo Pareto* (California, 1987), pp. 73, 96–110 misunderstands Pareto's argument, regarding 'residues' as denoting solely the behaviour, as opposed to the derivative utterances or beliefs, which indicate underlying sentiments. This is simply wrong. As we have

seen, the term 'residue' strictly understood has a broader frame of reference than this. It is thus untrue that Pareto's classes of what he calls residues can be more clearly regarded as different categories of sentiments (ch. 7), for Pareto does not know this for sure. He clearly states that a theory of sentiments was beyond him (para. 1690, note). This mistake is related to the nature of Powers' whole project to offer a propositional and hence deductive version of Pareto's theory. Without a firm understanding of the sentiments underlying human behaviour, this is impossible. Since Pareto did not presume that he had such knowledge, indeed it is hard to know how one could attain it, he had to stick to the inductive approach. Powers's attempt to streamline Pareto's doctrine is thus vitiated from the start.

107 Pareto, *Trattato*, para. 889.
108 Ibid., para. 2183.
109 Ibid., paras 2025–6, 2227.
110 Ibid., para. 2178.
111 Ibid., paras 2053–9.
112 Ibid., paras 2178–9, 2227, 2235–6, 2053–9. For a pertinant application of Pareto's thesis of the links between economics and politics to what he calls the protectionist cycle see paras 2208–22.
113 V. Pareto, *La trasformazione della democrazia*, in *Ecrits sociologiques mineurs*, pp. 955–6.
114 Pareto, *Trasformazione*, pp. 975–6.
115 Ibid., ch. 2. See too the letter to Pantaleoni of 2 May 1921, in *Lettere a Maffio Pantaleoni*, no. 704, III, pp. 279–80.
116 Pareto, *Trattato*, paras 825–7, 2466, n. 1. This criticism is made by Finer in his 'Introduction' to Pareto, *Sociological Writings*, p. 75.
117 Pareto, *Trattato*, para. 2251.
118 Ibid., paras 2237–44.
119 Ibid., paras 1843, 1864, 1866.
120 A. Sen, 'The Impossibility of a Paretian Liberal', *Journal of Political Economy*, 78 (1970), pp. 152–7. Sen's famous example involves the choices of Lewd and Prude concerning who should be allowed to read *Lady Chatterley's Lover*. Prude's favoured ranking is (n), that no one should read it; (p) that he should read it, thereby preventing gullible Mr Lewd being corrupted; and finally (l) that Lewd should get his hands on it. Lewd's preferences, in contrast, are first (p), that Prude should read it ('it will do him some good'); second (l), that he should read it ('shame to let a good book go to waste'); and finally (n), that no one should read it. On grounds of individual freedom, the liberal would prefer (l) to (n), since Lewd wants to read it; and (n) to (p), because Prude does not. However, the book cannot be handed over to Lewd as the liberal wants because (p) is Pareto superior to (l). Sen has responded to his critics in 'Liberty, Unanimity and Rights', *Economica*, 43 (1976), pp. 217–45.
121 Pareto raises this difficulty himself in *Trattato*, paras 2133–7, 2140–6.
122 See his letter of 22 May 1921, in *Lettere a Maffeo Pantaleoni*, no. 705, III, pp. 281–4.
123 Letter to Lello Gangemi, 13 Nov. 1922, *Correspondance*, no. 1261, II, p. 1114.
124 V. Pareto, 'Il fascismo' (1922), in *Ecrits sociologiques mineurs*, pp. 1078–89 and letter of 26 Nov. 1920 to Pantaleoni, in *Lettere a Maffeo Pantaleoni*, no. 697, III, pp. 273–4.

125 Pareto, *Lettere a Maffeo Pantaleoni*, 17 June 1921, no. 708, III, pp. 285–6, Letters to Vincenzo Fani, 11 Oct. 1922, A. Linaker, 19 Nov, 1922 and E. Lolini, 23 March 1923, in *Correspondance*, nos 1249, 1263, 1309, II, pp. 1106, 1116, 1141.
126 Pareto, *Trasformazione*, p. 927.
127 *Lettere a Maffeo Pantaleoni* no. 733, 23 Dec. 1922, III, p. 320.
128 B. Croce, 'Contributo alla critica di me stesso' (1915), in *Etica e politica*, 2nd edn economica (Bari, 1973), pp. 334–5.
129 B. Croce, 'A proposito del positivismo italiano. Ricordi personali', *La critica*, III (1905), pp. 169–72.
130 G. W. F. Hegel, *Philosophy of Right*, tr. T. M. Knox (Oxford, 1952), p. 10. Knox translates the Hegelian phrase as 'What is rational is actual, and what is actual is rational', pointing out its activist non-conservative nature, as discussed below. For a similar analysis, see S. Avineri, *Hegel's Theory of the Modern State* (Cambridge, 1974), p. 126.
131 B. Croce, *Ciò che è vivo e ciò che è morto della filosofia di Hegel* (1906), in *Saggio sullo Hegel* (Bari, 1913), p. 41 and 'Una pagina sconosciuta degli ultimi mesi della vita di Hegel' (1948), in *Indagini sul Hegel e scharimenti filosofici* (Bari, 1952), p. 10.
132 B. Croce, 'Per la interpretazione e la critica di alcuni concetti del marxismo' (1897), *Materialismo storico*, p. 98 and note.
133 B. Croce. 'Sul principio economico; due lettere a Prof. V. Pareto' (1900), *Materialismo storico*, pp. 209–30.
134 B. Croce, 'Sulla forma scientifica del materialismo storico' (1896), in *Materialismo storico ed economia marxistica*, 3rd edn economica (Bari, 1978), p. 15.
135 Croce, 'Come nacque e come morí il marxismo teorico in Italia 1895–1900', in *Materialismo storico*, pp. 274–5.
136 F. De Sanctis, *Storia della letteratura italiana* (1872–3) (2 vols, Milan, 1978), II, p. 864.
137 B. Croce, Autobiographical fragment of 1912, posthumously published as *Memorie della mia vita* (Naples, 1966), p. 39.
138 See B. Croce, 'Introduzione', *La critica*, I (1903), pp. 1–5.
139 For more detailed studies of this period of Croce's career, see R. Bellamy, 'Liberalism and historicism: Benedetto Croce and the political role of idealism in modern Italy 1890–1952', in A. Moulakis (ed.), *The Promise of History*, (Berlin New York, 1985), pp. 69–109, E. E. Jacobitti, *Revolutionary Humanism in Modern Italy* (New Haven London, 1981), and Bobbio, *Profilo ideologico*, ch. 6.
140 E.g. B. Croce, Review of G. Sorel, *Saggi di critica del maxismo*, in *La critica*, I (1903), pp. 226–8, 'Cristianeismo, socialismo e metodo storico', *La critica*, V (1907), pp. 317–30. This latter, an overview of Sorel's thought, was later used as a preface to the Italian edition (1909) of the *Reflections sur la violence*.
141 B. Croce, 'G. D'Annunzio', *La critica*, II (1904), pp. 1–28 and 'L'odio contro il D'Annunzio', *La critica*, IV (1906), pp. 165–6. See too G. Prezzolini's enthusiastic review of Croce's *Estetica*, 'L'uomo-dio', *Leonardo*, I (1903), pp. 3–4 and his notice on 'La critica', *Leonardo*, IV (1906), p. 362.
142 B. Croce, 'Alfredo Oriani', *La Critica* V (1907), pp. 1–28.
143 E.g. B. Croce, Review of L. Luzzati, *La libertà di coscienza e di scienza*, in *La critica*, VII (1909), pp. 287–92 and an interview on the same theme in *Marzocco*, 7 Nov. 1909, now in G. Castellano (ed.), *Pagine sparse*, 1st series 2

vols Naples, 1919), II, pp. 242–3, 'Mentalità massonica', *Giornale d'Italia*, 6 Oct. 1910.

144 B. Croce, 'Di un carattere della più recente letteratura italiana', *La critica*, V (1907), pp. 177–90. For later polemics see the section 'Contro gli atteggiamenti artistici, mentali e morali dei cosidetti "giovani" ', in Castellano (ed.), *Pagine sparse*, 1st series, II, pp. 357–78.

145 B. Croce, 'Leonardo, rivista di idee, a. IV ott.–dic. 1906', *La critica*, V (1907), pp. 67–8. The quotation comes from G. W. F. Hegel, *Enciclopedia delle scienze filosofiche in compendio*, tr. B. Croce (Bari, 1907), part iii, para. 396.

146 B. Croce, 'Fede e programmi', *La critica*, IX (1911), pp. 390–6, reprinted in *Cultura e vita morale*, 2nd edn (Bari, 1926), p. 162.

147 B. Croce, 'Per la rinascita dell'idealismo', *La cultura*, XXVI (1908), pp. 1–8, in *Cultura e vita morale*, pp. 35–6.

148 B. Croce, 'La morte del socialismo', *La Voce*, III (1911), 9 Feb., pp. 501–2. The 'interview' (Croce wrote both questions and answers himself), was given the day after the Milan Conference of the PSI had confirmed the ascendency of the reformist tendency within the party.

149 Croce, 'Fede e programmi' and 'Il risveglio filosofico e la cultura italiana', *La critica*, VI (1908), pp. 161–78.

150 B. Croce, 'E necessaria una democrazia?', *L'unità*, I, no. 7, 27 Jan. 1912, p. 26 and 'Il partito come giudizio e come pregiudizio', *L'unità*, I, no. 17, 6 April 1912, p. 66.

151 B. Croce, Review of G. Mosca, *Elementi di scienza politica*, 2nd edn (Turin, 1923), in *La critica*, XXI (1923), pp. 374–8. Croce's view of patriotism is in many respects very similar to that put forward by Alasdair MacIntyre in his lecture 'Is Patriotism a Virtue?', The Lindley Lecture, University of Kansas, 26 March 1984.

152 B. Croce, Review of T. Mann, *Betrachtungen eines Unpolitischen* (Berlin, 1919), in *La critica*, XVIII (1920), pp. 182–3.

153 B. Croce, 'Programma del Fascio dell'ordine', 4 July 1914, in Castellano (ed.), *Pagine sparse*, 1st series, II, p. 400.

154 See Croce's important new preface to the 1918 edition of *Materialismo storico*, pp. xiv–v. Ironically, Croce's first writing on Marx had been an attack on the evolutionary interpretation of Loria.

155 B. Croce, 'Ritorno sulle postille precedenti' (1916), in G. Castellano (ed.), *Pagine sparse*, 2nd series, *Pagine sulla guerra* (Naples, 1919), p. 131.

156 B. Croce, quoted in D. Coli, *Croce, Laterza e la cultura europea* (Bologna, 1983), pp. 147–8.

157 B. Croce, 'Lo stato come potenza' (1915), in Castellano (ed.) *Pagine sulla guerra*, p. 74.

158 Croce entirely approved of the inclusion of fascists in the government block in a general election held during his last months of office. See G. De Ruggiero, *Scritti politici 1912–26*, ed. R. De Felice (Bologna, 1963), p. 31.

159 B. Croce, 'Liberalismo e fascismo – intervista', *Giornale d'Italia*, 27 Oct. 1923.

160 B. Croce, 'Le elezioni e il ritorno alla vita politica normale – intervista', *Corriere italiano*, 1 Feb. 1924.

161 B. Croce, 'La situazione politica – intervista', *Giornale d'Italia*, 10 July 1924.

162 Ibid., July 1924.

163 G. Gentile, 'Croce e il suo liberalismo', *L'epoca*, 21 March 1925. For similar views see the article by Giulio de Montemayor in *Educazione politica*, May

1926 and G. Prezzolini's preface to U. Benedetto, *Croce e il fascismo* (Rome, 1967), pp. 2, 11.

164 G. Gentile, 'Il fascismo e la Sicilia', speech at Palermo, 31 March 1924, in *Che cosa è il fascismo?* (Florence, 1925), p. 50.

165 E.g. B. Croce, Review of N. Machiavelli, *Il principe*, ed. F. Chabod, *La critica*, XXII (1924), pp. 313–14.

166 B. Croce, 'Lo Stato e l'etica' (1924), in *Etica e politica*, p. 187.

167 B. Croce, 'Liberalismo', *La critica*, XXIII (1925), p. 126.

168 B. Croce, 'La concezione liberale come concezione della vita', in *Etica e politica*, p. 235.

169 G. W. F. Hegel, *Lectures on the Philosophy of World History: Introduction*, tr. H. B. Nisbet (Cambridge, 1975), p. 71.

170 B. Croce, *La storia come pensiero e come azione* (1938), 4th edn economica (Bari, 1978), p. 51.

171 Croce, 'La concezione liberale', pp. 239–42.

172 Croce, *La storia*, pp. 47–51, 227–8.

173 B. Croce, 'Storia economico-politica e storia etico-politica' (1924), in *Etica e politica*, p. 231.

174 For Croce's debt to Mosca see his review of G. Mosca, *Elementi di scienza politica*, 2nd edn (Torino, 1923), in *La critica*, XXI (1923), pp. 374–8.

175 B. Croce, 'Principio, ideale e teoria della libertà' (1939), in *Il carattere della filosofia moderna* (Bari, 1941).

176 B. Croce, *Storia d'Italia dal 1871 al 1915* (1928), 3rd edn economica (Bari, 1977), p. 205.

177 E.g. B. Croce, *Una famiglia di patrioti e altri saggi storici edn critici*, 2nd edn (Bari, 1927), *idem Vite e avventure di fede e di passione* (Bari, 1936).

178 B. Croce, *Storia del regno di Napoli* (Bari, 1925).

179 Croce, *La storia*, pp. 33–4.

180 B. Croce and L. Einaudi, *Liberismo e liberalismo*, ed. P. Solari (Naples, 1957), p. 152.

181 B. Croce, *Storia d'europa nel secolo decimonono*, 4th edn economica (Bari, 1981), p. 316.

182 C. Rosselli, 'Liberalismo socialista', *Rivoluzione liberale*, III (1924), in L. Basso and L. Anderlini (eds), *Le riviste di Piero Gobetti* (Milan, 1961), pp. 227, 231–3.

183 P. Gobetti, Comment on G. Prezzolini, 'Per una società degli apoti', *Rivoluzione liberale*, I (1922), in *Le riviste di Piero Gobetti*, p. 281.

184 G. De Ruggiero, 'Il problema di autorità', *Il paese*, 8 Dec. 1921, in *Scritti politici 1912–26*, pp. 421–2.

185 Calogero's writings are usefully collected together as *Difesa del liberal-socialismo ed altri scritti*, nuova edizione di M. Schiavone e D. Confrancesco (Milan, 1968). See especially pp. 76, 199, 222.

186 B. Croce, 'Revisione filosofica dei concetti di "libertà" e "giustizia"', in *La critica*, XLI (1943), pp. 276–84, and *idem*, *L'idea liberale contro le confusioni e gl'ibridismi* (Bari, 1943).

187 B. Croce, *Il partito liberale, il suo officio e le sue relazioni con gli altri partiti. Discorso tenuto al primo congresso del Partito Liberale Italiano in Napoli il 4 giugno 1944* (Bari, 1944).

188 B. Croce, 'Una parola desueta: l'amor di patria', in *Scritti e discorsi politici* (2 vols, Bari, 1963), I, p. 95.

189 B. Croce, preface to the 1947 edition of his *Storia d'Italia dal 1871 al 1915*.
190 For further discussion see my articles 'Hegel's Conception of the State and Political Philosophy in a Post-Hegelian World', *Political Science*, 38 (1986), pp. 99–112 and 'Hegel and Liberalism', *History of European Ideas*, 8 (1987), pp. 693–708.
191 See my 'Hegel and Liberalism' for a full discussion of this point.
192 G. De Ruggiero, *Il ritorno alla ragione* (Bari, 1946), and Croce's review in *Quaderni della critica*, II (1946), p. 79.
193 B. Croce, 'Agli amici che cercano il "trascendente"' (1945), in Etica e politica, pp. 378–84.

Chapter 4   Germany: Liberalism Disenchanted

1 J. P. Mayer, *Max Weber and German Politics: A study in Political Sociology*, 2nd edn (London, 1956), pp. 33, 109, 117, 119. A similarly Machiavellian interpretation of Weber is offered by R. Aron, 'Max Weber and Power Politics', in O. Stammer (ed.), *Max Weber and Sociology Today* (Oxford, 1971), pp. 83–100, e.g. p. 85).
2 W. Mommsen, *Max Weber and German Politics 1890–1920* (New York, 1967).
3 Although R. Dahrendorf, *Society and Democracy in Germany* (New York, 1967) cites Mommsen in support of his own view that 'Weber was, if anything, more "nationalistic" than Bismarck' (p. 57), Dahrendorf goes on to use Weber as evidence for the 'strange liberalism' of the Germans.
4 E.g. Mommsen, *Max Weber*, pp. 40, 189.
5 In adopting this interpretation I follow the work of D. Beetham, *Max Weber and the Theory of Modern Politics*, 2nd edn (Cambridge, 1985), who stresses against Mayer and Mommsen that Weber's thought transcends its immediate German context to face the problems confronting liberalism within modern societies generally (e.g. pp. 3, 7, 12).
6 Dahrendorf, *Society and Democracy*, p. 14.
7 This thesis has been particularly boldly stated by Dahrendorf, *Society and Democracy*, esp. chs 1–4, whose arguments this paragraph largely summarises. Its political dimensions have been developed and refined by historians of the 'Kehrite' school, whose views form the basis of the next paragraph, e.g. E. Kehr, *Battleship Building and Party Politics in Germany 1894–1901: A Cross Section of the Political, Social and Ideological Preconditions of German Imperialism* (Chicago and London, 1975), F. Fischer, *War of Illusions: German Politics 1911–1914* (London, 1974), H.-U. Wehler, *The German Empire 1871–1918* (Leamington Spa, 1985) and V. R. Berghahn, *Germany and the Approach of War in 1914* (London, 1973). More generally, see A. Gerschenkron, *Economic Backwardness in Historical Perspective* (New York, 1965) and B. Moore jun., *Social Origins of Dictatorship and Democracy* (Harmondsworth, 1966), esp. chs VII and VIII.
8 Dahrendorf, *Society and Democracy*, p. 35. For further comparisons between the growth rates of the British and German economies see V. R. Berghahn, *Modern Germany: Society, Economy and Politics in the Twentieth Century* (Cambridge, 1982), pp. 1–9 and table 9 p. 260.
9 Dahrendorf, *Society and Democracy*, p. 39.

10 For examples of this genre see H. Kohn, *The Mind of Germany* (London, 1961), F. Stern, *The Politics of Cultural Despair* (Berkeley 1961) and G. L. Mosse, *The Crisis of German Ideology* (London, 1966). Rather more sophisticated versions of this thesis inform what are nevertheless the two best studies of German liberalism: L. Krieger, *The German Idea of Freedom: History of a Political Tradition* (Boston, 1957) and J. J. Sheehan, *German Liberalism in the Nineteenth Century* (Chicago, 1978).

11 Krieger, *German Idea of Freedom*, p. 86.

12 Ibid., pp. 86–7.

13 R. Aris, *History of Political Thought in Germany from 1789 to 1815* (London, 1936), pp. 97, 101. Aris also calls Kant 'the first representative of liberalism in Germany' (p. 104).

14 T. Mann, *Betrachtungen eines Unpolitischen* (Berlin, 1918).

15 Krieger, *German Idea of Freedom*, p. ix.

16 E.g. Wehler, *German Empire*, pp. 42, 46. Kehr, who died in 1933, was deeply influenced by Weber's writings.

17 This point is well made by H. Williams, *Kant's Political Philosophy* (Blackwell, 1983), p. 157.

18 See especially E. Gellner, *Nations and Nationalism* (Oxford, 1983).

19 For a masterly synthesis of German liberal ideas, see Sheehan, *German Liberalism in the Nineteenth Century*, esp. chs 1–3.

20 The following account draws heavily on the work of D. Blackbourn and G. Eley, especially their joint work *The Peculiarities of German History: Bourgeois Society and Politics in Nineteenth Century Germany* (Oxford, 1984) and their earlier essays collected in G. Eley, *From Unification to Nazism: Reinterpreting the German Past* (Boston, 1986), esp. chs 2, 3, 5 and 6, and D. Blackbourn, *Populists and Patricians: Essays in Modern German History* (London, 1987), esp. chs 4 and 7. See too R. J. Evans (ed.), *Society and Politics in Wilhelmine Germany* (London, 1978) for a selection of articles reflecting the new revisionism.

21 Blackbourn and Eley, *Peculiarities of German History*, p. 230.

22 E.g. P. Anderson, 'Origins of the Present Crisis', *New Left Review*, 23 (1964), pp. 26–54, T. Nairn, 'The British Political Elite', *New Left Review*, 23 (1964), pp. 19–25 and M. J. Weiner, *English Culture and the Decline of the Industrial Spirit (1850–1980)* (Cambridge, 1981). E. P. Thompson's reply to Anderson and Nairn, 'The Peculiarities of the English', reprinted in his *The Poverty of Theory and Other Essays* (London, 1978), provided obvious inspiration for Blackbourn and Eley's revision of German history.

23 See A. J. Mayer, *The Persistence of the Old Regime: Europe to the Great War* (New York, 1981).

24 M. Weber, 'Capitalism and Rural Society in Germany' (1906), in *From Max Weber: Essays in Sociology*, eds H. H. Gerth and C. Wright Mills (London, 1948), p. 383.

25 For an excellent account of Kant's liberalism see Williams, *Kant's Political Philosophy*, esp. ch. 6. The best single source of Kant's views is the essay 'On the Common Saying: "This May be True in Theory, But It Does Not Apply in Practice"' in *Kant's Political Writings*, ed. H. Reiss (Cambridge, 1970). The creation of a bourgeois quasi-Kantian 'public sphere' within German civil society is classically analysed by J. Habermas, *The Structural Transformation of the Public Sphere: An Inquiry into a Category of Bourgeois Society* (Cambridge, 1989), esp. chs 9, 10, 11, 13.

26 Mommsen, *Max Weber*, pp. 7–9.
27 W. Mommsen, 'Max Weber's Political Sociology and His Philosophy of World History', *International Social Science Journal*, 17 (1965), pp. 23–45 and *idem, The Age of Bureaucracy: Perspectives on the Political Sociology of Max Weber* (Oxford, 1974), ch. 1.
28 W. Hennis, *Max Weber: Essays in Reconstruction* (London, 1988), esp. ch. 3. See too K. Tribe, 'Introduction' to *idem* (ed.), *Reading Weber* (London, 1989).
29 M. Weber, *Roscher and Knies: The Logical Problem of Historical Economics* (New York, 1975), pp. 71, 199–210.
30 Mommsen, *Max Weber*, p. 36, remarks that this lecture 'should be judged as the most significant documentation that we have of Max Weber's political philosophy until the war years'.
31 For full details of this work and its intellectual and political context, see Mommsen, *Max Weber*, ch. 2, Beetham, *Max Weber*, pp. 36–44, D. Kasler, *Max Weber: An Introduction to his Life and Work*, (Cambridge, 1988), ch. 3, and K. Tribe, 'Prussian Agriculture – German Politics: Max Weber 1892–7' and M. Riesebrodt, 'From Patriarchalism to Capitalism: The Theoretical Context of Max Weber's Agrarian Studies (1892–3)', chs 4 and 5 respectively of Tribe (ed.), *Reading Weber*.
32 The following account draws on the secondary sources cited in note 31 and two articles by Weber: 'Developmental Tendencies in the Situation of East Elbian Rural Labourers' (1894) and the Freiburg inaugural on 'The National State and Economic Policy' (1895) both translated in Tribe (ed.) *Reading Weber*, as chs 6 and 7 respectively.
33 See Hennis, *Max Weber*, pp. 117–25.
34 Weber, 'National State', p. 198.
35 Ibid., p. 203.
36 Ibid., pp. 204–5. This remained a persistent theme in Weber's writings, see P. Baehr, 'Max Weber as a Critic of Bismarck', *European Journal of Sociology*, 29 (1988), pp. 149–64.
37 For details see Kasler, *Max Weber*, pp. 66–73.
38 Weber, 'National State', p. 202–7.
39 Mayer, *Max Weber*, p. 20 goes so far as to say that' the *Machtstaat* idea is the *Leitmotiv* of Max Weber's political sociology.'
40 Cited, along with a host of similar quotations from different periods, in Mommsen, *Max Weber*, p. 43 n. 32.
41 Weber, 'National State', p. 204.
42 Weber, 'Capitalism and Rural Society in Germany', p. 373.
43 For a discussion of Chamberlain's attempted realignment of British liberalism, see A. Hooper, 'From Liberal-Radicalism to Conservative Corporatism: the Pursuit of "Radical Business" in "Tory Livery". Joseph Chamberlain, Birmingham and British politics, 1870–1930', in Richard Bellamy (ed.), *Victorian Liberalism: Nineteenth Century Political Thought and Practice* (London, 1990), ch. 11. See too H. G. C. Matthew, *The Liberal Imperialists* (Oxford, 1973).
44 Weber, 'National State', p. 207.
45 See note 7. Wehler, *German Empire*, esp. pp. 46, 94–100, offers a useful summary of their position.
46 Reply to naval questionnaire of the *Allgemeine Zeitung*, cited in Eley, *From Unification to Nazism*, p. 127. This paragraph draws extensively on Eley's interpretation of this period in chs 5 and 6 of this collection.

47 E. Franke, 'Weltpolitik und Sozialreform', in G. Schmoller and M. Sering (eds), *Handels- und Machtpolitik* (Stuttgart, 1900), I, p. 131, cited in Eley, *From Unification to Nazism*, pp. 127, 161.

48 Mommsen, *Max Weber*, p. 70.

49 Cited in ibid., p. 101.

50 For Brentano's views see J. Sheehan, *The Career of Lujo Brentano: A Study of Liberalism and Social Reform in Imperial Germany* (Chicago, 1966).

51 Sheehan, *Career of Lujo Brentano*, pp. 161–3; Mommsen, *Max Weber*, pp. 117–22.

52 M. Weber, 'Germany as an Industrial State' (1897), in Tribe (ed.), *Reading Weber*, pp. 213, 214, 218.

53 Reply to the naval questionnaire of the *Allgemeine Zeitung*, quoted in Beetham, *Max Weber*, p. 135.

54 Proceedings of the 1896 Protestant Social Congress, cited in Beetham, *Max Weber*, p. 134.

55 M. Weber, *Economy and Society* (2 vols, Berkeley, 1978), II, pp. 910–21.

56 M. Weber, 'Parliament and Government in a Reconstructed Germany: A Contribution to the Critique of Officialdom and Parliamentary Parties' (1918), translated in *Economy and Society*, II, as Appendix 2, part iv 'Bureaucracy and Foreign Policy', pp. 1431–42.

57 M. Weber, 'Bismarcks Aussenpolitik und die Gegenwart' (1915), in *Gesammelte Politische Schriften*, 2nd edn (Tubingen, 1958), pp. 117, 124.

58 For details, see Mommsen, *Max Weber*, pp. 59–60.

59 Weber, 'Bismarcks Aussenpolitik', pp. 125–6.

60 Weber, 'Deutschland unter den europäischen Weltmächten' (1916), *Politische Schriften*, pp. 170–2.

61 Max Weber, 'Zwischen Zwei Gesetzen' (1916), *Politische Schriften*, p. 140.

62 Weber, 'Bismarcks Aussenpolitik', pp. 120–1 and *idem*, 'Deutschlands Aussere und Preussens Innere Politik' (1917), *Politische Schriften*, pp. 173–8.

63 Weber, *Economy and Society*, I, pp. 397–8.

64 Ibid., I. p. 395.

65 Ibid., II, p. 922.

66 Weber, 'Politics as a Vocation' (1918), in *From Max Weber*, p. 78.

67 Weber, *Economy and Society*, p. 902.

68 Weber, 'Deutschland unter den europäischen Weltmächten', pp. 164–5.

69 M. Weber, 'The Meaning of "Ethical Neutrality" in Sociology and Economics', in E. Shils and H. Finch (eds), *Max Weber on the Methodology of the Social Sciences* (Illinois, 1949), p. 47.

70 E.g. Mommsen, *The Age of Bureaucracy*, ch. 2 and Mommsen's 'approving' discussion of Aron, 'Weber and Power Politics' in Stammer (ed.), *Max Weber*, pp. 109–16. An important corrective to these interpretations, which informs my own account, is provided by Beetham, *Max Weber*, ch. 5.

71 Weber, 'Politics as a Vocation', p. 116 (amended translation).

72 Weber, *Economy and Society*, II, p. 926 marginal note added about 1913.

73 'The three rational components of a national boundary: military security, economic interest, community of national culture, do not come together like that on the map' (Weber, 'Deutschland unter den europäischen Weltmächten' p. 169).

74 Weber, *Economy and Society*, I, p. 398.

75 D. Miller, 'The Ethical Significance of Nationality', *Ethics*, 98 (1988), pp. 647–62 offers a similar argument for the importance of nationality for social solidarity, which I have found very useful in explicating Weber's views.

76 E.g. A. D. Smith, *The Ethnic Origins of Nations* (Oxford 1986).

77 M. Weber, 'Die Lehren der Deutschen Kanzlerkrisis', in *Politische Schriften*, p. 213.

78 Weber, 'Politics as a Vocation', p. 78.

79 Mommsen, *The Age of Bureaucracy*, ch. 5.

80 The centrality of this theme in Weber's writings is a commonplace which has given rise to a vast secondary literature. My own interpretation is particularly indebted to K. Lowith's classic *Max Weber and Karl Marx* (London, 1982) and the various studies of Mommsen.

81 For a fine analysis of these articles, on which my own examination draws, see Beetham, *Max Weber*, pp. 44–9 and ch. 7.

82 M. Weber, 'The Prospects for Democracy in Tsarist Russia', in *Selections in Translation*, ed. W. G. Runciman (Cambridge, 1978), pp. 282–3.

83 Weber, 'Prospects for Democracy', p. 281.

84 Ibid., p. 283.

85 Ibid., p. 281.

86 Ibid., p. 282.

87 M. Weber, 'Ruslands Übergang der Scheinkonstitutionalismus' (1906), in *Politische Schriften*, p. 107.

88 Max Weber, 'Socialism' (1918), in Max Weber, *The Interpretation of Social Reality*, ed. J. E. T. Eldridge (London, 1971), pp. 191–219.

89 M. Weber, *The Protestant Ethic and the Spirit of Capitalism* (New York, 1958), pp. 17–18, 21, 26.

90 Ibid., pp. 53, 78.

91 See his 'The Social Psychology of the World Religions', in *From Max Weber*, pp. 267–301.

92 Weber, *Protestant Ethic*, p. 85.

93 Ibid., pp. 90–2.

94 Ibid., pp. 21–5, 16–17 and A. Giddens, *Capitalism and Modern Social Theory* (Cambridge, 1971), pp. 178–80.

95 Weber, *Protestant Ethic*, p. 76.

96 M. Weber, 'Science as a Vocation' (1918), in *From Max Weber*, pp. 138–44, 147–55.

97 M. Weber, ' "Objectivity" in Social Science and Social Policy' (1904), in Shils (ed.), *Methodology*, p. 57.

98 Weber, 'Science as a Vocation', pp. 152–3.

99 Weber, *Protestant Ethic*, pp. 104–5.

100 Ibid., pp. 180–1. For a good discussion of Weber's distinctiveness in this respect see H. Liebersohn, *Fate and Utopia in German Sociology, 1870–1923* (Cambridge, Mass., 1988), esp. ch. 4.

101 Weber, *Protestant Ethic*, p. 181.

102 The following account of Weber's theory of bureaucracy is indebted to Beetham, *Max Weber*, ch. 3 and W. Mommsen, *The Political and Social Theory of Max Weber* (Cambridge, 1989), ch. 7. Most of this analysis draws on Weber's discussion of bureaucracy in ch. XI of *Economy and Society*.

103 Weber, *Economy and Society*, p. 223.

104 Bureaucracy became more perfect, Weber observed, 'the more it is "dehumanised", the more completely it succeeds in eliminating from official business love, hatred, and all purely personal, irrational and emotional elements which escape calculation' (*Economy and Society*, p. 975).

105 Weber, *Economy and Society*, p. 973.

106 Ibid., pp. 974–5.

107 Weber, 'Parliament and Government', p. 1400.

108 For details see Beetham, *Max Weber*, pp. 63–7 and D. Lindenlaub, *Richtungskampfe im Verein für Sozialpolitik (1890–1914)* (2 vols, Wiesbaden, 1967), ch. 3.

109 A. Weber, 'Diskussionsbeitrag in der Debatte uber die wirtschaftlichen Unternehmungen der Gemeinden' in *Schriften des Vereins fur Sozialpolitik*, vol. 132 (Leipzig, 1910), pp. 239–40, 243 quoted by E. Demm, 'Max and Alfred Weber in the *Verein für Sozialpolitik*' in W. Mommsen and J. Osterhammel (eds), *Max Weber and his Contemporaries* (London, 1987), p. 95.

110 M. Weber, 'Diskussionsbeitrag', pp. 281ff. A not entirely reliable translation of his contribution appears as Appendix I 'Max Weber on Bureaucratisation in 1909' to Mayer, *Max Weber*, pp. 125–31. Quotations from this speech in this paragraph have been modified in accordance with suggestions found in Mommsen, *Age of Bureaucracy*, ch. 3 and Beetham, *Max Weber*, ch. 4. I have also drawn on Weber's discussion of the bureaucratic official in *Economy and Society*, pp. 958–63.

111 E.g. M. Weber, 'A Research Strategy for the Study of Occupational Careers and Mobility Patterns' (1908), in Weber, *Interpretation of Social Reality*, pp. 104–16.

112 Weber, *Economy and Society*, p. 1000.

113 Weber, 'Parliament and Government', pp. 1417–18 and *Economy and Society*, pp. 992–3.

114 Weber quoted in Beetham, *Max Weber*, p. 74.

115 Weber, *Economy and Society*, pp. 225, 998–1001.

116 Weber, 'Parliament and Government', pp. 1431–8.

117 Weber, 'Socialism', pp. 206–13.

118 Ibid., p. 199.

119 Weber, 'Parliament and Government', p. 1459.

120 Ibid., p. 1394.

121 This view was common at the time. For an overview of these arguments, see D. Lavoie, *Rivalry and Central Planning: The Socialist Calculation Debate Reconsidered* (Cambridge, 1985) and A. E. Buchanan, *Ethics, Efficiency, and the Market* (Oxford, 1985).

122 Weber, *Economy and Society*, pp. 104, 109–13.

123 Weber, 'Parliament and Government', p. 1394.

124 M. Weber, 'Deutschlands Künftige Staatsform' (1919), in *Politische Schriften*, p. 448.

125 Weber, 'Parliament and Government', p. 1402.

126 Ibid., p. 1402.

127 Ibid., p. 1402.

128 H. Marcuse, 'Industrialism and Capitalism', in Stammer (ed.), *Max Weber*, pp. 133ff.

129 For example, this view mars David Held's otherwise fine analysis of Weber's political sociology in *Models of Democracy* (Cambridge, 1987), ch. 5.

130 Weber, 'The Meaning of "Ethical Neutrality"', p. 27. Hennis, *Max Weber*, p. 59, goes so far as to call this 'Max Weber's "central question"'. I have adopted Keith Tribe's, Hennis's translator, modification of Shils's rendition of this passage.
131 Beetham, *Max Weber*, p. 96.
132 Weber, 'Politics as a Vocation', p. 104. See M. Ostrogorski, *Democracy and the Rise of Political Parties* (1899), tr. F. Clarke (London, 1902). Curiously, Weber does not mention Graham Wallas, *Human Nature in Politics* (London, 1908), which was to prove so essential to J. Schumpeter's rethinking of democracy in *Capitalism, Socialism and Democracy* (1943), 5th edn (London, 1976), pp. 256–64.
133 Weber, 'Wahlrecht und Demokratie in Deutschland' (1917), in *Politische Schriften*, pp. 254, 279; *idem*, 'Politics as a Vocation', pp. 83–7; *idem, Economy and Society*, pp. 291–2, *idem*, 'Parliament and Government', pp. 1442–9.
134 Weber, *Economy and Society*, p. 284.
135 Ibid., pp. 291–2, 951–2; *idem*, 'Parliament and Government', pp. 1443–9; *idem*, 'Politics as a Vocation', pp. 100–4.
136 Weber, 'Politics as a Vocation', pp. 109–10.
137 Weber, quoted in Beetham, *Max Weber*, p. 108.
138 Weber, 'Politics as a Vocation', p. 106.
139 Ibid., p. 106. For a modern interpretation of Gladstone as a charismatic party leader, see C. Harvie, 'Gladstonianism, the Provinces, and Popular Political Culture, 1860–1906', in Bellamy (ed.), *Victorian Liberalism*, ch. 9.
140 Weber, 'Parliament and Government', p. 1457.
141 See Beetham, *Max Weber*, pp. 102–5, 111–14 and especially P. Baehr, 'The "Masses" in Weber's Political Sociology', *Economy and Society*, 19 (1990), pp. 242–65, for discussions of Weber's view of the mass, on which I have drawn below.
142 Weber, 'Parliament and Government', pp. 1450–1.
143 Ibid., pp. 1428–9, 1460–1.
144 D. Beetham, 'Mosca, Pareto and Weber: A Historical Comparison', in Mommsen and Osterhammel (eds), *Max Weber*, pp. 139–58 draws interesting parallels between these three thinkers. Although they gave no overt evidence of knowing each others' work, Michels openly drew on all three and worked with both Mosca and Weber. Michels's relationship with Weber is explored in Mommsen, *Political and Social Theory*, ch. 6.
145 Weber, 'Parliament and Government', p. 1414.
146 Weber, *Economy and Society*, II, p. 952.
147 Ibid., II, pp. 285, 287; *idem*, 'Parliament and Government', p. 1445.
148 Weber, 'Parliament and Government', pp. 1452–3.
149 For Pareto's progressive disillusionment, see chapter 3. Michels, a former socialist, took a similar path to fascism, charted by D. Beetham, 'From Socialism to Fascism: The Relation between Theory and Practice in the Work of Robert Michels', *Political Studies*, 25 (1977), pp. 3–24, 161–81. Mosca ultimately compromised with modern forms of mass democracy, but retained a preference for liberal notable politics, see R. Bellamy, *Modern Italian Social Theory* (Cambridge, 1987), ch. 3.
150 Weber, 'Parliament and Government', p. 1443.
151 Weber, *Economy and Society*, pp. 286–7.
152 Ibid., p. 288.

153 Weber, 'Parliament and Government', p. 1459.
154 Ibid., p. 1458.
155 Weber, Letter to Michels of 4 August 1908, quoted in Mommsen, *Max Weber*, p. 395. See too Weber, 'Parliament and Government', p. 1456 for the same example.
156 Weber, 'Parliament and Government', p. 1450.
157 Ibid., p. 1450.
158 Ibid., p. 1416.
159 Ibid., p. 1410.
160 Ibid., p. 1408.
161 Ibid., p. 1418.
162 Ibid., p. 1409. The 'negative integration' of the SPD has formed a theme of modern historians of the movement. See in particular, C. E. Schorske, *German Social Democracy 1905–17* (New York, 1955) and P. Nettl, 'The German Social Democratic Party 1890–1914 as a Political Model', *Past and Present*, 30 (1965), pp. 65–95, although Eley, *From Unification to Nazism*, ch. 7 disputes this thesis.
163 Weber, 'Parliament and Government', p. 1420.
164 Ibid., p. 1413.
165 Ibid., p. 1424.
166 Ibid., p. 1408.
167 Ibid., p. 1420.
168 Ibid., p. 1457.
169 Ibid., p. 1452. Beetham, *Max Weber*, pp. 113–16 has been particularly influential in insisting on the last function of parliament, as a protector of liberty.
170 Sheehan, *German Liberalism*, esp. chs 10, 11, 15 and 16.
171 Weber, 'Wahlrecht und Demokratie', pp. 254–8 and *idem*, 'Parliament and Government', pp. 1460–2.
172 R. Michels, *Political Parties* (1911) (New York, 1962).
173 Weber, 'Parliament and Government', p. 1460.
174 Weber's views of the Social Democrats are dealt with in detail in Mommsen, *Political and Social Theory*, ch. 5.
175 For an examination of this stage of Weber's career see Mommsen, *Max Weber*, ch. 8.
176 Weber, 'Parliament and Government', p. 1404.
177 The following discussion draws on a joint article on Weber's essay written with Peter Baehr, whose wording I have often borrowed, 'Personality and Passion', *Times Higher Education Supplement*, 23-3-90.
178 Weber, 'Politics as a Vocation', p. 115.
179 Ibid., p. 115.
180 Ibid., p. 78.
181 Ibid., pp. 121–6; *idem*, 'Science as a Vocation', pp. 147–8.
182 Weber, 'Politics as a Vocation', p. 120.
183 Ibid., p. 116.
184 Ibid., p. 127.
185 Mommsen, *The Age of Bureaucracy*, p. 91, quoting with approval the opinion of Arnold Bergstaesser, 'Max Weber's Akademische Antrittsrede', *Viertel jahreshefte für Zeitgeschichte*, 5 (1957), p. 209.
186 M. Weber, 'The Reich President' (1919), *Social Research*, 53 (1986), pp. 128–32.

187 For a full analysis, on which I have drawn, see P. Baehr, 'Weber and Weimar: The 'Reich President' Proposals', *Politics*, 9 (1989), pp. 20–5.
188 E.g. Mommsen, *Max Weber*, chs 9 and 10.
189 Weber, 'Reich President', p. 130.
190 Ibid., p. 129.
191 Ibid., p. 132.
192 Ibid., pp. 129, 131.
193 Beetham, *Max Weber*, pp. 234–5, 237–8.
194 Weber, 'Politics as a Vocation', p. 113.
195 C. B. Macpherson, *The Life and Times of Liberal Democracy* (Oxford, 1977), p. 89.
196 Held, *Models of Democracy*, pp. 161–2.
197 Mommsen, *Max Weber*, ch. 10. Ironically, Mommsen also provides the evidence for rebutting this charge, see note 198.
198 Mommsen, *Max Weber*, pp. 348–54, 376–8.
199 Baehr, 'Weber and Weimar', p. 24.
200 Mommsen, *Max Weber*, pp. 381–9, 410. Schmitt acknowledged the debt to Weber in *The Crisis of Parliamentary Democracy* (1923), (Cambridge, Mass., 1988), p. 4.
201 Weber, *Economy and Society*, pp. 866–75; *idem*, 'Prospects for Democracy', p. 281.
202 Translation of the German term *Herrschaft* is fraught with difficulty. Roth and Wittich, translators of *Economy and Society*, use 'domination' and 'legitimate authority' interchangeably. Mommsen, *The Age of Bureaucracy*, p. 72 n. 1, prefers the consistent use of 'domination'. However, in referring to *Herrschaft* as involving voluntary obedience requiring neither coercion nor reasoned argument (*Economy and Society*, pp. 212–13), Weber is clearly invoking the standard attributes political philosophers associate with the concept of authority (e.g. R. B. Friedman, 'On the Concept of Authority in Political Philosophy', in R. E. Flathman (ed.), *Concepts in Social and Political Philosophy* (London, 1973). Hence, Weber's careful distinction between *Herrschaft* and *Macht* (power) (*Economy and Society*, p. 53), which Mommsen rather cursorily passes off as 'extremely formalistic'. Mommsen's suggested modifications of the Roth translation do not alter the substantive point Weber clearly makes.
203 Weber, *Economy and Society*, p. 215. See too *idem*, 'Politics as a Vocation', pp. 78–9.
204 Weber, *Economy and Society*, pp. 241–5, 1115–17.
205 Weber, 'Parliament and Government', p. 1405.
206 Weber, *Economy and Society*, pp. 246–54, 1121–7.
207 Ibid., pp. 266–71; *idem*, 'Parliament and Government', p. 1457.
208 Mommsen, *The Age of Bureaucracy*, pp. 83–4.
209 Weber, 'Politics as a Vocation', p. 79, and see note 202.
210 I owe this point to M. Warren, 'Max Weber's Liberalism for a Nietzschean World', *American Political Science Review*, 82 (1988), pp. 41–3.
211 R. W. Krouse, 'Classical Images of Democracy in America: Madison and Tocqueville', in G. Duncan (ed.), *Democratic Theory and Practice* (Cambridge, 1983), pp. 76–7, as quoted in Held, *Models of Democracy*, p. 144.
212 Weber, 'Parliament and Government', p. 1403.
213 For the influence of Nietzsche on Weber's thought, see in particular

E. Fleischmann, 'De Weber à Nietzsche', *European Journal of Sociology*, V (1964), pp. 190–238 and R. Eden, *Political Leadership and Nihilism: A Study of Weber and Nietzsche* (Tampa, 1983). Chapter 6 of Eden's book rehearses the standard liberal objections to Weber's Nietzschean liberalism, developing the line of criticism classically expounded by Mommsen, *Max Weber*, esp. ch. 10 For a more right-wing version see L. Strauss, *Natural Right and History* (Chicago, 1953), ch. 2. D. Beetham, 'Max Weber and the Liberal Political Tradition', *European Journal of Sociology*, XXX (1989), pp. 311–23 offers a negative judgement – this time from a left-wing perspective. Two positive accounts of Nietzschean liberalism that I have found very useful are W. Connolly, *Political Theory and Modernity* (Oxford, 1988), ch. 5, and M. Warren, *Nietzsche and Political Thought* (Cambridge, Mass., 1988). Warren extends his arguments to Weber in his article, 'Max Weber's Liberalism', pp. 31–50.

214 The comparison is made explicitly by Beetham, 'Max Weber and the Liberal', pp. 314–16, but is implicit in the criticisms of Eden and Mommsen.

215 Weber, 'Politics as a Vocation', p. 118.

216 Weber, 'The Meaning of "Ethical Neutrality"', pp. 17–18.

217 As Beetham, *Max Weber*, p. 5, writes, 'Weber's philosophical and sociological perspectives thus reinforce one another in a pluralist restatement of the liberal tradition.'

218 Weber, *Economy and Society*, p. 1117.

219 Weber, '"Objectivity" in Social Science', p. 55.

220 Warren, 'Weber's Liberalism', p. 39, relates this point directly to Habermas's 'discourse ethics' in *The Theory of Communicative Action*, vol. 1 (Cambridge, 1984).

221 Weber, *Economy and Society*, pp. 951–2.

222 Ibid., p. 949.

223 Held, *Models of Democracy*, p. 181.

224 See D. Miller, 'The Competitive Model of Democracy', in Duncan (ed.), *Democratic Theory*, pp. 133–55.

225 I owe this point concerning the link between voluntary associations and Weber's individualistic liberalism to S. Seidman, *Liberalism and the Origins of European Social Theory* (Oxford, 1983), pp. 266–7 and Lowith, *Weber and Marx*, pp. 56–60.

226 Weber, 'National State', p. 207 (amended translation).

227 Hennis, *Max Weber*, p. 146 quotes Weber as remarking that one can only understand modernity through Marx and Nietzsche.

Chapter 5 Contemporary Liberal Philosophy: Liberalism Neutralized

1 E.g. S. M. Lipset, *Political Man* (New York, 1959).

2 An account of the context of post-war liberal thought can be found in A. Arblaster, *The Rise and Decline of Western Liberalism* (Oxford, 1984), chs 18 and 19. I have traced the post-war development of liberal political philosophy in more detail in my article 'Rinascita della filosofia politica anglo-americana?', *Teoria politica*, V (1989), pp. 93–102 and, somewhat more briefly, in the editorial introduction to R. Bellamy (ed.), *Liberalism and Recent*

Legal and Social Philosophy, Archiv für Rechts- und Sozialphilosophie (1989), Beheift Nr. 36.

3 This point has been made in different ways by D. Miller, *Social Justice* (Oxford, 1976), esp. Introduction and Conclusion, and B. Barber, *The Conquest of Politics: Liberal Philosophy in Democratic Times* (Princeton, 1988).

4 For a selection of articles illustrating the debate see M. Sandel (ed.), *Liberalism and its Critics* (Oxford, 1986).

5 E.g. A. Gutmann, 'Communitarian Critics of Liberalism', *Philosophy and Public Affairs*, 14 (1985), pp. 308–22.

6 I. Kant, 'On the Common Saying: 'this may be true in theory, but it does not apply in practice', in H. Reiss (ed.), *Kant's Political Writings* (Cambridge, 1970), p. 73.

7 See in particular, F. A. Hayek, *The Constitution of Liberty* (Chicago, 1960); *idem*, 'The Principles of a Liberal Social Order', *Studies in Philosophy, Politics and Economics* (London, 1967); *idem, Law, Legislation and Liberty* (3 vols, London, 1973–9); R. Nozick, *Anarchy, State and Utopia* (Oxford, 1974); B. A. Ackerman, *Social Justice in the Liberal State* (New Haven, 1980); R. Dworkin, 'Liberalism', in S. Hampshire (ed.), *Public and Private Morality* (Cambridge, 1978), pp. 113–43; and J. Rawls, *A Theory of Justice* (Oxford, 1971).

8 J. Raz, *The Morality of Freedom* (Oxford, 1985), pp. 110–33.

9 For more general analyses of the New Right, which examine it as a political movement as well as a system of ideas, see S. Newman, *Liberalism at Wits' End* (New York, 1984) and D. King, *The New Right: Politics, Markets and Citizenship* (London, 1987).

10 Nozick, *Anarchy, State and Utopia*, esp. ch. 7.

11 These remarks are inspired by O. O'Neill, 'The Most Extensive Liberty', *Proceedings of the Aristotelian Society*, 80 (1979/80), pp. 45–59, and J. Gray, 'Liberalism and the Choice of Liberties', reproduced in his collection of articles, *Liberalisms: Essays in Political Philosophy* (London, 1989), ch. 9.

12 The articles by David Lyons and Hillel Steiner in J. Paul (ed.), *Reading Nozick: Essays on Anarchy, State and Utopia* (Oxford, 1981), reveal how Nozick's argument can prove self-defeating in this respect.

13 See Nozick, *Anarchy, State and Utopia*, p. 178, where he leaves it as an open question 'whether or not Locke's particular theory can be spelled out so as to handle various difficulties'.

14 Ibid., p. 153.

15 Ibid., p. 25.

16 Hayek, 'Principles of a Liberal Social Order', p. 162; *idem, Law, Legislation and Liberty*, 1, pp. 36–7.

17 See King, *New Right*, pp. 97–100 for a brief discussion of this problem.

18 Hayek, *Constitution of Liberty*, pp. 285–6.

19 Hayek, *Law, Legislation and Liberty*, 3, p. 152.

20 Ibid., 2, p. 28.

21 Hayek, 'Principles of a Liberal Social Order', pp. 160–3.

22 C. Kukathas, *Hayek and Modern Liberalism* (Oxford, 1989). My discussion of Hayek's philosophy largely follows Kukathas's analysis.

23 Hayek, *Constitution of Liberty*, p. 398.

24 The following discussion draws on Kukathas, *Hayek*, ch. 4 and Gray, *Liberalisms*, ch. 6.

25 Hayek, *Constitution of Liberty*, pp. 18–19.

26 Ibid., p. 19.
27 Ibid., p. 21.
28 Ibid., p. 153.
29 Gray, *Liberalisms*, p. 91. See too Kukathas, *Hayek*, pp. 142–3.
30 Hayek, *Constitution of Liberty*, pp. 153, 210.
31 For criticisms to this effect see J. Raz, *The Authority of Law: Essays on Law and Morality* (Oxford, 1983), pp. 210–32 and R. Hamowy, 'Law and the Liberal Society: F. A. Hayek's *Constitution of Liberty*', *Journal of Libertarian studies*, 2 (1978), pp. 287–97.
32 J. Gray, *Hayek on Liberty*, 2nd edn (Oxford, 1986), pp. 63–5.
33 Ibid., pp. 59–61.
34 E.g. Hayek, *Constitution of Liberty*, pp. 31, 44, 48, 259.
35 Kukathas, *Hayek*, pp. 191–201.
36 Hayek, *Constitution of Liberty*, p. 41.
37 R. Dworkin, 'What is Equality? Part 1: Equality of Welfare', *Philosophy and Public Affairs*, 10 (1981), pp. 197–226.
38 J. Raz, *The Morality of Freedom* (Oxford, 1986), pp. 117–18.
39 Dworkin, 'Liberalism', p. 127.
40 Ibid., p. 130.
41 Ibid., p. 134, *idem*, 'Why Liberals Should Care About Equality', in *A Matter of Principle* (Oxford, 1985), pp. 206–7.
42 The literature on Dworkin is now fairly extensive. I have found the following particularly useful: H. L. A. Hart, 'Between Utility and Rights', in A. Ryan (ed.), *The Idea of Freedom* (Oxford, 1979); V. Haskar, *Equality, Liberty and Perfectionism* (Oxford, 1979), pp. 258–69; J. Finnis, *Natural Law and Natural Rights* (Oxford, 1980), pp. 221–3; W. A. Galston, *Justice and the Human Good* (Chicago, 1980), pp. 131–6; W. E. Connolly, *Appearance and Reality in Politics* (Cambridge, 1981), pp. 90–119; M. Sandel, *Liberalism and the Limits of Justice* (Cambridge, 1982), pp. 135–47; J. Raz, 'Rights-based Moralities', in J. Waldron (ed.), *Theories of Rights* (Oxford, 1984); L. Alexander and M. Schwarzschild, 'Liberalism, Neutrality and Equality of Welfare versus Equality of Resources', *Philosophy and Public Affairs*, 16 (1987), pp. 185–210; and P. Jones, 'The Ideal of the Neutral State', in A. Reeve and R. Goodin (eds), *Liberal Neutrality* (London, 1989).
43 Dworkin, 'Why Liberals Should Care About Equality', pp. 206–7, *idem*, 'What is Equality? Part 2: Equality of Resources', *Philosophy and Public Affairs*, 10 (1981), pp. 283–345.
44 Dworkin, 'What is Equality? Part 2', p. 287.
45 Dworkin, 'Liberalism', p. 141.
46 Dworkin, 'What is Equality? Part 2', pp. 301–4.
47 Alexander and Schwarzschild, 'Liberalism, Neutrality and Equality', pp. 97–103.
48 E.g. Dworkin, 'Why Bakke Has No Case', in *A Matter of Principle*, p. 299: 'There is no combination of abilities and skills and traits that constitutes "merit" in the abstract; if quick hands count as "merit" in the case of a prospective surgeon, this is because quick hands will enable him to serve the public better and for no other reason.'
49 The failed economies of the former 'actually existing' socialist countries of the Soviet bloc provide no evidence for this view. Not only were they extremely inegalitarian in practice, their problems can be ascribed more

to the illiberal nature of their political as opposed to their economic systems.

50 See Miller, *Social Justice*, whose work has influenced these remarks.

51 Dworkin, *Taking Rights Seriously*, 2nd edn (London, 1978), p. 234.

52 Dworkin, 'Liberalism', p. 136.

53 I should perhaps underline that here I am making the quite general point that once neutrality is defined in terms of motivation then the ground is ripe for all kinds of sophistry. When pressed by Hart, 'Between Utility and Rights', Dworkin argued that fascists could be banned from campaigning in elections on the grounds that they intended to offend equality of respect and neutrality ('Do We Have a Right to Pornography?', in *a Matter of Principle*, pp. 365–72). This argument will not work. However, it would be perfectly coherent for him to say that the effect of their actions is to contradict neutrality.

54 Dworkin, 'Bakke's Case: Are Quotas Unfair?, in *A Matter of Principle*, pp. 301–2.

55 Dworkin, *Taking Rights Seriously*, p. 201 *idem*, 'Do We Have a Right to Pornography?'

56 Dworkin, *Taking Rights Seriously*, p. 198.

57 Ibid., p. 272.

58 Rawls, *Theory of Justice*, pp. 260–3, 584.

59 Ibid., p. 302.

60 For a collection of the earliest essays see N. Daniels (ed.), *Reading Rawls* (Oxford, 1975). Three important book-length critiques are B. Barry, *The Liberal Theory of Justice* (Oxford, 1973); R. P. Wolff, *Understanding Rawls: A Reconstruction and Critique of a 'Theory of Justice'* (Princeton, 1977); and Sandel, *Liberalism and the Limits of Justice*.

61 Rawls, *a Theory of Justice*, p. 312, regards our possession of these qualities as simply fortuitous, the result of being born with a given genetic make-up into a particular social and familial setting, and hence arbitrary from a moral point of view. However, the very charge of arbitrariness seems self-contradictory. The difficulty would seem to arise from the same confusion between the capacity and the conditions for autonomy we noted in Mill's theory in chapter 1.

62 E.g. A. Schwartz, 'Moral Neutrality and Primary Goods', *Ethics*, LXXXIII (1973), pp. 294–307; T. Nagel, 'Rawls on Justice', in Daniels (ed.), *Reading Rawls*.

63 See J. Rawls, 'Kantian Constructivism in Moral Theory' *Journal of Philosophy*, LXXVII (1980), pp. 515–72; *idem*, 'Social Unity and Primary Goods' in A. K. Sen and B. Williams (eds), *Utilitarianism and Beyond* (Cambridge, 1982); *idem*, 'Justice as Fairness: Political not Metaphysical', *Philosophy and Public Affairs*, 14 (1985), pp. 223–51; *idem*, 'The Idea of an Overlapping Consensus', *Oxford Journal of Legal Studies*, 7 (1987), pp. 1–25; and *idem*, 'The Priority of Right and Ideas of the Good', *Philosophy and Public Affairs*, 17 (1988), pp. 251–77.

64 This project has much in common with Habermas's attempts to revive the liberal public sphere. See Stephen K. White, *The Recent Work of Jurgen Habermas: Reason, Justice and Modernity* (Cambridge, 1988). This resemblance is possibly due to the fact that Rawls was influenced by Charles Larmore's political view of liberalism which explicitly draws on Habermas discourse ethics. See C. Larmore, *Patterns of Moral Complexity* (Cambridge, 1987), chs 3

and 4, and J. Rawls, 'The Priority of Right and Ideas of the Good', *Philosophy and Public Affairs*, 17 (1988), pp. 253–4 n. 2, 261 n. 16, 263 n. 19 where he acknowledges his debt to Larmore's book and the parallel with Habermas.

65 Rawls, 'Kantian Constructivism', p. 525.

66 Rawls, 'Overlapping Consensus', p. 4.

67 Rawls, 'Political not Metaphysical', pp. 230, 251.

68 Rawls, 'Overlapping Consensus', p. 13.

69 For detailed discussion of these points, see J. Raz, 'Facing Diversity: The Case of Epistemic Abstinence', *Philosophy and Public Affairs*, 19 (1990), pp. 3–46.

70 E.g. Richard Rorty, 'The Priority of Democracy to Philosophy', in M. D. Peterson and R. C. Vaughan (eds), *The Virginia Statute for Religious Freedom* (Cambridge, 1988).

71 E.g. Susan Moller Okin, 'Justice and Gender', *Philosophy and Public Affairs*, 16 (1987), pp. 3–46.

72 J. Rawls, 'Fairness to Goodness', *Philosophical Review*, 84 (1975), p. 549.

73 Rawls, 'Priority of Right', p. 265.

74 W. Galston, 'Pluralism and Social Unity', *Ethics*, 99 (1989), p. 718.

75 E.g. Okin, 'Justice and Gender'.

76 Rawls, 'Overlapping Consensus', p. 17.

77 E. g. Gutmann, 'Communitarian Critics of Liberalism'.

78 M. Sandel, 'Morality and the Liberal Ideal', *The New Republic*, May 7, 1984, p. 17.

79 M. Walzer, *Spheres of Justice* (Oxford, 1983), p. 7.

80 Walzer, *Spheres of Justice*, pp. 313–15.

81 Ibid., pp. 84–91.

82 Ibid., pp. 151–4.

83 Walzer's fullest account of his approach is in M. Walzer, *Interpretation and Social Criticism* (Cambridge, Mass., 1987).

84 Walzer, *Spheres of Justice*, pp. 224–6.

85 M. Walzer and R. Dworkin, '*Spheres of Justice*: an Exchange', *New York Review of Books*, 21 July 1983, p. 43.

86 W. Galston, 'Defending Liberalism', *American Political Science Review*, 76 (1982), p. 627. The works of rationalist communitarian/ethical liberals discussed here include Galston, *Justice and the Human Good*; Finnis, *Natural Law and Natural Rights*; C. Taylor, *Philosophy and the Human Sciences: Philosophical Papers 2* (Cambridge, 1985); J. Raz, *The Morality of Freedom* (Oxford, 1986). I am inclined to exclude A. MacIntyre, *After Virtue: A Study in Moral Theory* (London, 1981) because he does not wish to refound liberalism on a communitarian/ethical basis, but rejects it altogether. See his subsequent book: *Whose Justice? Which Rationality?* (London, 1988), ch. XVII. Most of my remarks would apply equally well to his views, however.

87 Finnis, *Natural Law and Natural Rights*, p. 222. More specifically, Finnis argues that: 'There is…no alternative but to hold in one's mind's eye some pattern, or range of patterns, of human character, conduct and interaction in the community, and then to choose such specification of rights as tends to favour that pattern or range of patterns. In other words, one needs some conception of human good, of human flourishing in a form (or range of forms) of communal life that fosters rather than hinders such flourishing' (pp. 219–20).

88 Dworkin, *Taking Rights seriously*, p. 91.
89 Finnis, *Natural Law and Natural Rights*, p. 220.
90 Raz, *The Morality of Freedom*, p. 214.
91 Finnis, *Natural Law and Natural Rights*, p. 154.
92 Raz, *Morality of Freedom*, p. 250.
93 Finnis, *Natural Law and Natural Rights*, p. 225.
94 H. L. A. Hart, *The Concept of Law* (Oxford, 1961), pp. 189–95.
95 S. Hampshire, *Morality and Conflict* (Oxford, 1983), p. 145.
96 Ibid., p. 148.
97 Raz, *Morality of Freedom*, p. 366.
98 Ibid., ch. 9 and pp. 295–9.
99 Ibid., p. 391.
100 Ibid., p. 215.
101 S. Mendus, 'Liberty and Autonomy', *Proceedings of the Aristotelian Society*, LXXXVII (1986/7), pp. 107–20.
102 Raz, *Morality of Freedom*, p. 215.
103 Ibid., p. 429.
104 Ibid., pp. 369–70.
105 I owe the following observations to the fine critique of Rawls in D. Zolo, *Complessità e democrazia: per una ricostruzione della teoria democratica* (Turin, 1987), ch. 11.

Conclusion: from Liberal Democracy to Democratic Liberalism

1 The following argument has been much influenced by the work of Danilo Zolo, particularly his *Democracy and Social Complexity: A Realist Approach* (Cambridge, 1992). I have also been inspired by the writings of Richard Rorty, particularly 'The Priority of Democracy to Philosophy', in M. D. Peterson and R. C. Vaughan (eds), *The Virginian Statute for Religious Freedom* (Cambridge, 1988), and Jean-François Lyotard, *The Post-Modern Condition* (Manchester, 1986). However, in my view, neither of these two theorists takes either their appeal to history and sociology to undermine contemporary meta-narratives or their attempt to separate justice from ethics and situate it within politics far enough. In common with other post-modern philosophers, such as Gianni Vattimo, *La società trasparente* (Milan, 1989), both seem remarkably sanguine about the continued plausibility of ethical liberalism.
2 David Held, 'Democracy, the Nation State and the Global System', in *idem*, *Political Theory Today* (Cambridge, 1991), p. 228. See too *idem*, *Models of Democracy* (Cambridge, 1987), p. 271 for an earlier version of his thesis.
3 The following discussion is greatly indebted to O. O'Neill, 'The Most Extensive Liberty', *Proceedings of the Aristotelian Society*, 80 (1979/80), pp. 45–59; *idem*, *Faces for Hunger: An Essay on Poverty, Justice and Development* (London, 1986), ch. 6; *idem*, 'Children's Rights and Children's Lives', *Ethics*, 98 (1988), pp. 445–63; and J. Gray, *Liberalisms: Essays in Political Philosophy* (London, 1989), esp. ch. 9 I have developed this argument further in R. Bellamy, 'Liberal Rights and Socialist Goals', in W. Maihofer and G. Sprenger (eds), *Revolution and Human Rights, Archiv für Rechts- und Sozialphilosophie*, Beiheft Nr. 41 (1990), pp. 249–64.

4 The attempt of liberal philosophy to exclude politics forms the subject of Benjamin Barber's lively collection of essays, *The Conquest of Politics: Liberal Philosophy in Democratic Times* (Princeton, 1988). Although I agree with many of his criticisms of contemporary liberalism, I do not share his neo-Aristotelian conception of politics.

5 See J. Rawls, 'Kantian Constructivism and Moral Theory', *Journal of Philosophy*, LXXVII (1980), pp. 515–72.

6 I have developed this argument in my 'Schumpeter and the Transformation of Capitalism, Liberalism and Democracy', *Government and Opposition*, 26 (1991), pp. 500–19.

7 K. Marx and F. Engels, *The Communist Manifesto, Selected Works*, vol. 1 (Moscow, 1969), p. 127.

8 The following criticisms are inspired by T. Campbell, *The Left and Rights: A Conceptual Analysis of the Idea of Socialist Rights* (London, 1983) and S. Lukes, *Marxism and Morality* (Oxford, 1985).

9 I owe these characterisations of civic republicanism and civic humanism to Q. Skinner, 'The Paradoxes of Political Liberty', in S. McMurrin (ed.), *The Tanner Lectures on Human Values*, VII (Cambridge, 1986), pp. 225–50. Skinner's account of the civic republican view of liberty has influenced more generally my conception of democratic liberalism.

10 Rawls makes this observation in 'The Priority of Right and Ideas of the Good', *Philosophy and Public Affairs*, 17 (1980), pp. 272–3. However, he is only willing to grant classical republicanism a supplementary role in securing the rights and liberties defined by the overlapping consensus. As Skinner, 'Paradoxes of Political Liberty', pp. 246–50, makes clear, contrary to Rawls, this limitation ultimately renders classical republicanism incompatible with his own rights-based version of political liberalism.

11 In some respects the French liberal tradition of de Tocqueville and Constant developed a democratic liberalism of this nature. See L. Siedentop, 'Two Liberal Traditions', in A. Ryan (ed.), *The Idea of Freedom* (Oxford, 1979).

12 For a fuller discussion see D. King, *New Right* (London, 1987), ch. 5.

13 B. Barry, *Political Argument* (London, 1965), ch. 4.

14 The above discussion is indebted to B. L. Crowley's critique of Hayek in *The Self, The Individual and the Community: Liberalism in the Political thought of F. A. Hayek and Sidney and Beatrice Webb* (Oxford, 1987), chs 3 and 7.

15 See D. Miller, *Market, State and Community: Theoretical Foundations of Market Socialism* (Oxford, 1989).

16 C. Larmore, *Patterns of Moral Complexity* (Cambridge, 1987), pp. 51–2.

Index